THE
Damnable
Question

THE
Damnable
Question

A HISTORY OF
ANGLO-IRISH RELATIONS

GEORGE DANGERFIELD

BARNES
&NOBLE
BOOKS
NEW YORK

1999 Barnes & Noble Books

ISBN 0-7607-1350-2 *casebound*
ISBN 0-7607-1349-9 *paperback*

Printed and bound in the United States of America

99 00 01 02 MC 9 8 7 6 5 4 3 2 1
99 00 01 02 MP 9 8 7 6 5 4 3 2 1

RRD-H

To Mary Lou Dangerfield

*my dear fellow traveler with Tony
from Dublin to Sligo, from London
to Oxford to Harpole*

This Book Is Dedicated with My Love

Foreword

"Inevitable," I think, is happiest as a meteorological term — when it applies to such phenomena as tornados, waterspouts and hurricanes. It at any rate has no place in history: in history an "inevitable" event is something which people do not wish to avoid or do not know how to avoid: it is not essentially unavoidable.

In history, events which have the appearance of inevitability are of the first importance, if only because they compel us to ask what sort of people wished to bring them about and why and how they did so. Conversely, we are prompted to inquire through the lack of what qualities — wisdom, compassion, foresight and so forth — people to whose disadvantage they happened were unable to prevent them from happening.

The Dublin Easter Rising of 24 April 1916 is such an event. As a military *coup* it was, and its leaders apparently expected it to be, a failure; it lasted only a week; and the Republic which it proclaimed outside Dublin's General Post Office did not appear until many years later and then in a very different form. Yet it has that peculiar and tragic dignity which we associate with the term "inevitability." Although the authorities could have prevented it with comparative ease, we feel that it *had* to happen. This is to enter into metaphysics; and here the historian discreetly retires to firmer ground.

At the heart of the Rising one can discover both Irish myth and socialist philosophy: in effect both Cuchulainn and Karl Marx fought in the General Post Office in Easter Week; and the historian is bound to inquire, and inquire very carefully, into what they were doing there. But his other and I think his larger preoccupation is with the train of events which led up to it from a distant past and then away from it into the immediate future.

I have heard the Easter Rising called "a point of no return": and so it was, but only in the sense that it was difficult, though not impossible, for the Irish people to return to the state of mind they were in before it occurred. Such points of no return are not only *not* inevitable, since they illustrate the human principle of change in which there is always an element of choice, but they are also very common occurrences.

I have given this book the subtitle of "A Study in Anglo-Irish Relations"; I have introduced the Easter Rising into its first paragraph; and the Easter Rising, though sacred as an Irish event in the Irish mind, is in fact central to the whole study of political Anglo-Ireland in modern history. It is much more than a point of no return; it is a great watershed. From the Rising the history of modern Irish revolution flows backward until it loses itself in the Act of Union of 1800–01, when Ireland lost its own parliament, such as it was, and became an integral part of a united kingdom. From the Rising this same history rushes forward until it begins to disappear in the Anglo-Irish Treaty of 6 December 1921 and its acceptance in Dublin on 7 January 1922.

Irish men and women have a tendency to live in their past, to cherish and to nurse it, because it is a past of indignities and oppressions, and has a more visceral and more poignant character to them than the English past has to their English neighbors. The English past, to be sure, is also full of indignities and oppressions, but these (except to Welsh, Scottish and Cornish Home Rulers) are no longer seen as inflicted by aliens, and they were accompanied by solid achievements. Thus the English think that the Irish sense of the past is redundant: in the sense that the Irish are always waking it up in order to sing it to sleep. Here the English are quite wrong, and yet they have very powerful reasons for being quite wrong: and I hope that this study will in some measure reveal these reasons.

The tragedy of the Irish Revolution which the Rising set in motion is that it was not allowed to complete itself. It destroyed the old respectable Irish Parliamentary Party; it set up a republican Dail, usually on the run; it fought the English to a standstill or at least a standoff in the Anglo-Irish war of 1919–1921; it exacted from an English Cabinet and English conferees terms which would have been simply unthinkable in 1916; but it failed to go one step further and refuse these terms as being insufficient. It had, therefore, no chance *under revolutionary conditions* to test the concept of an Irish Republic for a United Ireland. Probably it would have failed here, too: but to fail after an attempt is surely very different than to fail before one. The ratification of the Treaty in January 1922 left certain aspirations quite unappeased; it was followed by a Civil War, the wounds of which have not yet been healed; Anglo-Irish relations continued to move along the old road that once led away from the Union and now away from the Free State; and if these relations have today been reduced to a squalid and protracted death in the back streets of Belfast it is because the Anglo-Irish past has not yet been put to rest in a United Ireland. It is that past — the Anglo-Irish past — which in this book I have endeavored to explore and explain.

I wish to express my appreciation to the John Simon Guggenheim Memorial Foundation for granting me the fellowship which enabled me to continue my researches in London, Dublin and Oxford.

My gratitude is also due to Mr. Michael Heuson and the staff of the Division of Manuscripts in the National Library of Ireland; to Mr. Breandán Mac Giolla Choille, Keeper of State Papers in the State Paper Office, Dublin Castle, and to Miss Fitzgerald; to the staff of the Public Record Office in Portugal Street and Fetter Lane, London; to the staff and the late Miss Rosemary Brooks in that delectable and now vanishing oasis in St. Bride's Street, the Beaverbrook Library, and to its honorary director, Mr. A. J. P. Taylor; to Mr. Mark Bonham Carter, for permission to consult the Asquith Papers; to Mr. John Grigg, for permission to consult the papers of his father, the first Lord Altrincham; to Eilis Dillon (Mrs. Vivian Mercier) for a gracious loan of certain family materials; to Mr. Robert H. West, who permitted me to examine parts of his work in progress on the organization of the Irish National Volunteers from 1913 to 1915 and for other assistance of value; to Mr. Hubert Ribeiro, for helping me to bring light to the darkness of James Connolly's last industrial dispute in 1915–1916 and for his most painstaking work on the Joseph Plunkett Diary; to Mrs. Madeline Marina and Miss Elizabeth McGeough for their flawless expertise in deciphering and bringing order to two most disheveled typescripts; and to Professor David W. Miller for a singularly memorable walk from St. Bride's Street to Bayswater.

George Dangerfield
Santa Barbara, California
September 1975

Contents

ILLUSTRATIONS

"You will never get to the bottom of this most perplexing and damnable country."

> — Henry Herbert Asquith, writing to his wife from Dublin, May 16th, 1916

Part One

LOOKING BACK,
1800—1906

Chapter One

Famine

I

On Easter Monday, 24 April 1916, some eight hundred revolutionaries occupied certain key points in the city of Dublin in the name of the Irish Republic. On 29 April, greatly outnumbered, although their numbers by then had grown to sixteen hundred, hopelessly outgunned, with the center of the city in flames, the headquarters and one other detachment surrendered. The other detachments surrendered on the next day. This was Ireland's Easter Rising: and it seems that those who led it knew that they were doomed before they began. Only the gallantry of the rebels, one might have supposed, had saved it from becoming a rather lurid, a very sanguinary farce.

Yet this was not the case. When the Republic was proclaimed that Easter Monday from the steps of the post office in Sackville (O'Connell) Street, to a listless and perhaps uncomprehending group of bystanders, Ireland's flight from British imperial history had reached its decisive moment. The occupation, however incomplete, of such a city as Dublin, the proclamation, however unheeded, of such an entity as an Irish Republic — these, as it happened, were to be irreversible events.

Taking place near the heart of a great empire, when that empire was already reeling from the repeated shocks of a great war, the Rising could hardly have escaped an unwelcome notoriety; and even the citizens of Dublin, when the rebels were marched through their streets under guard on their way to prison, showed themselves to be either coldly apathetic or actively hostile. The fact that England was still thought to be fighting for the rights of small nations in general and of one small Catholic nation in particular; the pride that was taken in the famous Irish regiments now standing side by side with the English — these, it would seem, had condemned the Rising in Dublin. And was not the destruction there, though caused for the most part by English artillery and English incendiary shells, none the less due to those untimely rebels? But then began a series of courts-martial, conducted in secret; then began the announcement, day by day, of the execution not only of the leaders but of secondary figures as well. The city was soon filled with rumors of worse things to follow — surreptitious murders, mass arrests, a wholesale revenge. And suddenly the spirit of Dublin and the country at large underwent a profound and, as it turned out, a lasting change. What had been on the surface an unwanted and unpopular rising became the nucleus of a national movement; and men who had been mocked and even pelted with filth when they marched through the streets as prisoners of the British Army, were transformed into martyrs and heroes after they had died before its firing squads.

No doubt the imperial government had, and not for the first time, abetted Irish subversion with an act of helpful stupidity: in this instance by permitting a military mind, and no brilliant one at that, to decide the fate of the Irish leaders. But it would be absurd to believe, and no one has believed, that the executions alone produced so swift a revulsion in the feelings of the Irish people. The executions were at best a proximate cause. Beneath that rather shallow feeling of agreement with the English cause as against the German, there lay for most Irishmen, to put it mildly, an inveterate and incurable distaste for English rule.

"In political terms," it has been well said, "this [the declaration of the existence of an independent Irish Republic] was the principal achievement of the insurrection, the point of departure, it is hardly too much to say, for all subsequent Irish history."[1] In history a past bespeaks a future; a future imperatively demands a past. The Easter Rising of April 1916 rose up from the troubled depths of Irish history; it was even to some extent a product of the earthy spells of Irish mythology: it was also a bitter, exact and decisive gloss upon the long unhappy annals of Anglo-Irish relations.

II

Indeed, the Proclamation of the Provisional Government of the Irish Republic, read out by Padraic Pearse that Easter Monday, was above all an appeal to Irish history, which was seen as the matrix of republicanism. "Irishmen and Irishwomen," it began, "in the name of God and of the dead generations from which she receives her old tradition of nationhood, Ireland, through us, summons her children to her flag and strikes for her freedom."

A long backward look would be required to contain everything that the Proclamation thus summoned from the past and to retrace those steps by which England imposed upon a stubbornly Catholic people a Protestant garrison of landlords and clergy. The garrison itself was not always of one mind: the last great rebellion — the rebellion of 1798 — was largely the work of Protestant dissenting radicals in the northeast; and the Catholic rising which occurred simultaneously in Leinster and specifically in the county of Wexford was in sympathy with the Protestant rising but not usually with Protestants. Both were suppressed with extreme savagery: floggings, mutilations, torture, death. Had not the rebels counted on help from the French Directory? Had not General Humbert landed in Connaught? Had not a French fleet, carrying Wolfe Tone and three thousand soldiers, been intercepted off the coast of Donegal? Whether or not there had been any *rapprochement* between Catholic and Protestant dissidents, both had risen: in that era of revolution and repression, such a coincidence was intolerable.

The English answer, the Act of Union of 1800, was not really satisfactory to the leaders of the Protestant garrison, the landed and clerical interests: but if they had lost their Parliament in Dublin, they had retained (they supposed) their control of all that mattered in Irish affairs. The Catholic leaders may well have been happy with the thought that they were now to be admitted, without any revolutionary upheaval, into full political and civil equality: for what could the "United Kingdom of Great Britain and Ireland" mean if not that? What indeed? It was not until 1829 that the Catholics received Emancipation, and then only by sacrificing the very voters who had made it possible. As for the Protestant Ascendency, its foundations were, in

----

fact, weakened — as if by some earthquake — by the huge reverberations of
O'Connell's oratory and the tramping of the crowds which came to listen:
for Daniel O'Connell, with his Catholic Association in the 1820s and his
Repeal Association in the early 1840s, organized a formidable Catholic political nation, which he refrained only at the last moment from leading into
open defiance of the English Government. And then the Famine of 1845–50,
along with numberless more pitiful and innocent victims, consigned the
Protestant dispensation all unwitting, for it rarely perceived the implications
of anything, to a lingering and far from exemplary death.

It would be unnecessary here to recite in detail an unspeakably grievous
tale. Before the Great Famine (there had been many lesser ones) set its black
Malthusian stamp upon the whole process, Irish population had about
doubled itself since the 1780s, reaching in 1841 the immense figure of eight
million. There was no industrial outlet for this population; it was obliged to
compress itself into such arable land as there was, which in turn was sub-
divided into minute and yet minuter portions. Here the only food was the
irrepressible potato — irrepressible, that is to say, when it was not struck by
blight, after which it became the most treacherous of crops. Here they lived
for the most part in cabins which (said Sir Walter Scott) would scarce serve
for pigsties in Scotland.

This system of land tenure was, as often as not, left by an indifferent
landlord to the mercies of a "middleman," whose business it was to wring a
good rent from a pauperized tenantry, and to whom subdivision — which in
any case could hardly have been avoided — seemed the easiest means of
doing so. When the Famine struck in 1845, it is perhaps safe to say that the
Irish land system, such as it was, had got completely out of control.

It has been pointed out, and this is indeed of the greatest interest, that
Ireland had become the laboratory in the pre-Famine years for one or two
experiments in centralization, experiments which — though they reveal no
overall plan — were none the less ahead of the times. A system of public
education was initiated in 1831, a system of public health in 1805. The second
was a scheme for public dispensaries for the poor, and a plan for the speciali-
zation of hospital services which strikes one as being a good deal more
sophisticated than the services themselves could ever have been. The first
belied the intention of its founders by becoming more and more denomina-
tional. Yet the fact remains that two largely uniform and centralized plans
were actually in existence in Ireland, at a time when the tide of English
opinion was already flowing toward decentralization and *laissez-faire*.

What could this mean? In one sense, it meant that Ireland was a colony,

where social experiments could be performed for which English public opinion was not yet ready. (In this way, at the other end of the century, the
Sidney Webbs were in favor of the Boer War because they wanted the Boer
republics to revert to the position of a colonial laboratory.) But did it also
imply a deposit of idealism among all the forbidding strata of Irish administration? Undoubtedly it did. The public education scheme was a genuine
response to the desire of the Irish peasantry to obtain some schooling for
their children. The public health system (even if the dispensary side of it
remained largely on paper) was an equally genuine response to the helplessness of the agrarian poor.

This helplessness, in quite another form, was revealed in a more direct
form of centralization — one that might be described as less a response than
a comment. This was the Irish police system, and here comparisons are very
much in order.

In England, after the close of the Napoleonic Wars, there was riot and
misery enough, and the Government which responded with (for example)
the Six Acts of 1820 — on the whole a cruel effort to limit the right of
petition — can hardly be accused of imagination. On the other hand, this
Government was by no means wedded to efficiency. Its usual method of
keeping the peace, in times of disaffection and tumult, was to announce a
state of "Alarm," suspend the Habeas Corpus Act, and then sit back and
leave the restoration of law and order to the regulars, the yeomanry and the
justices of the peace. Upon these unpaid justices, in fact, the "gentlemen of
the parish" as Lord Liverpool called them, much of the responsibility for law
and order descended. It was these amateur magistrates, lay and clerical,
who could if necessary, without further consultation, call for military aid.
England still seemed to live in an age of Dogberry and Verges: almost of
Justice Shallow and Justice Silence. Its local government had hardly changed
since the days of the Tudors, and police, as we understand the term, scarcely
existed.

The ordinary Englishman recoiled from the very thought of a police
system. It conjured up visions of sinister European practices. Better to chance
a throat-slitting, a house-burning, a frame-wrecking, a riot, than to have the
minions of some Fouché spying on one's daily affairs or slyly tapping on
one's door at midnight. Informers, of course, there were: the Home Office
could not have got along without them. But the Home Office was as yet not
greatly respected; informers were anything but organized; and the absence
of a regular police was a matter for congratulation. As a parliamentary
committee of 1816–1818 put it: "the police of a free country was to be found

in rational and humane laws, in an effective and enlightened magistracy, [and] above all in the moral habits and opinions of the people."[2]

It is one of the curiosities, or rather one of the enduring conundrums of history, that the English common people — though sorely tried — should not have resorted to downright revolution in the early decades of the nineteenth century. Halévy's answer to this conundrum — the prevalence of an evangelical ethic among the people's natural leaders — has often been questioned but never demolished in detail. Or could it have been the genuinely amateur nature of local government which compelled a grudging respect? Or did the old Whig concept of Parliamentarism still retain some magical power? Whatever the answer, the people did not resort to revolution and, odder still, it was somehow or other hoped — one cannot exactly say "expected" — that they never would. Thus England waited until 1829 before a police force was instituted, and then only in London. In 1839, a Royal Commission recommended wider areas; but even in that year it was not daring enough to propose a national system; and none emerged until 1856.

Ireland, on the other hand, by the year 1825, had a fully fledged police system organized by counties; by 1836, through the work of Under Secretary Thomas Drummond, this had become a centrally controlled national force.[3] The difference need not be labored. In Ireland there could be no talk about the police being found "above all in the moral habits and opinions of the people." Nor was there much faith in "an effective and enlightened magistracy" if by "magistracy" one meant the local landowner or Anglican (Church of Ireland) clergyman. The first was considered a usurper, the second a heretic; neither had a genuine or even a presumptive stake in the welfare of the Catholic peasantry, in this world or the next.

In fact the parish could not be, as it was in England, the primary unit of local government. The Protestant gentry and clergy did not have that sort of deeply indigenous concern which would permit them to dispense even the rough-hewn local justice which prevailed in England. And so, in 1822, one finds that salaried magistrates were sent out into the Irish countryside to bolster up the justices of the peace. By 1836, these had been transformed into Resident Magistrates, well-paid functionaries, projections of the central administration in Dublin Castle. How effective they actually were is another question: but it is difficult not to see what kind of government this was. Act of Union or no Act of Union, it was the government of an alien and hostile people.

Those who were at all familiar with them readily admitted that the Irish peasants were a courteous, hospitable, and witty race. Their charm was recognized; their gaiety almost proverbial. And even Anthony Trollope, who lived for several years in Ireland as a postal inspector, and whose sympathies were with the landlords, admitted that "the [Irish] working classes [are] very much more intelligent than those of England." "But," he added, "they are perverse, irrational, and little bound by love of truth."[4]

This criticism seems to beg the question, by an appeal to that equally perverse and irrational abstraction "love of truth." Years of oppression had taught the Catholic Irish that they could not look to the law for protection; that every one of its representatives, from judge to juror, was an enemy; that to reveal what was really in their minds would be dangerous: that the truth, while great and prevailing, commonly prevailed against them. Under such circumstances, mere prudence suggested that it was best to say what was expected and would do the least harm. The real truth — what was really in the mind — was a secret, to be acted out, if at all, in dark and conspiratorial ways.

The secret societies, whose members roamed the countryside after sunset, the Whiteboys, Threshers, Blackfeet, and Ribbonmen, constituted indeed a *negotium perambulans in tenebris,* a terror that walketh by night, a dread and a warning to rackrenting landlords and tithing clergy. Their methods — particularly the maiming of animals — were usually disgusting: for the secret societies personified the ferocity which never lay far beneath the pleasing surface of the Irish character. They were helplessness on the prowl — the lawlessness, that is to say, of those who have been deserted by the law. But if it had not been for Ribbonism, the condition of the Irish tenant would have been even more wretched than it was.[5]

Thus it is natural enough that England should have celebrated the lawless and alien character of this people with Insurrection Acts, Arms Acts and Peace Preservation Acts, looming like monuments to misrule in the years between the Act of Union and the Famine. It certainly would seem that the Government in Westminster and Whitehall and its subsidiary in Dublin Castle had realized that to the Irish they were foreigners and the Irish foreigners to them.

And yet, to cite one famous example, they sometimes continued to act as if no such difference existed. In 1838, it was decided to introduce into Ireland the English poor law system, as embodied in the Poor Law Amendment Act of 1834.

This act was a recognition of the undoubted fact that the old poor law, which constituted a subsidizing of wages, had distributed the burden of outdoor relief among the ratepayers in a very inequitable manner. The new act, therefore, no longer (though there were many exceptions to this) permitted outdoor relief to the able-bodied poor. The able-bodied poor were now to be herded into workhouses, where the situation of the pauper, said the new Poor Law Commissioners, "must cease to be really or apparently so eligible as the situation of the independent labourer of the lowest class."

In England the Poor Law Amendment Act was deeply hated and bitterly resisted; but its harsh Benthamite logic seemed to work, at least to the extent that the English ratepayer was able to finance it. In Ireland, where two and a half million laborers were in a state of semi-starvation every summer, after the old potato crop had been consumed and before the new one came in, the new Poor Law made no sense at all. It was said to have been imposed upon Ireland to prevent the yearly migration of Irish workers into England; either for that purpose, or for a frankly genocidal one. The latter explanation, while inadmissible in fact, was at least compelling in fancy.

It was not that the Government had been left in the dark. A Royal Commission had been appointed in 1835 to consider the question of introducing the Poor Law into Ireland. Its report, issued after it had been sitting for three years, was a candid and enlightened admission that no comparisons could be made between English poverty and Irish poverty, or (for that matter) between English property and Irish property. It reported against workhouses, not merely because there were simply too many paupers to be accommodated, but also because the Irish ratepayer could not sustain them. It recommended instead a wide and enlightened scheme of land development: the reclaiming of the nearly three million acres of bog land known to exist, the passing of a drainage act for cultivated land, the replacing of cabins by better houses, the setting up of allotments for cottiers in waste land, and the establishment of model agricultural schools. Along with this proposal for the abolition of underemployment and undercultivation, it suggested that poor rates could afterwards safely be introduced for the relief of the sick, the infirm and the aged.[6]

The Government was proof against this sort of thing. After a brief visit to Ireland, George Nicholls, an English Poor Law Commissioner, reported in favor of the denial of all outdoor relief, the setting up of workhouses, and the division of the poor rate between owner and occupier. Since the Royal Commission had pointed out that an adequate workhouse system would cost £5,000,000 a year against a total annual rental of £10,000,000, it is clear that the Government was unable or unwilling to perceive that Ireland was not England.

A vast amount of authentic information had been produced before the great Potato Famine struck in 1845. A hundred and fourteen Royal Commissions, 61 parliamentary committees had, since the passing of the Act of Union, and up to 1833, sat down to consider and to report on the condition of Ireland.[7] All had foreseen the calamity that at length befell that unhappy land. The recklessness of the landlord, the avarice of the middleman, the steady growth of population, the crowding of more and more people upon less and less land — the commissions and the committees had duly reported all this. They had noted the fatal propensity of the potato to disease and of the land system to sub-division; they had pointed out the dangers of reprisal which confronted the "improving" landlord, the beggary and death which befell the evicted tenant. But their reports have benefited only the historian. The Government made no move until the Famine was upon it. Then and then only, when it was too late, did it inaugurate a policy of reclamation.

The Famine runs like a great *sudd* through Irish history, which can offer no single calamity to equal it. In 1841, the population had passed the eight million mark; in 1851 it had dropped to 6,500,000: such were the effects of death, disease and emigration. In other words, a population increase, aided and abetted by a land system which piled more and more people upon less and less land, had reached unbearable proportions by 1845 when, by a truly Malthusian trick of nature, at least one million died in the famine years, while others fled the sick and starving island.

For the Catholics who survived the Famine and resisted emigration, a great change was in store. This has been described as "The Devotional Revolution"[8] — that is to say, a disciplinary reform within the priesthood and a religious revival among the population.

In pre-Famine Ireland, the Catholic clergy were not in good odor with the Congregatio De Propaganda Fide, the great missionary organization in Rome: too many of them were given to avarice, drunkenness and unchastity. Into the archives of Propaganda, to be sure, reports of vice were more apt to find their way than were tales of virtue: but the condition of the Church was far from edifying. It has been estimated that, at the very most, only 40 percent of the Catholic population went to mass. As early as 1819, it is true, Bishop Doyle of Kildare and Leighlin had endeavored, not without success, to introduce a better discipline into his diocese; and in the late 1830s and early 1840s there were signs of a religious revival: but there were not enough priests or churches to cope with the religious needs of that overcrowded countryside, where people lived in unimaginable squalor on the dreary margins of subsistence.

It was in 1850 that Paul Cullen, Rector of the Irish College in Rome, was transferred to Ireland as Archbishop of Armagh: two years later, he was translated to Dublin. He was a disciplinarian with a strong missionary spirit — a new transmontane broom which swept away many abuses long sanctioned if not sanctified by custom — a great promoter of pilgrimages, processions, triduums, novenas and all the varieties of organized devotion.

In these labors, although hampered by much internal opposition, he was greatly assisted by the fact that he had been preceded by a Famine: for the Famine inevitably left those who remained in Ireland with a deep sense of sin and guilt. Otherwise, why had the land been so fearfully punished? Then again, the population had been so reduced by death and emigration in those dread years that the ratio of priests to laity, of pastor to flock, now greatly increased. In the third place, the conduct of the priesthood, as episcopal administration grew more efficient and austere, underwent a notable reform.

Moreover, the Famine was the focus of a cultural deprivation which had long been in the making. The Union, binding Ireland more closely to Great Britain, naturally tended to anglicize communications, both written and spoken, and the Famine did its part in driving the Irish language back into the West. This process, it has been argued, forced the Irish into something like an identity crisis, in which they began to look for a substitute language and to find it in the teachings and ceremonies of the Church. Thus, with the passing years, the devotional and practicing Catholics increased to more than 90 percent of the Catholic population, and the terms "Catholic" and "Irish" became virtually interchangeable. The significance of the Church as a cultural factor in the development of Irish nationalism cannot, of course, be overemphasized; and since the agrarian economy of Ireland, all through the later nineteenth century, was in poor shape, the Church's moderating influence — in the face of a Land League or even of a Plan of Campaign — must also be taken into strict account.

Nor must one forget another legacy of the Famine years. Before 1845 early marriages were customary and indeed encouraged — "They cannot be worse off than they are," said the Bishop of Raphoe in 1835, "and they may help each other" — but after the Famine late marriages became and remained the rule. Late marriage was indeed "the only method of birth control practicable in Catholic marriage";[9] it was also a tribute, if that is the right word, to the deep-seated trauma inflicted by the Famine.

Years later, the Gaelic League came into being as a reviver of the language and, in all innocence, as a nurse of revolution; but nothing revived the birth rate or discouraged the emigrations. In 1911, the population figures for the whole island, Catholic and Protestant, stood at 4,390,000.

It has been said with some justice that the English Government not only mismanaged the problem of famine relief, but mismanaged it in a bleak and unimaginative way. Governments in those days, of course, were not equipped to handle such a vast catastrophe: and indeed it has been claimed (and by one of the most brilliant of its critics) that, from the partial famine of 1845 until the summer of 1847, the English Government behaved with some generosity. "An elaborate relief organization was set up, public works were started on a scale never attempted before, and a very large sum of money indeed, more than eight million pounds, was advanced."[10] This was not enough; but it was in all probability as much as any other Government could or would have done.

In 1847, however, after a financial crisis in England, the dire edict went forth that famine relief was to be transferred to the Irish Poor Law. According to this law, in Ireland as in England, parishes had been grouped into Unions, and boards of guardians had been elected to carry out the policy of workhouse relief. Even in pre-Famine days, a large number of these Unions had been near bankruptcy, the poor rates had never been collected in full or at all or otherwise than by force, and the workhouses had, if built, as often as not been left unfurnished and unstaffed. How could anyone suppose that this travesty of a system, after a year and a half of famine, would be able to provide the necessary relief? Actually, what we are privileged to observe here is the darker side of the utilitarian mind at work. The Poor Law system, on paper, was a most rational construct: all one had to do was to postulate or invent an Ireland which could implement the system out of the rates; and, that feat accomplished, one could leave the real Ireland to her fate. Above the Whole Famine one might inscribe, as an appropriate motto, "the greatest happiness of the greatest number."

When all was over, there entered into the surviving Irish politics and Irish society a bitterness and a grimness unknown in O'Connell's heyday. One of the gravest charges was that, at the height of the famine, vast quantities of grain and oats were being *exported* from Ireland. Grain and oats were not consumer crops in Ireland; they were grown to pay the rent; and they had become a recognized part of Anglo-Irish exchanges. To turn them back for distribution would have been difficult if not impossible even for the reforming Tory government of Sir Robert Peel, not to mention its inactive Whig successor under Lord John Russell. Such exportations were, in fact, simply a reflection upon the land system and the governments which, for years, had made them compulsory. Republicanism, which seemed to have died out in the rebellion of 1798, was born again in the years of the Famine.

There had been a great deal of sympathy from England, much of it of a very practical kind: but there was also, it goes almost without saying, a Podsnapian feeling of repulsion, indeed of contempt. Might it not be said that the Irish had only themselves to blame? That they were irresponsible, ungrateful, treacherous? That, when all was said and done, they were "unfit to govern themselves, or even to enjoy the same constitutional rights as the rest of the United Kingdom?"[11] "How can such a people be assisted?" wrote Lord John Russell in 1848 — Lord John Russell, who had never lifted a finger to assist them.[12]

After the Famine, the Irish rebellion acquired what might well be called a new constituency. Irishmen had emigrated to the United States in pre-Famine days; the Erie Canal, for example, was dug largely (and with a horrid waste of life) by Irish labor: but it was not until the great migration of 1846 and 1847 that the United States harbored the beginnings of a distinctive Irish-American population — a population which nourished an enduring hatred for Britain. At first both hated and despised for their drunkenness and violence, they acquired in due time and with successive emigrations a new respectability and an important political influence, and became an object of grave concern to English statesmanship. They collected and transmitted funds to Ireland; they nurtured revolutionary anti-British societies; worse still, they touched a sensitive nerve in the highest places in American government. By the end of the nineteenth century, no English Government could think of them without a shudder. To a lesser extent, but in sufficient numbers to provoke a salutary concern, these Irish of the dispersal were to be found in Canada, in Australia, and indeed throughout the Empire.

Chapter Two

Disturbance

Because so many of those who fled or died were Irish-speaking, the Famine almost silenced the Irish tongue, and certainly drove it back into the Irish West. It also left a vicious land system unimproved and unrepentant. Between 1849 and 1852 there were 58,423 evictions, and after one has subtracted the families readmitted in one form or another the total still stands at 48,295 — a savage figure.[1] Even when better conditions returned, tillage prices did not rise at the same rate as animal prices, the number of small farms decreased, and those who were put off the land had no other prospect than emigration or death. Into these scenes the English Parliament continued to import its own form of misery.

An Encumbered Estates Act (1849) made the sale of debit-ridden estates much easier than was ordinarily the case when land changed owners, with the result that the peasants were often delivered into the hands of a new and more grasping set of landlords. A weirdly titled Civil Rights Act (1851) legalized the ejectment for arrears in the case of every tenant whose rent was less than £50. The Deasy Act (1860) gave the landowner an absolute power to dispose of his land as he saw fit. It was a fundamental belief with the Irish that anyone who undertook to till the soil became possessed of rights which could not be interfered with: the Deasy Act, blatantly establishing a free trade in land, challenged this sacred belief in the breast of every peasant affected, and produced a state of continual and increasing disturbance.[2]

As Patrick O'Farrell has put it: if England had her Irish question, Ireland most assuredly had her English question.[3]

Short of revolution, would there ever be an answer?

I

Both the Young Ireland movement in '48 and '49 and the Irish Republican Brotherhood in '67 made attempts at revolution. Young Ireland survived its two failures and lingered on as a most attractive ideology: its best prose writer, John Mitchel, had a profound influence on Arthur Griffith; the thoughts of Fintan Lalor, its most persuasive ideologue, still echo in the printed works of James Connolly and Padraic Pearse; its poet, Thomas Davis, became the bard of Sinn Fein and his work could never be "de-Davisized" out of Irish life. As for the Fenian Rising of '67, though strikingly ineffective, it did not altogether fail to have an effect. It was, said William Ewart Gladstone, "the first streak of dawn"[4] — a peculiar expression for an Englishman, but then Mr. Gladstone had a peculiar mind: and when he became Prime Minister after the Election of 1868, he succeeded in disestablishing the (Anglican) Church of Ireland and in passing a Land Reform Act in 1870.

These measures, to which incidentally the Irish Republican Brotherhood was totally indifferent, were at best symbolic. The alien Church lost standing rather than material endowments, and power of a spiritual nature — it was opposed by the Catholic National Association on the one hand and the Protestant Liberation Society on the other — it had wielded only to a limited extent. And the Land Act of 1870, while insisting that the Irish peasant had rights, did absolutely nothing to advance them. To borrow the language of the great O'Connell, the landlords could have driven — and in effect did drive — a coach and six through the Act of 1870; and Benjamin Disraeli was uttering only a truism when he predicted that it would lead to "increased bitterness and increased perils to society."[5]

The Irish peasant had one frightening weapon — agrarian disturbance: it remained only to take this weapon out of the hands of Ribbonism and put it under the control of an effective organization. Another catastrophe was required before this could happen; and in the three years 1877, 1878 and 1879 this catastrophe came slowly and horribly into sight.

In 1877 there was heavy rainfall, which damaged both planting and harvest. 1878 was somewhat more clement, although the essential potato yield was very poor. Then came the dread denouement. "It is impossible for the imagination to devise a worse combination of weather conditions than befell the Irish in 1879." The mean temperature of every month from January to September was far below the average; the rainfall in June and July was 100 percent above that of the preceding ten years; in July and August there was no summer heat. The estimated value of all crops in Ireland, which stood at £36.6 million in 1876, fell to £22.7 million in 1879.[6]

Elsewhere in Europe the years had been dreadful too. In England, for example, the combination of three bad harvests with an invasion of cheap American wheat dealt agriculture a blow from which it did not recover until well into the next century. In Ireland, where oats and barley were more typical crops, the impact of American wheat was not so severe: but the crop destruction coincided with a general fall in prices, and in parts of the country there was starvation as bad as it had been in the Famine years. To make matters worse, the customary exodus of Irish farm labor to England ceased, because England had no work to offer.

Low prices in Ireland meant eviction, despair and, of course, the reign of "Captain Moonlight" with its usual accompaniments. Ricks were burned; cattle maimed; graves dug before doors and sometimes filled as well. Persons whose property or profession accustomed them to the receipt of threatening letters now found that they had a new correspondent, one "Rory of the Hills, who always warns before he kills."[7] Among those who met this fate was Lord Mountmorris, despatched in his stronghold in County Galway. And so it went, growing worse and worse.

Into these calamities there stepped a certain Michael Davitt, who had lost an arm in an English factory and who — after seven years of hell in Dartmoor for his part in an attack on Chester Castle — had been released in 1877 on ticket-of-leave. A most compassionate man, one of the saints of Fenianism, Davitt conceived the idea of uniting the extreme and moderate wings of Nationalism in support of the oppressed peasantry; and actually succeeded in converting no less a man than Charles Stewart Parnell, the most conspicuous figure among a militant group of Irish M.P.s. "Conversion" is perhaps too strong a word: Parnell was fully awake to the political advantages in this strange connection.

When Davitt returned from America in 1879, with the blessing of John Devoy and the Clan na Gael, and founded his Land League in October, Parnell agreed to become its president. Thus began the "New Departure," a powerful and frightening combination between two very different kinds of agitation — parliamentary Obstruction and agrarian Disturbance.

The Land League proposed to create an organization of peasant farmers strong enough to bring about a significant reduction in rents, assist those who were threatened with eviction, and eventually wring from the Government a radical change in the land system. Although it was ostensibly a reforming movement, and therefore not acceptable to the orthodox leadership of the I.R.B., there were many Fenians in the League and John Devoy certainly saw the New Departure as the first step toward an armed uprising.[8]

This was not the aim of Davitt or Parnell. The former dreamed of a peaceful land nationalization; the latter hoped for a peasant proprietorship — two widely divergent views which neither revealed to the other. Davitt was a disciple of Fintan Lalor; Parnell had never read Lalor, and would not have approved of him if he had. These misunderstandings did not prevent the New Departure from becoming one of the most significant events in Irish history.

Parnell was always a constitutionalist, hoping to achieve his ends through legislation in Westminster. But just as the Land League, although its characteristic weapon was the boycott and its avowed purpose a peaceful resistance, was accompanied and sustained by a violent Ribbonism, so Parnell, after 1879, carried with him into the House of Commons the threat of an armed *jacquerie*. In England, in fact, the Land League was always seen as the forerunner of revolution, even as revolution itself. When Parnell acquiesced in the suppression of the Land League, when he entered into an understanding with the Liberals in 1886 and afterwards, the threat was still there. It was one of the sources of his extraordinary influence.

II

Charles Stewart Parnell was a Protestant landlord from County Wicklow. When in 1875, at the age of twenty-nine, he entered Parliament as the member for Meath, an impressive appearance seemed all he had to offer. Tall and beautiful, he sat in impenetrable silence, a graven image: the Home Rule Party of those days was quite content with that. By 1877, however, Parnell had found his voice and revealed his vocation, becoming the leader of an exotic radical wing of this decent entity. To him and his colleagues, each of the great English parties was suspect, to say the least: "odious" would be a better word. Their method of attack was "obstructionism," the skillful use of Parliament's rules against itself, thus making business difficult and even impossible. On one occasion they kept the House in continuous session for forty-one hours; and the unhappy Speaker was forced to invent and impose a new rule, curbing a hallowed freedom of speech. "We shall never gain anything from England," said Parnell, "unless we tread upon her toes."[9]

This extraordinary man, so eager to make a Judy out of the Mother of Parliaments and so successful in doing so, had been brought up in an atmosphere of eccentric Anglophobia. His maternal grandfather, a commodore in the United States Navy, had fought the British in the War of 1812. His American mother, although she danced attendance at the vice-regal Court in Dublin, and sent her sons to an English school and to Cambridge University (from which respectable institution Parnell was expelled for felling a debt collector), confessed herself an ardent admirer of the Fenian movement. If Parnell was feared in the Commons it was because, unlike the ordinary Irish member, who tended to be excitable or uncouth or both, he turned against the English gentlemen a weapon they considered to be exclusively their own — the dreaded *morgue anglaise,* an ineffable and freezing contempt. "His very passion was English," said Lord Cowper, "his reserve was English, his coolness was English."[10] Lord Cowper, however, had forgotten Parnell's pride — the pride of an Irish gentleman who considered that his English counterparts did not treat him with the proper respect.

In any event, his was a character unique in Anglo-Irish politics. A constitutionalist, a conservative, a rebel, with his cold *persona,* his aristocratic aloofness, and his passionate heart; a man of manifold superstitions; an introvert who shrank from the audiences that welcomed him; a great Irish patriot to whom the color green was almost physically sickening — there he stands in the eye of history, a Protestant landlord addressing those Catholic peasants, from many a green-draped platform and in the name of anti-landlordism.

To the conservative Irish peasants his manly form, his physical beauty, his very lack of oratory in a land where orators abounded — all these carried a unique appeal: nor had they any objection, historical or otherwise, to aristocratic leadership. To the English these Parnellite crowds inevitably recalled the days of O'Connell and the monster Repeal meeting at Clontarf, which O'Connell had called off only at the last moment. Another Clontarf and this time a successful one — was it possible? The thought of a great leader with a discontented peasantry at his back haunted Whitehall and Westminster, even if Parnell urged only a boycott, even if Davitt spoke only of "moral force," even if, in terms of context and character, O'Connell and Parnell were light years apart.

There followed, therefore, two predictable responses to the Land League agitation: the great Land Act of 1881 and a ferocious Coercion Act in the same year. The Land Act, by giving the southern and western tenant access to the Ulster custom of fair rent, free trade and fixity of tenure, put him into a state of "dual ownership" with his landlord, but of course ignored the fact that what he wanted was no landlord at all. The Coercion Act put Parnell into Kilmainham Gaol for language unbecoming an Irish subject of the Queen.

It was here, in jail, that Parnell agreed to the suppression of the Land League in return for a halt in coercion and substantial concession in the matter of arrears in Irish rent; his own release from prison was part of the "Treaty." This was collaboration with a vengeance, and he might well have lost his influence with agrarian activism if, on 6 May 1822, a new Chief Secretary (Lord Frederick Cavendish) and his Under Secretary (Mr. T. H. Burke) had not been murdered in Phoenix Park — slashed to death with surgical knives by a group of Fenian extremists known as "The Invincibles." This lamentable event was followed, as a matter of course, by renewed coercion; Parnell raised his voice in furious protest, although the murder itself had filled him with revulsion; and thus his prestige was restored.

The stars in their courses seemed to fight for him. His new National League of October 1882 — moderate, more dedicated to Home Rule than to land reform, not popular in America — was ill-advisedly condemned by the Vatican, a condemnation universally resented and producing an odd quasi-concordat between Parnell and the Catholic Church. There followed the Liberal Reform Act of 1884, which enfranchised the farm laborers of the United Kingdom and ironically tripled the Irish agricultural vote. "Ironically" because, in the election of 1885, the Liberals were driven out of every constituency they had held in Ireland and there came back to Westminster a highly disciplined Parnellite party of eighty-six members.

After a curious flirtation with the Conservatives, marked by profound misunderstanding on both sides, Parnell accepted from Mr. Gladstone, in 1886, a Home Rule Bill of great respectability and one which, if Parliament had agreed to it, would have gone a long way toward solving the Irish Question — always supposing that the generous land purchase bill which accompanied it had also been accepted. Such speculations are, however, quite useless: for the Conservatives were convinced that Home Rule meant the dissolution of the Constitution itself; the Liberal Whigs were of a like mind; and both Gladstone and Parnell had insulted Joseph Chamberlain, leader of the radical wing of the Liberals, who in any case was inclined to look upon Ireland as a kind of Birmingham slum. Indeed the Home Rule Bill was defeated even before the Conservatives, the Whigs and the Radicals voted it down on its second reading; after this defeat the Liberal Party seemed to lie in ruins, an unpedestalled armless statue.

And yet — it was odd but it was true — Parnell and Gladstone seemed undismayed. Each of these giants was deeply conservative; neither was afraid of radical expedients. They moved on together: not friends, barely on speaking terms, not quite arm in arm; on parallel lines. Parnell survived a landlord-industrialist attack on him, led by the London *Times*, which published some letters suggesting that he had condoned the murder of Lord Frederick Cavendish. The letters were shown to be forgeries; and with that it seemed as if the tide had turned and that the Gladstone-Parnell entente would bring Home Rule to Ireland before the century was out.

The complexities of Parnellism, both within itself, and in its relation to English politics, are very subtle and very important: they have been unraveled and rewoven many times, and once especially by a master hand.* Here it has been necessary only to dwell upon one aspect of Parnell's influence: and one must now, as a final example of this one aspect, recall the Irish scene of the mid-1880s.

A new agricultural depression had settled in in the winter of 1885–86; violent resistance to eviction broke out in many places; and in the autumn of 1886 the "Plan of Campaign" was instituted.

The plan proposed that tenants on rackrented estates — for rackrenting persisted despite the Land Act of 1881 — should organize and agree upon a reasonable rent; each of their committees should offer the rent to the landlord on the next "gale" day; and if the offer were refused the rent should remain in the hands of the committee until the landlord came to terms. It was in truth a formidable arrangement; it was endorsed by the Parnellite National League; Parnell's chief lieutenants, John Dillon (the son of a Young Ireland journalist) and William O'Brien were deeply involved in it and went to prison for their pains.

* Conor Cruise O'Brien, *Parnell and His Party* (Oxford, 1957).

Parnell himself had gone into retirement. Ill-health, the companionship of Mrs. O'Shea, a growing attachment to mystification, made him less and less visible, more and more Yeats's "Great Comedian." When the Conservative Government (which regarded the Plan of Campaign, with its frantic scenes of riot and repression, as another prelude to revolution) passed a fearful Coercion Act in 1887; when the viceroy "proclaimed" the National League as a dangerous and illegal association; when police brutalities, often enough the result of great provocation, culminated in the killing of several rioters at Mitchelstown in October — even then Parnell maintained his singular detachment. Privately he disapproved of the Plan of Campaign: publicly, he neither endorsed nor disavowed it. But when the plan began to run down in 1889, he showed that he had not discarded his earlier self of the Land League days. He organized a Tenants' Defence Association — to keep the plan alive with new funds, to protect "tenants threatened by the landlord conspiracy," to import into this agrarian upheaval a renewed and radical demand for "combination and organization."[11]

The importance of this cannot be overlooked. Here was a great Parliamentary leader, with an angry peasantry at his back, whose position was clearly this: — if England delayed too long in granting Home Rule, there was still the alternative of an agrarian rising. "The most advanced section of Irishmen," he said in May 1889, "as well as the least advanced have always understood that the parliamentary policy was to be a trial."[12]

Nobody of any consequence could overlook the menace in that: and indeed nobody did. In 1889 the political sentiment in England was turning towards a Parnellite Home Rule, as the lesser of two evils.

The end was in strict accordance with Victorian morals. For years it had been known that Katharine O'Shea was Parnell's mistress. Captain O'Shea knew it, the leaders of the Irish Party knew it, Mr. Gladstone and Mr. Chamberlain knew it. Indeed, it was an open secret; and certainly no unusual one. Once exposed to the press and to public opinion, however, it was transformed at once into an open sewer. In 1890, Captain O'Shea — possibly urged on by that unforgiving enemy, Joseph Chamberlain — instituted divorce proceedings. Parnell, who believed that money would be found (it was not) to buy O'Shea off, did not contest them. He was consequently placed in the most disagreeable light by O'Shea's lawyers; Mr. Gladstone's nonconformist following raised a fierce outcry; Mr. Gladstone announced that he could not work with Parnell as leader of the Irish Party; and the Irish bishops realized that it was no longer possible to remain silent.

At this the Irish Party, after some fearful scenes in Committee Room 15 of the House of Commons, scenes of towering rage and tragic recrimination, at last, on 6 December 1890, split into two unequal parts. The majority (it included the gift-tormented T. M. Healy and the honorable John Dillon) voted to unseat Parnell as chairman: amidst the small minority stood a Wicklow squire called John Redmond.

In three Irish by-elections in 1891, Parnell fought back. He began with a manifesto, in which he repudiated the Liberal Party. Could this have been mere opportunism, or could it have represented what in his heart of hearts he had always felt? Whatever the answer, there now emerged the rebel whose presence the English had always suspected and always feared: for in his speeches he began to call on the hillside men — on Ribbonism itself — to come to his assistance. Of course it was too late. The Irish cared nothing for the nonconformists, and not too much for Mr. Gladstone: but the Church had spoken, and spoken in terms of morality not of politics. Parnell was hooted on many a platform, he was pelted in many a town; on one occasion lime was thrown into his eyes. On 27 September he spoke in Galway in a pouring rain and neglected to change his clothes. On 6 October he died, in Brighton, in the arms of Katharine O'Shea, now Katharine Parnell. He died of exposure, exhaustion and disgrace. On 11 October he was buried with solemn honors in Parnellite Dublin's Glasnevin Cemetery, an occasion on which his enemies thought it the better part of valor to remain indoors. He ascended rapidly out of politics and into myth: but he left behind him for the next ten years a divided nation and a divided party.

He also took Home Rule with him into the grave, from which it emerged, briefly and to no avail, between 1912 and 1914.

III

Although Mr. Gladstone, during the short Liberal interregnum of 1892–95, steered a Home Rule Bill through the House of Commons by a margin of 32 votes, the House of Lords — with no Parnell to overawe them — threw it out by 419 to 41.

Parnell had no adequate successor. How rarely does a Joshua succeed a Moses! The influence of his death upon the Irish Party — essentially a fatal one — can best be discerned in quite another quarter.

In English eyes both the Land League and the Plan of Campaign had Parnellite overtones. The English knew, as we think we know, that Parnell would much rather achieve his ends through Parliament than through revolution: but it is no oversimplification to say that his threatened alternative was not lost upon them. The Conservative leadership, therefore, perceived as early as 1885 that the best way to undermine the cause of Home Rule was to dig away at the roots of agrarian discontent. The Ashbourne Act of that year, the first piece of legislation which seriously encouraged tenant farmers to purchase their holdings through government financing, was the work of a caretaker Conservative Government.

Then again, while A. J. Balfour, Lord Salisbury's elegant philosophical nephew and Chief Secretary for Ireland from '87 to '91, enforced the new Coercion Act of 1887 with a cold-hearted ferocity, he had still the wit and indeed the wisdom to acknowledge the power of a discontented peasantry, especially when it had the blessing of Irish politicians in the House of Commons.

It was in this spirit that "Bloody Balfour" created the Congested Districts Board, designed to resettle uneconomic estates, promote local industries, and improve conditions generally in the west and southwest. And it was Balfour who endeavored to relieve agrarian distress with such public works as light railways: he probably enjoyed the predictable quips about light railways and heavy punishments.

Under his successor and brother, Gerald Balfour, the Conservatives went one step further with the Local Government Act of 1898. This replaced the old grand juries, as far as their administrative and fiscal duties went, with county councils, urban district councils and rural district councils. Since the old grand juries were invariably dominated by Protestant landlords, and the new elected councils were filled with Nationalist attorneys, publicans and shopkeepers, the Irish Party believed that it had come one step nearer to Home Rule through its new control of local government. The Conservatives, on the other hand, hugged to their bosoms the thought that they were "killing Home Rule with kindness."

Neither side was correct, since Home Rule survived, in a fashion, long enough for the Conservatives to kill it without any kindness at all; and since, in 1898, a new agrarian disturbance began which was destined to introduce a land reform very adverse to the influence of the Irish Party.

It so happened that the Congested Districts Board, so admirable in so many respects, had created a bitterness among the peasants because it had no powers of compulsion. There was no way in which a bankrupt or inequitable landlord could be forced to sell his holdings to the Board. It was out of this situation that the United Irish League erupted into history in 1898. Its founder was William O'Brien, a passionate, unstable, most attractive man, and one of the heroes of the Plan of Campaign. He had recently acquired a home near Westport in County Mayo, where the peasants lived huddled together — hence the term "congested" — not only at the bare level of subsistence but on the margins of wide, rich, empty grass farms. To O'Brien the solution to this uncivilized state of affairs was the compulsory purchase and resettlement of the grass farms; and it was to bring pressure upon the Congested Districts Board and the Government that the new League was founded.

Its success was immediate. It spread from Mayo and turned itself into a general movement in favor of compulsory purchase — a movement which whetted the land hunger of the Irish peasant and generated such violence that between 1901 and 1902 thirteen Irish M.P.s had been sent to prison and nine counties and two cities had been "proclaimed" as in a state of grave disorder. To O'Brien all this was most encouraging, but John Redmond, the new chairman of the Irish Parliamentary Party, saw it in a very different light. Only "apathy and chaos," he told this enthusiastic colleague, would be the result of "preaching practically universal boycotting."[13]

Redmond was too uncertain of his leadership and possibly too "constitutional" to wish to identify himself with such a movement: but he was right, at least with respect to "chaos." While the landlords as a body considered that coercion was the only remedy, a small and relatively enlightened group responded to what must now be recognized as a historic pressure. Meeting with Mr. Redmond and three other Irish Nationalists in December 1902, they produced a report which, among other useful recommendations, proposed that the government should immediately institute a grand scheme for land purchase. The report was enthusiastically endorsed by George Wyndham, the incumbent and romantic Chief Secretary; and also by his formidable Under Secretary, Sir Antony MacDonnell, whose previous service as an Indian administrator had earned him the title of "The Bengal Tiger."

The main features of the proposed Act were as follows: If three-quarters of the tenants on any given estate agreed and the landlord consented, the Commissioners under the Act were empowered to purchase the estate and resell it to the tenants for annual payments at a rate less than their present rent. To induce the landlords to sell — there was no compulsory clause — they were to be given a bonus of 12 percent on the sale price.

Here again the lack of compulsion was a grave weakness; the financial provisions needed constant revision; and the landlords had been treated with a suspicious generosity. Nevertheless the Wyndham Act was truly constructive — the pinnacle, one might say, of Conservative reform in Ireland. If it had not been for the unwavering support of A. J. Balfour, now Prime Minister, it might not have got through the Cabinet, let alone the Parliament: but it passed a stormy third reading in the Commons in July 1903; was handled with surprising mildness by the Lords (the 12 percent bonus may have had something to do with this); and received the Royal Assent in the middle of August.

If the Irish Party had a preference, it was obviously for Home Rule first and land purchase thereafter. They had been caught in a cleft stick; and nowhere is this more clearly illustrated than in a speech which John Dillon made to the Commons on 5 May 1903. He began by rejecting cooperation with the landlords who — whether enlightened or not — were all Unionists. "Where did the policy of land purchase as the only and final settlement of the land question really take its origin? *It took its origin from the Land League.*" As Dillon's biographer reminds us, no one who heard them *could* escape the meaning of these words. The policy of land purchase, or peasant proprietorship, owed its success not to cooperation with the landlords but to "sustained pressure and agitation."[14]

Later on in this speech, however, he changed his tune and, after a series of delicate transitions from one theme to another, ended by praising the proposed Act as one of "real benefit and a means of restoring peace to Ireland."[15] What else could he do at this juncture? To accept the Act was to weaken the Party, since Home Rule depended upon *not* settling the land question; to condemn the Act was politically impossible, since it conferred substantial benefits upon a historically oppressed majority of the Irish people.

Its immediate effects were spectacular. John Dillon almost left the Party because of its cooperation with the land interests; William O'Brien, who now discovered that only cooperation would do, actually did leave it;[16] the United Irish league became the organ and uneasy conscience of the Irish Parliamentary Party; and George Wyndham, never forgiven by the Unionist diehards for saving them from their own excessses, was caught in a political mistake — for which the Bengal Tiger was chiefly responsible — and hounded out of public life.

The Wyndham Act created an invidious distinction between tenants whose landlords agreed to sell and tenants whose landlords did not; it paid no attention to the plight of the landless peasant; it might have collapsed if the Liberals had not come to its aid in 1909. But, and this was the point, it was a gigantic and irreversible step toward a peasant proprietorship; it had thus deprived the Home Rule party of its most cogent argument — a discontented peasantry. By 1905, parliamentary leaders like John Redmond had come to see this; but, not being gifted with second sight, they could not grasp its full implications. They were, after all, in unshaken control of Ireland, outside the Protestant northeast — the political control, that is, and the political control only. Their claws had been pared by the Wyndham Act. The essential fighting spirit was departing from them, and had already begun to express itself through other groups and in other voices.

Chapter Three

The Troubling of
the Waters

When the eighty-one members of the Irish Parliamentary Party were reunited in 1900 under the chairmanship of John Redmond, they proposed to return the Party (it has been written) to what it had been in Parnell's prime — "predominantly Catholic but not subservient to the Church . . . genuinely national without being either sectional or sectarian."[1]

If this was the case, then Mr. Redmond was in for a difficult time of it: for the Church was in no mood to smile upon a Catholic leader who put his national above his sectarian interests and who — with Home Rule as his great objective — was obliged to maintain a *liaison* with the Liberal Party. The Church had a tendency to construe the word "Liberal" in European terms — as implying all sorts of disagreeable qualities such as anticlerical, freethinking and materialist: and it was inclined to shudder at the sort of Home Rule which might emerge from such an alliance.

John Redmond, a devout Catholic but one to whom Nationalism came first, would therefore be in need of all his firmness. It was here that historical process was very hard on Mr. Redmond. He was to be made the sport of Tory passions and Liberal hesitations which are to this day very difficult to understand and which served to bring out the weakest side of his political character — his readiness to obtain Home Rule at almost any price.

More magnanimous than the great Parnell, more generous and probably more honest, John Redmond was far less passionate, elusive and commanding. He had a melodious voice and a genuine gift for oratory: but it was not for these that he had earned the respect of the House of Commons, but rather for his strong common sense, his lack of excitability, his grasp of detail. He in turn had been known to say that Parliament, while "always ignorant and nearly always unfair" in its treatment of Ireland, was "dominated by a rough and ready sense of manliness and fair play."

Manliness and fair play . . . such words sound a little odd on the lips of an Irish leader. And if he was weighty and formidable — it was not altogether in jest that he was called "the Leviathan" — yet he carried into the stiffest debates and imported into the sternest speeches something of the air of a man who, though his principles would never be compromised, might come to accept compromise as a principle. This was a dangerous lesson for an Irishman to learn: it was a lesson which the House of Commons was only too happy to teach.

A stocky man, with an impressive hawklike nose and rather owlish cheeks, John Redmond came from a long line of Catholic gentry, whose estates in County Wexford had been confiscated under the Penal Laws and who had won their way back to a modest affluence through commerce. His father had been an M.P. when Isaac Butt was leading the Home Rule Party; he himself had been educated at Clongowes and Trinity College, Dublin; he was a member of both English and Irish bars; he had never practiced law. M.P. for New Ross, for Wexford and now for Waterford, he lived like a country squire in a former hunting lodge of Parnell's, called Aughavannagh, among the wilds of the Wicklow mountains. His home in London was a modest flat among the wilds of Kensington: here he spent far more time than he did in Wicklow.

Indeed, this was a very usual complaint — that he spent too much time among the English. Then again, he was too reserved, too private, and — when approached for information or advice — too oracular. He had few close friends in the Party; and he was out of touch with the younger members.[2] From London society, as befitted an Irish leader, he held himself aloof:

but, in a peculiarly intimate manner, not from the Empire or from England. He had married, first an Australian and then, on her death, an English-woman.

As far as the Union was concerned, he could if necessary be very bitter. "For us," he said in 1905, "the Act of Union has no binding or legal force. We regard it as our fathers regarded it before us, as a great criminal act of usurpation carried by violence and fraud, and we say that no lapse of time and no mitigation of its details can ever make it binding upon our honour or our conscience."[3] Whether the Home Rule Bill, as presented in 1912, was much more than a mitigation of the details of the Act of Union is arguable: but we may take it for granted that he expected Home Rule to develop into something more muscular than it appeared to be in 1912. It was only when Home Rule began to slip from his grasp, and his life work with it, that his compromise with a banal imperialism became really pronounced.

In any event, Redmond was not an inconsiderable man: far, far from it. But he cherished the fatal belief that, even in the midst of change and crisis, a certain constitutional propriety was required of an Irish leader. And this in its turn — did it perhaps betoken a lack of cultural sensitivity, a closed mind, an inattention to what was going on behind his back?

For Ireland was experiencing a wonderful upheaval in the years before World War I. Though sometimes harsh or strident or contradictory or quarrelsome, it represented a sense of revival, a renewal of hope. The Irish Literary Renaissance, the Gaelic League, the Sinn Fein movement, the Irish Ireland of D. P. Moran, the resurgence of the Irish Republican Brother-hood — all these were, in a sense, a reaction to the squalor and bitterness of Irish politics after the fall of Parnell: but the fall of Parnell, with the strong emotions which it released, can only be said to have *added* to the general ferment we are now to examine.

The Irish Literary Revival, for example, was of the first importance to Ireland's revolutionary future simply because it happened, because it troubled the waters of national life. By 1910, Dublin had become a literary capital of importance and promise among the capitals of Europe; and the Revival which had accomplished this is naturally full of questions, not all or any of them easy to answer.

These questions can be examined here only when they touch that vital area where the Revival and the revolution meet. The Revival begins with Stan-dish O'Grady's *History of Ireland: Heroic Period,* published in 1878: and O'Grady's *History* is somewhere at the heart of the Easter Rising of 1916. In this work, the marvelous Ulster Cycle, or that part of it known as the Tain

Bo Cuailagne, was released from the grip of a scholarship which had preserved the Irish myth, like a splendid fly, in a kind of philological amber. Among the released prisoners was the great hero Cuchulainn, who defended Ulster against hosts and stratagems of Queen Maeve of Connaught. From then onward this hero must be accounted one of the seminal figures in Irish history. There are many variations of the Cuchulainn myth, some of them far from edifying; but it was an immaculate Cuchulainn who inhabited Padraic Pearse's school, St. Enda's, and was one of the shadowy heroes (another was Karl Marx) who fought side by side with the living in the General Post Office during Easter Week.

It is easy to imagine what effect the work of O'Grady *ought* to have had from the very beginning. When it appeared the Irish nineteenth century was for the most part a discouraging waste. The Great Famine was still a living memory; a new famine seemed about to begin. The Rebellion of 1867 had been a grim fiasco; Parnell had yet to join hands with Davitt. The national tongue, now driven by the Famine back into the West, had long been of little or no interest, even to Irish-speaking patriots such as Daniel O'Connell; and the national features had been degraded by the Victorian English cartoonist into those of a simian with a billycock hat.

O'Grady had to wait till after Parnell's death before he was really recognized. Then began the unlocking of one of the richest mythologies in Europe; then, in the peasant's prehistory, there started to move those lords and queens, heroes and charioteers, through a god-swarmed, demon-haunted, magical, magnifying landscape. The effect was to bring the peasant before the imagination in a way that was simply not available, for example, to the poets of Young Ireland; and since a myth is a call to action, the Irish Literary Revival culminated in Synge's masterpiece, *The Playboy of the Western World,* an intense and provoking celebration of the Irish countryman, his present life and (by implication) his marvelous provenance.

Standish O'Grady was a Unionist landlord and many of the leading figures of the Literary Revival came from the land-owning Ascendency class: most of them were Protestants. To their eyes the countryside was not a melancholy place from which one wrested a grim living: it had (which of course it did have) a singular and romantic beauty. Possibly the Home Rule movement in 1886, and the various Land Acts and rural reforms, had seemed to these gentlefolk like a writing on the wall, where they could read the doom of their class: in which case they were most unlike the majority of Irish landlords. But it is altogether more probable that the Revival was possessed by a far more complicated form of nationalism.

Its greatest figure — if one excepts James Joyce, who turned his back on Ireland, though never on Dublin, in 1910 — was William Butler Yeats, and Yeats came from a background, not of landed gentry, but of Protestant clergy and merchants. He was not too remotely derived from Yorkshire and Cornwall, paternal Yeats and maternal Pollexfen — a powerful mixture which drew from his father the only eulogy ever (said Yeats) to turn his head: — "By marriage with a Pollexfen we have given a tongue to the sea-cliffs." He had spent much of his childhood in Sligo and "everyone I knew well despised Nationalists and Catholics, but all disliked England with a prejudice that has come down from the Irish Parliament."[4]

It is not surprising that a man so derived — who spoke of Ireland with a proprietary air, as one from a possessing class, though not the "best" class — should have developed a nationalism that was distinctly exclusive. He learned to be a conscious Nationalist from his youthful friendship with John O'Leary, the splendid old Fenian, who had returned to Dublin in 1885 and used to frequent the Contemporary Club, at the corner of College Green and Grafton Street. In 1886 O'Leary said to an audience in Cork: — "It is one amongst the many misfortunes of Ireland that she has never yet produced a great poet. Let us trust that God has in store for us that great gift." A little later he told the Contemporary Club that "Young Yeats is the only person in this room who will ever be reckoned a genius."[5]

O'Leary held that a cultural revival must always support and in Ireland's case precede a political revolution, and he said that revolutionists above all men should "appeal to the highest motive, be guided by some ideal principle, be a little like Cato or like Brutus."[6] He had lived to see and deplore the change (which Dostoevski had explored for Russia in *The Possessed*) where Irishmen who had been of O'Leary's party — "and oftener their sons" — preached assassination and the bomb or, more dreadful still, followed after constitutional politicians with such low morals "that they would lie, or publish private correspondence, if it might advance their cause."

Brutus had not published private correspondence, but he had certainly practiced assassination. Could any revolution have succeeded on O'Leary's lofty terms? Somewhere there must be the hateful "Invincibles," somewhere the unarmed policemen shot down in the Castle gateway. But the attraction of such teaching is undeniable.

In the end, Yeats wrote those famous lines: "Romantic Ireland's dead and gone/ It's with O'Leary in the grave." That was in 1913, six years after O'Leary's death — "September 1913" is the title of the poem — and by that time he had begun to see the Catholic Irishman in the shape of William

Martin Murphy, a wealthy businessman and newspaper proprietor, who refused a gallery to Sir Hugh Lane's collection of paintings, and who had been a leading anti-Parnellite in the days of Parnell's downfall. "Romantic Ireland" to Yeats went back to a dream he had quite recently cherished of "an ancient ideal of [Irish] life" which would find — so he told a New York audience in 1903 — its fulfillment in an Ireland where "if there are few rich, there shall be nobody very poor."[7] The crude materialism of the Catholic middle class, in his eyes, in 1913, was just as destructive of this dream as the "provincialism" of Protestant Anglo-Irish had seemed to be in 1903.

His early nationalism, the nationalism of the Celtic revival, was rendered somewhat feverish by his love for the splendidly tall and beautiful Maud Gonne, whom he courted in vain and at some inconvenience, since she was a wild and active republican. It was for her that he wrote his one-act play *Cathleen-ni-Houlihan,* which was first performed at the opening of the Abbey Theatre in 1904, with Maud Gonne as the old woman who has lost her "four beautiful green fields" (Ulster, Munster, Leinster and Connaught) and who lures a young man away from his own wedding in order to fight and die for her in the rebellion of 1798. It ends with the lines:

Did you see an old woman going down the path?
I did not; but I saw a young girl, and she had the walk of a queen.

Those who were present have testified to the electrifying effect of these lines; and Yeats in his old age wrote that he could not sleep at nights for wondering:

> *Did that play of mine send out*
> *Certain men the English shot?*

And this was no otiose question, for *Cathleen-ni-Houlihan,* unlike most Revival literature, is in the very canon of the Irish Rebellion.

But Yeats did not stay with *Cathleen-ni-Houlihan.* In the first place, Maud Gonne married Major John MacBride, "a decent County Mayo soldier," who had fought for the Boers against the English, and whom Yeats never forgave. Even in his *1916* he characterizes MacBride as a "drunken vainglorious lout." *Post hoc ergo propter hoc* is never much of an explanation: but it is true that after the Gonne-MacBride marriage Yeats's nationalism became more and more aristocratic and elitist. The marriage may have precipitated what must have occurred sooner or later. To Yeats, it was impossible for a national poetry to stay where the Young Ireland poets had left it: that is to say, as a poetry which considered the message of more importance than the voice. He wanted to rid it of the romanticism which was still popular and usable, the romanticism which turned all the past, as he put it, "into a melodrama with Ireland for blameless hero."[8]

No literary judgment is being made here, of course: only the very simple statement that the Irish Literary Revival pointed quite naturally to the creation of an Anglo-Irish literature which should be read and admired outside as well as inside Ireland, and to a sense of nationality (of what it is to be a nation) which was capable of self-criticism. The Irish Literary Revival reached its peak with the performance of *The Playboy of the Western World* in 1907, and with the riot in the Abbey Theatre which that masterpiece touched off. It was, really, not so much a riot as a confrontation between two quite incompatible senses of nationality. On the one hand, there were the middle- and lower-middle class Catholic Dubliners, not long removed from their rural past, a past to which they had no desire to return, but which they wished to see purged of all that was disreputable or indecent, or, indeed, human. On the other side was a sense of nationality which perceived this past, really an adopted past, as something wildly heroic and imaginative, but still capable of presenting itself as a criticism of life.

In other words, while Synge's tragi-comedy exasperated the audience because it was not genteel, in the sense that the audience is said to have broken up in disorder at the mention of a woman's shift, this was not the only or the deepest insult. The point is that it projected an image of Ireland which at that stage of Irish nationalism — if nationalism may be defined as a specific form of consciousness conveying a sense of destiny, mission, and superiority — was bound to give offense. Synge and Yeats had a right to be furious at the brutal reception given the play: but the audience had turned itself into a mob of nationalist *enragés* because it had a right to be enraged.

Yeats and the Irish Literary Revivalists made their place in the world by deploying a literature of great distinction, flexibility and beauty: but they did not fully answer the question, "What is Anglo-Irish?" It could be the language that was caught by Douglas Hyde's *Beside the Fire* or Lady Gregory's "Kiltartan" — the language of the indigenous Irish, which consists of an English vocabulary superimposed upon a Gaelic syntax. Or it could be the kind of literature which Professor Daniel Corkery, in his *Synge and Anglo-Irish Literature* (Cork, 1955), that severe but significant work, excludes from his strictures — English written by men who lived in Ireland and wrote for the Irish people. Such writers would include Young Ireland's poet, Thomas Davis: they would not quite include William Butler Yeats.

Yeats, indeed, hoped to "de-Davisize" Irish history and letters — to remove from it that vein of nationalist propaganda with which the poetry of Thomas Davis was seamed. And it is here that the Literary Revival (which Augustine Birrell thought would eventually have "killed by ridicule insensate revolt")[9] parted company with the Gaelic League, the very nurse of revolt, insensate or otherwise.

The Gaelic League, founded in 1893 by Douglas Hyde and Eoin MacNeill, was intended to "de-Anglicize Ireland" by reviving the Irish language, which seemed doomed to extinction. Hyde was no revolutionary, and MacNeill turned out to be a very reluctant one: their original purpose was to unite all Irishmen, Catholic and Protestant alike, in what might be properly described as a neutral, nonpolitical union. Out of this would arise an Irish nation which, while presumably remaining under English rule, would rid itself of all that was cheap, enervating and commonplace in the English dispensation. How such a cultural union could be effected without a genuine Irish politics seems more perplexing in retrospect than it did to Hyde.

He was a Protestant, the son of a clergyman of the Church of Ireland, born in County Sligo, and brought up in the neighboring County Roscommon. Here, as a small boy, he learned to speak and to love the Irish language. He was a charming, gentle personage, a living testament to the fact that the terms "gentleman" and "scholar" are not incompatible. At Trinity College he had belonged to the Society for the Preservation of the Irish Language; from here he removed to the Gaelic Union, where he wrote his first poems in Irish; and so on to the Pan-Celtic Society, a tiny group whose imagination was turned toward a literature, written in English, but inspired by the Irish past.[10] With Yeats he founded the Irish Literary Society in London in 1891; this was followed by the National Literary Society of Dublin in 1892, where Hyde delivered his lecture on "The Necessity for De-Anglicizing Ireland" that November. He had already published his *Beside the Fire* (1890), in which he addressed himself to the problem of adapting folk speech to literary ends. Here he avoided "all tenses not found in Irish, and by using those similarly wanting in English, as well as the phrases commonly substituted for the unfamiliar tenses, he produce[d] a pleasant sense of reality."[11] In other words, he tried to reproduce the English of those who thought in Irish.

Beside the Fire is one of the seminal books of the Irish Literary Revival, because Hyde's folk idiom "gave Irish prose writers a medium by which they could keep their distance from English writers."[12] His *Love Songs of Connacht* (1893) was of even greater importance: like his prose tales of *Beside the Fire,* his folk songs were collected from the lips of the Connaught peasantry or from old neglected manuscripts; and in these translations, he tried to preserve the rhyme and meters of the original Gaelic. No man had done more to show what a beautiful poetry lay waiting for the student of Gaelic; or what could be done with the Anglo-Irish idiom. He himself had once hoped that Irishmen could get rid of the English influence by reading such poets as Tom Moore and Thomas Davis: but he abandoned this sterile hope, as he afterwards abandoned his commitment to Anglo-Irish, when he and MacNeill founded the Gaelic League.

The aim of the Gaelic League was to preserve Irish, written and spoken, as the national language; to study and publish all the existing Gaelic manuscripts; and to promote a modern Irish literature. Despite the fact that Hyde himself was neither Nationalist nor Unionist, nor political in any way, the Gaelic League was to be of the first importance to Irish nationalism.[13]

Although Hyde's version of an Irish Ireland, his dream of a bilingual nation with Irish as the national language, was designedly temperate, it became a haven for political activists as will be shown, even though Hyde more or less successfully resisted them until 1915. His first objective was to extend the teaching of Irish: bilingually in Irish-speaking districts; as an approved subject in others. In 1896, one finds Eoin MacNeill and Father Peter O'Leary passing a resolution congratulating the Christian Brothers on their success in teaching Irish for the Intermediate Examinations. The Christian Brothers might have done better if they had paid less attention to the Intermediate Examinations and more to the realities of education: but, even so, it was through their hands that most of the leaders of the Irish revolution passed.[14] In 1904 the League certainly made some impression on the Intermediate Board (Padraic Pearse's "Murder Machine"), but its greatest success was in 1910 when it won its battle to have Irish made a compulsory subject for matriculation in the new National University of Ireland. By that time it had produced six hundred branches and was still growing.

The League seems always to have appealed to townsmen rather than to countrymen, which by no means interfered with its revolutionary tendencies, but gave it a more pendantic air than might otherwise have been the case. An earlier and more earthy organization, the Gaelic Athletic Association, founded in Parnell's days, was probably even more effective: it is said to have "spread like wildfire into every parish in the south and west."[15] Its founder was Michael Cusack, an Irish speaker from County Clare, a bulky, impressive, disputatious man, whom Joyce immortalized as The Citizen, and who talked his way out of the GAA less than two years after he founded it. Seven men attended its founding on 1 November 1884, in Thurles; and four of these were Fenians.[16] Since neither hurley nor Gaelic football is for faint-hearted people, the GAA's connection with extreme nationalism is fairly obvious; but that was not at first visible. Archbishop Croke, for example, spoke of it in warm if singular terms: it would, he said, help to counteract the influence of "such foreign and fantastic field sports as lawn tennis, polo, croquet, cricket and the like." The prospect of lawn tennis, polo, croquet and cricket finding their way into Irish villages was, to say the least, remote: but at the funeral of Parnell, who was a cricketer, two thousand hurley players marched with draped sticks, in the belief (perhaps correct) that in his last year he had gone over to extremist politics. By them, the mere carrying of the *camán,* the hurley stick, could be a sign of resistance to authority.

Since the Church was one of the authorities whom the GAA seemed disposed to resist, it lost the favor of Archbishops Croke and Walsh. It was reconstituted by quieter minds; it welcomed even the mildest form of nationalist belief; but it never lost its appeal for physical force men, and it always retained its character as a nursery for activists.

Of all the varieties of extraparliamentary nationalism the strangest, however, and, by a curious quirk of fate, eventually the most conspicuous was Arthur Griffith's Sinn Fein movement. Sinn Fein means "Ourselves," and it became in the course of time a portmanteau word for every kind of extremism, including the very physical-force extremism which Sinn Fein professed to decry.

Or did it? Arthur Griffith, the founder of Sinn Fein, is a sphinxlike figure, but one who becomes sphinxlike only when he endeavors to answer his own riddle. Since he employed a lean, lucid and incisive prose, this might seem odd: but the point is that somewhere at the very heart of his thinking there lay a darkness which even the most careful studies have not altogether penetrated. Griffith's style has been said to owe something to Swift — although Swift is really inimitable — and much to John Mitchel, the prose writer of Young Ireland. Here he did not stop at the development of a style, for Mitchel's xenophobia awoke a response in Griffith's harshly conservative mind. There are, indeed, many Mitchels, as Owen Dudley Edwards has pointed out;[17] and the Mitchel whom Griffith chiefly followed was one who preached a passive resistance, not the Mitchel whom Padraic Pearse and James Connolly hailed as the apostle of revolution. Then again, and this shows how little he could care for the Irish Literary Revival, he reposed the greatest faith in the nationalism of Thomas Davis, who (he said) demanded that the Irish should turn their faces from "the false lights of cosmopolitanism."[18] Had not Davis taught national self-reliance? But national self-reliance also has many aspects, and in the first issue of his first paper, *The United Irishman,* in November 1899, we find Griffith advocating "the nationalism of '98, '48 and '67," that is, the nationalism of armed insurrection.

This kind of statement leads us into many enigmas. Griffith, born in Dublin in 1871 and brought up in the printing trade, had been driven by necessity to South Africa just before the outbreak of the Boer War. He had just time to predict that it would take the whole strength of England to win this war when, no doubt fortunately for himself, he was called back to Ireland to edit the new weekly *United Irishman.* The words quoted above, therefore, may reflect the Anglophobic influence of the Boer War: but it is equally possible that they rose from deeper sources.

Griffith had been brought up in a time when "de-Anglicizing" Ireland was all the thing, but (unlike the Gaelic Leaguers) he wanted to give de-Anglicizing a political character: and before he left for South Africa he had been in trouble with the authorities because of his vigorous objection to recruiting for the British Army and to Queen Victoria's visit as a part of that campaign. Politics was essential to him; and when he founded his new organization the Cumann naGaedheal in 1900, he required of those who joined it that they should be the advocates of an Irish republic.

Two years later, at a convention of the Cumann naGaedheal, he proposed that the Irish M.P.s should abandon their "useless, degrading and demoralising policy" and, following the lead of the Hungarian deputies of 1867, refuse to attend the English Parliament. He need not have gone to the Hungarian past for this policy: O'Connell and Davis had advocated it in 1843 and 1844, and it had been urged on Parnell in the winter of 1881.[19] It was, in fact, respectably Irish, except for the important fact that the Hungarians had and the Irish had not put it into practice.

In 1904 Griffith published six articles in the *United Irishman,* which afterwards appeared in book form as *The Resurrection of Hungary: A Parallel for Ireland.* Here he demonstrated the force of the truism that for political purposes the best way to handle any past is to misinterpret it. The autonomy which Hungary achieved in 1876 was by no means as complete as Griffith maintained. On the other hand, it undoubtedly had been brought about by Franz Déak's organization of a boycott of the Imperial Diet by the Hungarian representatives. Although T. M. Kettle attacked Griffith's Hungarian policy with great force in *New Ireland* in 1905, he described it as "the largest idea contributed to Irish politics for a generation";[20] and Griffith agreed that this was so. He proceeded to infuse into it a plan for the nurture of Irish industries through the policy of Protection: a policy equally odious to English Liberals and (if applied to Ireland) to English Tariff Reformers, far from popular with the ordinary Irish businessman, and borrowed by Griffith from the German economist Friedrich List. He thought that protected industries would produce — though he did not explain how they would support — an Irish population of twenty millions.

In 1905, at a Convention called by the National Council, which had come into being as a protest against Edward VII's visit to Ireland, Griffith laid before a small but enthusiastic audience the main features of his economic nationalism, and added for good measure the proposal of a *de facto* Parliament composed of M.P.s who refrained from sitting in Parliament and of delegates elected from local bodies of one kind or another. Here for the first time was heard the term of "Sinn Fein." A few months later the extreme republican Dungannon Clubs of Ulster amalgamated with the Cumann na-Gaedheal to become the Sinn Fein League: and in the by-election at North Leitrim in February 1908, the League actually put up a candidate who was soundly beaten by the Irish Party's man by 3103 to 1157. John Redmond thought that this was the end of the Sinn Fein League, which he called "the temporary adhesion of isolated cranks," but John Dillon did not: and, in fact, in September the Sinn Fein League united with the National Council to become simply "Sinn Fein."

The Sinn Fein's Constitution was distinctly enigmatic. While it called for the re-establishment of Ireland as an independent nation, it declared also — or seemed to declare by demanding a return to the Renunciation Act of 1783, that it would be satisfied with the so-called "Constitution of 1782," which provided Ireland with a Parliament, where no Catholic could sit, and where the Crown retained a silent veto on all legislation. If it had not consented to abolish itself in the Act of Union, this body would presumably have developed into something nonsectarian, semi-independent and ultimately independent; but that was not a substantial argument in 1908.

There were many IRB men in Sinn Fein, who saw the movement as a temporary shelter, and who perhaps agreed with Griffith that the Dual Monarchy concept would meet with public approval. But Griffith himself declared that he could not play the role of political leader in a Dual Monarchy movement, because he was a follower of Wolfe Tone;[21] and a follower of Wolfe Tone would have nothing to do with a monarchy, however dual. This contradiction at the heart of his thinking was submerged as he turned more and more toward passive resistance: but was it ever dissolved? He was a great admirer of Parnell—the Parnell, that is, who obstructed Parliament and advocated the boycott: and one agrees with Professor Mc-Cartney that his passive resistance would not have objected to "occasional excursions into the domain of active resistance at strategic points."[22]

Even so, this was scarcely a dynamic state of mind: and it is small wonder that Sinn Fein began visibly to decline in the last year before the War. Griffith was not, after all, cut out to be the builder of a political party. He was a political propagandist, and his propaganda never carried a very wide appeal. He was, also, a proud, peppery and quarrelsome man: his short, sturdy figure, with the head thrust forward and upward, and the bristling mustache, reminds one irresistibly of a terrier about to bite. His intimate friends were devoted to him; he always remained a personage with whom to reckon; and if his *Sinn Fein* failed as a daily newspaper in 1909–1910, it continued on in its original form as an organ for separatist opinion. It is perhaps because nobody knew exactly where he or it stood that "Sinn Fein" became a generic term for active separatism long before the 1916 Rising, and that the Rising itself was known as the Sinn Fein Rebellion, although Griffith totally disapproved of it. It is quite typical of Griffith, however, that, once the Rebellion had started, he tried to join in.

Among those who disapproved of Sinn Fein was the astringent and dogmatic D. P. Moran. It was not Griffith's economic nationalism which called down Moran's wrath, it was the fact that Sinn Fein was a political movement. Moran was born in Waterford, learned his journalism in London, and had been since 1900 the owner and editor of Dublin's *The Leader*. He dedicated *The Leader* to the nourishing of an Irish Ireland but in terms of a nationality which he thought almost dead — in terms, that is, of an Irish mind and spirit. The primary instrument for achieving this he took to be a spoken Irish, in all its varying dialects and with all its different spellings: only in this way could an effectively bilingual nation come into being. He thought the Gaelic League too pedantic, too wrapped up in language for its own sake: but in the main and with numerous misgivings he approved of it. What he wanted, and wanted so passionately that it led him into many extravagances and much bitterness, was an Ireland that should cease thinking about political independence and concentrate rather upon thinking about itself.

To Moran, the Fenian movement with its insistence upon independence first was totally wrong-headed; and to call the Irish Literary Revival a genuine awakening was — if only because it expressed itself so beautifully in the English tongue — "one of the most glaring frauds that the credulous Irish people have ever swallowed."[23] Was it not, in effect, a stultifying paradox — an effort to revive an Irish interest in the legendary past by the very means which must be removed if that past were to survive? As for Sinn Fein, by turning political it had put the cart before the horse, and the cart itself was not of Irish make. He could not resist this opportunity to use his sharp pen; Sinn Feiners (he wrote) were "the green Hungarian band." Griffith was not the man to take this lying down; and the dust of battle soon obscured the fact that, whatever their differences, the two were engaged in at least one mutual endeavor — that of undermining the Irish Parliamentary Party.

It is hardly necessary to say that to a mind like Moran's political leaders such as John Redmond and John Dillon were simply outcasts. Moran was in a hurry to remove everything — social evils, industrial backwardness, English tastes, Westminster politics, but surely Westminster politics was the worst of all. What had Irishmen to do with such a game of make-believe; such a worthless charade? With his harsh provincial wit, his genuine intensity, his biting pen, Moran did more damage to the Home Rule cause than most of his contemporaries; and the constitutionalists themselves did not realize, until it was too late, how very hurtful his ridicule had been. Among others who came under Moran's lash, in the course of time, was Sir Horace Plunkett, the champion of agricultural improvement, the loquacious and illustrious father of Irish cooperation. Sir Horace was a younger son of the nineteenth Lord Dunsany, who headed the Protestant branch of an ancient Irish family. He had been sent to Eton and to Oxford, had gone ranching in the United States, and had returned on his father's death in 1889 to manage the family estates. From this vantage point he surveyed the Irish agricultural scene and came to the conclusion that cheap foreign food was the source of its distress. There were products such as butter and eggs, in which Ireland could easily compete with the outer world if only they were efficiently marketed. The answer to this was cooperation, and to cooperation Plunkett turned his redoubtable energies.

The obstacles that lay ahead of him were equally redoubtable. Reforming landlords were still suspect; the Irish farmer was profoundly conservative; the local shopkeeper and the local usurer were bitterly jealous; and Plunkett himself had a genius for making enemies, owing to his incurable habit of saying what was in his mind. And what was in the mind of an agricultural reformer in Ireland was, as often as not, best left unsaid.

Nonetheless, in spite of these and other difficulties, Plunkett's ideas prospered. In 1892, he became the Unionist M.P. for South Down and (although the electors soon realized that they had caught a tartar) was successfully reelected in 1895. This was the decade of the Congested Districts Board, a decided help to the spread of his gospel, and cooperative societies began to appear, chiefly in the West. In 1894, he founded the Irish Agricultural Organisation Society; in 1895, largely at his instance, the famous Recess Committee of Parliament was founded, which led in due time to the creation of an Irish Department of Agriculture and Technical Instruction, with Plunkett for its vice-president. Meanwhile, in 1887 he obtained, as editor of his journal *Irish Homestead,* the services of the poet AE, alias George William Russell.

Russell, a thirty-year-old clerk in Pim's Drapery Store in Dublin, was a big, gentle human being, whose strongly bearded features and even stronger feelings for the supernatural and its manifestations were one day to earn for him (from D. P. Moran) the unkind nickname of "The Hairy Fairy." But a sense of what was numinous in the soil and its emanations did not preclude, and in Russell seemed positively to enhance, a very positive and objective approach to the problems of those who made their living from it.[24] Under his editorship the *Irish Homestead* became well-known far beyond the shores of Ireland.

The partners' differences in temperament and social philosophy — for Russell believed in self-help and Plunkett inclined toward state aid — did not prevent their working together in harmony and introducing a new hopeful spirit into the Irish countryside. And yet their very success was an invitation to obstruction and defeat. The Department of Agriculture and Technical Instruction, with its three advisory boards and its increasing staff, was too much for Sir Horace's limited powers of administration; it began to compete with and even oppress the Irish Agricultural Organisation Society; and only his membership in the House of Commons, where he was almost a junior minister, gave Plunkett the power to maintain some kind of order. In 1900, however, he lost his seat at South Down; and this calamity was compounded when, in 1904, in *Ireland in the New Century,* he claimed that cooperation was necessary because the Irish character was lacking in self-reliance. The Catholic Church, said the injudicious Sir Horace, was partly to blame for this: she had been too much of a mother and a nurse.

The Church used her influence; the Press was suitably outraged; and D. P. Moran who once, for nonpolitical and businesslike reasons, had been ready to support cooperation, was now, on religious and racist grounds, anxious to disavow it. Sir Horace himself had grown weary of the battle, and when the

Unionists fell from power in the landslide election of 1906, he knew that his resignation would be demanded. Although never one to slight his own worth, he was not sorry to go. Behind him he left the Irish Agricultural Organisation Society and, as a solitary but sufficient monument to the efforts of himself and George William Russell, the Irish dairy industry. Russell went on to merge himself into AE, one of the best known and most loved figures in literary Dublin; Plunkett became a necessitarian Home Ruler, an illustrious thorn in the side of friend and foe.

No doubt they had attempted an agricultural revolution, one that would have instituted, not only new methods of distribution, but also many technical refinements in production. But it was a revolution which, once it had overcome the stubborn resistance of the farming community, could only have produced a contented countryside: and among those who unworthily criticized the cooperative movement not the least vocal and effective were the leaders of the Irish Parliamentary Party.

It was the Party's fate, here as elsewhere, to resist, or ignore the efforts of a new world as it struggled to be born. Looking back at these efforts, from the Gaelic Athletic Association to the Literary Renaissance, from D. P. Moran to Arthur Griffith, from Hyde to Plunkett, one can see how these extra-parliamentary movements represented change, hope and creation. Irish Ireland, Anglo-Irish "cosmopolitanism," Young Ireland poetry, Hungarian solutions, no more cricket and croquet — they all jostled together, by no means amicably, not without eccentricity, sometimes with genius itself, toward a new world. The Irish Parliamentary Party represented a solid majority of the Irish people: it was doomed, nonetheless, to move in another direction until, in 1918, it disappeared from sight . . . the sport of English parties, the last and saddest victim of the politics of Home Rule.

Part Two

IRISH LEADERS AND ENGLISH PARTIES, 1906—1914

Chapter Four

The Liberals—
David Lloyd George

I

In the General Election of 1906, the Conservative Party went down to an ignominious defeat. There were many reasons for this: a slow, depressing, almost genocidal victory in the Boer War: an Education Act with a Church of England bias; anti-labor sentiments; the use and abuse of Chinese coolies in South Africa; and, above all, Tariff Reform, or the proposed introduction of protective duties into an English economy long inured to free trade.

Then again, the Conservatives had been in power too long; with one Liberal interim of two and a half years they had been governing the country since 1886; they had come to resemble a rather clumsy device for keeping one or two great Tory families in power; and the collapse of their vote-gathering machinery in the late election was a clear sign that the time had come for them to retire and regroup their forces.

The Liberals who succeeded them — on the whole a middle class party with a moderate center, imperialist and radical wings, a stern tincture of religious Dissent, and an understanding with left-wing labor — did so with a majority of 132 over the three other parties (Conservative, Irish and Labour) combined; and for the last time in their history they enjoyed a majority in England itself. Whether all this represented a vote of confidence or a pressing desire to get rid of the Conservatives is another question — the Liberals were notoriously at odds with themselves when they solicited the voters' approval in 1906.

On the other hand, there was something indistinctly but undeniably attractive about them. In their famous Newcastle Conference of October 1891 they had begun to speak with tongues: and amidst the usual clamor about the usual causes it took no particularly keen ear to detect the high wild notes of municipal socialism and collectivist reform. Mr. Gladstone's contribution, in this respect, had been vague and depressing:[1] to him Irish Home Rule was the paramount consideration.

Home Rule was lost again in 1893; Mr. Gladstone retired and was heard no more: not so the voices he had endeavored to silence at Newcastle. To the post-Gladstonians, "the destructive work of *laissez-faire* was over; the constructive work must begin through the removal of social and economic obstacles to equality. It was essential to turn from constitutional questions to a firm social policy."[2]

The principle of *laissez-faire* had often been honored only in the breach, but as a somewhat abstract answer to state intervention it was still very much alive. The post-Gladstonian Liberals, therefore, although they seemed in 1906 to be poised on the edge of a Promised Land — today we should call it the Welfare State — and were not without precedents to support them as they moved into it, knew that it was a dangerous terrain. In two of their measures, an Old Age Pensions Act (1908) and a National Health Insurance Act (1911) — although the first was niggardly and the second barely salubrious — they seemed to be advancing with some confidence. Their Budget of 1909, as will be seen, was on the whole a progressive event. In other fields, however, such as sweated industries, or national unemployment insurance, or the minimum wage, they proceeded with a caution which was akin to timidity and which positively invited reprisal and revenge.

At the very outset, before this vein of caution had become visible, Mr. A. J. Balfour, the defeated Prime Minister, had openly suggested that the nation's affairs could still be run by the huge Conservative majority in the House of Lords. Mr. Balfour had been affronted as an aristocrat and dismayed as a Conservative by the new Liberal majority, with its shabby social background and its formidable labor tail. Under his direction, the Lords restrained themselves from tampering with Welfare legislation, sorely as they were tempted to do so: but Liberal measures, an Education Bill which restored the religious balance, a (liquor) Licensing Bill, a Plural Voting Bill, they crippled or vetoed in the most bare-faced manner.

Nor was the hereditary chamber the only problem: far from it. The Liberals had not been long in office before they were confronted with a severe economic recession; unemployment percentages rose above the tolerable limit; and by-elections began to go against the Government. Could this mean that Tariff Reform — that child of Joseph Chamberlain's which should have died of exposure in the bleak Election of 1906 — was actually still alive, and not only alive but kicking?

Tariff Reform meant building a wall of protective tariffs around the United Kingdom, and then knocking holes through which Empire goods could pass. It had badly divided the Conservatives, many of whom were obstinate Free Traders, and it had alarmed the poorer classes with its threat of "stomach taxes" — that is, duties on imported foodstuffs not of Empire origin. In 1908, however, it was being touted as *the* antidote to unemployment; and it was to prove that Free Trade could finance the nation's needs more efficiently and more equitably than Protection that David Lloyd George, Chancellor of the Exchequer, put together his so-called People's Budget of 1909.

The Budget paid small deference to peace, retrenchment and [political] reform, those Liberal deities who had presided over the Party in its Victorian heyday. It had to find money for the swollen naval estimates, a political expenditure which had little to do with Peace, and for the recently enacted Old Age Pensions, a social reform which had no relation to Retrenchment. Mr. Lloyd George, moreover, had been deeply upset by the un-Liberal character of the naval program, and had carefully improved its appearance, not to mention his own, by making it the vehicle for future and more extended social benefits. He offered, for example, along with the usual assaults upon brewers and distillers, such progressive measures as supertaxes on incomes over £5000 and greatly increased death duties; and to these he appended some heavy duties upon land — old radical nostrums, probably unworkable, but very dear to his heart, for he was an open enemy to the landed interest.

To Lloyd George, in fact, the land taxes were radical in more senses than one, for they were deeply rooted in the forbidding memories of his Welsh childhood, where the landlord was the local tyrant and "the silhouette of the gamekeeper," as he put it, "stood beyond every wood and stream."[3] Born in

Manchester in 1863, he was brought up in Llanystumdwy, a little Welsh village, chiefly by his shoemaker uncle, Richard Lloyd, a man whom he revered above every other human being. His childhood was spent in a poverty so drab, so severely Baptist, that he once vowed that he would rather die than have to live it over again: but Richard Lloyd, a man of more prominence than substance, pinched and scraped to get him started as a solicitor's clerk and to find the extra money which would pay for his "articles."[4] He grew up to be a short man with a large head of which he was inordinately proud, black hair, intensely blue eyes, inescapable charm. At twenty-seven he was elected to Parliament for Carnarvon Boroughs, a seat he won by eighteen votes and held for fifty years.

No man was more forthright in his denunciations of the Boer War than this Welsh attorney: so much so that on one occasion, through a back door and disguised as a policeman, he was just able to escape the attentions of a wicked Birmingham mob, unanimously bent upon tearing him limb from limb. He was a natural radical and a born orator, now ingratiating, now violent, and often, in the intensity of his emotions, breaking out into his native Welsh. No personality so greatly gifted, so merry, so moody, so captivating and potentially so dangerous had ever come out of Wales into the Westminster Parliament.

By the time he had become Chancellor of the Exchequer, by way of the Board of Trade, he was apparently indispensable. The young pro-Boer, the bitter enemy of imperial tyranny, had in some measure accepted the golden mean: if he had not been taught this by the Birmingham mob, he had learned it from Parliament. He was highly regarded as a mediator. He had settled a railway strike in 1907, without actually giving the strikers what they wanted; he was to do the same thing in 1911. In the polished arts of evasion and duplicity — their enemies might have said — he was more Liberal than the Liberals. Yet, in many respects, he was not a Liberal at all.

Years later, John Maynard Keynes wrote:

How can I convey to the reader, who does not know him, any just impression of this extraordinary figure of our time, this syren, this goat-footed bard, this half-human visitor to our age from the hag-ridden magic and enchanted woods of Celtic antiquity? One catches in his company that flavour of final purposelessness, inner irresponsibility, existence outside and away from our Saxon good and evil, mixed with cunning, remorselessness, love of power, that lend fascination, enthralment and terror to the fair-seeming magicians of North European folklore.[5]

This is all rather mischievous; but in its slanted way it is very true. The Anglo-Saxon mind could not comprehend Mr. Lloyd George, not simply because he was Welsh, but rather because — among the attributes that attach themselves to any successful politician (cunning, remorselessness, love of power) — one could detect also "a final purposelessness, [an] inner irresponsibility," which was really purpose and responsibility masquerading as something else. And what was this purpose? To what did he owe this responsibility? The answer can be found in two sentences. "Lloyd George fed upon power," Alfred Gollin has written. "His qualities swelled with the exercise of it."[6] In talking about Lloyd George one does not talk about "love of power": one must talk about enslavement to power. The great slaves to power, such as he, may do good with it and they may do evil, in succession or together: but the end is almost always the same. In the end it will destroy them.

Of course, Lloyd George had his secondary allegiances and distastes: it is these which give him his fascination and his ambiguity. He was deeply concerned for the poor, whence he came, although it is doubtful if he really understood the industrial worker. He genuinely despised aristocracy, and at the height of his power took a cynical pleasure in selling peerages. There was nothing factitious about the antiwar sentiments which so nearly cost him his life. A curious fate awaited him. The champion of the poor became a friend of the rich; the quarry of the Birmingham war mob became one of the greatest of war prime ministers; the despiser of aristocracy died an earl.

II

The People's Budget is nowadays accepted as a serious effort in the cause of Liberal finance. At the same time, considering Lloyd George's character, with its infinite capacity for double-dealing, one cannot help wondering if this is all that the Budget was. Could he have inserted those land-taxes — in which (unlike almost all the Cabinet) he seriously believed — for some other purpose as well? Could they also have been a trap for the House of Lords — the House of Lords which had used its veto in the most shameless manner for the sake of Church of England schools, and drunkenness, and privilege?

The landed interest, which had never recovered from the ruined and ruinous harvests of the late 1870s, had found its last fortress in the House of Lords, and here it was prepared to make what, to its overheated mind, was a final stand. Even so, could the Lords be persuaded, would they actually dare to throw out a Finance Bill? It was true that they had a constitutional right to do so: but they had not exercised this right for more than two hundred years; and customary behavior — one of the tutelary gods of the constitution — was all against their exercising it now. In spite of this, there were rumors that they intended to perform this despotic act; Mr. Lloyd George, while still hoping and perhaps expecting his Budget to survive, could not refrain from goading them on with intemperate words; the impeccable Mr. Balfour then lost his head and advised a draconian reply; and on 30 November 1909, a date as famous as constitutional history can make it, the Lords vetoed the Budget by a vote of 350 to 75.

This was really the curtain-raiser — and surely no insufficient one — to the more and more violent politics which became one of the characteristics of prewar England. There followed two General Elections, one of January and one of December 1910, and between them the death of Edward VII, the accession of George V, a constitutional conference which was doomed from the start,[7] and an abortive effort by Mr. Lloyd George — never a good party man — to form a National Government by abandoning Irish Home Rule, Free Trade and military voluntarism in return for a continuing program of social reform.[8]

In one way or another, this was a very mixed and *mouvementé* year: but nothing, it seemed, could impede the onward march of Liberal history. General Elections are not referendums: in January and December the whole Liberal policy was passed in review, and from both Elections the Liberal Government emerged with a working majority. It was, of course, obvious that if the Liberals won the first election the Lords would have to accept the Budget which they had thrown out in November 1909: and accordingly they did so. It was equally obvious that if the Conservatives lost the December election, the Lords would be expected to pass a Parliament Bill which not only restrained them from vetoing a Budget but also reduced their power over other legislation from an absolute to a mere suspensory veto, good for two years. (In other words, a Bill passed by the Commons in three successive sessions of Parliament, and not necessarily the same Parliament, and three times rejected by the Lords, would become law.) Threatened with a royal creation of several hundred brand-new Liberal noblemen if they did not accept this Parliament Bill, the Lords — or those peers who dared to vote at all — voted away their absolute powers by a close margin on a hot and famous night in August 1911.

The significance of this for Irish history lay in the Election figures for January and December 1910. There were, for January: Liberals 275; Conservatives 273; Labour 40; Irish Nationalists 82. For December: Liberals 272;

Conservatives 272; Labour 42; Irish Nationalists 84. Such figures were like historical *graffiti,* the naughty calligraphy of Fate itself; for the Government henceforth depended for its majority upon Mr. John Redmond and (not counting eleven dissidents) the seventy-three votes he now commanded in the House of Commons.

It is no wonder that all Conservatives now answered to the name of Unionists. According to the Parliament Act which the Lords had accepted in 1911, a Home Rule Bill presented to the Commons in April 1912 could receive the royal assent as early as June 1914. And was it not all too clear that the price of further Irish support would be, precisely, a Liberal Home Rule Bill?

The Unionists could not deny that a majority depending upon Irish Nationalist votes was still a constitutional majority. Little as they cared for most of her inhabitants, it was one of their cardinal beliefs that Ireland was and must remain a member of the United Kingdom. And yet . . . a constitutional majority, which played such havoc with the Constitution, was not that, to all intents and purposes, a contradiction in terms, a political chimaera? From now on they bent all their efforts to bring about, at all costs, this majority's dismissal, if not its destruction, and the onward course of Liberal history was abruptly checked.

III

The Irish Nationalists, on their side, had not been happy with the People's Budget. Its liquor and licensing taxes, it seemed to them, struck too hard at the distillers and publicans who were the background of their party: and it was rumored — "in grossly distorted fashion" said the Prime Minister — that such taxes would undermine the Irish revenue and with it the fiscal prospects of Home Rule.

Then again, the Budget had imposed a 20 percent tax upon the unearned increment of land (or the difference between its rated and its real value) whenever land changed hands. It was based upon Lloyd George's belief that low rating of land was a brazen cheat; and it could not have been accomplished without a complete revaluation of land throughout the United Kingdom. The consequent effect upon the sales and annuities contemplated under the revised Wyndham Act might be very serious. The Irish Party leadership, little as it cared for the Wyndham Act, could not let this threat pass unchallenged; indeed Mr. William O'Brien, with his recently inaugurated All-for-

Ireland League,[9] would not have allowed it to do so; nor would Mr. Tim Healy and his backer, the *Irish Independent*. Mr. Redmond, therefore, attempted to put pressure on the Government. All he got for his pains was empty promises (the Chancellor of the Exchequer) and bland excuses (the Prime Minister).[10]

Hitherto, it is true, the Liberals had behaved very well with regard to an entity which might be called constituency Ireland — an imaginary Ireland, content to remain for ever within the United Kingdom. They had done something for urban housing, they had resettled three thousand evicted tenants and, in 1909, they introduced and enacted a bill which made the purchase of estates more easy than it had been under the original Wyndham Act and which opened up whole areas for sale through compulsory purchase.

In 1908, moreover, they had produced and enacted an Irish Universities Bill, creating a National University out of the three University Colleges at Dublin, Cork and Galway and a Queen's University out of the Queen's College at Belfast, while Dublin University (Trinity College) remained untouched. In deference to the scruples of English Protestantism, the Act declared that no religious tests should be given to the staffs of the two Universities: but everyone knew that the National University would be Catholic and the Queen's University Protestant. All this was, in effect, very much in the Conservative vein of "killing Home Rule with kindness."

The Catholic hierarchy, although it caviled at many details, was truly gratified at getting a university of its own. Nobody has ever supposed that the Catholic bishops thought as one, although beneath their many varieties of political thought there lay a common social conservatism: but in the matter of control of learning they were as nearly unanimous as any group of humans can hope to be. And now, with this new victory, their interest in Home Rule might be expected to diminish. As the fruit of an alliance between Irish politicians who seemed unduly secular and a Liberal Party with its sadly suggestive name and its new leaning toward a welfare state, Home Rule cannot have seemed very attractive to the bishops. Thus the Irish leadership drifted a little more out of the current of national life; the Liberals were the ones who had pushed it there.

The only way back was Home Rule itself; but this was precisely the kind of constitutional question in which the post-Gladstonians had little genuine interest. (One must remember that the question of the Lords' veto was not to them, as it was to the Conservatives, strictly a constitutional matter. They left the House of Lords quite unreformed as regards its composition and its hereditary character. They merely defined its relation to Finance Bills and qualified its veto, so that they could get on with the business of every day Liberal life.) Home Rule, in fact, they regarded as a legacy of debts, and in 1907 they had endeavored to discharge these debts with an Irish Councils Bill — "a modest shy humble effort [wrote the Prime Minister, Sir Henry Campbell-Bannerman] to give administrative powers to the Irish people." It was condemned by an angry convention of the United Irish League; the bishops, who had detected a secularizing education clause coiled like a snake among its provisions, added their denunciations to those of the U.I.L.: whereupon, humbly and shyly, it dropped out of sight.[11] "Home Rule we could not have," wrote the Chief Secretary for Ireland, Mr. Augustine Birrell, in strict privacy, "and we should have contented ourselves with Land Reform and the University Question."[12] When Herbert Henry Asquith succeeded Campbell-Bannerman as Prime Minister in 1908, these words still represented the attitude of the Government.

The Lords' rejection of the 1909 Budget changed all that. When a General Election was called for January 1910, there was a sudden alteration in the party's prestige. The Election was expected to be a close one and John Redmond, formidable at last, threatened the Government with the loss of every Irish vote in England if the Prime Minister did not openly commit himself to Home Rule. After heavy pressure from Mr. Birrell and from the Secretary for India, Lord Morley, who had twice been Chief Secretary for Ireland, Mr. Asquith agreed.[13]

On 10 December, accordingly, when he opened his campaign in the Albert Hall, he pledged himself to a policy which "while explicitly safeguarding the supremacy and indefectible authority of the Imperial Parliament, will set up in Ireland a system of full self-government in regard to purely Irish affairs." When the result of the January election made it clear that the Government depended upon Irish votes for its further existence, Mr. Asquith's careful words took on rather more force and resonance than perhaps he had intended to give them. He did not repeat them in the Election of December. Every Conservative election address, on the other hand, made it clear that Home Rule would be the consequence of a Liberal victory.[14]

After the Parliament Bill had been passed in August 1911 and had received the royal assent, no other course was open; and on 11 April 1912 Mr. Asquith presented a Third Home Rule Bill to the House of Commons.

Chapter Five

The Liberals—Birrell, Asquith and Home Rule

The Irish Government, which the Third Home Rule Bill should (ideally) have transferred into the hands of Mr. Redmond in 1912, actually survived — unchanged, incorrigible, in English hands — until the English left the island in 1922, taking most of its archives with them.

It was a perfect monument to the anomalous character of the Act of Union. Why, for example, should a portion of the United Kingdom need a viceroy? Yet a Viceroy or Lord Lieutenant (he answered to either title) stood at the head of the Irish Government, assisted in his duties by a Chief Secretary.

Whether the Viceroy or the Chief Secretary was actually or nominally at the head was, however, quite another question. In the latter part of the nineteenth century their relative positions depended upon which of the two had a seat in the Cabinet. Sometimes the Viceroy had been in and the Chief Secretary out; sometimes the Chief Secretary in and the Viceroy out: but in Augustine Birrell's time it was generally understood that the Viceroy's duties should be ceremonial and the Chief Secretary's those of a modern Prime Minister — understood, that is, by everybody but the Viceroy.

Mr. Birrell, in short, since he had a seat in the Cabinet and Lord Aberdeen, the Viceroy, did not, was *de facto* the supreme personage in Ireland. It was a Chief Secretary's duty not only to administer the Irish Government but also to explain and defend the Cabinet's Irish policies in the House of Commons. A Chief Secretary, therefore, was usually in England while Parliament was in session and usually in Ireland when it was not: and for this reason the routine work of administration was in the hands of an Under Secretary. It was because he had failed to distinguish between administration and policy that Under Secretary MacDonnell had involved George Wyndham in a political error and brought about his downfall: and, indeed, the distinction was not always too easy to make.

I

In Mr. Birrell's day the Irish Government consisted of forty departments functioning in Ireland. Of these eleven were the Irish branches of United Kingdom departments, and twenty-nine were departments concerned solely with Irish affairs and operating only in Ireland. The Chief Secretary himself moved between his Chief Secretary's Office in Dublin Castle and the Irish Office in Whitehall.

Of the twenty-nine departments functioning solely in Ireland, seven were nevertheless controlled by United Kingdom departments, while ten were under the immediate supervision of the Chief Secretary. These naturally dealt with matters of law and order: they also took care of benefit societies, statistics, heraldry and lunatics. The Chief Secretary was, in addition to these interesting duties, technically head of the Congested Districts Board, the Local Government Board and the Department of Agriculture and Technical Instruction. The other departments were quite autonomous and thirteen of them were governed by boards — fit only, it was said, to make a coffin for Ireland and little else — some being paid and some unpaid.

A kind of centralization existed, in that seventeen of the departments submitted their estimates through the Chief Secretary's Office. A kind of liaison was also maintained through propinquity and gossip, since some of the departments were housed in Dublin Castle, the others were very near it, and all the higher officials were members of the same clubs.[1]

Taking it all in all, a more exasperating form of government has rarely been devised: and although the ordinary methods of entrance were by competitive examination, it was universally held to be the nurse, not only of sheer inefficiency, but also of jobbery in many ingenious forms.

It will be seen from this that much depended upon the personality of the gentleman from whose office, as Chief Secretary, radiated whatever centralizing energy this peculiar government possessed. As much depended upon the degree of confidence which existed between the Chief Secretary and the Under Secretary and upon the latter's character. With Sir Antony MacDonnell, the Bengal Tiger, Birrell never got along; with MacDonnell's successors, Sir J. B. Dougherty and Sir Matthew Nathan, and particularly Sir Matthew, Birrell managed smoothly enough.

Birrell had been Campbell-Bannerman's President of the Board of Education, and had piloted the Liberal Education Bill through the Commons with great skill. The House of Lords then reduced the Bill to rubble, from the midst of which, in 1907, Birrell was rescued by Campbell-Bannerman, dusted off, and sent to Ireland in place of James Bryce, the historian. A Baptist of very flexible religious views, and of mixed Northumbrian and Scottish blood, Birrell combined a pleasantly cynical view of the human race with a genuine fondness for its eccentricities. No doubt he had need for both in Dublin Castle.

He was a large, untidy, clumsy man, with a sensitive and humorous face, a keen mind, a charming manner and a loyal nature. In Ireland he stayed away from the hangers-on at the frugal Viceroy's shabby court and shabbier festivities; he never went near the Kildare Street Club, the recognized headquarters of Irish Unionism; he soon ceased to inhabit the Chief Secretary's Lodge in Phoenix Park. He was, indeed, happiest outside the city, since he developed a fondness for the rural Irish and liked to travel about their island.[2]

He was not there as often as he should have been. The illness of a beloved wife was one reason for his staying away. Another — he was no sailor — was the Irish Sea, a notoriously turbulent stretch of water, with an unquantifiable but undoubtedly a souring effect upon the history of Anglo-Irish relations.

In spite of his absences, in spite of his rather offhand manner — he was sometimes known as the Playboy of the Western World — he was a serious and able Chief Secretary, and his eventual disgrace was due far more to circumstance than incapacity. In 1909, as has been shown, it was he, along with Lord Morley, who saw the need for a commitment to Home Rule: and one is tempted to think that this was not due to political considerations so much as to his adoption of the cause of Constitutional Ireland — the Ireland, that is to say, which hoped to coax or bully Home Rule out of an English Parliament.

In 1908, when Mr. Asquith became Prime Minister, this was not yet the case: Birrell had then begged to be given some other post, and only after a severe struggle agreed to remain. "In Ireland," as he afterwards put it, somewhat ruefully, "at least you are never dull."

II

Between the Chief Secretary and the Prime Minister there grew up a strong affection. Birrell was civilized, literate and loyal, and Mr. Asquith, who could extract loyalty and even love from men not much addicted to either, had no difficulty in capturing and returning the affections of the Chief Secretary. The two gentlemen were very Liberal in a special sense: they took a somewhat dispassionate view of the world, as if they expected the millennium, should it ever arrive, to be run by people very much like themselves. Ambition, power, progress itself — all were necessary, but all should be moderate.

Mr. Asquith could be ruthless if need be, and he was fond of power — no man fought harder than he to retain it when it was slipping from his grasp in 1916 — but it was not power as Mr. Lloyd George, for example, knew it. If Lloyd George was a slave to power, Asquith was a slave to place. He believed that it was his destiny to rise to the top, and to remain there — securely, even comfortably. As Prime Minister he ran his Cabinet like a chairman of the board; he was the implementer rather than the originator of ideas and policies; his personal standards were, for a man in his position, unusually high. No one has doubted his courage or capacity in the face of usual dangers and predictable difficulties: but if the dangers ceased to be usual or the difficulties to be expected — what then?

Herbert Henry Asquith was undoubtedly a most gifted man. Born in 1852, the son of a Yorkshire manufacturer in a small way, he had been an outstanding classical scholar at Oxford's Balliol. He had then deserted Oxford and the humanities for a solid career at the Bar, and long before that career was established — Trollope's Mr. Low would have thought it very reckless — had entered Parliament as the member for East Fife.

This was in 1886; and the fact that six years later he became Home Secretary under Mr. Gladstone is sufficient indication that the recklessness was merely the sign of a faultless instinct. Asquith was made for Parliament.

He had a copious mind, a most efficient intellection, a superb memory, a style of speaking which, disdaining oratorical flourishes, was lucid, cool and, above all, effective. "He succeeded in assuming," Roy Jenkins has written, ". . . and this is perhaps the main characteristic of a front bench style, that the interest of a statement lay in the fact that he was making it and not merely in its own inherent wisdom."[3] His calmness under attack or in difficulty was famous: it was only in his later years that it took on some of the quality of stone, which not only does not move but cannot. Self-satisfaction, the effect of long success, was one of the elements in this curious petrifaction: self-satisfaction and — in spite of his many gifts — a certain lack of imagination. He did not have the resourcefulness or the flexibility with which to turn an unexpected crisis to his own account. It is no wonder that he has been called "the last of the Romans" — an impassive figure, standing in the breach against a future that overwhelmed him.

He was Home Secretary under Lord Rosebery as well as under Mr. Gladstone; he was Sir Henry Campbell-Bannerman's Chancellor of the Exchequer. No one was more available, deservedly available, than he. When Campbell-Bannerman fell ill in 1908, it was Asquith whom Edward VII summoned to an overstuffed suite in a Biarritz hotel, in which equivocal setting he kissed hands as Prime Minister.

In 1894, a middle class Congregationalist, a widower with five remarkable children, Asquith married Margot Tennant, the febrile, witty, exasperating, social daughter of an industrial baronet. Very few Prime Ministers have ever been fashionable and Mr. Asquith — who was if anything faintly Bohemian — was certainly not one of them. But then "fashionable" was not what Margot Tennant was looking for in a husband. She was looking for fame, and in Asquith she believed she had found the way to it. He, for his part, liked to relax in the company of well-bred handsome women who did not talk shop — *that* he reserved for a single confidante — and he got along contentedly enough in the world to which she introduced him.

Perhaps he was too fond of it in a quiet detached way. His was the kind of mind which could get through a great deal of work in far less time and with far more thoroughness than most men's: but one gets the impression that, as the years went on, he never did more than suited his own convenience. The weekend was now a sacred period for the governing class: for Mr. Asquith it was to become sacrosanct. The dinner table was also a special oasis; and Mr. Asquith, coming down to the House of an evening, would often — to the embarrassment of his colleagues — betray all the endearing symptoms of having dined too well. But this never showed up in his next morning's work. In short, he was a very comfortable, indeed an eminent success: but success is not the same as power.

The times themselves were now demanding that men who claimed to be statesmen should put forth more energy, courage and skill than usual. In 1906, when the Liberals took office, this had not been the case: the social atmosphere *then* was still an autumnal mixture of complacency and apprehension, of which John Galsworthy's fiction gave a good example.[4] From 1910 onwards this *fin de siècle* atmosphere was visibly permeated by a more and more violent unrest — great labor strikes, suffragette militancy, a Unionist excursion into treason or something very like it. If these phenomena had anything in common — and the present writer has long believed that they had — it could only be explained in terms of an effort, by no means entirely rational, to escape from inert ideas, moral shibboleths, inhibiting standards, disgraceful conditions — in brief from all that was obsolescent in the great Victorian legacy. It was as if some vivid organism had struggled out of its chrysalis, only to be smashed in August 1914 by a universal thumb.

Liberalism, for its part, still strove to present an orderly, intelligent and rational advance into the future: and Mr. Asquith was, in this respect, one of its finest products. Between an eruption and an advance, however, while there may have been no difference in direction, since both presumably moved forward, there was indeed a difference in urgency. Surely a violent labor uprising on quasi-syndicalist lines, or the efforts of brave and strident women to connect a suffrage objective with a great female principle, or the brutal defiance of Parliament by Unionist politicians — these, however dissimilar, were evidence of a vital discontent, a desperate optimism, which the Liberal faith could neither assuage nor assimilate.

It was against such a background that Mr. Asquith presented the Third Home Rule Bill to the Commons on 11 April 1912: and the background had not left him untouched. The utter intransigence of a coal strike had already, that very February, reduced him, of all men, to tears on the floor of the House; and the suffragettes, to his mind a species of harpy, rarely gave him any peace on public occasions. As for Home Rule, it also was already little more than a troublemaker. As he told the King on 6 February, the Cabinet had decided that the Bill must be for all of Ireland, but that if it became clear from "fresh pressure of public opinion" that some special treatment must be given to the Ulster counties, then Government would be ready to accept the necessity "either by amendment of the Bill *or by not pressing it on under the*

provisions of the Parliament Act."[5] Either compromise or surrender: these
were to be the heroic alternatives!

III

With a few refinements and a hint of Federalism (Home Rule for Ireland,
Scotland, Wales and England with an Imperial Parliament over all) in some
quite unforeseeable future, the bill was not too different from the Second
Home Rule Bill which Mr. Gladstone had introduced in 1893.

The Irish Parliament was to consist of a Senate and a Lower Chamber,
their relations so arranged as to give protection to Protestant interests in the
northeast; and it was to have jurisdiction over all internal affairs. The Imperial Parliament would retain full control over all matters relating to the
Crown, peace or war, treaties and foreign relations, and new customs duties.
The Irish Parliament could raise new taxes, but could not add more than 10
percent to the income tax, death duties and customs duties imposed by the
Imperial Parliament. The Royal Irish Constabulary was to be placed under
the Imperial Parliament for the next six years, scarcely a sign of confidence.
A Lord Lieutenant would continue to represent the Crown. Questions of
vital importance, such as the question of what really constituted an Irish
revenue, were to be left to the decision of an Exchequer Board, composed of
representatives from both England and Ireland. Ireland was to send forty-
two members to the Imperial Parliament — one for every hundred thousand
inhabitants — presumably to maintain the principle of no taxation without
representation; but this reduction in membership (it had already been arranged) would not take place until after the next General Election.

To neither Nationalist nor Unionist could this have seemed a strong bill.
With no power over customs or excise, obliged to hunt hither and yon for
new subjects for taxation, with no control over the police for six years —
what sort of self-government was this? Why then did John Redmond hail it
as "a great measure . . . a great measure and we welcome it?"[6] His reasons
began to appear when he discussed the financial aspects of the bill. "Admittedly," he said, "it is a provisional settlement." When the time came for
"revision," as it would, "we will be entitled to complete power for Ireland
over the whole of our financial system."[7]

There was a good deal more to this than meets the eye: and it is of the first
importance to know what it was. In 1908, when Old Age Pensions were
enacted, Ireland still contributed more to the Treasury in revenue than she

received in services; in short, she was overtaxed. Social reform had changed all that. In 1911, chiefly because of expenditures on Irish Old Age Pensions, the surplus had been changed into a deficit of more than £1,000,000. Among John Redmond's papers there are some calculations by Mr. Birrell — undated but clearly made in 1912 — which show that in 1913–1914 (Mr. Birrell optimistically called this "the Home Rule Year") the deficit would have become, with the addition of health insurance benefits, at least £2,000,000.[8]

For this reason, according to the Third Home Rule Bill, expenditures for Old Age Pensions, Health Insurance, Unemployment Insurance and Labour Exchanges should continue to be met by the Imperial Parliament. On the other hand, a subsidy of £500,000 would at once be given to the Irish Parliament to make up for any deficit between its revenue and the nonwelfare expenditures allocated to it. The subsidy was to diminish year by year until the Irish Government had put its financial house in order: and in that year — the year of "revision" — it would be permissible for the Irish Government, on giving twelve months' notice, to take over the welfare expenditures also, if it wished to do so.

What then did Mr. Redmond really mean by "complete power over our whole financial system?" He was not a Protectionist, like Arthur Griffith; so far from wishing to raise tariffs, he had requested the power to *reduce* and had been turned down by the Cabinet.[9] Nor was he interested in the welfare state, even in its present rudimentary form: the Irish leadership was not city-minded, and welfare (to its way of thinking) was chiefly adapted to the needs of an industrial and urban population in which — this was a great weakness — it was really not interested.[10] Nonetheless, Nationalist pride demanded that the English Government should *not* give welfare handouts to the Irish people, once the Irish people had a working Parliament of their own. Mr. Redmond, therefore, had simply to wait until his Government was firmly established ("the year of revision"); he could then demand that welfare expenditures could be turned over to the Irish Parliament; and these expenditures could be either materially reduced or even, and not too gradually, abolished altogether.

This was not without a precedent. In 1911 a Committee, headed by Mr. A. W. Primrose, had been requested by Mr. Asquith to look into Irish finances in the event of Home Rule; and the Committee had come up with a most ingenious scheme whereby aged Irish men and women, who reached the age of seventy *after* Home Rule had been enacted, would receive no pensions at all. Indeed the whole welfare concept, applied to Ireland without what it euphemistically called "adaptation," must inevitably (said the Committee) lead to "a grievous waste of public money, if not to a serious demoralization of Irish life."[11] It therefore proposed that the Irish Government should have full power over the raising of revenue as well as over all expenditures.[12]

This is what John Redmond had in mind when he referred to "complete power over the whole of our financial system" — he was demanding the gradual expulsion of the welfare state from Ireland. In this he had support from another and very powerful quarter. The Primrose Committee's Report had been enthusiastically endorsed by the Bishop of Ross, who was on the Committee, and the Bishop of Raphoe, who was not. In January 1912 they were both calling for "fiscal autonomy," and John Dillon — although he agreed with them — dissuaded them only because he feared the Cabinet would turn them down.[13] And this is what the Cabinet did, in effect; since it rejected the Report on the grounds that it would make further representation at Westminster unnecessary, and also — and more so — that it was financially unsound.[14]

If Catholic bishops endorsed a plan to deprive aged Irish men and women of a few shillings a week, it was not because they were inhumane. They genuinely believed that a community of peasant proprietors would be demoralized by welfare: for, like the Irish Nationalist leaders, they were not urban minded. On the other hand, they had come to dread the Liberal welfare state, even in its present quite tentative form, because they were convinced that it presaged further, more expensive and more widely spread benefits; that this would mean the refusal of further funds to Irish education; and that Irish education would then be forced to go on the rates — a form of secular control that the Catholic bishops had so far managed to fend off, and which they unanimously deplored.[15]

Thus, for the first time, there seemed to be grounds for a genuine accord between the Church and the Party; and there is no question that the Party, if Home Rule had been enacted, would have regained all the prestige it had recently been losing. Nor does there seem any question that Mr. Redmond, while he had no wish to leave the Empire, would have expected to remain in it on more and more independent terms.

It is one of the ironical notes of these times that the Unionists should have ignored the socially conservative side of the Irish Party. But in truth they did not trust the Irish; their eyes were focused exclusively on independence, to which the Third Home Rule Bill was seen as a first step; and here, of course, they were right. Where they were wrong was in their belief that Union was very nearly if not quite the keystone in the arch of Empire, and that without it the whole thing would collapse.

This was not an entirely sane conspectus, but it existed; and there were other considerations. For religious and economic reasons they feared for the safety of the "loyal" Irish Northeast; they prophesied that Ulster Protestants and Ulster industries would both be mistreated by a Parliament in Dublin with a large agrarian and Catholic majority.

Religion, economics and politics, mixed together, make an explosive substance; and in this instance it was not the less dangerous for being exposed to the strange atmosphere which pervaded the United Kingdom in 1912. And this was not all. To their fears for the Empire and for Ulster Protestantism, the Unionists now added some quite cynical calculations of party advantage. It seemed to them that they could bring the Ulster question to such a pitch of violence, verbal or otherwise, as to bring about the dissolution of Parliament, a new Election, and the defeat, the exile, and — who could tell? — the virtual extinction of the Liberal Party. And so, while the Home Rule Bill made its slow first journey through the Commons — it was not passed until February 1913, to be at once rejected by the Lords — they turned away from Parliament and, in quite a shameless manner, began to beat the Ulster drum.

Chapter Six

The Orange Drum—
1911—1912

On 25 September 1911, some six weeks after the surrender of the House of Lords, a conference of Unionist Clubs and Orange Lodges met in Belfast. "Recognizing that the public peace of this country is in great and imminent danger by the reason of the threat to establish a Parliament in Dublin and knowing that such a step will inevitably lead to disaster to the Empire and absolute ruin to Ireland," it demanded that arrangements should be made for a Provisional Government for Ulster.[1]

At the time there was still a disposition in England to believe that such a conference — since it could not achieve its objective without help from England — did not mean what it said. This was unwise. Ireland is an island which encourages the long memory, and Ulster had a formidable past.

I

The settlers who moved into Ulster under James I, after the Tudor mutilation of that "fighting arm of Ireland"; who were persecuted by Laud; who sided with the Scots against the Long Parliament; were "apt to be independent with a distinctive flavor of frontier radicalism."[2] They were mainly dour Lowlanders, the sons of Calvin and of Knox; they readily absorbed the fighting tradition of the unhappy islanders upon whom they had been planted. As the generations passed, moreover, through intermarriage, through environment, they looked upon themselves as Irishmen too.

When William III defeated James II on 1/12 July 1690 at the Battle of the Boyne, the event had one meaning in England and quite another in Ireland: for in passing from one national history to the other we have to go through a looking glass. In England it was a great and solemn victory; in Ireland a tragic prelude to the Penal Laws which attempted to eradicate the Catholic gentry and the Catholic religion: and in time it brought to the plantation Presbyterians, precisely because they *were* Presbyterian and therefore dissenters from the Anglican faith, their own share of disabilities — a far less grievous share, but still a very heavy one.

In the last quarter of the eighteenth century, therefore, there was an attempt to separate religion from politics in the Protestant Northeast. The Irish Volunteers, who forced the Parliament in London to bestow a quasi-independence upon the Protestant Parliament in Dublin, were organized in Belfast and were mostly Presbyterian. They were succeeded by the United Irishmen, whose leaders — with some exceptions, such as Wolfe Tone and Thomas Russell — were Presbyterian. While the great Rebellion of 1798 was complex in its origin and horrid in its expression, it may well be called great because one can find in it a radical ideal to combine all Ireland into one island nation, without respect to race or religion.

In Ulster, however, there was already a deeply rooted enmity between the Protestant and the Catholic peasantry. This was especially the case in County Armagh, where their numbers were almost equal and there was a severe pressure on the land. In 1795 the Protestant "Peep O'Day Boys," after a victorious skirmish with the Catholic "Defenders," were persuaded to found an Orange Society, dedicated to the memory of William of Orange and his victory over James II at the Boyne. Despite its humble origin, men of the governing class began to join it, as well they might, since it was formed to defend the rights and privileges of the (Anglican) Church of Ireland, which looked down upon Presbyterianism as a second-class underbred sort of religion. In fact, when the United Irishmen staged their rising in Counties Down and Armagh, members of the Orange Society were prominent among those who helped the Government suppress it.

The radicalism of the Presbyterians and the bigotry of the Orange Society tended at one time to go in different directions. The former almost generated a tolerant religious attitude, as evidenced by the Reverend Henry Montgomery in his (losing) battle with the Reverend Henry Cooke in 1829; while the latter became more and more virulently anti-Catholic. There was, however, always a strong urge to unite them, and this was very marked after the Catholic Emancipation of 1829. The Orange Society had by then become so fanatical and in a political sense so unreliable that it was suppressed in 1836 by a valiant Chief Secretary, Thomas Drummond. It lingered on, unrepentant, unreconstructed, in the hearts of small Protestant farmers, agricultural laborers, city workers: only the Protestant *elite* stayed away. It was not until the Land Act of 1881, the first threat to the Protestant Ascendency since Emancipation, that Orangeism became respectable: although it never exorcized — and has not to this day — the lingering spirits of the United Irishmen, on the one hand, or the Reverend Henry Montgomery, on the other.

Orangeism in its heyday was far more popular than "loyal"; far more pro-Union than pro-Government; and though it was draped in the Union Jack, that respectable piece of bunting could not disguise the fact that nineteenth century Orangemen had been known to express a wish to kick Queen Victoria's crown into the Boyne. With the Anti-Repeal Union of 1886; with the embryonic Irish Unionist Party of that year; with the Ulster Defence Union of 1893, a response to Mr. Gladstone's Second Home Rule Bill — this grim movement had got into full swing. Indeed the Defence Union and its founder, Colonel E. J. Saunderson, a dour wit, very popular in the House of Commons, became the first — though unfortunately not the last — to urge an armed and disciplined resistance to Home Rule.

When Ulster Unionism was finally consolidated in 1905, it took the form of an Ulster Unionist Council, composed of two hundred members — one hundred nominated by the Unionist Associations, fifty by the Orange Grand Lodges, and fifty consisting of M.P.s and peers. Designed to work hand in glove with the (Southern) Irish Unionist Alliance and the somber (English) Union Defence League, it was from the start a force to be reckoned with.

Colonel Saunderson died in 1906, and his place as leader of the Irish Unionists was taken by Walter Long, an English county (Hampshire) gentleman of ancient family who sat for South Dublin in the Commons and had been Chief Secretary for some eighteen months after George Wyndham's resignation. A stubborn and backward man, with a strong bump of self-esteem, Mr. Long had conceived a genuine devotion to an ideal Ireland; with the real Ireland he was commonly in a state of irritation. He had inherited from Colonel Saunderson a somewhat fractious Protestant Ulster, for under the Colonel's nose there had arisen an Independent Orange Order, half populist, half puritan, which forced his resignation from the Grand Mastership of the Orange Order. Indeed Belfast itself, sadly in need of social regeneration, seemed for a while on the verge of expelling the orthodox Unionists. With the threat of a new Home Rule movement, however, this reforming impulse died away; and when Long resigned the leadership of the Irish Unionist M.P.s, he left behind him a strong Protestant Ulster for which he could take little credit. He was succeeded — it was a unanimous choice — by Sir Edward Carson.

II

There was no Ulster in Sir Edward Carson's past. He was born in Dublin in 1854, and both sides of his family had lived in Southern Ireland for more than two centuries. In religion he was attached to the low church Anglicanism of the Church of Ireland. A graduate of Trinity College, Dublin, he was called to the Irish bar in 1877; and he first became prominent during the Plan of Campaign struggles, when, amidst desperate scenes of riot and eviction, William O'Brien and John Dillon waged a Fair Rent battle against the might of Lord Salisbury and his Chief Secretary and nephew, Arthur ("Bloody") Balfour. Balfour, as has been shown, developed a policy which consisted of "resolute" government and rational reform. But "resolute" government came first.

"Resolute" was the seventeenth-century "Thorough," adapted to the conscience of the nineteenth century. It kept as far as possible within the confines of the law, but, confronted as it was by a huge agrarian disturbance, it needed to make these confines as elastic as possible. Carson had a legal mind bold enough to attempt this feat, and he did not flinch from the consequences of exercising it. "He was quite fearless," said Mr. Balfour. "Everybody right up to the top was trembling [but] Carson had nerve . . . I sent him all over the place, prosecuting, getting convictions."

In return for these services, Carson was appointed Solicitor General for Ireland in 1892; got himself elected to one of the two seats for Dublin University; and took his place in the House of Commons and at the English Bar. He had looked upon his English sojourn as a brief exile, a necessary first step to a seat on the Irish Bench. But he stayed on, to become a famous advocate, a frightening adversary, a dour and relentless cross-examiner. Those who heard it never forgot his destruction of Oscar Wilde, a more brilliant personage on every count.

With his gifts, his energy, his charm — for charm he had when he cared to use it — where might he not go? His appearance, too, was of a piece with his reputation. His tall body, his rather brutal face, the dark eyes brooding over the long jaw and heavy chin, put one in mind of a pirate — a pirate, or was it a puritan? Or both? One could not be sure.

He looked like a vigorous man in mind and body: but those who knew him well knew that he suffered from a bad digestion, bad nerves, insomnia and melancholy. It is hard not to give these symptoms a place in something more fundamental, something which provides a clue to his success and his failure. In spite of the strain of altruism in his character, his was in truth a profoundly negative personality.

He was one of those not so rare people who flourish only in opposition. When he was elevated to Cabinet rank, he never could do anything with it. His political career, with its many disappointments, reflected the Nationalist concept of Ireland as a "seamless garment": he merely stood this concept on its head. The Union, he said, was seamless; and in order to preserve it in that condition he was ready to draw his sword. And yet he was a former Law Officer; he had a vested interest in law and order. Deep inside him, they too had their claims. To this day it is uncertain whether Sir Edward Carson, when in 1914 he seemed poised upon the verge of rebellion and civil war, was the leader of his fanatical lieutenants or their most important captive.

Such was the interesting personage who, in the summer of 1911, was asked to become the leader of the Irish Unionist M.P.s and head of the Ulster Unionist Council. He did not hesitate long. He was willing to sacrifice a part of his large income, his peace of mind, even perhaps his professional future, in order to immerse himself in Orange politics. The place he took in the Unionist Council was readily yielded by Captain James Craig, of the whiskey firm of Dunville's, once a British officer in the Boer War with a reputation for courage, now a millionaire distiller. Captain Craig was a red-faced gentleman who looked like a stolid farmer. His manners were courteous and benign. He had a keen, cold, narrow mind, as the Catholics of Ulster were one day to learn to their cost.

III

The Province of Ulster, after all, was anything but a solid Protestant entity. Of its nine counties, three (Donegal, Monaghan and Cavan) had large Catholic majorities, while two (Fermanagh and Tyrone) had small ones. The political population of the province was so equally divided that it returned seventeen Unionists to Parliament as against sixteen Nationalists, and in 1913 this position was actually reversed by the victory of a Redmondite Home Ruler in a by-election in Derry City.

It was in the four northeast counties of Antrim, Armagh, Down and Derry that Protestant majorities held sway and Belfast was their stronghold — Belfast which had already become a satrapy of the manufacturing and shipbuilding empire of northeast England and southwest Scotland. One might even have said that Belfast, so far from being Ireland's industrial capital, was really nothing of the sort. Its raw materials were virtually all imported; its markets were overseas. As a shipbuilding center it should have been Liberal, to the extent at least that shipbuilding and Free Trade traditionally went hand in hand; and the chairman of the Harland & Wolff shipyards, Lord Pirrie, had already turned himself into a Home Ruler. The ordinary Belfast businessman, however, professed to believe that Home Rule would force him to exchange his lucrative share in the British complex for a monopoly of the domestic exchanges of an impoverished rural South — in other words that Belfast actually *would* become the industrial capital of Ireland. How he derived this from the concept of Home Rule it would be hard to say: but then he believed, and this was no profession, that Home Rule would be nothing more than a Liberal effort to shuffle the Irish deficit off on to Irish shoulders. And he was, he said, convinced that a Dublin Parliament — through malice or muddle or both — would soon succeed in crippling industrial Ulster.[3]

Into this suspicious community there was introduced, on 23 September 1911, the portentous phenomenon of Sir Edward Carson.

The thousands who gathered to hear him at Craigavon, Captain Craig's estate outside Belfast, were not disappointed in this new leader. Speaking in vibrant tones and in accents seldom heard north of the Boyne, he told them exactly what they had come to hear. "We will yet defeat the most nefarious conspiracy that has ever been hatched against a free people . . . We ask for no privileges . . . We ask for no special rights, but we claim the same rights from the same government as every other part of the British Empire, and Heaven help the men who try to take them from us."[4]

Whether a Protestant minority was not claiming a privilege and a special right when it demanded to be free of the decisions of a majority in Ireland and in the Imperial Parliament — this was a delicate question into which Sir Edward and his audience made no pretence of entering. Sir Edward had also spoken of the "Protestant Province of Ulster," which was an odd way of describing a province whose population was nearly half Catholic. Belfast itself had a large Catholic population: it began moving in with the Union, increased after the Famine, and was now settled in the west of the city. Here reigned "Wee Joe" Devlin, political boss, publican, and M.P. for West Belfast, who deployed and controlled the energies of the Ancient Order of Hibernians, an organization which, though never much in favor with the Church, endeavored to counteract the Orangeism of its Protestant neighbors.

The whole sad question of Protestant and Catholic differences in Ulster — enthusiastically fostered by Belfast industrialists — lent itself to misconception. Centuries of enforced misunderstandings, of martyrdoms and massacres, sieges and battlefields, stood between the two groups. Their aversions had been exploited by statesmen and capitalists, landlords and clerics; and when they entered the twentieth century, with their train of unappeasable memories, these differences seemed almost beyond understanding, let alone adjustment.

They were not, it would seem, by any means wholly religious differences. To the men who composed Sir Edward's audience at Craigavon their Catholic neighbors were an inferior caste of conquered people. "Croppies lie down!" was one of their more popular adjurations. "The crown of the causeway on road or street," ran one of their favorite spells, "and the Papishes under my feet." Every anniversary of the Battle of the Boyne, on 12 July, the Orange Lodges decked themselves in bowler hats, dark suits, white gloves and orange sashes; unfurled their scriptural banners and their replicas of William III; beat their dull massed drums and vilified the Pope. Each side, with reason, feared the bigotry of the other. To Ulster Catholics the Protestant religion in its various forms was quite meaningless, but Protestants were living symbols of an old and continuing injustice. To the Ulster Protestant, the Catholic Church was an institution to which the most sinister plots were attributed. Indeed, to an unlettered Protestant, the Pontiff himself was highly gifted in the art of breaking and entering; and it was confidently expected that, even before Home Rule arrived, he would find his way into Dublin Castle. Behind all this there was a deeper, more urgent and scarcely more rational local fear. If an all-Ireland Parliament, with its Catholic majority, were actually established in Dublin, what revenge might not Wee Joe Devlin and his cohorts take upon their Protestant neighbors behind the Shankill Road in Belfast?

Sir Edward himself never descended to sectarian arguments and never encouraged men to riot: but how thrilling his reference to "a nefarious conspiracy" and the like must have been to Protestant ears: and how strange, how small his sense of responsibility when he allowed himself to utter it!

IV

When a former Solicitor-General like Sir Edward beat the Orange drum, the sight (not to mention the sound) was somewhat incongruous: when the leader of His Majesty's Loyal Opposition and his colleagues joined him in this exercise, it became frankly grotesque. Yet this is what happened after 8 November 1911. On that day, Mr. A. J. Balfour announced that he was formally resigning the leadership of the Conservative-Unionist Party. Politics, he had been heard to say, had become odious; the Party had treated him badly; his ambitions in any case were all satisfied.[5] He had led the Party to three defeats; he had mismanaged the Budget and the Parliament Bill crises. His was no longer an impressive record. He excused himself with the thought — for he was something of a positivist — that the future lay with science not politics. But it was only an excuse; the truth lay elsewhere. He was tired; he was probably bored; but that was not all. After the 1906 Election he had, with remarkable prescience, foreseen a kind of politics and a kind of Parliament in which he would find the role of leader less and less congenial.

The choice of his successor lay first between Mr. Austen Chamberlain and Mr. Walter Long, who were not on speaking terms. Mr. Chamberlain had an impressive exterior and a fussy and father-haunted mind: he was also upright and loyal. Mr. Long belonged by birth and even spirit to Disraeli's "many-acred squires," who on that disastrous night of 25 June 1846 had gone into the hostile lobby against Sir Robert Peel: indeed, his own ancestor, "the pleasant Walter Long," had been one of them.[6] A living reminder of that vanishing class, he could still command a following in the Conservative Party: it is for this reason, doubtless, that one finds him occupying office after office in Conservative and Coalition cabinets — a political rolling stone, and one which always gathered moss. The leadership, however, was to escape him; and the prize went to a compromise candidate, Mr. Andrew Bonar Law.

When Mr. Asquith introduced the Third Home Rule Bill in April 1912, Mr. Bonar Law accused him, first of selling his conviction, and then of not having any, and all in language so abrasive that the Prime Minister remarked — "We are getting on with the new style."[7] And "the new style" has since been inseparably connected with Andrew Bonar Law and his unfortunate, not to say unforgiveable behavior during the last two years before the Great War.

He was by birth a Canadian, by occupation a Glasgow ironmaster and metal broker. His father, a Presbyterian minister, had once left his Ulster manse for a Canadian one, and then left Canada to return to Ulster. The son had climbed no higher than Secretary to the Board of Trade, but he had made quite a reputation for himself as a tough debater and had even acquired a small following.[8] In private he had a sense of fun and Lloyd George — who was fussy in such matters — always enjoyed his company when at last they became colleagues: but in public he was dour and without unction. Mr. Asquith described him as "meekly ambitious" — a description which somehow fits his sad eyes and crumpled face — and certainly one cannot read Lord Blake's biography of him without realizing that Law never genuinely desired the highest place.

The party leadership was an extremely delicate position for such a man, a man who did not know how to give or even enjoy a good dinner, a man who was a reflection of that shift in membership which was bringing the businessman and the inhabitant of suburbia out of the Liberal and into the Conservative ranks. He was not the kind of gentleman whom the Conservatives normally chose for their leader, and of course he knew it. In any event, Mr. A. J. Balfour — with his affable and elegant manners, his knifelike wit and his stony heart — would not have been an easy man to follow, whatever his shortcomings. Was the "new style," as Bonar Law used it, the effect of a quality which a leading historian has called "hardness"?[9] Was it an attempt to compensate for a sense of inadequacy? Or was it a response to the urgency of a party game which the Unionists were turning into a deadly and quite uncharacteristic feud — a feud which no parliamentary system and no political democracy could long sustain?

Sir Edward Carson had also been drawn into this feud — to the extent at least of using Ulster not merely as a preservative of Union, but also as a means of drumming the Liberals out of politics. Theirs, he said, was "a craven government, a wretched, miserable, time-serving lot."[10] Such language came more naturally from his lips than from Mr. Law's: but there is no mistaking what it was. It, too, was "the new style."

Chapter Seven

The New Style—
1912—1914

T he "new style" took several forms during the next two years, not all confined to the Unionists. They were: Verbal menace; Pressure on the King; Inter-party collusion; Military disaffection. And between them they brought party politics to the verge of collapse.

I

Verbal Menace

On 10 April 1912, for example, Sir Edward Carson said that if the people of England permitted the coercion of their "kith and kin" in Ulster, the British Army would never stand the strain. In June, Mr. Bonar Law stated that there were stronger influences than parliamentary majorities, and that a Government which ordered troops to enforce Home Rule would stand more chance of being lynched in London than Loyalists would stand of being shot in Belfast. On 27 July, at a monster meeting held outside Blenheim Palace, Bonar Law declared that he knew of no lengths to which Ulster Unionists might go where the Unionist Party and the public at large would not follow them "in sympathy." This was a little too mild for F. E. Smith, the brilliant youngish Conservative lawyer, a product of Lancashire and Oxford, who, much to Mr. Balfour's disgust, had been made a Privy Councillor by Mr. Asquith in the Coronation Honours List of June 1911. (His gratitude to the Prime Minister on that occasion was profuse but short lived. Six weeks later he joined Lord Hugh Cecil in a successful attempt to shout Mr. Asquith down in the House.) Arising in great and calculated excitement, he now cried: "Should it happen that Ulster is threatened with a violent attempt to incorporate her in an Irish Parliament, I say to Sir Edward Carson, 'Appeal to the young men of England.' "[1]

In the late autumn, looking back at such speeches, and there were many of them, the Prime Minister said: "This reckless rhodomontade [has] furnished for the future a complete grammar of Anarchy."[2] He did not add "and of Treason" because — as a cultured Liberal — he simply could not take mere verbal threats very seriously.

Even the Ulster *Sacramentum* — a bowdlerized version of the old Scots Covenant — could not have been taken very seriously either. Signed by Carson and a long line of prelates, peers, Privy Councillors and Members of Parliament, some on their knees, several in their own blood, in the city of Belfast on 29 September 1912, the Covenant pledged its signatories "throughout this our time of threatened calamity" to use all necessary means to defeat "the present conspiracy to set up a Home Rule Parliament in Ireland." By the end of November, it was claimed that in Ulster alone 218,206 men and 228,991 women had put their names to it: and later on it was introduced into England with even more spectacular results from men and women alike. But it was no great threat. It committed them, at most, to a state of mind. Anyone who wished to sign it could have done so, in hot blood or in cold, without a qualm.

II

Pressure on King George V

King Edward VII died on 6 May 1910, in the middle of the Veto crisis. He had returned from a holiday at Biarritz late in April with a heavy cold which turned into bronchitis. "It was that awful Biarritz," said Queen Alexandra, who considered this resort a second Babylon, "that finished him off." Others more politically minded attributed his death to worry and, by indirection, to the Liberals. Actually King Edward had been on good terms with his two Liberal Prime Ministers — far better, as it happened, than with Mr. Balfour, whom he suspected of laughing at him up his sleeve. In the crises ahead, at any rate, the King would probably have been more of a help than a hindrance.

Of the new King, George V, little was known. A sailor, with a salty quarterdeck vocabulary when aroused, he was otherwise a philistine of great propriety and dullness. He had, with genuine reluctance, for such a mass creation was fundamentally preposterous, agreed to create several hundred new peers if the Lords refused to accept the Parliament Bill. But his patience (he was a true-blue Conservative) had been severely strained, and under further stress he might not behave well.

On 12 May 1912, at Balmoral, Mr. Bonar Law informed the King — in language so very much in "the new style" that he was never forgiven for it — that it was his duty either to refuse his assent to the Home Rule Bill when it came before him in June 1914 or else to dismiss his Liberal ministers before this occurred. "In either case," added Mr. Law dourly," half your subjects will think that you have acted against them."[3]

In September, he again told the King that before he assented to a Home Rule Bill he had the right to find other ministers — in other words, Mr. Law and his colleagues — who would permit the question to be settled at a General Election.[4]

This was, of course, doctrine of the most dubious kind; and if the times had been less tense and feverish would not have been poured by a responsible leader of the Opposition into the ear of a constitutional King. Mr. Law, however, was not alone in his misdemeanors. Early the following year, as if to illustrate the strangeness of the political atmosphere, one finds an astonishing exchange of letters between Mr. St. Loe Strachey, editor of the *Spectator* and an influential Free Trade Conservative, and A. V. Dicey, a former Vinerian Professor at Oxford. Both admitted that there was "a tendency to force the King" into reviving the royal veto. Mr. Strachey was totally opposed to this: but Professor Dicey, generally considered the country's leading constitutional authority, was not so sure. "We shall have to fight the usurpation of a party machine," he wrote. "We cannot afford to give up an old and clumsy weapon." He might have been talking of the culverin, for the last exercise of the royal veto had taken place in the reign of William III, who twice refused his assent to bills creating triennial parliaments. On the whole, however, Professor Dicey preferred another device — namely that the King should arbitrarily dismiss his ministers and "call to office a Unionist Ministry wholly and solely for the purpose of referring the Home Rule Bill [to the people] for their sanction or rejection." Here he was lending his authority to an argument which was far from candid but of which the Unionists were becoming very fond — namely that the people had not been given an opportunity to pass on Home Rule.[5]

George V was beginning to feel that he himself was in much the same predicament. A joint memorandum from Mr. Bonar Law and the Marquess of Lansdowne, the Unionist leader in the Lords, had severely shaken him. They argued, once again, that he had a right to dismiss Mr. Asquith;[6] and in an agitated letter to the Prime Minister, four thousand words long and all in his own hand, the King set forth his state of mind, or of indecision. Mr. Asquith who, strange to say, was being consulted for the first time on this interesting matter, replied with a classical orchestration of the theme "The King can do no wrong." The Cabinet (wrote Mr. Asquith) not the King must take full responsibility for the advice it offered him, advice which it was the monarch's constitutional duty to accept. To this His Majesty answered, courteously and ominously, that he had a "residual" right to dismiss his ministers.[7]

This was written on 22 September 1913 and its sentiments, if pursued, might have cost George V his throne. The truth was that he had again been listening to Lord Lansdowne. The marquess seems rather miscast in the role of Lorelei, since he was usually a temperate and reasonable man: but, being a great Irish landowner, he was neither the one nor the other when it came to Home Rule. On 6 September, at Balmoral, he urged George V toward the rocks of veto or dismissal or *insistence* on a dissolution; the King, very nearly won over, suggested that the Archbishop of Canterbury might be brought in to persuade Mr. Asquith; and on 9 September, when Lansdowne left the castle, told him, in the strictest confidence, that no less a man than Mr. Birrell had reported that the Ulster Unionists were not bluffing.[8]

If the King turned back to the paths of correct behavior, this was, in fact, due to the recklessness of Mr. Bonar Law and the cold intransigence of Sir Edward Carson. On 28 November, for example, Mr. Law suggested to an audience of Dublin Unionists that the Army would mutiny if it were asked to coerce Ulster. In January 1914 Sir Edward refused even to consider the generous compromise "Home Rule within Home Rule" after three meetings with Mr. Asquith.[9] On the 26th of that month, when Bonar Law wrote to

Lord Stamfordham, the King's private secretary, once again demanding a dissolution, Stamfordham replied that the King was not prepared to share Mr. Law's "pessimistic view."[10] Although George V wavered now and then thereafter, this deliberate snub was also final.

Thus the Unionist leadership had tried verbal menace and solemn mummery — the treasonable speeches of important men, the hollow rituals of the Covenant; and they had tried to put pressure on the King. All these expedients had failed. There remained two more: a weird collusion with the Liberals, and military disaffection itself.

III

Collusion

By "collusion" one means simply this: that, just as an outsider caught in a family quarrel is likely to be set upon by both sides, so the Irish Party, involved through no fault of its own in English party politics, could expect to receive little consideration from one side and less mercy from the other. This would have been the case, perhaps, if politics had remained the serious game which — under the ordinary conditions of political democracy — it usually was. But now conditions were very far from ordinary: in 1914 politics, at least on the Unionist side, had reached a pitch of intensity and even of malice never before equaled in modern British history.

On 2 February, for example, there took place a momentous interview — "my Leviathan interview" in Mr. Asquith's words — between the Prime Minister, Mr. Birrell and Mr. Redmond. Here Mr. Asquith exploded what — in a note to his confidante, Miss Venetia Stanley, he afterward, with quite unseemly merriment, called his "bomb." He told the Irish leaders that certain contingencies might arise which would oblige the King to dismiss his ministers and send for the Unionists to form a new Government. Under Mr. Redmond's questioning, he admitted that a Unionist attack was to be made on the Army Annual Bill.[11]

The Army Annual Bill, a legacy from the Glorious Revolution of 1688–89, was the law which annually regulated the code of discipline for the Army, the law which gave Parliament legal control over the armed forces of the Crown. If it were *not* passed the Government would be unable either to control or to pay the Army, which would virtually cease to exist.

As Mr. Asquith unfolded the plot, the Unionists in the Commons would, "probably with the connivance of the Speaker," create such a disturbance that the Bill would be held up; or else, if it passed the Commons, the Lords would use their suspensory veto and reject it out of hand, or amend it out of shape. The King would then have no choice but to break the deadlock by calling on the Unionists to form a new Government.[12] In the ensuing Election the Unionists, especially since they had jettisoned Tariff Reform in 1912, would most likely sweep the country. The postponement of Home Rule for many years would be the necessary consequence.

The idea of Unionist interference with the Army Annual Bill, either through rejection or amendment, had been in the air since 1912; but it was not seriously considered by the Unionists' leadership, according to the evidence now available, until December 1913. It was then suggested to Mr. Balfour and Lord Lansdowne, and Mr. Balfour replied that it was "ingenious" and should be passed on to "Headquarters," in other words to Mr. Bonar Law.[13] Toward the end of January 1914 Mr. Law was in favor of a crippling amendment in the Lords; on 1 February Lord Lansdowne agreed "although I rather dread the step"; on 2 February Lord Hugh Cecil had come into the plot and was calling for secrecy, since there had been hints in the *Daily News;* and on 3 February Mr. Balfour told Mr. Bonar Law that the proposal was one of "extraordinary interest."[14]

On 4 February, a special committee composed of Sir Edward Carson, Lord Robert Cecil, Lord Halsbury, Sir George Cave and Sir Robert Findlay began to consider how best to frame an amendment. On 10 February, Lord Willoughby de Broke, a sporting peer who had fought the Parliament Bill down to the last ditch, spoke openly of the plan in the Lords. Eight days later, Professor Dicey gave it his blessing: it would be a constitutional use of their legal powers, he told Bonar Law, if the Lords passed the Army Annual Bill with the proviso that the Royal forces were never to be used to coerce Ulster.[15]

The Annual Act was of course susceptible to routine amendment to keep it up to date: but never, surely, in its long history to such an amendment as this!

The whole plan had obviously been leaked to Mr. Asquith on 1 February, as it had to the *Daily News,* in the hope that he would be intimidated into calling for a dissolution of Parliament before it was too late. To Mr. Bonar Law's way of thinking the Liberal Government was now at the end of its tether. Its known dissensions over the Naval Estimates; the terrific battering it had received from other quarters during the past two years; the very fact that Lord Loreburn (a former Lord Chancellor and a most rigorous Home Ruler) had written to the *Times* in September suggesting a compromise with Orange Ulster — what were these if not signs of weakness and portents of collapse? Mr. Law had already had three secret meetings with Mr. Asquith, and had come to the conclusion or misunderstanding — for two more dissimilar minds could hardly have been found in public life — that the Prime Minister was a weak and faithless man.

Mr. Asquith put little stock in the Army Annual Bill plot: his was not a combustible imagination. To give him his due, as an accomplished and experienced parliamentarian, he *may* have realized that the Tory back-benchers, gladly as they welcomed a resistance to Parliament in Ulster, would not feel kindly toward a tampering with the Army in England: which, as will be shown, is what happened.

This was simply not true, however, of Mr. Redmond and his colleagues. In the first week of March, and with the magical assistance of Mr. Lloyd George, the Prime Minister persuaded Messrs. Redmond, Dillon and Devlin to accept a six years' exclusion from Home Rule of six of the nine Ulster counties.

The idea was not new. It had been raised by Mr. Churchill in 1912;[16] it had been the subject of an amendment in the Commons early in 1913; it had appeared in the course of the abortive Asquith-Bonar Law discussions late in that year; in October and November Lloyd George had tried in vain to urge it on Mr. Redmond; and in late December and in January, Carson had told Asquith that nothing but exclusion would do.[17]

Why then had Redmond given way, in March 1914, to proposals he had sternly rejected in the previous November? The answer can only be the "Leviathan interview": the interview when Asquith exploded his "bomb" and Redmond — as Miss Stanley was told — "shivered visibly."[18] The interview had had, as Mr. Asquith put it, its "salutary" effect; it had forced the Irish leaders into making concessions in the hopes of placating the Opposition and the Orange Unionists. These concessions were little short of calamitous. To agree to special conditions for Ulster under an all-Ireland Parliament in Dublin was one thing: to accept the exclusion of six Ulster counties from the control of that Parliament, even on a temporary basis, was quite another. It made a rent in the ideal of the "seamless garment" — it was the first Nationalist obeisance to that principle of Partition which afterwards became a great stumbling block to peace in Ireland.

When Mr. Asquith presented the six years' exclusion plan to Parliament on 9 March, Sir Edward Carson contemptuously dismissed it as a "sentence of death with a stay of execution of six years."[19] In Ireland, *Sinn Fein* and *Irish Freedom* condemned it out of hand, and Cardinal Logue confessed that he found it hard to consider becoming, even temporarily, a virtual foreigner in his cathedral city of Armagh.

The Irish Party's reluctant sacrifice of principle to expedience had been made, therefore, and it had been made in vain: the damage to its reputation had been incalculable. In short, the Unionist leaders had used the Army Annual Bill plot to bring about, they hoped, a dissolution of Parliament and the end of Home Rule: the Liberal leaders had used it for precisely the opposite reasons. Caught in this crossfire, this curious form of interparty collusion with regard to Irish interests, Mr. Redmond had become the most prominent casualty. The other, to be sure, was the Liberal Government, whose weakness had now been exposed to the whole political world.

IV

Military Disaffection

The Ulster Volunteer Force was founded in January 1913, when the Unionist Council decided that the various groups which had been marching and drilling (with haphazard enthusiasm, wooden rifles, and the blessing of the Belfast magistrates) should be united into one body, limited to men between seventeen and sixty-five, and organized by counties, divisions and districts. Since the Peace Preservation Act of 1881 had been allowed to lapse in 1907, it was now legal to import arms.

On 13 April 1913, Mr. Birrell addressed a long and important memorandum to the Cabinet in which he dismissed as totally unfounded an anonymous report — which he traced back to Colonel R. H. Wallace, Grand Master of the Belfast Orangemen — that the arms available, besides some one hundred thousand revolvers, amounted to eighty thousand rifles and a few Maxims. He thought that Major Frederick Crawford, of the firm of Alexander Crawford and Sons, might have imported some one thousand rifles; he also admitted that there was talk of civil war: but what he really feared, he said, were the riots which would take place in Northeast Ulster, after Home Rule had been enacted, and while the first elections to the Dublin Parliament were taking place.[20] In spite of his good intentions, and a disposition to cheerfulness, Mr. Birrell had not written an encouraging report.

The Ulster Volunteer Force, in fact, made a deeper and deeper impression on public opinion as the spring passed into summer. It had even acquired a Commander in Chief on the suggestion of no less a personage than Field Marshal Earl Roberts, the Army's most famous soldier: his name was Lieutenant General Sir George Richardson.

General Richardson had done most of his active service in long-forgotten expeditions — Wazari, Tirah, the Zhol Valley — he had led a cavalry brigade against the Boxers in Peking — in 1908 he had retired as a division commander in Poona.[21] There was little of the firebrand left in this elderly warrior, who now commanded some fifty thousand men of no military experience but unbounded enthusiasm: but he was very useful as propaganda. And it was in the form of propaganda that the UVF exerted at this moment its chief influence. It let it be known that it was extremely well organized for the day when it would spring to arms.

That day, to be sure, had still to dawn. In spite of the disappearance of the Peace Preservation Act there were technicalities which made the legal importation of rifles difficult; and up to the autumn of 1913 the number of imports was relatively small and the rifles themselves were of varying caliber and obsolete design.

The Government reimposed its Arms Embargo in December, which only encouraged smuggling; and it was really not until 11 March 1914 that it aroused itself from its torpor and began to look around. On that day Mr. Asquith appointed a small Cabinet committee to examine certain rumors which (he told the King) were being wafted out of Ulster.[22] These rumors concerned the Ulster Volunteer Force, now 85,000 strong. Its transportation, communications and medical corps were all still largely on paper; it lacked artillery; it possessed only six machine guns: but its number of usable rifles was steadily increasing. (By the end of March, the police reported, they amounted to twenty-one thousand, of which thirty-five hundred were of the latest design.[23]) Earlier in the year, its staff had drafted a "No. 1 Scheme," a three-page document which called for a sudden and paralysing blow at all railway communications, all telegraph, telephone and cable lines, and all avenues of approach into Ulster.[24] A copy had found its way to the police at Omagh and thence to the Chief Secretary's office,[25] where it was not taken too seriously: but it was this scheme to which the Cabinet Committee was supposed to find an answer.

The Committee was composed of five members, but it was dominated from the start by Colonel J. E. B. Seely, the vain and flamboyant Secretary for War, who had fought the Boers as a colonel of yeomanry and by Winston Churchill, First Lord of the Admiralty, an ex-hussar who had seen action in a cavalry charge at Omdurman. Mr. Churchill, whose tragic father had coined the sentence "Ulster will fight and Ulster will be right," had himself deserted his father's party on the question of Free Trade and, crossing the floor of the House, had converted himself into a Lloyd George radical. He was now in the early stages of a second and slower metamorphosis which, years later, was to transform him back into a Conservative. While the Liberals had been generous to this brilliant convert, many of his colleagues thought him at best a necessary evil, and the rest did not think him necessary.

On 14 March he redeemed his reputation for being shaky on Carsonism with a rousing speech at Bradford, in which he spoke of a "treasonable conspiracy," and declared that "there are worse things than bloodshed, even on an extended scale." "If Ulster is to become a tool in party calculations," he said in his peroration, "if all the loose wanton and reckless chatter we have been forced to listen to these many months is in the end to disclose a sinister and revolutionary purpose, then I can only say to you, 'Let us go forward together and put these grave matters to the proof.' "[26]

He had in fact already gone forward. On 11 March he ordered the Third Battle Squadron, then cruising off the coast of Spain, to hold its exercises at Lamlash, in the Firth of Forth, about sixty miles from the Irish coast, there to be joined by eight destroyers from Southampton Water. Mr. Asquith was not told of this order until the Cabinet of 17 March; and even then, becoming more and more imperturbable, he did not ask *when* the move was to be made and was not informed that it had already begun.[27]

As for Colonel Seely, he too had marched forward, *pari passu* with his vigorous colleague at the Admiralty. On 14 March, he sent Lieutenant General Sir Arthur Paget, Commander-in-Chief in Ireland, a letter of instructions requiring him to take specific precautions for guarding the weapons depots at Armagh, Omagh, Carrickfergus and Enniskillen — four strategic points for an investment of Ulster.

General Paget was a grandson of the famous cavalry leader, Lord Uxbridge, who lost his leg at Waterloo: he himself had a reputation for losing his head; and was not, everything considered, quite the man to be commanding in Ireland in these difficult times. After transmitting by letter and telegraph his reluctance to send troops into Ulster, he hurried over to London and was soon in conference with the Cabinet Committee and members of the Army Council.

He was now ordered to send two battalions of infantry into Ulster and to order a third, already in Belfast, to move out of its vulnerable barracks to a safer location outside the city. When he raised his two chief objections — that a movement of troops might create a disturbance in Ulster, and that the Great Northern Railway, whose workers were Orange to a man, might refuse to carry his two battalions northward — he was told that large reinforcements would, if necessary, be sent him from England, and that naval vessels would stand by, ready to carry his troops by sea should the railroad decline to take them.[28]

At a final conference, on 19 March, alone with Colonel Seely and Sir John French, Chief of the Imperial General Staff, he suddenly betrayed an extreme bellicosity and was told not to be "a bloody fool."[29] He then more soberly discussed the possibility, since professional soldiers were almost all Unionist, that many of his officers might object to taking part in operations against the Ulster Volunteers. He was instructed to tell them that officers domiciled in Ulster would be permitted to "disappear"; but that all others must obey their orders or accept instant dismissal. With these extremely odd orders, *which were never put into writing,* General Paget left London on the night of 19 March.

At Dublin on 20 March he summoned his senior officers to a conference: among them was Brigadier General Hubert de la Poer Gough, the popular and fiery commander of the Third Cavalry Brigade. Into their astonished ears he now poured a rambling disquisition, the gist of it being that troops were to be moved into Ulster, and that the whole Province might soon be in a blaze. He had warned "those swine" in the Government that they were playing with fire, but they would not listen. They had promised him ships and reinforcements and he was prepared to do his duty. He then repeated his instructions. Officers actually domiciled in Ulster could "disappear": all others must either obey their orders or accept instant dismissal.[30]

By the evening of 20 March 1914, at their headquarters in the Curragh Camp near Dublin, Brigadier General Sir Hubert Gough, his three colonels and fifty-five of his officers in the Third Cavalry Brigade, had decided that they would accept dismissal rather than move against loyalist Ulster. Cavalry officers, it was generally considered, were not among the brightest members of His Majesty's armed forces. But if they were not among the brightest, they were socially among the smartest; in those weeks Unionist and Liberal hostesses had been vying with one another in what was called "war to the knife and fork"; and the connection between the Curragh Mutiny (for mutiny it was) and the squabbles of privileged society was all too soon being made.

Of course these officers had a genuine excuse: no professional soldier either wants or ought to be given a choice in the matter of obeying orders; and, in fact, only the coolness of Major General Sir Charles Fergusson, commanding the Fifth Division, prevented the trouble from spreading to the infantry. As it was, the two infantry battalions left for the North as ordered, one from the Curragh, one from Mullingar, and were received in Ulster without incident, indeed with enthusiasm.[31]

General Paget's actions also were not entirely without excuse. It has been said by the best writer on the Curragh affair, that all he had been instructed to do was to move two battalions of infantry and that he had been "assured by experienced Ministers that this could in all probability be done without engendering any excitement."[32] But, like many other professional soldiers, Paget had little faith in the experience of Ministers; and the instructions conveyed to him — as indeed they do to us — the idea that Seely had something more in mind than the safeguarding of military stores. Had he known of Churchill's orders to the Third Battle Squadron and the eight destroyers, he would have been more certain still.

The news of what Gough and his officers had decided reached the War Office at 7:30 the same evening, and was in all the morning newspapers the next day, 21 March, where the King first learned of it. On this day, too, Mr. Asquith first heard that the Third Battle Squadron was on its way to Lamlash, and at once countermanded the order. The unrepentant Gough and his three colonels arrived in London the next morning; and on the following afternoon, 23 March, owing to the carelessness of Seely and the eagerness of French (who, of course, only wanted conciliation) they were given the disastrous pledge that "the troops under our command will not be called upon to enforce the present Home Rule Bill in Ulster, and that we can so assure our officers."[33] On the following day they returned in triumph to Ireland.

It was in vain that the Prime Minister, who had absented himself from these proceedings, when he heard of the pledge at once disavowed it. It was in vain that he accepted the resignations of Seely and French; in vain that he decided to take over the War Office himself; in vain that he survived, with his customary skill, some awkward scenes in Parliament. The damage had been done. The stable door had been locked by a practiced hand with skill and precision; the horse had gone. An impression had been created that the armed forces of the Crown could not be relied upon to do their duty and — which was a good deal nearer to the truth — that the Government was now helpless.

V

The Party Game Collapses

Mr. Bonar Law had already carried his unseemly plot against the Army Annual Bill one step further from Parliament: he had enlisted the support of Major General Henry Wilson, Director of Military Operations at the War Office. General Wilson, besides being the tallest, the ugliest and possibly the cleverest officer in the British Army, was also the most conspiratorial. Although he professed a contempt for politicians, whom he called "the frocks," they exercised an unusual fascination on him. Despite the fact that he had spent much time in arranging for the cooperation of the British and French armies in the event of a war with Germany, he swallowed without compunction Mr. Law's idea of a crippling amendment to the Army Annual Bill. A disturbance in the Commons, it is true, struck this peculiar soldier as likely to create an unfortunate effect in Europe; but an amendment in the Lords (he assured Mr. Law) "gets over my difficulty": and the two became firm allies.

Thus, when General French returned from his meeting with the Seely-Churchill Cabinet Committee on 18 March and told General Wilson in confidence that the Government proposed "to spray troops all over Ulster as if it were a Pontypool coal strike," the faithless Wilson reported every word, first to Bonar Law that afternoon, and then to Sir Edward Carson, Lord Milner and Sir Lysander Jameson that night at dinner.[34] The latter three agreed that the Lords had now no choice but to cripple the Army Annual Bill when it appeared in their House.

General Wilson was a fanatical Unionist, and for conspiring with the Opposition he had as his excuse, such as it was, the fact that he came from a family of well-to-do Protestants in County Longford. Lord Milner's Unionism was also fanatical, but of quite an opposite kind. Intensely loyal, immensely able, Lord Milner offered his loyalty to an England which existed, to some degree, only in his own mind. His grandmother was German; his father had been born, raised and buried in Germany; he could never rid himself of the feeling (said his disciple L. S. Amery) that in people's eyes "he was not quite English." The more he tried to dispel this appearance, the more, by some psychological sleight of hand, he seemed to assume it. His oversized and overschematic thinking, his intense belief in the superiority of the British race, his known contempt for the Constitution — these were, to say the least, uncomfortable traits.

And yet he was influential (Mr. Asquith, an old friend of Balliol days, used to listen to him), he was supremely efficient, he was greatly admired, he had been rewarded. He had risen to be High Commissioner of South Africa and Governor of Cape Colony; he was one of the architects of the Boer War; he was raised to the peerage. Retiring from South Africa under a cloud, at least in Liberal eyes, for having condoned the flogging of Chinese coolies on the Rand, he gathered around him a variegated group of young intellectuals interested in his "New Imperialism." They called themselves The Round Table, but were usually known as Milner's Kindergarten. Not seated at this Arthurian Table, but just as ardent a Milnerite, was General Henry Wilson.

Sir Edward's resistance to Home Rule had touched the imagination of Milner's Kindergarten; and Milner himself, besides circulating a British Covenant among the civilian populace, was already using the National Service League to spread disaffection — or so he hoped — among the officers of the Regular Army and the Reserves. Moreover, he was arranging for the collection of large secret funds from wealthy sympathisers in London, with which he expected to finance Sir Edward's Provisional Government when it came into being and the Ulster Volunteer Force even before this blessed event. The canvassing for these funds is believed to have begun in March.[35]

It is a tribute to the violence of the times that there should have been this underground Unionist movement, headed by the proconsular Milner, financed by his wealthy friends, spreading into the War Office and the armed services, and ready to go to any lengths in support of Orange Ulster.

General Wilson, when he heard of the Curragh incident, was filled with excitement; called on Bonar Law at 9:30 A.M. to urge him to "back Hubert [Gough]"; meditated resignation; and then decided that it was still his duty — Milner called it "saving the Empire"[36] — to spread disaffection around the War Office. When the peccant Gough and his colonels arrived in London, it was Wilson who coached them in what they ought to say. Behind him stood no less a figure than the venerable "Bobs" (Field Marshal Earl Roberts of Kandahar, the people's idol and the Army's), who cut General French in the street for the "infamy" of associating himself with a Liberal

Government.[37] It was a little before this interesting moment that the party game began to fall apart, or — which was much the same thing — to get completely out of political control.

A motion of censure against the Government had been set for 19 March; London was already filled with rumors that bench warrants would be issued for the arrest of Carson and the other Ulster leaders; and Carson came down to the House that afternoon, well primed with War Office information from his dinner with General Wilson the night before.

He told his friend Walter Long, who recorded it in a memorandum, that he could not stay to wind up the debate. He had just time to listen to Mr. Asquith's speech and to make a bitter and most effective one himself. "Having all this time been a Government of cowards," he said, "they are going to entrench themselves behind His Majesty's troops. They have been discussing over at the War Office the last few days how many men they require and where they should mobilize."[38] He then accused the Government of attempting to provoke an insurrection; strode from the House while the Opposition rose to cheer him; telephoned his servant to meet him at Euston station and — with Walter Long to see him off — just caught the 5:55 Belfast mail. It was generally supposed that he had gone to set up his Provisional Government.[39]

This was not the case: he had gone to escape a possible arrest. The next morning he went directly to Craigavon, which had been turned into an armed headquarters: and from here he reported at once to Bonar Law. He said that he had found the city and its surroundings "very excited," that troops were reported on the move everywhere, and that the Government "are under the impression that our people are going to take action — or it may be that they desire to provoke an outbreak. It is all a strange message of peace, and really one would have thought it impossible in a country like ours."[40] One cannot mistake the note of despondency in this letter. Carson was beginning to lose his taste for adventure: to his negative mind an armed outbreak was more useful as a threat than as a fact, and so, for that matter, was a Provisional Government.

On the same morning, Friday 20 March, Mr. Bonar Law sat down to write a letter to the editor of the *Scotsman*. Along with his recklessness, it seems, he still preserved a working modicum of prudence. Since February he had maintained that he would not recommend a tampering with the Army Annual Bill unless he had a united party behind him. He now discovered that the troglodytes of the party, with Ian Malcolm of the Defence Union League at their head, actually deplored any unpatriotic meddling with the

Bill; and on 19 March wrote to the editor of the *Spectator* to say that he could not honestly assert there was much chance of the Bill's being amended, since it was "not likely or possible that there could be an undivided party."[41] On the next day he told the editor of the *Scotsman* that he feared he must give up the plan,[42] and he wrote this letter some hours before the first news of the Curragh mutiny came to London. He, too, was beginning to lose his taste for an unconstitutional or at least unprecedented foray against a precious and venerable Parliamentary bulwark — a foray which, when the Curragh news *did* arrive, at once became unnecessary.

At their first meeting on 14 October 1913, Mr. Asquith and Mr. Bonar Law had agreed on just one thing. Mr. Asquith had boasted that the Irish Party needed the Liberals far more than the Liberals needed the Irish Party; and Mr. Bonar Law, not to be behindhand, had replied that "it was the certainty of British support which made the strength of Ulster resistance." In other words, the game was still in the hands of the two great English parties: with this difference, that Mr. Asquith had usually lived up to the rules, and that Mr. Bonar Law had usually broken them. At their next meeting, significantly enough, they agreed that things might yet pass into the control of people who cared nothing for English politics or English parties.[43]

Both Sir Edward Carson's letter to Mr. Bonar Law of 20 March, and Mr. Bonar Law's of the same date to the *Scotsman's* editor, seemed to indicate that this had indeed happened; that the party game was now over; that if the Government was helpless, so too was the Parliament; and that the destiny of Ireland, whether with the Union or with Home Rule or with some more extreme dispensation, was now passing away from Westminster and Whitehall and into the control of Belfast and Dublin.

Part Three

THE EASTER RISING, 1914—1916

Chapter Eight

Dublin: November 1913– March 1914

O n 25 November 1913, at the Rotunda Rink in Dublin, there appeared a new movement calling itself The Irish National Volunteers. From this movement sprang, as its extremist wing, those Irish Volunteers who fought in the Easter Rising; and many of the leaders in that seminal event were present at the Rotunda Rink on 25 November. This date, therefore, is itself of great importance in Irish history: not least because the movement which it commemorates was instigated and managed by the Irish Republican Brotherhood, at last aroused from a long sleep.

I

The Irish Volunteers and the Irish Republican Brotherhood

The Irish Republican Brotherhood owed its existence to two refugees from the Young Ireland Rebellion of '48 and '49, James Stephens and John

O'Mahoney, who met in Paris and were soon in touch with revolutionaries from every part of Europe. In 1856, O'Mahoney left for America, where he founded the Fenian Brotherhood (from the *Fianna,* a mythical host of Irish warriors). It was dedicated to the total overthrow of English rule in Ireland. In spite of a baffling capacity for reproducing itself in different forms, the Fenian movement never died out in America, and became a frightening element in the background of Anglo-Irish history.

Stephens, an inspired organizer, founded his own secret-oathbound Brotherhood in 1858, in Dublin. Becoming in due time the Irish Republican Brotherhood, it gathered in such famous names in insurrectionary history as Jeremiah O'Donovan Rossa, John O'Leary, Charles Kickham, Thomas Clarke Luby and John Devoy. After its abortive insurrection in 1867 — which Stephens, who had a practical turn of mind unusual in Fenian circles, considered inopportune and was condemned for cowardice on that account — the Irish Republican Brotherhood gradually frayed out into terrorism and, at last, into insignificance. Its very constitution, as revised in 1873, insisted that "the IRB shall await the decision of the Irish nation, as expressed by the majority of the Irish people, as to the fit hour of inaugurating a war against England."

What revolutionary movement had ever awaited such a decision? From 1885 to 1910 the will of the majority of the Irish people, as expressed in six General Elections, was presumably to follow the lead of the Irish Parliamentary Party. It is not surprising that the IRB should have entered the twentieth century in a condition resembling the trance of death itself. Its membership was said to be so small that it would scarcely have filled a large-sized concert hall. Since the eleven Supreme Councilors were widely scattered, the power came to reside with the Council's President, Secretary and Treasurer. These offices were filled by three elderly and bibulous conservatives called Fred Allen, P. T. Daly and John O'Hanlon.[1] The troubling of the Irish waters, in the wonderful renaissance years, was bound to reach even these sleepy guardians of revolution and shake their repose.

In Belfast, once the nursery of revolution, there were in fact three young men who were determined to revitalize this moribund Brotherhood. They were: Denis McCullogh, whose father was a Fenian publican and who was initiated into the IRB in dismal circumstances at a pub's back door; Bulmer Hobson, a middle class Quaker, and a name to conjure with in insurrectionary history; and Sean MacDiarmida, son of a Leitrim farmer, who became a bartender in Glasgow and then in Belfast, and whom Hobson and McCullogh had recruited. Hobson and MacDiarmida moved to Dublin, where Hobson worked as a journalist and MacDiarmida as a Sinn Fein organizer, while McCullogh remained in Belfast. One by one they were co-opted into the Supreme Council: by 1912 McCullogh had been joined by Hobson, and with them, as younger members, were P. S. O'Hegarty (for the South of England), journalist and historian, and Major John MacBride (for Connaught), who was soon succeeded by Sean MacDiarmida.[2] In 1911, MacDiarmida was stricken by polio and came out of his ordeal with a badly crippled leg, but this did nothing to weaken those two characteristics which, in rather frightening combination, have always been associated with his name — a deadly purpose and a devastating charm.

The first task of these younger members was to get rid of their elderly leaders. In 1910 P. T. Daly was expelled for alleged misuse of American funds: which, since by that time the Redmondite United Irish League of America was taking all the money, amounted to a driblet of £300 a year. In 1911, Allen and O'Hanlon resigned over the question of Hobson's *Irish Freedom*, a militantly republican sheet to which they objected and which marked the IRB's break with Sinn Fein. These maneuvers would not have been successful, however, without the support of Thomas James Clarke.

The character and destiny of this man, one of the key figures in the Easter Rising, can be discerned if one reads his *Glimpses of an Irish Felon's Prison Life*. Born in 1857 of a Galway father and a Tipperary mother, Clarke had been sworn into the IRB in the Land League days and had fled to America because of his part in a riot against the police. He had been sent to England by the Fenian Clan-na-Gael in 1881, to take part in the "dynamite war"; he was captured in 1883 and sentenced to penal servitude for life; and of this sentence he served fifteen and a half years in Chatham and Portland prisons. In Chatham Prison, a particularly sinister bastille, the treason-felony Irish prisoners, the "Special Men," were subjected to a "scientific treatment of perpetual and persistent harassing, which gave officers a free hand to perse-cute us just as they pleased . . . This system applied to Irish prisoners, and to them only, and was specially designed to destroy us mentally and physi-cally — to kill or drive insane." Here he saw and heard things, he wrote, which "are ineffaceable in the memory, they burn their impress into a man's soul."[3]

Released from prison, with his reason somehow intact and his resolution unimpaired, he married Katherine Daly, the daughter of the Fenian leader; migrated to America; became assistant to the Fenian John Devoy, once an assistant to Stephens; and, in 1907, hearing that there was a revival among the younger members of the IRB, returned to Ireland and set up a newspaper and tobacco shop in North Great Britain Street (now 75A Parnell Street) in Dublin. A small and deceptively mild personage, with a big bald forehead and a walrus mustache, he was a fanatic of the first order, who stood out for the young against the old — "easily the first and the best of us," wrote P. S. O'Hegarty, "the embodiment of Fenianism, an impregnable rock."[4] He had been co-opted into the Dublin Centres' Board — a Centre was the head of a local Circle — soon after his arrival, and *Irish Freedom* had been his idea before Bulmer Hobson took it up.

The method of recruiting for the IRB began at this time to bypass the old porous system. A prospective candidate was now subjected to a scrutiny so thorough as to make it virtually impossible for an undesirable to get in or for information to leak out. Here was Tom Clarke, for example, a man known to be seditious; here was his tobacco shop with his name in defiant Irish over its door; here he was on the Castle "B" list, which meant that his every move and visitor was presumably watched; and yet so ingrained was the official belief that the IRB had sunk into indolence and apathy that Clarke was taken for granted, like an inflammable substance assumed to be safe because it has been correctly labeled.

In 1913, with Carsonism rampant in the Northeast, the new leaders thought that the time had come to make a positive move. It was in this year for example that they attempted to politicize the Gaelic League. The League encouraged the growth of national industries and village crafts and had begun the movement for bilingual street signs. To this extent, in all innocence, it created a shadowy political infrastructure, and was the natural focus for a new and unwelcome nationalism. Much to his distress, Douglas Hyde detected the beginnings of a left wing in the League, and in July forced himself to name certain men — among them Thomas Ashe and Eamonn Ceannt — as "dangerous . . . the Gaelic League Irreconcileables"; while his conservative supporters put it about that there was a sinister plot to unseat him for the Presidency.[5]

Far more than the Gaelic League, of course, the Ulster Volunteer Force held the fascinated attention of the IRB. As a paramilitary force, designed to resist an Act of Parliament, it was "setting us a splendid example," said Tom Clarke. In July, the IRB began drilling in secret in the National Foresters' Headquarters in Parnell Square.

The Irish Parliamentary Party did not encourage volunteering: but in Athlone, in September 1913, something called The Midland Volunteer Force had been organized by a Redmondite group, specifically for defense against an invasion of Carsonites from the North. The Midland Volunteer Force excited the admiration of Laurence Ginnell, M.P. for Westmeath; Laurence Ginnell was a friend of Bulmer Hobson; and early in October Hobson advised the Dublin Board of Centers that the time had come to launch a Volunteer Movement for all of Ireland outside the Orange counties.[6]

The assistant editor of *An Claidheam Soluis* (The Sword of Light), official organ of the Gaelic League, was another good friend of Bulmer Hobson's. He was Michael O'Rahilly, or The O'Rahilly, head of an ancient Kerry family which (like the Redmonds) had repaired its ruined fortunes in the business world. Attractive, romantic and radical, The O'Rahilly was too much of an individualist to join the IRB: but he had written for *Irish Freedom* under the *nom de guerre* of "Rapparee"; although he had escaped the denunciations of Douglas Hyde, he was a member of the Gaelic League's political wing; and at this opportune moment he was in virtual control of the editorial policy of *An Claidheam Soluis.*

At Hobson's suggestion, he now approached Eoin MacNeill, Professor of Early and Mediaeval Irish History at University College, Dublin, one of the League's original founders, and a Redmondite of moderate views. What he wanted, he said, was an article "of general interest" for the 1 November issue: and it is altogether too much to suppose that he did not at least hint at volunteering as a possible subject. An article on volunteering, at any rate, is what he got.

Entitled "The North Began," it was not quite the sort of thing that a respected scholar of moderate views should have written. It said, in effect, that the Ulster Volunteer Force had been founded by the Unionist remnants of a feudal aristocracy; but that its rank and file — the "Orange democracy" and the "Presbyterian rural party" — were "home rulers in essence and in principle," and that they constituted "the most decisive move toward Irish autonomy that has been made since O'Connell invented constitutional agitation." He readily admitted that Ulstermen claimed to hold Ireland for the Empire: "but really," he wrote, "it is no matter whether Ireland is to be held for the Empire or the empyrean . . . What matters is, *by whom is Ireland to be held?*" He then invited Sir Edward Carson to march his Ulster Volunteers to Cork where — he hoped — they could be met "in all amity" by ten times their number of National Volunteers.[7]

A few days after this article appeared, Hobson and The O'Rahilly presented themselves at MacNeill's house. Would the professor act on his own suggestion and institute a Volunteer Movement in Dublin? Years later MacNeill wrote: "I had no doubt in my mind that these two men came from the old physical force party" — he was wrong about The O'Rahilly — "whose organization was the IRB, and I had little doubt of the part I was expected to play."[8] Nonetheless, after consulting his wife, this kindly talkative man agreed to play it. A meeting was arranged for 11 November; and although Hobson absented himself because of his known extremism, of the twelve men present four — Eamonn Ceannt, Sean MacDiarmida, James A. Deakin (who soon withdrew) and Pieras Beaslai — were IRB members and a fifth, Padraic Pearse, was soon to be sworn in.

As a result of this and subsequent conferences, there was a huge overflow meeting at the Rotunda Rink in Dublin on 25 November 1913, where the stewards were all IRB men from the Gaelic Athletic League, and where the Irish National Volunteers were launched with much triumphant oratory. This included a speech by MacNeill in which he said that the Volunteers (they soon lost the "National," perhaps in deference to the UVF) were being organized, not for aggression, not for domination, and certainly not to fight the Ulster Volunteers — had not Ulster led the Volunteers in 1782, organized the United Irishmen, and fought in Down and Antrim in 1798? The object of the Irish Volunteers was simply to resist the English politicians who were attempting to make a football out of Home Rule.

A Provisional Committee was formed to run this new movement: its Chairman was Eoin MacNeill and its Treasurer was The O'Rahilly; but the Secretary, Bulmer Hobson, was IRB; so were twelve of the thirty Provisional Committeemen; and the office staff — Liam Mellows, the paid secretary, Eimar O'Duffy and Barney Mellows — was IRB too.[9] The movement, which enrolled three thousand on the opening night and steadily increased until in May 1914 it numbered around seventy-five thousand and was still growing, had been well infiltrated from the top and the outcome could be awaited with some confidence. Even the Government's ill-timed reinstatement of the arms embargo in December, although aimed at the Ulster Volunteer Force, gave these new Volunteers an added feeling of importance and identity, since they were sure it was aimed at them.

Indeed, the only dissident note in all this was sounded at the very beginning. When Laurence Kettle attempted to read the Volunteer Manifesto at the Rotunda meeting of 25 November, he was greeted with jeers and catcalls from a small group of working men, who had come to the Rotunda carrying clubs and hurleys. These men were not interfering because they disapproved of the Manifesto so much as because it was being read by Lawrence Kettle.

The Kettle family had been accused of employing scab labor on a farm in which it had an interest, and Kettle's hecklers were all members of a small force called the Irish Citizen Army, the defensive arm of the Irish Transport and General Workers Union, which had recently organized the agricultural laborers of County Dublin. The Union was now in the throes of a general strike and lockout, and was fighting a losing battle against a majority of the Dublin employers and their unofficial allies, the Dublin magistrates and the Dublin Metropolitan Police.

The leaders of this strike were James Larkin and James Connolly. James Larkin founded the ITGWU in 1909; James Connolly led the Irish Citizen Army into the Easter Rising of 1916.

II

The Origins of The Irish Citizen Army: James Larkin

James Larkin came from a family of Catholic farmers in County Armagh. His grandfather had fled to Liverpool, the second Irish capital in those days, as a result of the Famine and its clearances; his father had died of tuberculosis, after struggling to bring up a family of six on a wage of twenty shillings a week; and he himself had begun to make his living, at the age of eleven, in one of the most viciously slum-ridden and criminal cities in Europe.

Bellicose and imaginative, vindictive and compassionate, Larkin was a marvelous extrusion from that dreadful environment, above which he rose by sheer force of character, and which he longed to dispel. He learned his socialism at open air meetings in Liverpool and became himself a notable speaker. "He kept his attention," writes Emmet Larkin in his superb opening chapter of *James Larkin,*

> focused sharply on the abominable realities of a decaying industrial system, singing a song of undiluted discontent, and Shelley, Whitman, Francis Adams and William Morris were his poets. In these years on the hustings he learned all the tricks of demagogy, the theatrics, the repartee, the rhetoric and the poetry that were to make him one of the most successful mob-orators of his day.[10]

In 1906, at the age of thirty, he was elected General Organiser of the National Union of Dock Labourers; in 1907 he was sent to Belfast to organize the docks. Here, in the days of the populist Independent Orange Order, he seemed to have a chance: but he fell foul of "Wee Joe" Devlin, National-ist boss and head of the Ancient Order of Hibernians, who publicly dis-avowed him in Ulster Hall. In 1908, he and his family moved on to Dublin.

He was a tall, ungainly man, with blue-black hair and burning eyes. He had a quick wit, an immense voice, a marvelous rhetoric, all uttered in a harsh Liverpool accent. "You cannot argue with the prophet Isaiah," said one Dublin employer, after an unprofitable exchange of words with Larkin: but if ever a social Isaiah was needed, surely he was needed here.

Nearly 26,000 families out of a city of 300,000 were huddled together in the Dublin slums, the verminous haunts of drunkenness, immorality, disease and crime. Of the 5,332 tenement houses, 1,516 were said to be structurally sound and fit for habitation, 2,288 were on the borderlines of unfitness, and 1,518 were not only unfit but absolutely beyond the possibility of reclamation. Baths were unknown; water was located only in the yards; the few privies were disused and choked up. It is no wonder that the Dublin death rate was a horrible 24.8 per thousand, chiefly due to infant mortality and tuberculosis. If the former had begun declining by 1910, the latter was constant, and both were higher than anything that could be found in Great Britain, itself no sanitary paradise.[11] And at the root of all this there lay unemployment, casual employment, sweated labor, social indifference, and the Dublin Corporation, one of the most corrupt city governments in all Europe.

It is not hard to imagine how inconvenient, to say the least, was the proletarian voice of James Larkin, echoing and re-echoing in such an en-vironment. The Dublin Dock Labourers, a body of proven respectability, angrily suspended him not long after his arrival; whereupon he founded his Irish Transport and General Workers Union which (he hoped) by enlisting all the unskilled laborers in Ireland would eventually realize an industrial commonwealth. In June 1911, after many trials and tribulations, including a term of imprisonment for "Criminal Conspiracy," he was firmly entrenched in the Dublin Trades Council, he controlled the parliamentary committee of the Irish Trade Union Congress, and he was editor of the *Irish Worker and People's Advocate,* a lively muck-raking journal, with a weekly circulation of twenty thousand.

The year 1911 was Irish labor's *annus mirabilis,* when the great English unrest spilled over into Ireland, employers and workers fought one another up and down the land, and Larkin's special gifts for agitation and leadership came into their own. The English railway unions, however, the ones most in need of Irish cooperation, showed themselves more anxious to receive help than willing to give it: and it was in this year that Larkin conceived a nationalist repugnance for English union leadership.

Giving aid to Larkin was, of course, no laughing matter: for Larkin was a virtuoso in the use of sympathetic strikes, to which Dublin as a trading city was especially vulnerable and which (ideally) needed English cooperation and English funds whenever they were called. It was for his deployment of such strikes and for his belief in one big union that Larkin was labeled a Syndicalist — a heady word in those days.

Whether he really was one is another matter. He was known to call himself an Irish patriot, invoking the name of Cathleen ni Houlihan, and Syndicalism claimed that the worker had no fatherland. When it suited his purpose, he also used political methods, and Syndicalism — in contradistinction to Marxism — denied the validity of political action. The report that he learned his philosophy from the elegant Guild Socialism of A. R. Orage makes one wonder if the term Syndicalism, elastic though it is, can be made to contain him: and yet, since it meant "Trade Unionism" and implied a belief in class warfare as a fact of life, in the primacy of production, and in the crying need for economic activism, then in these terms Larkin was a Syndicalist indeed. One thing, at any rate, is certain: his importance to the history of Irish insurrection is that he brought revolution into Dublin and this revolution had a distinctly nationalist tendency.

His famous Transport Strike of 1913 was directed against the Dublin Tramway Company and its owner, William Martin Murphy. It was timed for Horse Show Week, when the city would be filled with visitors: whereupon Murphy summoned the four hundred-member Dublin Employers' Federation and demanded a lockout of all employees who would not sign a document abjuring the Irish Transport and General Workers Union. The strike began on 26 August 1913; the lockout on 3 September; by 22 September the number of men locked out had reached twenty-five thousand. Under Murphy's leadership, the employers made it clear that — so far from negotiating — they intended to starve the men into an abject surrender. Even a Board of Trade enquiry, headed by Sir George Askwith, could not persuade them to take a more humane position: and the Court of Enquiry's report, issued on 6 October and mildly critical of the sympathetic strike, put the blame for refusing a settlement squarely upon the employers.

Murphy was Dublin's richest citizen. He was a contractor, a railroad and tramway tycoon with interests reaching into Africa, a drapery magnate and the owner of the *Irish Independent* and a chain of newspapers. A tall, elderly man, with silvery hair and a most benevolent appearance, Murphy was the very embodiment of those Catholic entrepreneurs who had flourished under the kindly shadow of the Land League — who, in other words, had profited from the boycotting of their Protestant competitors.[12] As Conor Cruise O'Brien has pointed out, Murphy was the economic head and T. M. Healy, K.C., the political and legal brains of the "Sullivan Gang" from Bantry, County Cork, a group associated with the social and economic activity arising from the Parnellite boycott.[13] After the divorce scandal, however, the group turned against Parnell and became the lay spearhead of the clerical assault upon him.

It was for this reason, among others, that the poets in Dublin to a man raged against Murphy, for they were all Parnellites. After the Court of Enquiry's Report had been published, there appeared in the columns of the Irish *Times,* no less, a furibund letter from AE, accusing the employers of insolence, ignorance and "a devilish policy of starvation." W. B. Yeats wrote a poem, dated 29 September, and published in 1914, in which he tells Parnell's spirit — the poem is called "To a Shade" — not to revisit Dublin because his enemies are at their old tricks again and especially picks out "an old foul mouth" (Murphy-plus-Healy, the Board of Trade's Enquiry having opened on 29 September). He had already written his "September 1913," with its refrain "Romantic Ireland's dead and gone," a harsh attack upon the materialism of the rising Catholic entrepreneur. In November he wrote a message for Larkin's *Irish Worker and People's Advocate,* in which he assailed the employers for their cruelty: the *Irish Worker,* needless to say, would not ordinarily have been the vehicle for Mr. Yeats's thoughts. Among other poets who joined in these attacks were Padraic Pearse, Padraic Colum, James Stephens, Sheamus O'Sullivan, Joseph Plunkett and Thomas Mac-Donagh.

On the other hand the IRB leadership, much to the disgust of Sean O'Casey, offered no help to Larkin: divisive battles must wait until after the English had been driven out of Ireland. Arthur Griffith also disapproved of the strike, although he sympathized with the plight of the workers, because industrial disturbance interfered with one of Sinn Fein's ideals, the advance of Irish industry. The Church also disapproved: it associated Larkinism with socialism and socialism with irreligion, nay atheism itself: and the priesthood, with its strong back-to-the-land sentiments, had no great sympathy with the factory worker or the dweller in the slums. Nonetheless, Archbishop Walsh, who had roundly condemned a Larkinite effort to send hungry children to temporary Catholic homes in Protestant England, was soon obliged to issue pleas for a fund to relieve these small victims of Mr. Murphy. And public opinion in general, once the starvation strategy became clearer, began to swing around toward the ITGWU.

Nonetheless, neither sympathy nor disapproval could greatly affect that doomed adventure. Murphy and the Dublin Employers' Federation were all-powerful and intended to remain so: had they not watched Larkin with dismay as he organized the stevedores earlier in the year, and persuaded six of the most important steamship companies to sign a contract with his Union, and intimidated the building trades, and organized the farm laborers? And had he not, as it were, put himself into their grasp when he dared to strike the Tramway Company: or if not into their hands into those of William Martin Murphy, which was much the same thing?

The strike, therefore, was a desperate, anguished and brutal affair. As early as 30 August there was a night of rioting, a slum explosion, in which two strikers lost their lives: on the next day, "Bloody Sunday," there was a police riot, when participants and mere onlookers at a forbidden Larkinite meeting were clubbed down, men, women, and children, without any semblance of mercy or even discrimination. As a result of this and the previous night's explosion, over four hundred civilians and police were treated in the hospitals, and the arrests amounted to more than one hundred. A Commission composed of two King's Counsel was appointed to inquire into the behavior of the police on "Bloody Sunday": five months later its report completely exonerated them.[14]

In the end, what broke the ITGWU's resistance was sheer famine, aided and abetted by a withdrawal of support by the British Trade Union Congress, voted at an unprecedented special meeting on 9 December 1913. The English labor leaders disliked the idea of an independent Irish labor movement; they detested Larkin for his efforts to appeal to their followers over their heads during a "fiery cross" campaign in England in November; and they were exasperated at the closing of the Port of Dublin in the same month, which spread before their eyes a prospect of endless sympathetic strikes. They were, in fact, preparing for their own General Strike: it was to take place — it never did — in the winter of 1914: they were no longer willing to deplete their treasuries for the sake of Irish agitators such as James Larkin, a man in whom they detected not merely an agitator but a revolutionary.

The Port of Dublin was closed when the Dublin Steampacket Company — the only company operating between Dublin and the ports of Great Britain — was struck in direct violation of an agreement in May: and those employers who had endeavored to stay out of the disturbance by using the Steampacket Company were now forced to join hands with the rest. Larkin took this rather desperate measure on the advice of James Connolly.

III

The Irish Citizen Army: James Connolly

James Connolly had arrived from Belfast on 29 August 1913, in response to a telegram from James Larkin. He was almost immediately arrested for a "seditious" speech on the steps of Liberty Hall, the ITGWU headquarters in Beresford Place; refusing to give bail, he was sentenced to three months in prison. On 6 September he went on hunger strike and was released in poor shape seven days later.

A stocky, rather taciturn man who looked like a respectable publican, a self-taught intellectual, a profoundly revolutionary soul, Connolly is one of the great figures in the history of modern Ireland. His best known work, *Labour in Irish History* (1910), is a Marxist interpretation of the Irish past, although the introductory chapter is written throughout in a Gaelic mood. Indeed, he called this book a contribution to the Gaelic revival. One must not go to Connolly in search of consistency: it would be better to describe him as one who had an experimental faith in Marxism, a faith simple enough to be submitted to the claims of imagination and the needs and nature of time and place.

Marxism before 1917 was far more pliable than it became once it had hitched its wagon to a particular star. Connolly the Marxist is a great man as much for what he was and for what he dreamed as for the brief revolution he helped to bring into being; but his memory still touches a revolutionary nerve and presumably will continue to do so until that millennial day when revolutions become unnecessary.

He was born in Edinburgh in 1868, of parents who came from County Monaghan: he was raised in the deepest poverty. It is probable that he received no formal education of any kind. He is known to have served in the English Army and to have left it without the formality of a discharge. He reappears as a married man, who settled in Edinburgh as a Corporation carter: it was here that he studied scientific socialism at the feet of James Leslie, who persuaded him — the Corporation having dismissed him for Socialist activities — to migrate to Ireland as an organizer for the Irish Socialist Republican Party. From 1896 to 1903 he labored in this unpromising vineyard — the Irish worker was still glumly wedded to the Irish Parliamentary Party — and endeavored to cultivate not merely that combination of political with economic action which he had learned from the Scottish Labour Party, but also a strain of revolutionary nationalism. This union of socialism with nationalism haunted him for the rest of his life.[15] Even after hunger drove him and his family to America in 1903, and he had broken with Daniel De Leon's Socialist Labour Party and become an organizer for the syndicalist I.W.W., it would not leave him alone. In his Manifesto for the Irish Socialist Federation and in his writings for *The Harp* he revealed an unshakable belief that Irish workers would be all the better international revolutionaries if they first identified themselves with their national being.

In 1910 he returned to Ireland.

He now saw the Irish working class party as the offspring of a marriage of convenience between the political action of the Marxists and the direct action of the Syndicalists: but he also believed — if his 1912 Manifesto for the Irish Labour Party is anything to go by — that it would have to make an opportunist appeal to those who cared for neither. In 1912 he was sure that Home Rule was on its way, and he wanted Irish labor to be represented in the new Irish Parliament, for Home Rule to him was a sordid but necessary stage in an inevitable process. Had not the Wyndham Act driven out the old garrison of landlords? Would not Home Rule bring in a garrison of capitalists? And would not Home Rule in due time surrender to the Workers' Republic?[16]

The Irish Parliamentary Party, therefore, seemed as transient and futile to Connolly as, for very different reasons, it did to D. P. Moran. The Irish Parliamentary Party, in turn, was just as unaccommodating. John Dillon, who had once gone to prison as an agitator for the agrarian "Plan of Campaign," was quite typical in this respect: he saw men like Larkin and Connolly simply as rabble-rousers. "Murphy is a desperate character," he wrote; "Larkin is as bad. It would be a blessing for Ireland if they exterminated each other."[17]

When he returned to Ireland, Connolly had told a friend: "My first mistake was to go to America, my second was to leave it." As an organizer for the Socialist Party of Ireland, he was nearly mobbed in Cork, on the grounds that the Party stood for atheism and free love. A strict monogamist who never denied being a Catholic and who detested propagandist atheism, Connolly found this kind of thing deeply dispiriting. Nor was he really at home when he became, in 1911, secretary to the Belfast branch of ITGWU.

Readers of *Labour in Irish History* will notice that he allows the Protestant worker to slip altogether out of his account of the nineteenth century, and although in actuality he did his best to create an alliance between the Protestant and the Catholic dockers, he seems never to have been comfortable in Belfast.[18]

Larkin for his part was not too happy with the more methodical and stable Connolly. He professed to be disappointed with the poor showing of the Belfast ITGWU; he overlooked Connolly's work in organizing the Belfast textile workers or the foundry workers in Wexford, both branches of the ITGWU. The great Transport Strike changed all that. In Dublin in 1913, at last and for all time, Connolly came into his own.

Larkin had been sentenced by E. G. Swifte, Chief Divisional Magistrate in Dublin, to seven months' imprisonment for seditious libel, a sentence which many people thought should more properly have been given to Sir Edward Carson and Mr. F. E. Smith. There was a great protest meeting in the Albert Hall on 3 November; on 9 November a by-election at Reading, normally a Liberal seat, went to a Unionist; on 11 November Lloyd George told the National Liberal Club that this defeat was largely due to Jim Larkin; on 13 November Larkin was released and set out almost at once for his "fiery cross" campaign in England.

And on 13 November at a great rally to celebrate this solitary triumph, Connolly proclaimed what he called a state of war. "Listen to me," he said; "I am going to talk sedition. The next time we set out for a route march, I want to be accompanied by four battalions of trained men. I want them to come out with their corporals and their sergeants and people to form fours. Why should we not drill and train in Dublin as they are drilling and training in Ulster?"[19] Thus, thirteen days before the founding of the Irish Volunteers, the Irish Citizen Army came into being.

Among those who sat on the platform with Connolly on this occasion were two persons who, if their upbringing had been permitted a voice in their affairs, would not have been there at all. One was Captain J. R. White, D.S.O., who had propounded the idea of a strikers' army the day before. He was the son of Field Marshal Sir George White, the almost legendary hero of the siege of Ladysmith. The other was Constance Countess Markievicz.

The Countess Markievicz, besides possessing a genuine concern for people in poor circumstances — she was known among her father's tenants as a "wild, kind girl" — was greatly attracted to anything militant or aggressive. In 1908 she had experienced a sudden conversion to extreme nationalism after reading Robert Emmet's speech from the dock. She had thereupon joined Maud Gonne's nationalist organization for women, Ingidhe Na hEireann, where she caused no little embarrassment, since she was a hyper-typical daughter of the Anglo-Irish Ascendency — beautiful, brilliant, well-born, reasonably well married to a Polish count, and talking in a loud high voice in the accents of the English upper class.

The eldest child of Sir Henry Gore-Booth, fifth baronet of Lissadell in County Sligo, she was connected through her mother with some of the leading families in England. Her family on her father's side had come adventuring to Ireland with the Reformation. They were now substantial land-holders, dividing their time between Dublin, London and the great stone house of Lissadell on the north shore of Sligo. She had been expected to occupy herself with the usual pursuits — parties, balls, hunting — until she married and settled down. But neither these nor art nor theatricals nor the Suffragette Movement nor marriage itself could assuage a restlessness which — like her sister Eva who fled into labor politics — drove her out of Ascendency Ireland and, at the age of forty, into the extremes of Irish nationalism.

W. B. Yeats used to visit Lissadell when he was becoming known as a writer and did not need to observe the line that was drawn, to their mutual satisfaction, between county and merchant families. He was greatly attracted to the beauty of both sisters and celebrated it years later in the wonderful opening lines of his poem "In Memory of Eva Gore-Booth and Con Markievicz."

> *The light of evening, Lissadell,*
> *Great windows open to the south,*
> *Two girls in silk kimonos, both*
> *Beautiful, one a gazelle.*

The poem is a very strange one because, after the hush and wonder of these opening lines, it plummets into sheer hatred, damning both sisters for their descent into the "common" fight for lower-middle-class nationalism and lower-class labor politics. But Yeats has left it on record that, every time he recovers from a spasm of hatred, the images in his poetry become so pure and luminous that they would "like a country drunkard who has thrown a wisp of hay into his own thatch, burn up time."[20] And so in the poem he returns to the innocence and beauty of the early lines, the innocence and beauty whose only enemy is time, and asks the shades of the two sisters to command him to strike a match "and strike another till time catch."

The poem has always seemed to the present writer a work of the first importance, not only in the primary sense for being what it is but also in the secondary one for its comment on the strange history of those days. For the Irish Revolution, which emerges once and for all on the platform with James Connolly on 13 November 1913, has a strong romantic and even eccentric side from that moment on until its tragic collapse in the Dail Cabinet in December 1921.

Constance Markievicz, after all, was not so out of place as some people — Sean O'Casey for example — seemed to think her. With Larkin, the great actor of the strike, she got on very well. She was no doctrinaire, she was a creature of strong impulses and few ideas, as often as not expressed in a very histrionic manner. Yet impulses, ideas, manner — all could be put to use if allowed to combine in their own way. In 1909, for example, she made an interesting variation upon Sir Robert Baden-Powell's patriotic gospel of Scouting when she instituted her own Boy Scouts — her Fianna na hEireann — after Bulmer Hobson's defunct organization and (for he is everywhere in the Irish pre-Revolution) with Hobson's help. The boys were taught Irish history, took their orders in Gaelic, and were trained to be commandos in some future war against the English. The IRB recruited them after they were seventeen; two faced a firing squad after the Easter Rising; many became leaders in the revolutionary days that followed. This is hardly an adaptation that would have gratified Baden-Powell.

Captain J. R. White was a less spectacular and more transient figure. His experiences during the Boer War, where he had been decorated for gallantry, had upset his hitherto conventional notions of the fitness of things. On retiring from the Regular Army he had gone to Ulster, and when Carsonism raised its head and its Union Jacks, he had endeavored to explain — as MacNeill had later attempted in "The North Began" — that the Ulster Volunteer Force did not necessarily represent a loyalist movement. Now, a recent arrival in Dublin, he had been greatly stirred by AE's letter to the *Irish Times* and on 12 November, at a meeting of the newly formed Civic League, a meeting attended by the poet Thomas MacDonagh, he proposed a scheme for drilling the strikers, to which he offered his time and his professional skill. Connolly's speech the next day contained his response to this proposal.

On 19 November, at a second meeting of the Civic League (each time within the precincts of Trinity College), White read a telegram from another Ulsterman, Sir Roger Casement, offering support for the drilling scheme; and at the same meeting the name "Transport Union Citizen

Army" was adopted. The Army was originally intended to be a defense force, to protect the strikers from the attentions of the police. On 23 November, enough men to form two companies appeared at Croyden Park, the ITGWU's recreation center at Clontarf. When the Irish Volunteers were organized at the Rotunda two days later, it was a detachment of the Transport Union Citizen Army which protested against the appearance of Laurence Kettle. Thereafter the Irish Citizen Army (it soon dropped the "Transport Union") drilled from time to time, armed chiefly with the *camán,* under Captain White in Croyden Park.

When the great Strike collapsed from starvation in February 1914, the Irish Citizen Army dwindled away — according to Sean O'Casey — to no more than a single skeleton company.[21] In March 1914, a reorganization was suggested to Captain White: and on 22 March, at Liberty Hall, a public meeting put this into effect. The new Army Council had White for Chairman; its honorary secretary was Sean O'Casey; its honorary treasurers were Richard Branigan and the Countess Markievicz. Its vice-chairmen ranged all the way from the flamboyant Jim Larkin to the pacifist Francis Sheehy-Skeffington. Its Constitution stood foursquare upon "the first and last principle . . . that the ownership of Ireland, moral and material, is vested in the people of Ireland."[22] On the next day, according to William O'Brien of the Tailors' Union, who was present and counted them, there were 250 marchers at an ICA review in Croyden Park.[23]

Reorganizations are apt to be deciduous: and the first to fall off was Captain White, who had never got along with Larkin and who now disagreed with Connolly over his (White's) plan of affiliation with the Irish Volunteers. He was followed by Sean O'Casey, after losing by a single vote — the lady thoughtfully voting for herself — a fight to oust the Countess from the Army Council. Later on Francis Sheehy-Skeffington, gentlest and most determined of Socialists, found that he could not abide the growing belligerence of the ICA. As for Larkin, his passionate hubristic soul had never quite recovered from the agonies of the Strike; and the leadership of the ICA seems to have passed to Connolly long before Larkin's departure for America in October. Though its fame and its brief life are inseparably connected with Connolly and the Easter Rising, one can never forget Larkin's central role in creating the environment which brought it into being.

Chapter Nine

Belfast and Dublin: March–August 1914

When, in March 1914, Major General Sir Nevil Macready was appointed to supersede Brigadier General Count Gleichen as General Commanding the Belfast District, his appointment was actually part of the Churchill-Seely program for the investment of Ulster: and only a slight and perhaps a politic indisposition had kept him in London until after the program had fallen into limbo. An even-tempered officer, with no sympathy for either Nationalists or Orangemen, General Macready was now quite prepared to keep the peace if necessary, did not entertain much doubt about the obedience of his officers or his men, and regarded Sir Edward Carson as something between an anomaly and a joke.

I
Carson and the Lion

When Macready appeared at Craigavon, now converted into an armed camp, to pay what his colleagues in the War Office called his "state visit" to

Sir Edward, he seems to have caught a glimpse of something which is far more visible today, at least as a reasonable supposition — namely that his state visit had been paid to a prisoner of state.[1] This does not mean that Carson was under some kind of deferential house arrest, with Captain Craig as head jailer and UVF sentries posted as much to keep him from getting out as to prevent undesirables from getting in. Far from it: he was (once the arrest scare had passed) as much needed in London as in Belfast. But it does mean that he was in danger of becoming the victim of his own conspiracy; that he was more and more at the mercy of such Orange hotheads as Major Robert McCalmont and Captain F. P. Crozier, men who were ready to attempt any wild *coup,* even the one which Churchill's and Seely's plan was supposed to forestall.[2]

That particular *coup* never was brought off: instead there took place a more expensive and even more elaborate feat. On the night of 24 April, shipments of arms for the UVF were landed at Larne, Bangor and Donaghadee. This was the work of Major Frederick Crawford, a persistent and ambitious fanatic, who had once planned to kidnap Mr. Gladstone on the promenade at Brighton — an escapade which, one somehow cannot help regretting, was never attempted through lack of encouragement. His plans for a gunrunning, on the other hand, had received Carson's blessing long before the Curragh affair; it was well financed by the Carson Defence Fund, by the Union Defense League, and by Lord Milner's private fund-raising among his wealthy friends;[3] and it was one of those exploits which Carson could have disavowed or even discouraged only at the cost of losing all prestige and all control.

The arms had been purchased in Hamburg and consisted of ten thousand brand new Mannlicher rifles, with short bayonets, and ninety-one hundred Mauser rifles, model 88, with longer bayonets: both model 1904 and model 88 were 7.9 caliber and used the same ammunition. The total cost had been estimated at £45,640, and this included two million rounds of ammunition. It was presumed that £5,000 would buy a steamer and pay for the packing. Crawford also purchased several thousand old Vetterli rifles, as perilous to friend as to foe, with a further one million rounds. Another £4,500 went into the purchase of the steamer *Clydevalley,* into which the arms were to be transshipped before the final run to Larne.

In spite of Crawford's addiction to overcomplex maneuvers, the voyage of the *Fanny* (she ended up as the *Doreen*), the transshipment into the *Clydevalley* (she became the *Mountjoy II*), and the distribution of the arms at Larne, all were carried out with resolution and resourcefulness. They demonstrate that the staff work of the UVF was in excellent condition. Nonetheless, if the police had not remained in their barracks, mute but sincere friends to the whole illegal enterprise, it would have had a very different ending.

The single word "Lion," telegraphed to Sir Edward Carson at his house in Eaton Square, told him that the gunrunning had succeeded and that he was one step nearer to the abyss. The Cabinet, after meeting on four successive mornings and discussing many countermeasures of a spectacular and horrendous nature, at length decided to take no measures at all. It was now quite helpless: and on 29 April, when the Opposition's demand for a full inquiry into the Curragh incident was given a debate, Sir Edward spoke in a more conciliatory tone than the Commons had heard from him in many a month.[4]

Clearly he hoped, although he dared not admit it, that this embarrassing profusion of arms would never be used in anger. He offered once again the permanent exclusion of Ulster "until Parliament shall otherwise determine," but now he added his fervent hope that should Home Rule — "much as I detest it" — be enacted on these terms, the Government of Ireland for the South and West would prove such a success that "notwithstanding all our anticipations . . . *it might even be for the interests of Ulster itself to move towards that Government and come in under it.*"[5] This was hardly a concession; but it struck a note of genuine indecision. And, of course, it came too late.

For the success of Ulster and the helplessness of the Liberal Government were having their own effect upon Eoin MacNeill's Volunteers. As Augustine Birrell put it: "The recent gun-running exploit of the Ulster Volunteers excited as much admiration among the lodges of the Ancient Order of Hibernians as in those of the Orange faction. 'Well done Ireland' was the general verdict." He thought that the mere fact of eighty thousand men enrolled in the Irish Volunteers, "among them thousands of old soldiers and tens of thousands of the strongest young fellows in the South and West and North-West" made many a pious Presbyterian in the Northeast breathe the prayer, " 'Would that once more we could *all* be United Irishmen' "[6]

How soon would it be, in other words, before the Irish Volunteers got out of hand?

II

Redmond's Coup

Lack of arms in Southern Ireland, due more to want of funds than to the Government's embargo, was a serious embarrassment to those who felt that, as a response to Larne, it was now the Irish Volunteers' duty to get out of hand. On 8 May 1914 there was a meeting at the house of Alice Stopford Green in Grosvenor Road, Westminster, to discuss this problem.

Mrs. Green, widow of J. R. Green the historian, and daughter of a Protestant Archdeacon of Meath, had published in 1908 her *History of Modern Ireland and Its Undoing*. She had charm and wit, a scholarly cast of mind, a gregarious nature: her intense belief in Irish nationalism, for example, did not preclude her from numbering among her friends that delightful bachelor and cold-blooded Unionist, "Bloody" Balfour.

On this 8 May, she met with Eoin MacNeill, Darrell Figgis (who lived in Meath but had turned London journalist) and Sir Roger Casement; they were discussing the possibility of running guns for the Irish Volunteers.

Sir Roger Casement, born in 1864 at Sandycove near Dublin and brought up in an atmosphere of rigid Protestantism among the glens of Antrim, had joined the Consular Service in 1892. The Foreign Office was not too popular with this junior Service: and Casement's conventional imperialism might have been disturbed by the Boer War, an experience not uncommon in consular circles, if he had not "loathed" the Boers — so Brian Inglis tells us in his fine biography — as the oppressors of the Bantu.[7] Later on, his exposure of the cruelties practiced upon the helpless natives of the Belgian Congo earned him the friendship of E. D. Morel, "the first radical of the twentieth century who took up foreign affairs as a wholetime interest";[8] while his investigations of the Putumayo horrors earned him a knighthood. Knighthood or no, he was gradually reaching the conclusion that the Foreign Office was a soulless entity and, for more esoteric reasons, that England was destined by a just Providence to succumb with her Empire to the might of Germany.

Long before this his Irish nationalism had been awakened by the ubiquitous Bulmer Hobson; he had begun the study of Irish history as early as 1905; his friendship with Mrs. Green did the rest. He contributed to the Countess Markievicz's Fianna; he warmly supported the Irish Citizen Army; he even gave up his dream of retiring to a South African farm.[9] He agreed with Eoin MacNeill that there was an affinity between the Ulster and the Irish Volunteers, of whose Provisional Committee he had become a member. He had, in fact, supported MacNeill at an interesting meeting in Cork when that intrepid scholar had called for three cheers for Sir Edward Carson and the audience — though subsequently pacified — had with some difficulty been dissuaded from rushing the platform.

A confirmed bachelor, Sir Roger looked to Mrs. Green for that disinterested friendship and advice which such a woman could give him in his many difficulties. On her side the relationship, although entirely platonic, was no doubt all the more piquant through his being a very handsome man. She was now saying that £1,500 could be raised for buying guns, and Casement and Figgis agreed that the rifles should be bought first and transportation arranged for afterwards; that The O'Rahilly should come to London to advise them about European arms merchants; and that Figgis should set out for Europe to start negotiations. MacNeill was soon brought around to their way of thinking and departed for Dublin on his mission to keep Mr. Redmond in the dark.

His idea of putting the Irish leader off the scent was to suggest that a new Council of Six should supersede the Provisional Committee and that William Redmond, John Redmond's popular brother, should be asked to become a member. The offer was made through Joseph Devlin on 13 May:[10] but, instead of putting John Redmond into a relaxed and friendly mood it had quite the opposite effect. Taking the offer to be a sign of weakness, Redmond at once demanded that two other members of his own choosing should join the proposed Council. Misunderstanding was piled upon misunderstanding[11] until at last, on 9 June, Mr. Redmond, who sometimes behaved as if he were the Chairman, not just of the Irish Party, but of Ireland herself, issued an ultimatum in his most imperious manner. The Provisional Committee, he announced in the newspapers, must be "strengthened by the addition of twenty-five representative men from different parts of the country at the instance of the Irish Party and in sympathy with its policy and aims."

"Strengthened" has an odd sound in the light of the Party's known distaste for volunteering. In fact, as MacNeill observed, under the Party's leadership the Volunteers would be "dissipated or allowed to melt away."[12] The Provisional Committee was of a like mind and made no answer. At this, Mr. Redmond issued a second ukase: he would create another Volunteer authority if the Committee did not yield at once.

It is true that Mr. Redmond had been losing ground ever since the exclusion crisis; but he was still immeasurably more powerful than Professor MacNeill. He had said that he would disrupt the movement and disrupt it he would. On 16 June the Provisional Committee, "acting under a deep and painful sense of responsibility," accepted "the alternative which appears to them the lesser evil" and bowed to Mr. Redmond's demand.[13]

Feelings within the Committee were very bitter; eight members (six of them IRB men) at once published an angry dissent; and Bulmer Hobson, who had led the reasonable argument that Redmond's proposal must be accepted as a lesser evil, was repudiated by Tom Clarke and Sean Mac-Diarmida and forced to resign from the editorship of *Irish Freedom*. He was too prominent a man to be expelled from the IRB or the Dublin Board of Centers, but Clarke and MacDiarmida never trusted him again. He had for some time, he wrote, been criticized because of his association with Casement and even with MacNeill, men "who belonged intellectually and socially to a different world," and Clarke had been heard to say that Casement (whom he met at Buswell's Hotel on 15 June to beg him in vain not to vote for Redmond in the Committee) was nothing but a British spy.[14]

As for John Redmond, he could hardly have relished being called the lesser of two evils, but he had won his case, such as it was: a strong dose of moderation and sheer incompetence had been injected into the Volunteers' veins. When his twenty-five nominees were received into the Provisional Committee during the first week in July, John Gore, a Dublin lawyer who was one of them, ventured to observe that many of them had hitherto taken no part or interest whatsoever in volunteering![15] Nor were they exactly "representative": as a list in the Redmond Papers shows, the majority came from Dublin or Belfast, while the Provinces were poorly represented and the interior scarcely at all.[16]

III

Buckingham Palace

It remained to be seen whether events would be as accommodating as the Provisional Committee.

On 25 May, after some disturbance, the Home Rule Bill received its third reading in the House of Commons. No matter what the Lords did or did not do, it would now be ready for the Royal Assent on 25 June. Professor Dicey had once wrapped himself in the shreds of constitutional respectability by declaring that any help given to rebellion in Ulster *after* Home Rule was enacted "would, I can hardly doubt, be treason."[17] He now repeated this injunction to Lord Milner, and Lord Milner was urging immediate action upon Sir Edward Carson.[18]

There was even a growing belief that Carson, that reluctant Cataline, would set up his provisional government in Belfast, treason or no treason, on the day Home Rule received the Royal Assent. The Lord Mayor of Belfast let it be known that, in such an event, he would call upon the Ulster Volunteers to maintain order; and General Wilson assured Lord Milner that "if Carson were sitting in City Hall and we"—his War Office clique—"were ordered to close the Hall we would not do it."[19]

Mr. Birrell was also convinced that Belfast would become the scene of anarchy: but General Macready, who was not in Wilson's confidence, believed—or so he confessed in his memoirs—that what he most feared was fighting between the Irish Volunteers and the Ulster Volunteers in outlying parts of the six counties.

Macready's thinking seems to have undergone a singular transformation. When it came to fighting, he said, the Irish Volunteers—simply because they were less disciplined—would "indulge in an orgy of riot and murder"; his own soldiers would obey his orders to intervene; and the result would be the "serious bloodshed" which always happens when "troops have to rely on their weapons rather than their numerical strength."[20] One notices how the Irish Volunteers have now, almost imperceptibly, become the enemy whom Macready's men would have to kill. Although every allowance must be made for the fact that these words were written some eight or nine years after the event, when Macready's mind had been warped by his experiences in Dublin in 1920 and 1921, they cannot be disregarded. They tend to illustrate that the affairs of Ireland were passing into nationalist hands; that it was no longer the Protestant Northeast which had to be considered as dangerous but also, and more so, the Catholic South and West and Northwest; and that the founding of the Irish Volunteers had been and remained a cardinal event.

As it happened the Royal Assent was not given to the Home Rule Bill on 25 June, because the Liberals were already in full retreat, carrying with them, as part of their *impedimenta,* the rueful leaders of the Irish Party. The Cabinet now agreed that since the Home Rule Bill itself could not be amended, it also could not be enacted: at least not until a new Amending Bill had been passed to qualify its provisions. This, strange to say, was the very same bill which Sir Edward Carson had once called a sentence of death with a stay of execution; it gave six of the Ulster counties the option of excluding themselves from Home Rule for six years; and Lord Crewe introduced it into the House of Lords on 23 June.

In the ensuing debate the venerable Earl Roberts announced, and not for the first time, that any attempt to coerce Ulster would result in the utter disintegration of His Majesty's Armed Forces. Whether in response to this prediction or for reasons even more arcane, their lordships then proceeded to amend the Amending Bill in such a way that it excluded *all nine* of the Ulster counties *without either option or time limit* — in effect, forever. This irresponsible, not to say demented bill, was sent down to the Commons on 14 July.

At this, John Redmond at last dug in his heels. He said that any further concessions would force him to vote against the Amending Bill on its second reading, bringing (he predicted) the bulk of the Liberals and all the Labour members with him. The Lords' amendments must be rejected, therefore, or the Government would fall.[21]

Into the middle of these events, on 28 June, had already come the news that the Archduke Franz Ferdinand of Austria had been assassinated at Sarajevo. General Wilson at the War Office — the Government had not dared remove him for fear of starting another "incident" there — at once stepped up his nearly completed plans for mobilizing an army which, if Home Rule were enacted, he still hoped to immobilize. Over all these peculiar plans and far from petty treasons, however, there now began to brood and gather an immense surmise.

Only Mr. Asquith continued to make Ireland his central concern and "the eastern problem," as he called it, the peripheral one.[22] He might, even at this late date, have withdrawn the Amending Bill and advised His Majesty to give his assent to Home Rule: might have, that is to say, if he had altogether trusted the King, or had shared General Macready's belief that the Army would do its duty, or had not been so amenable to extraparliamentary pressures; in short, if his Liberal pigeons had not come flocking home to roost. Instead, he took a more prudent and, in these unprecedented circumstances, an even more impractical maneuver. He advised the King to call a conference at Buckingham Palace; and George V, all compliance, suggested that Speaker Lowther should be in the chair.

On 21 July, therefore, Messrs. Asquith and Lloyd George for the Government, Mr. Bonar Law and Lord Lansdowne for the Opposition, Messrs. Redmond and Dillon for the Nationalists, Sir Edward Carson and Captain Craig for the Ulster Unionists, and Mr. Speaker (like a latter-day Uncle Tom Cobley) were all received at the Palace. His Majesty did not improve the occasion by remarking in his welcoming speech that the cry of civil war "is on the lips of the most sober and responsible of my people" — thus conferring soberness and responsibility upon the Unionist extremists, and conferring them in public, for the remark was unfortunately published in all the next day's newspapers.

The conference itself was held in the strictest secrecy: but both Mr. Bonar Law and Mr. Redmond have left their accounts.[23] Both agree that the Unionists and Conservatives wished to begin by discussing the time limit and that the Liberals and Nationalists refused to proceed unless the area to be excluded was first determined. Bonar Law's "Conference Memorandum" then declares that Redmond and Dillon "implied" that they would be willing, if a satisfactory area were agreed upon, to grant that area a permanent exclusion. Of this there is no sign in Redmond's "Private Note."

The conference, in any case, never got around to the question of permanent or temporary exclusion since the conferees could not agree upon the area to be excluded — according to the Prime Minister (in a note to Miss Stanley) they were bogged down in the middle of Tyrone. They were, indeed, endeavoring to settle by Act of Parliament what could only have been decided by Act of God: for Tyrone was so liberally pockmarked with Catholic and Protestant communities that nothing short of an earthquake or a general conversion could have drawn a boundary line.

The conferees were even reduced (in the Bonar Law "Memorandum") to gazing at one another in complete silence, like hapless co-conspirators: and on 24 July, to no one's surprise, they broke up with nothing accomplished. The King sadly bade them good-bye. Mr. Redmond went up to Sir Edward Carson and asked him to have "a good shake-hands for the sake of the old days on the circuit." It was not refused. Captain Craig, although he had never spoken to him before, did the same to Mr. Dillon. "Aren't they a remarkable people?" wrote Mr. Asquith. "And the folly of thinking that we can ever understand, let alone govern them!" According to Irish computation, this timely remark had been made seven hundred years too late.[24]

Mr. Asquith was now determined — at least, so he confided to Miss Stanley — to proceed with an Amending Bill which granted *permanent* exclusion to six of the nine counties, and he actually presented this unheroic, indeed perfidious, idea in the form of an ultimatum to Messrs. Redmond and Dillon. "This," he wrote Miss Stanley, "after a good deal of demur they reluctantly agreed to persuade their party to accept."[25] Mr. Asquith's extraordinary statement, so casually inserted in a note to a confidante, means on the face of it that the Irish leaders were ready to abandon everything which they had spent their adult lives in trying to accomplish. It also, of course, supports the "implication" in Bonar Law's "Memorandum." Is it not apparent, however, that they simply agreed to pass this preposterous ultimatum along to their party? In such desperate times they might have gone as far as that.

In the Cabinet, later on that day, ministers were wearily discussing the various points raised and dismissed in the conference. They were about to separate when the quiet voice of Sir Edward Grey began reading aloud a document just brought him from the Foreign Office. It contained the terms of Austria's fatal note to Serbia. "He had been reading or speaking for several minutes," wrote Winston Churchill in an immortal passage, "before I could separate my mind from the tedious and bewildering debate which had just closed . . . but gradually as the sentences followed one another, impressions of a wholly different character began to form in my mind . . . The parishes of Tyrone and Fermanagh faded back into the mists and squalls of Ireland, and a strange light began immediately, but by perceptible gradations, to fall and grow upon the map of Europe."

It did not, or not in the same way, fall and grow upon the map of Ireland.

IV

Bachelor's Walk

The Nationalist gunrunning, which had been planned originally in Mrs. Green's house in May, was a very modest affair, although spectacular as a feat and tragic in its outcome. Only £1,524 had been raised, a sum just sufficient to purchase fifteen hundred rather antiquated rifles from Messrs. Max and Moritz Magnus of Hamburg.[26] There was nothing left to pay for the chartering of a ship: but Erskine Childers offered his yacht *Asgard* and Conor O'Brien his yacht *Kelpie*. They were to collect the rifles from a Hamburg tug off the mouth of the Scheldt. O'Brien was to transship his quota into Sir Thomas Myles's schooner *Chotah* off the coast of Wales: Childers was to carry his rifles directly to Howth Harbor outside Dublin, and land them at noon on 26 July.

The whole exploit sounded a curiously Anglo-Irish note. Conor O'Brien, a grandson of Young Ireland's William Smith O'Brien and a cousin of Lord Monteagle, was a product of Winchester College and of Dublin and Oxford

Universities: he was also a Sinn Feiner, an Irish speaker, a local leader of Irish Volunteers, a Redmondite and a writer. Childers was the son of an English father and an Anglo-Irish mother. A near relative of his had served in Mr. Gladstone's first three cabinets. He himself had undergone a conventional education at Haileybury College and Cambridge University. He had volunteered for service in the Boer War; he had been Committee Clerk to the House of Commons. A less likely candidate for an illegal gunrunning into Nationalist Ireland it would, on the face of it, be hard to conceive.

But Childers combined a sternly logical mind with a vaulting imagination: his *The Riddle of the Sands* is one of the classical mystery stories of pre-War England, indeed of any England. Then again, he had spent many happy hours in his mother's Wicklow home. Around 1908 he began to conceive a sympathetic feeling for Home Rule and in 1911 wrote a most able book in its defense. On the whole, in the controversy over the Provisional Committee, he supported John Redmond. In World War I he fought loyally in the Royal Naval Reserve. Almost anything might have come out of all this: what did happen was that Childers boxed the political compass and, in 1922, a captain in the service of the Irish Republic, died with quiet composure before the rifles of a Free State firing squad. ("Come closer, boys," he said to his unnerved executioners. "It will make it easier for you.")

Both O'Brien and Childers were splendid sailors. They made an accurate rendezvous with the Hamburg tug near the Roentgen Lightship, and O'Brien landed his rifles in the *Chotah* at Kilcoole on 1 August. Childers's crew included his crippled American wife, Mary, and their friend Mary Spring-Rice, daughter of Lord Monteagle and niece of the British Ambassador to Washington: of that dangerous voyage in an overloaded vessel and heavy seas, Miss Spring-Rice has left a vivid account. At 12:45 P.M. on 26 July, having passed through the British fleet on review at Spithead, and now just three quarters of an hour behind schedule, the *Asgard* brought her nine hundred rifles into Howth.[27]

The Irish Volunteers had marched out of Dublin that morning between seven and eight hundred strong, on what most of them believed to be an ordinary route march. Among them were Arthur Griffith, the poets Padraic Colum and Thomas MacDonagh, and "a little man with a back like a ramrod" named Cathal Brugha, a purveyor of ecclesiastical candles who was to fight like a tiger in the Rising. They were led by Bulmer Hobson and accompanied by Eoin MacNeill, Darrell Figgis and a detachment of Boy Scouts (Fianna na hEireann) with two handcarts, which the Countess Markievicz had prudently loaded with heavy clubs. Like their counterparts at Larne, the Volunteers were most punctual and none but a few coast-guards, who soon removed themselves, attempted to interfere.

Here all resemblance between the two gunrunnings abruptly ceased.

The Police-Inspector at Howth had telephoned Mr. H. V. Harrel, Assistant Commissioner of the Dublin Metropolitan Police; and Mr. Harrel not only called out the police but also — which was technically illegal — secured the services of two companies of the King's Own Scottish Borderers. The Volunteers and the Fianna encountered the police and soldiers at the Malahide Road. While Figgis, MacDonagh and Hobson engaged Mr. Harrel in a heated and discursive argument, the Volunteers melted away into the Christian Brothers grounds, where they hid with their rifles, and then reformed for a march to Father Matthew Park. The police, already upset at the presence of soldiers, dispersed; the soldiers were marched back to their barracks, followed by a small but angry crowd, armed (it would seem) with stones and brickbats. As the soldiers debouched onto the quays at Bachelor's Walk the stones began to fly and Major Haig ordered his rearguard to block the narrow roadway; and the rearguard, untrained in riot procedures, opened fire. Three persons were killed instantly and thirty-eight were wounded, fifteen seriously, of whom one died later.

Comparisons between Larne and Howth cannot help being odious. At Larne twenty thousand rifles were unloaded without interference; at Howth nine hundred rifles brought out soldiers and police. At Larne, one UVF messenger died of a heart attack; after Howth four civilians were killed and thirty-seven wounded. The amount of official attention crudely reflected the usual mathematics of political democracy: it was in inverse proportion to the amount of money expended; for Larne, all told, had cost £60,000 and Howth and Kilcoole £1,500 between them.

As for the rifles brought in by the *Asgard* and the *Chotah*, they turned out to be "11mm. Mausers of rather antiquated pattern [wrote Padraic Pearse] without magazines and are much inferior to the British service rifle and even to those which Carson's men have. Moreover the ammunition landed is useless. It consists of explosive bullets which are against the rules of civilized war and which, therefore, we are not serving out to the men."[28]

As a consequence of Bachelor's Walk, by the evening of 27 July the Irish Volunteers had been increased by every unenrolled reservist in the South and West: and the situation along the Ulster borders had become very tense indeed. On that day John Redmond demanded and received a formal adjournment of the House and the second reading of the Amending Bill was postponed until 30 July. On 28 July, Austria declared war on Serbia. On 30

July, therefore, the Prime Minister and Mr. Bonar Law, "in the interest of the international situation," agreed to postpone the Amending Bill indefinitely.[29] On 31 July, Colonel Maurice Moore (late of the Connaught Rangers), Inspector-General of the Irish Volunteers, brother of George Moore, and son of a Mayo landlord who had been a great firebrand in his day, wrote to Mr. Redmond, proposing that all Irish reservists and all members of the Special Reserve should refuse to join the colors unless the King gave immediate assent to Home Rule.[30]

Mr. Redmond called this letter "a bombshell," but he already knew how to defuse it: or so it seemed at the time. He had received a letter from Mrs. Asquith, urging him to offer all his soldiers to the Government: and — much as he disliked all political women and this one in particular — he had actually replied on 2 August that he expected to see Mr. Asquith on the next day and that "I hope I *may be able* to follow your advice."[31] He may have made an appointment with the Prime Minister for 3:00 P.M. the next afternoon:[32] but of any meeting there is no record at all.

Sir Edward Grey, at any rate, in the course of his speech,[33] made the following statement:

> One thing I would like to say: the one bright spot in the very dreadful situation is Ireland. The position in Ireland — and this I should like very clearly to be understood abroad — is not a consideration among the many things we have to take into account now.

How had he come to say these words if — as he afterwards told Mr. Denis Gwynn — he had had no interview with the Prime Minister or Mr. Redmond before saying them? Perhaps he was referring to a statement by Sir Edward Carson in the *Times* of 1 August — a statement to the effect that a large body of Ulster Volunteers would give their services for Home Defence and that many would be willing to serve anywhere they were required.

Mr. Redmond must of course have read Sir Edward Carson in the *Times*. His answer to Sir Edward Grey was — as his letter to Mrs. Asquith shows — at any rate not unpremeditated. These were the words which brought the Unionist benches cheering to their feet:

> While Irishmen generally are in favour of peace and would desire to save the democracy of this country from all the horrors of war . . . still if the dire necessity is forced upon this country, we offer to the Government of the day that they may take their troops away and that, if it is allowed to us, in com-

radeship with our brethren in the North, we will ourselves defend the coasts of our country.[34]

He listened impassively to the cheering, and when Mr. P. J. Hooper of the *Freeman's Journal* afterwards came up to congratulate him upon having provided all that day's news for the Irish papers, he answered only, "How do you think they will take it?"

Chapter Ten

Mr. Redmond's Rubicon: August and September 1914

Mr. Redmond's answer to Mr. Hooper has something in it of the *alea jacta est* — "the die is cast" — which Caesar is reported to have said before crossing the Rubicon. This disciple of Parnell believed — it was hardly a Parnellite position — that the very best way of achieving Home Rule at such a juncture was through amity, not menace. Nonetheless, he realized that he had taken a gamble; and, as we now know, he had not taken it without expecting to extract some compensation from the Prime Minister.

When he wrote to Mr. Asquith the next day — "I *must* break in on your other preoccupations," he began — he said that he had taken great risks in making his offer, and that if Home Rule was postponed the result might be "disastrous." Surely it was not too much to ask that the Home Rule Bill should receive the royal assent at once, with a promise that it would not be put into operation until an Amending Bill was disposed of in the winter session.[1] Sir Edward Carson, needless to say, in another letter of the same date, was demanding that the status quo should be strictly preserved.[2] That night, at 11 P.M., England was at war.

I

The Meaning of Prorogation

Arrangements had been made for Redmond and Carson to meet the next day, 5 August, in the Speaker's Library, in order to iron out their differences before Sir Edward left for Ulster. What Redmond said that morning put the Unionist in such a rage that he threatened to stay and obstruct the Appropriations Bill which gave formal approval to the Government's declaration of war. Mr. Redmond retorted, so he told Mr. Asquith, that if the Government allowed itself to be bullied, he and his party would raise a discussion on the second reading of the Bill of such a kind that "it would exhibit us to the world as torn into a hundred fragments and disaffected with the Government of the day."[3] This *was* a Parnellite position; and it remained to be seen if Mr. Redmond would have the resolution to keep it up.

What he had said to enrage Carson appears in a further letter which he wrote to the Prime Minister the next morning, and in which he asked what the Government proposed to do "with reference to adjournment or prorogation."[4] After passing the Appropriations Bill, Parliament would rise: and Mr. Redmond did not want it to be adjourned, he wanted it to be prorogued.

The difference between adjournment and prorogation was so little known that Professor Dicey had once been obliged to explain it to as experienced a journalist as St. Loe Strachey. It was this: — If Parliament were *adjourned* it would, when next it met, take up where it had left off. If it were *prorogued,* "the effect of prorogation is at once to suspend all business until Parliament is summoned again — so that every Bill must be renewed after Prorogation as if it had never been introduced."[5] Thus if, as Redmond requested, the King were advised to prorogue Parliament, the Amending Bill, which had come down from the Lords in July and had not yet received its second reading, would simply cease to exist, while the Home Rule Bill, having gone three times through all its parliamentary stages, would now be ready to receive the Royal Assent. With Home Rule for *all* Ireland thus enacted, Mr. Redmond would be in an extremely strong position *vis à vis* Sir Edward Carson when the Amending Bill was reintroduced in the winter.

Mr. Asquith was proof against arguments of this kind. Moreover he knew that the "Leviathan" in his speech of 3 August had, in effect, harpooned himself. It would take a man of iron courage and little respect for Parliament to raise a hullabaloo in the Commons at this most critical moment — and to raise it after having made such friendly offers of support. He therefore replied that Mr. Redmond need have no fear; the "domestic truce" brought on by war would not endanger Home Rule; the Cabinet was determined to place it on the statute book. "But to prorogue at the present moment," he continued, "would in the present circumstances be considered as a piece of sharp practice." He trusted that Redmond would be satisfied with these assurances, "to which, in view of all that I have done the last three years, I am sure you will give weight."[6]

Considering that the Prime Minister had driven the Irish leaders back to the line of a six years' exclusion of six of the Ulster counties, and that he had then begged them to abandon this barely tenable position in favor of no time limit at all, it was asking a good deal of Mr. Redmond to expect him to give weight to any Asquithian assurances of any kind. He replied with a brief and bitter expostulation: to adjourn and not prorogue, he said, would be universally regarded as an evasion. "The happiest moment in Irish history will be lost," he wrote. "Not only will Ireland be divided and distracted, but the same will happen in every colony in the Empire and throw the Irish into the arms of the German colonists there — and all for what? To avoid a protest from Carson, who would not have the Unionist Party behind him."[7]

The fact was that he had lost an important round in the parliamentary game and that — not being the sort of Irish leader who would follow the old rebellious rule and make an Irish opportunity out of England's difficulty — he shrugged his shoulders like the good parliamentarian he had become and turned to another quarter.

II

Lord Kitchener

Mr Redmond had originally hoped for an Irish Volunteer Force which would not be required to take the oath of allegiance and which would be employed in the defense of Ireland and never drafted overseas.

But it so happened that Mr. Asquith had, on 5 August, relinquished the office of Secretary of State for War and handed it over to Field Marshal Earl

Kitchener of Khartoum, who thus became the first soldier on active duty to sit in any Cabinet since the Restoration of 1660. To this formidable monolith, whose prestige with the whole British public was exceedingly high, and not altogether deservedly so, Mr. Redmond repaired on 7 August.

Lord Kitchener had been born in Ireland in 1850; his father was an English officer from East Anglia; and he had been brought up to regard himself as the member of a Protestant master race in an alien, hostile and superstitious land. It was not surprising, therefore, that this attitude toward Irish nationalism should have been uncompromisingly Unionist; or that, as a professional soldier with rigid views as to what was or was not fitting, he should have looked askance at an irregular militia composed of Irish Catholics. He also lacked any idea, or the slightest wish to entertain any idea, of the niceties and perplexities of Anglo-Irish relations.

To John Redmond's request, therefore, that the drill sergeants and reservists should not be withdrawn from the Irish Volunteers and that the Volunteers should be suitably armed, this unimpressionable man returned a blank negative. He told Mr. Redmond that all he wanted from Ireland was recruits and that, for the purposes of Irish defense, he thought of drafting English Territorials, a body of men for whom he was known to feel a profound contempt. In a furious letter to the Prime Minister, John Redmond said that this would be taken as a supreme affront.[8]

The single result of these representations was that Lieutenant General Sir Bryan Mahon, now commanding the 10th Division at the Curragh — "reliever of Mafeking," wrote the Chief Secretary, "and a *beau sabreur* of the first water" — was asked to talk to Redmond as the leader of the Irish Volunteers. "Cocker him up," said the sanguine Birrell, "and make his Irish heart glow within him."[9] It was all to no avail. "No number of soldiers sitting on the shores of Ireland," said General Mahon, "will save your country any more than England from German vengeance."[10]

For a brief while, Mr. Redmond returned in spirit to those far-off days when, an eager young man, he had "shed his blood" for the great Parnell. "He has become," wrote T. P. Gill, "as 'emotional' as those he criticises, only it is the emotion of hatred . . . of things dead and gone: the anti-English emotion. So he plays to the gallery and the 'Hungarian' [i.e. Sinn Fein] gallery at that. I am going to talk with him . . . for this sort of thing is only increasing the mischief."[11]

It did not last long. The gamble Mr. Redmond had taken on 3 August had apparently succeeded: except among the more ardent nationalists, the speech had been well received in Ireland. The Germans had invaded a small neutral

Catholic country: all but the most determined Anglophobes, it seemed, would now prefer England to Germany.

In such a heady atmosphere, how could so old a parliamentary hand as Mr. Redmond sustain his "anti-English" hatred? Besides this, he had been receiving a series of dithyrambic letters from Mr. Birrell. "Everything points to an immediate and satisfactory solution," was their burden.[12] On 15 September Mr. Redmond learned that the Government proposed to enact a Home Rule Bill at once, but also to pass a Suspensory Bill which would prevent it from coming into force until the end of the war. Even then it would have to wait until Parliament had the fullest opportunity of "altering, modifying or qualifying its provisions in such a way as to secure the general consent of Ireland and of the United Kingdom."

When the Prime Minister made this pronouncement in the Commons, Mr. Bonar Law replied with a violently abusive speech, and then led his party *en masse* out of the chamber.[13] "Bonar Law never sunk so low in his gutter as today," wrote Mr. Asquith: but it was all play-acting. Mr. Law had been given all that he could have asked for at such a time. The Home Rule Bill would become an Act, but an Act in a state of suspended animation: it could not be restored to life until it had been so modified as to secure the assent of Orange Ulster and its English adherents.

Mr. Redmond did not follow Mr. Law out of the House: he now surrendered to the Suspensory Bill with what grace he could. On 18 September, the Royal Assent was given to the Home Rule Bill. Except for the five Lords Commissioners, there was not a peer present in the House of Lords for the occasion, and among the M.P.s who crowded to the Bar to hear the Clerk intone "Le Roy le Veult," there were only eight Unionists.[14]

When this hollow ceremony was over, the M.P.s returned to their chamber and against all precedent began to sing "God Save the King." Then someone called out "God Save Ireland." "And God Save England too," shouted Mr. Redmond who, like Home Rule itself, had now become Parliament's prisoner, and would never be released.

III

Woodenbridge

On 20 September, returning to his Wicklow home, he stopped off at Woodenbridge to look at a parade of Irish Volunteers. At the conclusion of his brief impromptu speech he said: "Your duty is two-fold. I am glad to see such magnificent material for soldiers around me, and I say to you, 'Go on drilling and make yourselves efficient for the work, and then account yourselves as men, not only in Ireland itself, but wherever the firing line extends, in defense of right, of freedom, and of religion.' "

He had thus transformed the Irish Volunteers from a defense force which would never go overseas into a reservoir of recruits for the English Army. In his 3 August speech he had stood on the very banks of his Rubicon: he had now splashed across. How could this honest, this deluded leader tell that on the farther side lay revolution itself?

Chapter Eleven

The Military Council: September 1914–August 1915

I

On 20 September it was still believed that the war would be short. No one had as yet realized that the Battle of the Marne was "a last manoeuvre of the pre-war type,"[1] or that, when the Germans dug in on the Aisne, a dreadful stalemate had begun. Mr. Redmond still had his eye on the bargaining table across which he would face the hard eyes of the exclusionists when the war was over.

Sir Edward Carson had as good as offered his Ulster Volunteers to the British Army, with the unconcealed proviso that those who stayed behind would remain in being as a defense force against Home Rule. John Redmond wished to do the same for his Volunteers: those who did not enlist would remain in being to back him up should he refuse to accept an Amending Bill. He was saying this as late as August 1915,[2] when the Redmondite Volunteers had virtually collapsed. It may even be true, when he made his first recruiting speech specifically to a Volunteer audience, that he hoped to drive the extremists out of the Provisional Committee: which is what happened, only not with the results that he expected.

On the whole, however, he put most of his faith in Irish enlistment to give him the moral force he needed to resist a permanent partition when the day came. In September 1914 this was not an idle hope. The fighting still bore a romantic and ideal aspect: it was for the cause of a little Catholic country, even of all small nationalities. That autumn there was a wave of enlistment. But these were men who would have enlisted without any encouragement from Mr. Redmond; they did not represent, as the *Freeman's Journal* would have had its readers believe, the whole country. They were the men who lit the bonfires, and attended the rallies, and shouted down the critics of Mr. Redmond: and when they went to war and were devoured by it, Mr. Redmond lost a young, ardent and irreplaceable element among his followers.

The trouble which beset the Irish Volunteers was not experienced by their Ulster counterparts. The Ulstermen were well armed and well trained. The Irish Volunteers were poorly armed and the *cadre* of reservists which should have trained them had gone off to the war. On 16 September, the number of Irish Volunteers was said to be over 190,000;[3] the vast majority of these never enlisted and never intended to.

II

In spite of its apparent success in Ireland, Mr. Redmond's 3 August speech in the House of Commons had been, in fact, followed by a subtle deterioration in his own prestige and that of the moderate nationalism which he represented.

In the first place, Mr. Asquith conveniently forgot a promise he had made to form an Irish Army Corps for Irish recruits; the two division commanders in Ireland, Sir Brian Mahon (10th) and Sir Lawrence Parsons (16th), continued to send their Irish recruits away to England; the Divisions were not permitted distinctive badges; Sir Lawrence's officers were almost all Unionists and Protestants;[4] and Lord Kitchener's War Office blankly refused even to mention the exploits of Irish regiments in Flanders in 1914 or at the Dardanelles in the next year. Thus, to take only one example, the heroic stand of the Royal Munster Fusiliers at Étreux, covering Smith-Dorrien's retreat from Mons, was not allowed to touch the imagination of Irish youth. As T. M. Healy told the Prime Minister, this was having an evil effect not only on recruiting but also on the good will of the Irish people,[5] who were beginning to suspect that Carson's men were being kept at home in order to fight Home Rule after the war. In fact, the Ulster division was sent to France in October 1915, and its bloody end in a most gallant attack at Thiepval in July 1916 came too late to alter the suspicion.

Then again — although he had tried to persuade Mr. Asquith and himself that this was not the case[6] — Mr. Redmond's 3 August speech had been received in Irish-America with genuine horror. In a letter of 19 September, he attempted to justify himself to Michael Ryan, President of the United Irish League: but Mr. Ryan was married to a German-American, he was running for the Governorship of Pennsylvania, a state with a strong pro-German vote, and he himself (like most Irish-Americans) was more interested in the destruction of the British Empire than in the cause of Irish self-government. In a letter of 2 October he said that while he had no quarrel with Redmond's right to do what he thought best for Ireland, all his sympathies were with Germany, he believed that nine-tenths of Irish-America thought as he did, and though he had no use for the revolutionary Clan-na-Gael, he shared the "disgust of soul" with which Mr. Redmond's 3 August speech had been received by all persons of Irish descent. In short, he and the treasurer advised the termination of the United Irish League in America: and from that day onward no funds were received from it. Of its three chief officials only Michael Jordan, the secretary, remained faithful to Redmond, and he was helpless: and the *Irish World,* after sacking its business manager, the Redmondite Patrick Egan, turned frankly pro-German and took the rest of the Irish-American press with it.[7]

III

Ever since the 3 August speech, the Provisional Committee of the Irish Volunteers had been divided into two unequal camps. The larger (headed by John D. Nugent of the Ancient Order of Hibernians) was Redmondite; the smaller (headed by Padraic Pearse) strongly supported the Dublin County Board of Volunteers when it refused to lend *any* assistance to the English government. From then on, Pearse complained, he was never allowed to speak in Committee:[8] but it was not until the Woodenbridge speech had provoked a violent scene between Nugent and Pearse that the minority broke away and, seizing the Volunteer Headquarters in Kildare Street, issued a manifesto declaring "Mr. Redmond, through his nominees, no longer entitled to any place in the administration of the Irish Volunteers."[9] This was on 24 September. The dissident minority now became known as the Irish Volunteers, while the majority began to call itself the National Volunteers, a name less associated with revolution.

At their first convention, in the Abbey Theatre on 25 October, the new Irish Volunteers were told that, out of a membership of 168,000, it appeared that Redmond had retained about 156,000. The 150 delegates were not dismayed by these melancholy figures. In scenes of great enthusiasm they elected Eoin MacNeill Chairman and The O'Rahilly Treasurer, and turned the old pre-Redmond Provisional Committee into a General Council, to be joined by representatives of all thirty-two counties and the nine principal towns. After this they approved a new declaration of policy: it called for a permanent trained and armed Volunteer Force to defend the Irish people; and denounced partition, disunion, conscription and the system of governing Ireland through Dublin Castle and military power.[10]

All this was quite conventional and Augustine Birrell may be excused for telling the Cabinet that "the old Fenian strain . . . is worn very thin in Ireland."[11] Mr. Redmond was of the same mind. He called MacNeill and his followers nothing more than an impudent nuisance; told Alice Stopford Green (who had complained bitterly of his use of "impudent") that the new Volunteers, if not put down, would cover Ireland with contempt and ridicule;[12] and listened with complacency to the Redmondite press as it celebrated the pro-English spirit pervading the country.

John Dillon was of quite another mind, however. He had never approved of recruiting, and to him "the MacNeill crowd" was not impudent or ridiculous: far from it. "It has poisoned the country," he said in October, "with the story that we have entered into some secret agreement with Kitchener and the Government to turn the Volunteers into soldiers whether they are willing or not."[13]

The police seem to have concurred in this view of things. The Redmonite Volunteers, they said, were losing numbers "through dread of being called on for military service"; there was little or no drill for lack of instructors; and the response to Redmond's Woodenbridge speech had been "poor." The country was being flooded with anti-enlistment placards and handbills with a strong appeal to "young farmers, shop assistants, clerks, school teachers and others of that class who in this country rarely if ever join the army"; and if there was little pro-German feeling, the anti-English feeling was on the rise.[14]

In November and December, the Redmondite Volunteers were said to be untrained, poorly armed, and losing numbers. In December, the police consensus was that Mr. Redmond's recruiting appeal had had little effect. The enlistment figures up to 15 December were now given as 33,924, of whom 7,819 were National Volunteers, 16,435 were Ulster Volunteers, and 9,680 were not known to belong to either.[15] In terms of religion, 13,711 were Catholics and 20,223 Protestants: the former were far the more likely to respond to Redmond's pleas.

The figures for the whole of the following year (or from 15 December 1914 to 15 December 1915) show that there were 51,144 enlistments, far heavier at the beginning of the year than at the end. 31,412 enlistees were Catholics and 19,279 Protestants; and of these 10,794 were National Volunteers and 8,203 Ulster Volunteers.[16] These figures are respectable; they indicate that Redmond's drive reached its peak early in 1915; but they also indicate that enlistments occurred chiefly among those who would have enlisted even without a Woodenbridge speech or a Redmondite recruiting drive.

In the Protestant Northeast the Ulster Volunteers saved much of their energy for their own organization: this was by no means the case with the Redmondite Volunteers. Money from the United Irish League in America had dried up in October 1914. The RIC reported that there were in sober fact not more than 10,400 serviceable rifles among *all* the Irish nationalists — as compared to 53,340 said to be in the possession of the Ulster force — and that 1,500 nationalist rifles were the property of "the Sinn Fein Volunteers."[17] These figures cannot be disregarded. When one hears of large parades of armed National Volunteers — as, for example, the 25,000 who passed before Colonel Moore and Mr. Redmond in Phoenix Park in April 1915 — it would be prudent to wonder how many in such parades were actually armed and with what.

Colonel Moore had done his best to invigorate his headquarters with a Military Committee and a Finance Committee: but at the beginning of July he was obliged to report that he had only two officers to go around the country, training the various corps of the National Volunteers and bringing them together for maneuvers. He needed, he said, at least thirty. Their salaries combined were only £286; and if the auditors carried out their proposal to discharge one and tie the other to "the office stool," the result would be the collapse of the National Volunteers.[18] But Mr. Redmond, his eye on postwar Home Rule, was chiefly bent — as Mrs. Green once put it — "on getting men into the army and he does not give any thought to those who remain in the country."[19] In short, lack of funds, the hostility of the War Office, Mr. Redmond's indifference, the growing unpopularity of the recruiting campaign — all these had done their work. The National Volunteers still existed, they still paraded, and at the end of 1915 were supposed to number around 112,500: but by this time they were a demoralized and apathetic body of men.[20]

IV

The Irish Volunteers were, for their part, a very seditious body in the eyes of the police: but they were not taken seriously as a paramilitary force, if only because they were so poorly armed. Their numbers were given as 13,500 in mid-December 1914; they were said to be much the same at the end of 1915; and in mid-April 1916 they were supposed to have risen to nearly 16,000.[21] They had their women's organization, the Cummann na mBann, designed for ambulance and Red Cross work, and perhaps other duties. "I would not like to think of women drilling and marching in the ordinary way," said Pearse, primly, "but there is no reason [he added] that they should not learn to shoot."[22]

As the hard core of the nationalist movement, the Irish Volunteers were said to prefer, not so much a German victory, as an England weakened by war and unable to resist a demand for independence.[23] It was recognized very early that one or two of their organizers, such as Liam Mellows and Robert Monteith, were IRB men, but the amount of IRB infiltration was never known. In August 1914 the Supreme Council of the IRB came cautiously to the surface and an open conference was called for 9 September at 25 Parnell Square, the headquarters of the Gaelic League, where prominent nonmembers such as Arthur Griffith and James Connolly discussed what steps were to be taken as a result of the European war, and an Advisory Committee was actually formed to plan for a fight in the Dublin area. But the Committee was too large and indiscriminate; it was soon disbanded; and the IRB went underground again.[24]

The less visible it became, however, the more its interest in the Irish Volunteers increased. In December 1914, when the Volunteers set up a Headquarters Staff, the Chief of Staff (Eoin MacNeill), the Director of Arms (The O'Rahilly) and the Director of Training (Thomas Mac-Donagh) were not members of the IRB, but this was not the case with the Director of Military Organization (Padraic Pearse), the Quartermaster (Bulmer Hobson) and the Director of Military Operations (Joseph Plun-

kett). At a somewhat later date another IRB man, Eamonn Ceannt, was
added to the staff as Director of Communications. Under the General Staff
there was the General Council, supposed to meet once a month; and to this
there had been added an Executive Council or Central Executive which was
dominated by the IRB from the start.[25]

In the Supreme Council of the IRB itself, Thomas Clarke and Sean Mac-
Diarmida, as Treasurer and Secretary, had virtually unlimited powers when
the Supreme Council was not — and it usually was not — in session. Together with the President, they acted as the Executive: and if the President
were absent they could act on their own. In this way it was possible for
Padraic Pearse, as early as December 1914, to work out plans (as Director of
Military Organization) for the deployment of the Volunteers if the Government should bring conscription to Ireland, and for him to concert these plans
in secret with those of Clarke and MacDiarmida. All Volunteers would
agree to carry out such plans because, while all of them were not ready for
an insurrection on any terms, all were prepared to fight in the event of
conscription or disarmament.[26]

In July 1915, the IRB Executive in the Supreme Council set up a new
Council, with the express purpose of centralizing its secret control over the
Volunteers. To this Council, which originally consisted of Pearse, Joseph
Plunkett and Eamonn Ceannt, was committed the task of formulating the
plans for a Rising. It was by no means a properly appointed body; Sean
MacDiarmida was in prison for anti-recruiting speeches when it was formed;
and it seems (for "seems" is as far as one can go) that Thomas Clarke was
responsible for it, along with Padraic Pearse and Eamonn Ceannt. It was not
until September 1915 that the full Supreme Council knew of its existence, and
it never knew of its plans.[27] In this shadowy way there came into being the
famous Military Council, whose members constituted the Provisional Government of Easter 1916, and died to a man.

V

Eamonn Ceannt, as Sean Fitzgibbon put it, was "more naturally a physical
force man than any of the other leaders." He was born in Galway in 1881,
came to Dublin at an early age, was educated by the Christian Brothers in
North Richmond Street and worked in the City Treasurer's department of
the Dublin Corporation.[28] He was secretary to the National Council of Sinn
Fein and one of the left-wing group which (as has been shown) began to

politicize the Gaelic League in 1913. When Douglas Hyde denounced these dissidents in the 4 July *Freeman's Journal,* among those who replied was Ceannt in the 12 July *Sinn Fein.* No weapon should be discarded, he wrote, in the battle against those who opposed the use of Irish: and among the weapons not to be discarded he was careful to specify physical force. Ceannt went far to the left of Sinn Fein, and indeed of the IRB, in his support for Larkin's Transport Union in the great lockout of 1913; but by the end of the year he had joined the IRB.[29] It is not surprising to find this resolute man on the new Military Council.

Padraic Pearse's was altogether a different case. He was in some ways even more direct of purpose than Clarke or Ceannt or MacDiarmida, men who merely wanted an insurrection and did not much care how it came; in other ways, he was almost excessively complex. He remains, next to James Connolly, the most compelling figure in the immediate history of the Easter Rising. Nobody personified as well as he the mystical nationalism of the Gaelic Revival, once this nationalism was translated into physical force. In 1899, the Father of the Literary Revival, Standish O'Grady, said in his cups: "We have now a literary movement, it is not very important; it will be followed by a political movement, that will not be very important; then must come a military movement, that will be important indeed."

James Connolly believed in an Irish prehistory where all property was held in common, and he approved of the language revival because he saw it as a unifying factor: but his views, at least when compared with Pearse's, were practical and mundane. His whole experience as a labor organizer, agitator and leader insisted that they should be: and his greatness lies in his having given a universal meaning to a battle he fought and lost on the farthest edge of Europe. Pearse, like Connolly, looked back to a remote Ireland which, whatever its distractions may have been, was a cultural unity before the English came and broke it up. There the resemblance, such as it is, ceases.

Pearse's life was a surrender to myth in its most potent form, as a call to action. Although he was a gifted educator, the myth took over even his educational plans. This was the myth of Cuchulainn, the lordly hero of the Red Branch, who fought against the Champion and the host of Queen Maeve, often in a demon-haunted bronze chariot and in an atmosphere crowded with tutelary gods. In the end, mortally wounded, Cuchulainn bound himself to a pillar and, even then, even while he bled to death, seemed to his enemies to be immortal. "I care not though I were to live but one day and night, if only my fame and my deeds live after me," said Cuchulainn as a youth: and these words appeared around a fresco on one of the walls at St.

Enda's, Pearse's school for boys. As Desmond Ryan put it, Cuchulainn was an important member of the staff at St. Enda's.

Pearse was born in Dublin on 10 November 1879. His father, James Pearse, was an Englishman who came to Dublin as a monumental sculptor during the Gothic Revival; the figures on the National Bank are his; his work is said to be found in many of the churches built in the second half of the century. Although almost certainly born a Protestant, he was quite certainly a Catholic by the time he married his first wife, Emily Fox, in the early 1860s. His second wife was Margaret Brady, a girl from County Meath, whom he married in 1877, just before setting up in business for himself in what is now Pearse Street: and Padraic Pearse was the eldest son of this marriage.[30]

Pearse once said of himself that the dark side of his character, "the sombre and taciturn Pearse," was due to his English blood — an imputation which the English would certainly resist but which may have been a reflection upon his father, about whose filial relations nothing whatsoever is known, and who died when Pearse was twenty. The elder Pearse was a radical Home Ruler and the author of a Parnellite tract in 1886: but it was Padraic's mother who, in the romantic tradition of Irish nationalism, sang him Fenian songs when he was a little boy.

Pearse was educated (like most Irish revolutionaries) by the Christian Brothers, whom he never forgave for their anti-Parnell stand — the dead Parnell was a "dirty fellow," said Pearse's master at his school in Westland Row —[31] and for their eager submission to the Board of Intermediate Education. The Board, a product of the Education Act of 1878, bound secondary education to the sorry routine of stereotyped written tests, and gave statutory bribes to those schools which (like the Christian Brothers) "brought the examination technique to a fine art which had little to do with education."[32]

In 1908, having gained his B.A. through the old Royal University and entered and abandoned the law, which he called "the most wicked of professions," Pearse founded St. Enda's, a bilingual secondary school for boys at Rathmines. Here he fought his battle against the Intermediate (which he saw as an English plot to reduce all the varieties of Irish life to a stultifying and submissive sameness): nor did he fight it alone. At his back there stood a formidable band of heroes and saints, from Cuchulainn and the Boy-Corps of Eamhain Macha to St. Enda and his companions in Aran. He did not choose to accept the idea that the State could usurp the place of the teacher as "fosterer" — a pre-Christian concept taken up by St. Enda, by St. Kieran, by Finnian. To each of these men his pupils were collectively family, household and *clann;* to their schools at Cloard or Aran or Clonmacnois came "rich or poor, prince or peasant": so that "to the pagan ideals of strength and truth were added the Christian ideals of love and humility."[33] Like the pupils of the hedge schoolmaster of the nineteenth century, whom he called "the last repository of a high tradition," Pearse wanted every one of his boys to be, in some intimate personal way, the disciple of a master. Was not the primary duty of a teacher to "seek to discover the individual bent of his pupils, the hidden talent that is in every normal soul?" Once, when a father told him that his son was good at nothing but playing a tin whistle and asked, "What am I to do with him?", Pearse replied, "Buy a tin whistle for him." It was, he said, the obvious answer.[34]

Although his friends admitted that he had a curious gift for making people do what he wanted, Pearse was in private a gentle personage, who instilled truth-telling into his boys by the simple method of always believing what they told him. He had a youthful face with a charming profile, which is all his photographs were permitted to show, since he had a slight cast in one eye. His body was strong and stocky and usually dressed in black. He walked with a heavy step. Behind his kind and somewhat humorless exterior there stood — as his pupils well knew — a twentieth century Cuchulainn: and the man who could not bear to kill even a worm in his garden would daily hold forth in his classroom on the beauties of death in battle.

"When we were starting St. Enda's," he wrote, "I told my boys: 'We must re-create and perpetuate in Ireland the knightly tradition of Cuchulainn, "better is short life with honour than long life with dishonour" . . . the noble tradition of the Fianna [a prehistoric Irish army] "we, the Fianna, never told a lie, falsehood was never on our lips" . . . the Christ-like tradition of Columcille, "if I die it shall be from the excess of love I bear the Gael."'" And to these, he thought, should be added the "evangels" of such heroes as Wolfe Tone, Robert Emmet, John Mitchel and O'Donovan Rossa. "I have seen Irish boys and girls moved inexpressibly by the story of Robert Emmet . . . and I have always felt it to be legitimate to make use for educational purposes of an exaltation so produced."[35] This heady atmosphere became, if anything, even headier when, in 1910, St. Enda's was moved to The Hermitage at Rathfarnham, a locality closely identified with Robert Emmet. Here his younger brother, Willie Pearse, taught painting and sculpture; here Thomas MacDonagh taught comparative literature; here the school language was Irish, the games were Irish, and all other subjects except science and languages were taught bilingually.

Cuchulainn, needless to say, was something more to Pearse than an important member of the staff of St. Enda's. When J. J. Horgan, the lawyer and (Redmondite) author of *Parnell to Pearse,* denounced the Easter Rising as, from a Catholic point of view, simply wicked, he based this finding on the moral reasons for rebellion as set forth in *Moral and Pastoral Theology,* by the Reverend J. H. Davis, S.J.— not one of which reasons the Rising appeared to satisfy.[36] It is hard to conceive that Horgan's strictures were derived solely from a study of the moral theology of Father Davis. Pearse barely concealed his identification of Cuchulainn with Jesus Christ: and in his messianic utterances might well have seemed (to a mind like Horgan's) to have gone even further. In his play *The Singer,* for example, published in 1915, the hero McDara is made to say: "One man can free the people as one Man redeemed the world. I will take no pike, I will go into battle with bare hands. I will stand before the Gall as Christ hung naked upon a tree." What wicked, what ultimate blasphemy might not lurk in these words, should the playwright and McDara be one and the same? Pearse, of course, was too devout a Catholic to identify himself with Christ: but between identification and imitation there is — from a political point of view — no great difference; and the profound theme of Redemption is an important, in many ways *the* important element in the symbolism of the Easter Rising.

Pearse joined the Gaelic League when he was sixteen. In time he acquired a cottage in an Irish-speaking district, to perfect his Irish, although he was always more at home in the city. He was editor of *An Claidheam Soluis* from 1903 to 1909: but in 1913 he began to find the nonpolitical aspect of the League more and more irksome, and although he never ceased to proclaim his love for Hyde, he begged him to realize that men "were men not archangels."[37] The League still had work to do, he said, but politically it was "a spent force." The really vital work must be done by others, "men who had sprung from the Gaelic League or who had received from the Gaelic League a new baptism and a new life of grace."[38]

He had been a Home Ruler, a very bellicose Home Ruler, in public, as late as 1912, because he held the establishment view that the IRB was a group of wornout Fenians. The IRB, in turn, thought of him, if at all, as a Redmondite sheep in wolf's clothing. Only Tom Clarke, always on the side of younger men, descried a genuinely popular orator in Pearse; persuaded him to make the annual speech at the grave of Wolfe Tone in Bodesntown Churchyard in June 1913; and listened with pleasure while his new protegé characterized English rule as "this evil thing against which [Tone] testified with his blood."[39] This should have cleared up all misunderstandings, but not in an island of orators; and he still remained outside the fold.

It was the formation of the Irish Volunteers which constituted the turning point for Pearse: to him it could only have seemed like the lifting up of day. Although the date is still uncertain, it was somewhere between the Rotunda meeting of 25 November 1913 and March 1914, and probably just after January, that he was sworn into the IRB. The man who swore him in was (predictably) Bulmer Hobson.[40]

It was natural for Pearse to protest bitterly when John Redmond took control of the Volunteers in June 1914; and for him to have perceived in Redmond's 3 August speech to the Commons "either madness or treachery."[41] In October 1914, however, after the split, he still thought of insurrection as something which would take place only if the Germans landed or food became scarce or the authorities tried to disarm the Volunteers or if the leaders were arrested: contingencies which, to be sure, he thought quite likely. Even then, he told Joseph McGarrity of the Clan-na-Gael in America, "we are not ready, for we have no arms." Of the fifteen hundred rifles landed at Howth and Kilcoole in July, he said, the greater part had been "stolen" by Nugent and other Redmondites: the Volunteers had retained no more than six hundred. In August, however, the Government had withdrawn its Arms Proclamation; weapons were easier to come by; and of the $26,000 collected by the *Gaelic American*, $5,000 had already been received. If only the remaining $21,000 could be sent — not to MacNeill or The O'Rahilly because *"they are not in or of our counsels and they are not formally pledged to strike, if the chance comes, for the complete thing"* — but to himself or Clarke or MacDiarmida or Ceannt or Hobson, then all would be well.[42]

This is the first acknowledgment that the IRB intended to take secret control of the Irish Volunteer Executive; it is also the last time one hears a note of uncertainty from Padraic Pearse. In December 1914 he was planning insurrection with Clarke and MacDiarmida; and in mid-1915, when he joined the IRB's Military Council, no man was more certain that an insurrection would come.

VI

Pearse, Plunkett and Ceannt were all chosen by Clarke for the Military Council because they were members of the Volunteer Headquarters Staff. When Thomas MacDonagh was co-opted to the Council in 1916, it was for the same reason. It was merely a pleasing coincidence that Pearse, Plunkett and MacDonagh were serious practicing poets. Pearse was the most conventional, in verse though not in spirit. Plunkett was perhaps the most interesting as a poet, although Yeats claimed that MacDonagh was only coming into his own when he died. MacDonagh was a very gifted translator from the Irish — indeed his English version of Pearse's "Renunciation" (originally written in Irish) is better than Pearse's. He could not have written such a poem himself, since it celebrates the sacrifice of all five senses to some greater cause — "the death I shall die" — and MacDonagh was not the man to accept such a sacrifice, with or without all its curious implications.

MacDonagh was born in 1878, in Cloughjordan, County Tipperary. His mother was an Englishwoman, a Unitarian who had been converted to Catholicism. His father was a schoolteacher, "a kindly, indulgent man," who did not care for uncomfortable doctrines. " 'Great cry and little wool, like the goats of Connacht,' has been remembered as his description of patriots who were for action at any cost."[43] The young MacDonagh studied for the priesthood at Rockwell College, but found that he had no vocation; became deeply involved in the Gaelic League; taught at St. Kieran's, Kilkenny, and St. Colman's, Fermoy; and in 1908 gave up the modest comforts of this career for uncertain prospects of midwife to Padraic Pearse at the birth of St. Enda's.

By that time he had written and published two small volumes of verse: but neither of these had any striking success and one day one of the pupils of St. Enda's found him "stirring the last of them with a stick on a funeral pyre."[44] He had, however, according to Padraic Colum, prudently kept back a few copies. In October 1908 the Abbey Theatre produced a singular play of his, *When the Dawn Is Come,* in which the Irish have risen against England under seven captains of a Council of Ireland, each captain taking weekly turns at commanding the Army. The protagonist is Thurlough MacKieran, the captain for the week, who pretends to sell himself to the British in order to learn their plans. He is accused of treason but escapes to command the army which, offstage, between acts two and three, is totally victorious. Thurlough is of course mortally wounded: but survives into the third act to be acclaimed the savior of Ireland.[45] St. Kieran was a teacher, so that "MacKieran" is self-explanatory.

It was not a very finished piece of writing, or a very actable play. MacDonagh himself, handsome, outgoing and enthusiastic, had "an abundance of good spirits and a flow of wit and humor remarkable even in a Munster man":[46] but one gets from the recollections of those whom he taught, and who were fascinated by his flood of ideas, the impression of something unfocused in his personality. In 1910, he went to Paris — in search of a "desert," he said, where "I could begin again without shackles."[47] Here he wondered if his real mission in life was to be a painter; but his canvases steadfastly refused to show any signs of vocation,[48] and he returned to the life of a literary academic, with a lectureship in English at University College, Dublin, and a co-editorship of the *Irish Review*. In 1912 he married Muriel Gifford, and settled down with her in a small house near St. Stephen's Green: from every account it was an extremely happy marriage.

It might seem odd that such a man, so circumstanced, could have gone all the way into rebellion. Padraic Colum, who knew him well, seems to have provided the answer when he said that "what was fundamental in him did not go into what he wrote. The fundamental thing was an eager search for something that would have his whole devotion." His purpose was to find a purpose: and the sense one gets of something unfocused in his life and character, something not satisfied with teaching or writing and often disenchanted with the Gaelic League mind, began to disappear when he joined the Irish National Volunteers in 1913, and disappeared entirely after the movement split in October 1914. The Irish Volunteers now fulfilled his need for a cause which would have his whole devotion: or, as he put it, half his need. "I am ten years younger than when you saw me last," he wrote to a friend in May 1915, "or rather than I was a little before you saw me last, for half of it is due to my marriage."

> I have found [he wrote in this letter] a great thing to do in and with life outside the very real and wonderful interest a wife and two children give me. It is worth living in Ireland as one of the directors of the Irish Volunteers. Of course, none but the best metal has stood the test . . . those who under all circumstances and at all times must and will be Irish rebels. Zealous martyrs and so saviours and liberators, for I am confident we shall win this time, through peace, I hope, but if necessary by war . . .[49]

When he wrote this he was a member of the General Council, the Central Executive and the Headquarters Staff of the Irish Volunteers. He was Director of Training for the entire country and Commandant of the second battalion of the Dublin Brigade. He was not yet a member of the IRB. That came about in September, when Sean MacDiarmida swore him in.[49] When he wrote it, however, he had already attended a secret meeting which Pearse had called to discuss the possibilities of a rising in September, and of which Eoin MacNeill was never informed.[50] It is, therefore, unlikely that when he wrote of winning "through peace, I hope," he really meant what he said: or, indeed, that winning was really uppermost in his mind. Did not the words "zealous *martyrs*," cropping up so unexpectedly, convey the real truth?

MacDonagh began his friendship with Count Plunkett and his family when their son Joseph was brought to him in 1908 for tutoring in basic Irish. George Noble Plunkett was a papal Count, the head of the Catholic branch of an ancient family, director of the National Museum of Science and Arts, and a gentleman of strong nationalist views, which were considered only proper since the Catholic Plunketts had been crippled by the Penal Laws. Even the Dublin police looked upon his Sandymount Rifle Club with bland approval[50] until they felt obliged to change their minds in April 1916. His son Joseph Mary, born in 1887, one of seven children, soon conceived a great friendship for his tutor. He had always been delicate; and he had been sent to an English Catholic public school, Stoneyhurst, where the discipline and diet no doubt served to increase an already serious tubercular condition. After spending some time with MacDonagh, he was forced to go abroad in search of health. In 1909, he was in Italy, Sicily and Malta; in 1910 and 1911 in Algeria. His verse at this time owed a good deal to the mysticism of St. John of the Cross, whom he had studied in the hope of rescuing Irish poetry from the paganism and theosophy of Yeats and AE. Here one can trace the influence of MacDonagh. However, his work is more metaphysical, its imagery more convoluted, and its whole presence on occasion more mature, than anything of MacDonagh's.

He was a high-spirited, courageous, flamboyant personage, given to wearing large rings and bracelets, and affecting the airs of a stage conspirator. He was said to be deeply versed in military lore. He had a passion for adventure. This last was amply gratified in March 1915, when the Supreme Council of the IRB needed to send someone to Germany to begin concerting plans for German military aid in case of a rising: and since the easiest way to leave the country was to do so on the pretext of a search for health, Plunkett was the very man.

He left Ireland on St. Patrick's Day and, traveling by way of London, Paris, Barcelona, Genoa and Berne, arrived in Berlin on the morning of 20 April, under the alias of Johann Peters of San Francisco.

His diaried account of this perilous exploit is written partly in English and partly in a private language transcribed into ungrammatical Irish. As regards military aid, his talk with Graf Georg von Wedel of the German Office seems on the whole to have been friendly: but the German General Staff had the last word. On 10 June, Captain Nodolny contemptuously refused his request: arms, said the captain, must come from America — or "Jacob" in Plunkett's private language, meaning presumably the *fatherland* of *Joseph* McGarrity, a member of the Clan-na-Gael's Revolutionary Directory. This is confirmed by Sir Roger Casement in the second volume of his German diary.

Sir Roger had gone to Germany (as will be shown) in the fall of 1914; he had actually made a kind of treaty with the German Government, a treaty which included the formation of an Irish Brigade out of Irish prisoners of war in Germany; and it was part of Plunkett's mission to give him what help he could. Plunkett spent the whole month of May near Limburg, where the Irish prisoners of war had been transferred — only fifty-three had agreed to join the Brigade. By nature optimistic and festive, in spite of his health, Plunkett always refers to Sir Roger in glowing terms — as a good talker and a fine story teller; and he says nothing at all about the reiterated complaints of German insincerity and stupidity which (according to the Casement diary) Sir Roger dinned into his ears. Indeed their only disagreement, according to Plunkett, was an argument over what he called the "Declarat" — the manifesto to be put out by the Irish Brigade at Limburg. Plunkett left Germany on 24 June, apparently in wretched health and spitting blood. What report he made to the Supreme Council is, of course, not known: but as a member of the new Military Council, whose business it was to pull wool over the Supreme Council's eyes, he probably submitted a far from truthful one.[51]

VII

It has already been mentioned that a move to bring politics into the Gaelic League was well under way in 1913, and Douglas Hyde himself was reported as having said, in August 1914, that Ireland could have no freedom without arms.[52] Even D. P. Moran, who usually abjured political nationalism, was beginning to suggest that the League had been too inactive and that the time had come to link it with the politics of Irish independence.[53] Moran had welcomed the Volunteer movement and condemned the Redmond recruiting drive, which his "Irish Ireland" philosophy detested: but even with all this going on in the minds of men who were not committed to physical force, nothing could have been done inside the League if it had not been for the careful work of the IRB.

As Diarmid Lynch put it, by the summer of 1915 the League's left wing was determined to gain control of the Coista Gnotha, "not to use it for the purposes of Republicanism" — that was always too much to expect — "but to obviate the possibility of tactics contrary thereto."[54] He had, therefore, carefully circulated among those Leaguers who were also IRB men instructions to get delegates sent to the Ard-Fheis who were favorable to their point of view.

The Ard-Fheis gathered at Dundalk late in July, and a resolution was passed to the effect that one of the objects of the League was to work for national independence. Even then, Lynch thought, Hyde might have accepted a resolution so distasteful to him, if it had not been for the result of the elections for the new Coista Gnotha. When the name of Sean Mac-Diarmida appeared high on the list and was followed by that of another political prisoner — then and then only did Hyde throw down his papers and leave the meeting. Thus cultural nationalism was, for the time being, ritually dead: whereas one can see the beginnings of an alliance between Irish Ireland and physical force which was actively consummated in the Easter Rising.

A delegation was sent to Hyde to beg him to change his mind; he was universally popular and respected; and Eoin MacNeill, who became President of the League in his place, was by no means so useful as a front man. But Hyde had had enough.*

VIII

A far clearer and far more deliberate sign of disaffection was given in August, when the body of O'Donovan Rossa was buried in Dublin's Glasnevin Cemetery. The old Fenian hero had died in New York in July, and was brought back to Ireland to lie in state in City Hall. His funeral on 1 August was a national event; tens of thousands were in the streets; the British soldiers, the Dublin police were alike absent; the traffic was controlled by the Irish Volunteers and the Irish Citizen Army. For the first and last time the National Volunteers and the Irish Volunteers marched in the same parade, along with the Fianna na hEireann (now a direct training school for IRB commandos), the Cumann na mBann, the Citizen Army, and also with other less ardent groups.

The IRB was the organizer behind the huge committee which managed

---

* In the fullness of time, his devotion was suitably rewarded, and on 4 May 1938 this Protestant scholar was elected first President of the Republic of Ireland.

the whole affair and it was determined to let no chance escape of using this occasion for its own purposes. Padraic Pearse, who had been instructed by Tom Clarke to "throw discretion to the winds," gave the funeral oration. It was short and, to an English ear, Augustine Birrell's at least, mere fustian. "I do not suppose," the Chief Secretary said, when reading the newspaper reports of the funeral, "anybody in the whole concourse cared anything for the old fellow, who never cared for anything at any time." And O'Donovan Rossa, perhaps, could Pearse's words have reached him in the fields of asphodel, might have experienced some difficulty in recognizing himself: — "Splendid and holy causes are served by men who are splendid and holy. O'Donovan Rossa was splendid in the proud manhood of him, splendid in the heroic grace of him, splendid in the Gaelic strength and clarity and truth of him." But Mr. Birrell was abysmally wrong in thinking that Rossa never cared for anything or that nobody in the huge crowd cared anything for him. The speech was not directed to a mind like Augustine Birrell's, it was directed to a mind like Tom Clarke's. Its closing words are still remembered: —

The Defenders of this Realm have worked well in secret and in the open. They think that they have pacified Ireland. They think that they have purchased half of us and intimidated the other half. They think that they have foreseen everything, think that they have provided against everything; but the fools, the fools, the fools — they have left us our Fenian dead, and while Ireland holds these graves, Ireland unfree shall never be at peace."

Even James Connolly was moved by this, although Connolly had been heard to say before the funeral that he wished people would stop blethering about dead Fenians "and get us a few live ones for a change."

Chapter Twelve

Dublin, New York, Berlin: May 1915—March 1916

Ⅰn the midst of these events, in May 1915 the last Liberal Government in history came to an end, and a Coalition took its place. The war on the Western Front and in Gallipoli had been going badly; a shells scandal had begun to expose enormous flaws in Kitchener's regime at the War Office; the resignation of Lord Fisher as First Sea Lord was followed by an irresistible demand for the departure of Winston Churchill as First Lord of the Admiralty. Underneath these upheavals lay two things — a fear that the Liberal Government was not equipped to wage a global war and the existence of a profound division between the principles of voluntarism and compulsion.[1] Mr. Asquith had, in fact, rearranged his Cabinet with stern resolution, so as to maintain a balance between those who advocated one or the other of the two embattled principles, and thus to postpone the evil day when something positive would have to be done.

The Coalition of May 1915 did not on the surface change things very much. There were, it is true, eight Unionists in the Cabinet, but with the exception of A. J. Balfour, who went to the Admiralty, and Lord Kitchener, who was retained at the War Office with his powers greatly shorn, the Liberals kept all the key posts. Sir Edward Carson was admitted — and much against his will — as Attorney General, and Mr. Bonar Law appeared content with a virtual exile in the Colonial Office. The promotion of Lloyd George to the new Ministry of Munitions was the real portent. The ministry was the place where things were to be set in motion, where rumors of government unfitness were to be laid to rest. Mr. Asquith, although he refused to admit it, was not designed by nature to preside over the fate of battlefields or the management of the resources that go to feed them: and he had little more than a year to go before, as Augustine Birrell put it, he fell from his elephant.

To no one had the Coalition been more unwelcome than to John Redmond. On 18 May he had received a message from the Prime Minister that the ministry was about to be reconstructed on a broad national basis and "I am most anxious," wrote Mr. Asquith, "that you should join. The administration will be a war administration and will cease when the war is ended. . . . The opposition are anxious that Carson whose administrative gifts they value should be included."[2] Redmond replied that the principles and history of the Irish Party made an acceptance of the offer impossible: and he added, in a second message, that Carson's inclusion would do "infinite harm."[3] Was not Carson just as recalcitrant as ever about Home Rule? Then on 29 May there came rumors that James H. Campbell of Dublin was to be appointed Lord Chancellor of Ireland: Campbell, who was said to have signed the Ulster Covenant in his own blood, and who was generally regarded as a peculiarly odious example of a Unionist party hack![4] At this Redmond at last rebelled: "there is a limit to our patience," he wrote; and he enclosed a bitter Resolution of the Irish Party of 7 June and a letter from the Bishop of Killaloe who spoke of "the humiliation and ruin of Irish feeling." The rumor had indeed done the greatest mischief in Ireland, and on 9 June Asquith wrote to say that Campbell's "claim" to the chancellorship had been withdrawn. "We have all, in the face of the exigencies of the war," wrote the Prime Minister, "to make some sacrifices. I may fairly say that no one has made more than I have myself. Nothing but the most compelling sense of public duty could have induced me to be where I am, and surrounded as I am, and cut off as I am today."[5]

This was a genuine *cri du coeur*. It was more than distasteful for Mr. Asquith to be surrounded in the Cabinet by such new colleagues as Sir Edward Carson and Mr. Bonar Law and Mr. Walter Long. But Mr. Redmond's "sacrifices" had been greater: the Coalition, to him, seemed packed with enemies.

I

Augustine Birrell, also from the very beginning, hated the Coalition. He was the Liberal of Liberals; he had even become, now that Home Rule had been consigned to the end of some political rainbow, a more and more convinced Home Ruler; and the idea of serving with Unionists was a bitter one to him. Only his loyalty to a Prime Minister whom he loved, and to a Nationalist Party which had always been fair to him, kept him (he said) from resigning his post.[6] Nevertheless, although Parliament had become "detestable," although the Nationalist members — "my Irish friends" — rarely bothered to attend the House, although the ministerial Front Bench was now disfigured with prominent Tories, he was soon assuming, with his usual equanimity, his usual sway.[7]

It was essentially a mild one; and since October 1914 he had acquired in Sir Matthew Nathan an Under Secretary who suited him exactly.

Nathan, born in 1862, had been privately educated because his parents feared that the better-known public schools would not be comfortable for a Jewish boy. The Army was not so backward; he was entered at the Royal Military Academy, Woolwich; graduated very high on the list; and by way of service in Egypt, India, Burma and Sierra Leone became Governor of Natal with the rank of lieutenant colonel. He afterwards transferred his abilities to the Civil Service and was Chairman of the Inland Revenue Board, a post of great distinction which customarily carried a knighthood with it, when he was sent to Dublin to become, under Mr. Birrell, who was usually in London, the ruler of Ireland.

He was a handsome man, with charming manners and a fine voice, very attractive to ladies, whose advances he had resisted to the point of still remaining a bachelor, although he is said to have proposed to one of Lytton Strachey's sisters. He was hard-working, efficient and loyal: and, unlike Sir Antony MacDonnell, he did not attempt to initiate policies on his own.

Later on, in 1915, Mr. Birrell's lot was again made easier by the more or less forced retirement of the Lord-Lieutenant, the Earl of Aberdeen. The Aberdeens had not made themselves popular with the customary "shoneen" hangers-on because of the dinginess and frugality of their vice-regal court; and although the little earl was harmless enough, his large philanthropic countess was something of a political chimera, a cross between Mrs. Proudie and Lady Godiva (in mufti), who upset the Unionists by dabbling in democracy and the Administration by interfering with the departments. They retired to the consolations of a marquisate; and, in their place came Ivor Churchill Guest, Baron Wimborne. Like Lord Aberdeen, Lord Wimborne did not have a seat in the Cabinet, and was little more than a figurehead, a position he accepted with a very bad grace. At the time of his arrival, his chief asset was thought to be a charming wife.

Birrell and Nathan, therefore, were more or less able to set the tone of their administration without interference. They hoped that the Under Secretary could bring Dublin Castle more into touch with the current of national life;[8] and Sir Matthew Nathan made himself accessible to everyone who wished to see him. The trouble was that the current of national life was now liberally sprinkled with characters ("ruffians" in the Castle parlance) who did not wish to see Sir Matthew Nathan.

The information available to him and his chief came by way of the Crime Branch Special, a section of the Judicial Division, one of the seven main constituents of the Chief Secretary's Office. (The word "Special" referred to political as opposed to ordinary crimes, a distinction not always clear in Ireland.) This information was derived from the monthly confidential reports of the Inspector-General of the Royal Irish Constabulary, with their attached reports from the County Inspectors; from intelligence gathered by the Crime Department Special Branch of the Royal Irish Constabulary, the G. Division of the Dublin Metropolitan Police, and the Home Office; and the Crime Branch Special Files.[9] The General Office Commanding in Chief in Ireland, or Competent Military Authority, also had his Special Intelligence Branch, which communicated what seemed to it good.

Their problem very naturally was — how far should they use this information to push their governmental powers? If they had listened to Messrs. Redmond and Dillon, and to some extent they did, they would have not pushed them at all; and their own inclination was to give as little of the appearance of coercion as they could. To Birrell, and rather less to Nathan, wisdom required that one should not make unnecessary martyrs. Nonetheless, as the war became more and more unpopular, something had to be done. For example, the lower ranks of the Civil Service had been (Nathan thought) heavily infiltrated by "this undesirable organization Sinn Fein" — a term which the Under Secretary used for anyone or anything that savored of disaffection.[10]

Nathan himself suspected that the most treasonable elements were to be found in the Irish Post Office, a suspicion which he communicated — much to that gentleman's disgust — to Mr. Hamilton Norway, the head of the department. But Mr. Norway himself was soon disabused. He was told that two men on his own staff had actually joined the IRB. "Is it really a fact," he asked, "that that sinister body, a far more dangerous body than Sinn Fein, has come to life again?"[11] Sir Matthew replied that the IRB was indeed alive, but to the best of his knowledge of little importance except perhaps in Northern Ireland — an observation which would have been more to the point in 1907. He thought the best solution — and he persuaded a reluctant Birrell to get the Cabinet to approve it — was to issue a letter warning all Civil Servants that continued membership in the Irish Volunteers would bring with it instant dismissal.[12]

A greater difficulty, at least to Liberal minds, was the problem of the seditious press. There was a luxuriant crop of small publications, some very well written, all highly subversive. It was one of Mr. Birrell's idiosyncrasies that he considered the press, or a very large part of it, beneath his notice: and he saw no reason why one should bother to suppress these little sheets. Nathan was not so sanguine. The Irish, he said, were a very imaginative people, and they were more easily affected by what they read than a duller race would be.

After the publication of the Defence of the Realm Act Regulations in the Dublin *Gazette* on 2 December 1914, a number of suppressions certainly took place, all of which have been recorded in Mr. MacGiolla Choille's admirably edited *Intelligence Notes,* and among the victims was *Irish Worker,* which Larkin had bequeathed to Connolly on his departure for America in October 1914. But when Connolly's *Workers' Republic* began publication in May 1915, without bothering to register in the manner prescribed by the Newspaper Libel and Registration Act of 1881, no action was taken against it.[13] This argues a dispensation rather mild than otherwise, for the *Workers' Republic* was a highly provocative sheet. Each week, on its back page, it would discuss insurrection in terms of what had taken place other times in other countries; for example, in Moscow in 1905; or in the Tyrol in 1809; or at the Alamo — "one of those defeats that are often more valuable to a cause than loudly trumpeted victories."[14]

This last example deserves our attention: for Connolly was thinking in terms less of military victory than of military *action*. In 1915, he knew nothing of the tentative plans being made for a Rising in the spring of 1916; he was not a member of the IRB, still less of its Military Council. Moreover, his Transport Union, still recovering from its defeat in 1913, was showing few signs of the radicalism it was to develop in 1919 and 1920; and his Citizen Army, sole representative of a militant working class movement, cannot at this date have much exceeded the 250 members observed by William O'Brien in Croyden Park in March 1914. It had, however, acquired an able chief of staff in Michael Mallin, ex-soldier and former secretary of a silk weavers' union; its discipline had been tightened; and it had acquired some arms, chiefly British army rifles "whose owners had parted with them willingly or unwillingly."[15] It was to this exiguous force that Connolly began to look for the occupants of his Irish Alamo.

He had never been a quietist, even for the sake of policy. When he became acting General Secretary of the ITGWU in October 1914, he put a large streamer across the front of Liberty Hall: "We serve neither King nor Kaiser — but Ireland." In the laconic words of William O'Brien, of the Tailors' Union, "This attracted a good deal of attention and was taken down by the British authorities on 19 December 1914."[16] Connolly had, in fact, begun to ask himself whether the Irish movement for national independence might not be "in its own right" — always supposing it became responsive to the demands of the workers — "a factor making for the overthrow of European capitalism."[17]

It is a measure of this turn toward nationalism that he would sometimes give lectures on street fighting to the Volunteers: his Citizen army as a whole had little use for them. This antipathy was quite mutual; it was a difference between lower middle class and proletariat, between stout and porter; and MacNeill had even been known to remark that the "Volunteers had no need of an organization that had recently been in conflict with the police."[18] Connolly, for his part, lectures or no, became increasingly impatient with the Volunteers. At length, in November 1915 he took up the cudgels in *Workers' Republic:* "Revolutionists who shrink from giving blow for blow" he wrote, "until . . . they have every shoe-string in its place and every man has got his gun, — and the enemy has kindly consented to postpone action so as not to . . . disarrange their plans — such revolutionists only exist in two places — the comic opera stage and the stage of Irish national politics. We prefer the comic opera brand. It at least serves its purpose."[19] The epigraph for this article was from Clarence Magnan, the poet of '48: — "Youth of Ireland, stand prepared/Revolution's dread abyss/Burns beneath us all but bared." A month later, profoundly disturbed by peace rumors in the American press, he asked in the *Workers' Republic:*

"Where does Ireland come in? Why should Ireland come in? What has she done to deserve separate discussion in the peace terms?"[20] He was now convinced that nothing but an insurrection during the war would give Ireland her right to be heard at the peace table. Whether that insurrection was successful or not was beginning to be quite immaterial; indeed, he was getting ready to come out with his little Citizen Army, if the Volunteers did not make a move.

He was somewhat restrained by the fact that he was now conducting a strike on the Dublin quays: it began on 27 October 1915 when forty casual laborers came out at North Wall for an increase of daily pay from 5s 8d to 6s 2d, or sixpence a day. The English and Scottish companies came to terms, but the Dublin Steam Packet Company, owned by the reactionary Watson family, held out and blared its defiance in the 1 November issue of the *Irish Times*. Connolly, for his part, was demanding the recognition of his Transport Union by the Steam Packet Company: and "This might become serious," Nathan noted on the Dublin Metropolitan Police report before sending it on to the Irish Office in London, and "It looks like a row," was Birrell's response.*

The strike apparently reached a settlement on 15 April 1916: but long before that Connolly's patience was wearing very thin. In an editorial of 22 January 1916, called "What Is Our Programme?" he wrote:

"We shall continue to teach that . . . a defeat of England in India, Egypt, the Balkans or Flanders would not be so dangerous to the British Empire as any conflict of armed forces in Ireland, that the time for Ireland's battle is NOW, the place for Ireland's battle is HERE."

---

* The strike is well covered in a lengthy file (Chief Secretary's Office Registered Papers #5952) in the Dublin State Paper Office: or rather well covered until 4 April 1916, when the file abruptly and mysteriously ceases with a minute from Nathan to Sir George Askwith, Chief Industrial Commissioner in London, to the effect that nothing more can be done for the time being to bring it to an end. It is evident from the minutes in this file that Askwith had a very poor opinion of Edward Watson, who managed the Steam Packet Company; that he refused to employ the Munitions Act in Watson's favor; and that Nathan was proof against demands to seize Liberty Hall, confiscate the weapons of the Irish Citizen Army, deport Connolly to Edinburgh, and so on. The strike received a flurry of unfavorable attention on 21 January 1916 in the *Irish Times*, the *Freeman's Journal* and the *Dublin Express;* otherwise it was not mentioned in the Dublin press; and it received no attention whatsoever in the London papers. On 15 April 1916 a notice in the *Irish Times* announced the departure of the Steam Packet Co.'s ships from Dublin to Liverpool on 18, 19, and 22 April and from Dublin to Belfast on 19 April. This would *seem* to indicate that the strike was settled on 15 April: but on what terms it is impossible to discover or even exactly when (since the statistical department of the Board of Trade stopped publishing strike figures in 1916). Thus James Connolly's last industrial dispute has, to some extent, slipped through a hole in history: but it is to be noticed that he considered it — according to a speech reported in the file — an opportunity to strengthen the Citizen Army.

And he ended the editorial with a thrust at the "stupidity" of the Irish Volunteers.

The Military Council in the meantime had been immensely strengthened by the co-option of Tom Clarke and Sean MacDiarmida in August 1915. These two formidable men were really running the IRB by the end of 1915: when Denis McCullogh succeeded S. Deakin as President of The Supreme Council in December, he left everything to them. They proposed to control the Irish Volunteers through the two thousand or so IRB members who had been ordered to join that force, and not one of whom realized that its headquarters had been taken over by an inner group whose orders, not MacNeill's, they would have to obey when the Rising came.

Toward the end of 1915, the Military Council had agreed that the Rising should come on Easter Sunday, 23 April 1916.

Here Connolly became a genuine menace, since there were many indications that he would start a premature insurrection with the Irish Citizen Army and thus ruin all their plans. On 19 January Connolly disappeared, and whether he was kidnapped or went of his own free will is still a matter of dispute. When he returned to his friends on 22 January he was silent as to where he had been or what he had done; although it is now quite obvious that he met with members of the Military Council; that he was told for the first time of the Council's existence and of its plans for a Rising on Easter Sunday; that he was informed of the extent to which the IRB had infiltrated the Irish Volunteer Headquarters and the Volunteers themselves; that he was offered an alliance; that he accepted.[21] Membership in the IRB was not necessary, but co-option into the Military Council followed as a matter of course. His editorials in the *Workers' Republic* were now no longer dangerous in the eyes of the Military Council; indeed they served as a kind of smoke screen; and they became — particularly on 12 February and 25 March — if anything more militant than before.

II

Among the plans confided to Connolly were those for American and German cooperation in the Rising; and to understand these it is necessary to return to 1914.

If the United Irish League in America had become moribund as a result of John Redmond's speeches, the Clan na Gael had been restored to a new life with the coming of war. The Clan was a secret organization only in the sense that little was or is known of its numbers or financing. In spite of many fissions since its founding in 1867, it retained intact its belief in the future independence of Ireland and in physical force as a means of securing it. The Clan had attracted attention during the Boer War — more attention than funds, for its treasury was in poor shape. It was centered in New York but drew its support from all the great American cities; and one of its leaders was the Fenian John Devoy, editor of the *Gaelic American,* a paper which made up in force for what it lacked in refinement.

It was the *Gaelic American* which started an Irish Volunteer Fund in July 1914; by August, as Pearse told McGarrity, $26,000 had been pledged and $5,000 had actually arrived in Ireland. How much of the $44,000 eventually raised by the Fund was allocated to *direct* help cannot be ascertained,[22] although Devoy's recollection that the Fund, supplemented by the Clan na Gael's remittance to the IRB, made "in all fully $100,0000 supplied to the men of Easter Week,"[23] certainly indicates that the Clan became an important influence in the schemes of the Military Council.

Shortly before the outbreak of war, Sir Roger Casement arrived in New York and presented himself to Devoy. "I think," he wrote to Colonel Moore before he left, "money could be got where I am going shortly. This is in strict *confidence* — don't tell outsiders. That is my chief object in going . . . I hope to go soon, very soon — and quietly — and see only a few of the right ones and if funds can be got there we may carry on ourselves."[24]

Since Sir Roger had supported Redmond as a "necessary evil," and Colonel Moore was a Redmondite, if a captious one, this letter was hardly candid: for Sir Roger persuaded Devoy that he had come to America to raise funds for the anti-Redmondite minority — so persuasively, in fact, that the Clan's Revolutionary Directory at once accepted him as a personage of "proven sincerity," and he addressed meetings of Irishmen in Norfolk, Virginia, and in Philadelphia.[25]

With the outbreak of war, Casement threw off the mask of fund raiser and stood forth as a fanatical Anglophobe. The pleas that England had gone to war in defense of little Belgium meant less than nothing to him: he had seen what little Belgium could do in the Congo. "I pray for the salvation of Germany," he wrote, "night and day — and God Save Ireland is another form of God Save Germany." He now composed a memorial to Kaiser Wilhelm, setting forth the old argument that the freedom of Ireland was essential to the freedom of the seas, but setting it forth in language so fulsome that the Clan executives themselves were taken aback, although they all signed the document. It was apparently sent to Germany by diplomatic pouch.[26]

It so happened that a special Committee of the Clan, soon after the outbreak of war, had met with the German Ambassador, Count von Bernstorff, and his military attaché, Captain von Papen, at the German Club in New York City. Here it laid before the two Germans the hopes of its Irish friends to set up an independent government and their further hopes that Germany would supply them with military help. Von Bernstorff agreed to send a dispatch to Germany: and a handwritten copy of this dispatch eventually found its way to Tom Clarke's tobacco shop in North Great Britain Street.[27]

Sir Roger Casement had also, with the Committee's blessing, visited Captain von Papen to suggest that an Irish Brigade could be recruited from Irish prisoners of war in German prison camps — a suggestion that von Bernstorff relayed to Berlin as "a grand idea, if only it could be carried out."[28]

Casement now burned his boats by writing and sending to the Dublin *Independent,* which published it on 5 October, a letter calling on all Irishmen to refrain from bearing arms against Germany. Had not Ireland suffered at the hands of Great Britain "a more prolonged series of evils, deliberately inflicted, than any other community of civilized men?"[29] This letter so horrified Alice Stopford Green that she shifted her support to the National Volunteers, or so she told Colonel Moore, although she never abandoned her personal loyalty to Casement or her distaste for Redmond.[30]

Ten days after this letter's publication in Dublin, Casement left New York for Germany. He was now so excited that Devoy, who supplied him with the necessary funds, began seriously to doubt the wisdom of sending him at all. He left by the Norwegian steamer *Oskar II,* accompanied by a young Norwegian sailor named Adler Christiansen, who had accosted him on the streets of New York; and in order to disguise his striking appearance he had shaved off his beard and washed his face in buttermilk to get a fair complexion.

In Christiania he escaped (it was long believed or suspected) an attempt on the part of the British Minister, Mr. Mansfeldt Findlay, to have him kidnapped and even murdered. It has now been established that the facts were just the other way around — that Christiansen tried to betray his master to Mr. Findlay, and that he was put off by a subordinate in the legation with a few kroner.[31] Christiansen later slipped into Norway and extracted a written promise from Mr. Findlay (to whom Casement had now become an interesting traitor) that he would receive £5000 if he brought about his capture. Casement knew nothing of this: to him Mr. Findlay was and remained a murderous villain who tried in vain to bribe his faithful companion.

He had come to Germany convinced that he would find there "a peace-loving, harmless Germany, wishing only to be allowed her modest place in the sun."[32] There had indeed been some preliminary courtesies — Herr Zimmermann, Graf von Wedel, Chancellor von Bethmann-Hollweg listened politely while he poured into their ears his accusations against Mr. Find-lay — accusations which, with the peculiar fraternity among professionals which existed even in wartime, they did not in the least believe and never intended to use. At the end of December 1914, however, Casement actually signed a "Treaty" with the German Government — or at any rate a document which bore a German seal although it was never ratified by any Irish body. Its ten articles were predicated upon the existence of an Irish Brigade, to be fed and equipped but not paid by the German Government, to be furnished with an Irish uniform and to fight only under the Irish flag; and its tenth article promised to recognize Ireland as an independent nation once its Government had been established.

Its sixth and most delusive article read in part as follows:

In the event of a German naval victory affording the means of reaching the coast of Ireland, the Imperial German Government pledges itself to despatch the Irish Brigade and a supporting body of German officers and men, in German transports, to attempt a landing on the Irish coast.[33]

Little dependence could be put upon (1) a German naval victory of sweeping proportions and (2) less upon the formation of an Irish Brigade. The German authorities may be excused for not guessing at the inner quiddities of the Irish soldier's mind: and Sir Roger had all the innocence of a true fanatic. Otherwise, how could he have supposed that Irish prisoners of war, all old soldiers, all belonging to famous regiments, all survivors of heroic engagements such as Mons and Étreux, would succumb to the blandishments of an Antrim civilian with an English accent? The prisoners of war were all moved to camp at Limburg, but out of the more than two thousand men, only fifty-three yielded to Sir Roger's solicitations.

Thus Joseph Plunkett's mission in April–June 1915 received no encouragement from the German General Staff, because the concept of an Irish Brigade was falling apart and because he had no definite plans to offer. By September 1915, however, the Military Council in Dublin had agreed that a landing of German arms and (if possible) soldiers could be made in Tralee Bay: and, later on, at some unspecified date in the early winter, Tom Clarke sent Devoy an Ordnance Map upon which the harbor of Fenit was clearly marked; and Devoy had sent a map of Kerry to Berlin with the same marking,[34] which, when at length it arrived, at once became decisive.

On 5 February 1916, two weeks after Connolly's "disappearance" and his meeting with the Military Council, Tommy O'Connor, the ship's steward, brought to New York a message from the Council, undated, unsigned and in cipher. It began with a description of British military strength in Ireland, and said that the Military Council could not expect the authorities to remain inactive much longer. It had therefore decided to strike on "Easter Sunday" (in Devoy's version). The message then "proceeded to state," writes Devoy, "that they wanted us 'to send a shipload of arms to Limerick Quay between April 20 and 23' . . . They wanted German military help after they had struck the first blow and did not in any way request it until they themselves had risen . . ."[35]

Devoy is not altogether clear; but there exists, on this point, a more reliable source. *Documents Relative to the Sinn Fein Movement,* a white paper put out by the British Government in 1921, contains some documents seized in a New York raid on a German agency in April 1916. It also contains something more to the point. Captain Reginald Hall and his brilliant staff at Room 40 in the Admiralty in London had broken the German codes, and the ciphered messages passing between the German Embassy in Washington and the Wilhelmstrasse in Berlin were, if intercepted, as clear as day. Thus we find in the *Documents* that Devoy's "Confidential Report" — the message brought by Tommy O'Connor — was sent to the German Embassy for "telegraphic transmission [to Berlin]" on 10 February. It reads in part: "We have decided to begin action on Easter Saturday. Unless new circumstances arise we must have your arms and munitions between Good Friday and Easter Saturday. We expect German help immediately after beginning action. We might be compelled to act earlier." This was not sent by wireless, but dispatched by S.S. *Sommelsdyk* to a cover address in Rotterdam. On 17 February, however, Ambassador von Bernstorff attached to a wireless message concerning the *Lusitania* negotiations the following words in code: "The Irish leader, John Devoy, informs me that a rising is to begin in Ireland on *Easter Saturday.* Please send arms to [arrive] at Limerick, west coast of Ireland, between Good Friday and Easter Saturday. To put it off longer is impossible. Let me know if help may be expected from Germany."[36] This message was intercepted and decoded by Room 40.

On 12 February, Miss Philomena Plunkett arrived in New York: she had come to assist her mother, Madame Plunkett, in advancing the canonization of the Blessed Oliver Plunkett, and, as part of her baggage on this mission, she carried a duplicate of the message brought by O'Connor, together with some additional information. When the German armament vessels neared the Irish coast, they were to wireless "Finn" if all was well, "Brann" if there was danger: and if the trawlers were not fitted with wireless these messages were to be sent from Germany and picked up by private receiving stations in Ireland. "Finn" would then mean that the cargo had left on time; "Brann" that it had been postponed.[37] As Devoy points out in his *Recollections,* he detected the mythological hand of Padraic Pearse in this romantic and amateur arrangement, since Finn was Fion, chief of the mythical Fianna, and Brann was his dog, who always scented danger first and gave warning.[38]

On 15 February, as Professor Alan J. Ward discovered, Devoy transmitted the news brought by Miss Plunkett, and added a request for a German flotilla carrying one hundred thousand rifles, together with artillery and German officers.[39] To this the Germans made no direct answer; but in a message from the Wilhelmstrasse, dated 1 March, and replying at last to Count von Bernstorff's message of 17 February, they said: "Between 20th. and 23rd. April, in the evening, two or three steam-trawlers could land 20,0000 rifles and 10 machine guns, with ammunition and explosives, at Fenit Pier in Tralee Bay. Irish pilot-boat to await trawlers at dusk, north of Innistookert, at the entrance of Tralee Bay, and show two green lights close to each other at close intervals."[40] They had evidently studied Devoy's map of Kerry with Fenit marked on it: and Fenit was certainly a probable and Limerick an improbable landing place. It appears that Room 40 failed to intercept this message: but such was not the case with the answer, a code message sent on 12 March by wireless from the German Embassy to a "Banker Max Moeblius" in Berlin. Decoded, it read: "Irish agree to proposition. Necessary steps have been taken."[41] This represents Devoy's decision to accept German arms without German soldiers: but it forced Captain Reginald Hall to reveal, in the most cautious fashion possible, something of what he knew. He therefore issued a report to General G. M. W. MacDonagh, Director of Military Intelligence, and General MacDonagh, on 22 March, citing "an absolutely reliable source" as his authority, told Field Marshal Lord French, Commander-in-Chief of the Home Forces, that there might be a rising on Saturday 22 April and that the Germans were to bring arms to Limerick on that day. On 23 March, General L. B. Friend, the Competent Military Authority in Ireland, was shown General MacDonagh's report: but he was not told of the identity of the "absolutely reliable source"; nor was Lord French: and as for Lord Wimborne and Mr. Birrell, who met with French in London that day, they were not told anything at all. Captain Hall was naturally anxious about preserving in the greatest secrecy the fact that his cryptographers had broken the German codes: and to him, as to General MacDonagh, politicians were as leaky as sieves. On the whole, Captain Hall would have chanced a rising all over Ireland rather than give the Germans an inkling of the truth; and any loose civilian talk about "absolutely reliable sources" might have proved disastrous. Mr. Birrell and Sir Matthew Nathan, therefore, along with the Viceroy, were left entirely in the dark: and when General Friend, himself only half informed, asked Sir Matthew what he thought of Lord French's proposals to increase the Irish garrisons and replace jury trials with courts-martial, the innocent Nathan replied — "I do not believe that [the] leaders mean insurrection or that the Volunteers have sufficient arms if the leaders do mean it."[42] That was on 10 April 1916, with the insurrection just two weeks away.

All through 1915, Mr. Birrell and Sir Matthew Nathan had pursued their policy — on the whole a very sensible one — of "minimum action and maximum inaction." Why stir up trouble in that excitable land? As Dr. Leon Ó Broin has shown, in his distinguished writing on this period, neither Lord Wimborne (who did not count for much) nor General Friend (who did) could persuade them into such strong measures as "proclaiming" the Irish Volunteers. The silence of Dublin Castle in the face of deliberate provocation at the funeral of O'Donovan Rossa is an example of the kind of government they were trying to run.

As 1915 grew older, however, they grew more apprehensive. Recruiting was running down, the incidence of violent speeches and hostile demonstrations was increasing, money was being openly collected for the purchase of arms, the influence of Mr. Redmond was on the wane, and the war was becoming steadily more awful. In England, Mr. Asquith was in deep trouble. It was not until November that he was able to set up a new War Council, while Lord Kitchener was away in Gallipoli: it consisted of himself, Mr. Balfour, Mr. Bonar Law and two mutual enemies, Mr. Lloyd George and Mr. Reginald McKenna. French was relieved of his command on the Western Front and his place was taken by a cooler personality and suppler politician, Sir Douglas Haig. Lord Kitchener, returning from the Dardanelles, found his apparatus dismantled and his powers transferred to the Chief of the Imperial General Staff, Sir William Robertson, a bluff and formidable master of all the arts of professionally sticking in the mud — in more senses than one, alas, since he was a firm believer in the primacy of war in the Western Theater. Lord Kitchener loyally agreed to remain at the War Office, his functions curtailed to "feeding and clothing the army."[43] These changes soon registered nothing more than a weird oscillation between coherence and collapse. Composed only of departmental ministers (in itself a fatal disadvantage), the War Council was also subjected, as its court of last resort, to what Mr. Asquith called the "plenum" of the Cabinet — to the bemused deliberations (as L. S. Amery put it) "of twenty-three gentlemen assembling without any purpose and without any idea of what they were going to talk about."[44]

The Chief Secretary was haunted by the fear that all this portended the fall of his beloved Asquith: by this fear and yet another — he was gravely alarmed by the threat of compulsory military service and by the possibility that it might be extended to Ireland. In December the Cabinet's "plenum" almost broke in two over the question of compulsory service for bachelors and by the related and even more vexing problem of the allocation of human resources: and among those who threatened to resign was Birrell himself. The crisis was averted with only the loss of Sir John Simon: on New Year's Eve Mr. Birrell was able to assure Mr. Redmond that the danger was over;[45] and when a conscription bill for bachelors was passed on 18 January 1916 there was no reference in it to the bachelors of Ireland.

And yet the horrid specter of Irish conscription could not be exorcized — it never was until the end of the war. In March 1916 it appeared again, conjured up by Sir Edward Carson and the Unionist back benchers; even Mr. Lloyd George, whose attitude had been hitherto somewhat ambivalent, was said to be joining in. In short, something more inclusive than the bachelor compulsion act was being called for; the news was sedulously spread throughout Ireland; and there were signs of disturbance everywhere. On 17 March there was even a St. Patrick's Day rally of Irish Volunteers along College Green: they had gone through a series of military drills and had then marched past their Chief of Staff, Eoin MacNeill. All this took two hours, during which traffic was simply brought to a stop, usually by men armed with rifles and bayonets, while Dublin Castle maintained its customary silence.

Mr. Birrell, indeed, was no longer too apprehensive. Looking back over the past twelve months, he could even congratulate himself upon having maintained a judicious balance between conciliation and firmness. In spite of the untrustworthiness of juries, had not Sean MacDiarmida been sentenced to six months for anti-recruiting speeches? Had not Irish Volunteer organizers such as Ernest Blythe and Desmond Fitzgerald been put away for other offenses against the Defence of the Realm Act? Had not Liam Mellows, another organizer, been imprisoned — he was one of a small group whom Birrell called the "banishees" — for refusing to obey a deportation order? He was not surprised to hear of continuous disaffection in Kerry and Galway, in Cork and Clare: but such reports were often exaggerated.

Even the Dublin Metropolitan Police informers added to this air of false security. On 16 March a certain "Chalk" told the DMP's G Division that the young men of the Irish Volunteer Brigade in Dublin were anxious to "start business" at once; that they were strongly backed by Connolly and the Citizen Army; and that "things look as if they are coming to a crisis." On the other hand, said "Chalk," who had a baffling propensity to hedge his bets, the leaders of the Irish Volunteers were "against a rising" for the time being, saying it would be madness to attempt such a thing "if the help promised by Monteith were not forthcoming." Monteith was a former clerk in the Ordnance Department, who had become an Irish Volunteer organizer and had disappeared in November 1915. He was reported to have reappeared in Germany in December as an assistant to Sir Roger Casement.[46] As for the "help promised," the G Division of the DMP took little stock in that.

On 20 March the Irish Volunteers in Tullamore — or the "Sinn Fein party" as the District Inspector called them — fell foul of the local branch of the Gaelic Athletic Association over (of all things) a display of Union Jacks by soldiers' wives celebrating the return of their husbands from the front. Pursued by an angry crowd, the Volunteers locked themselves into the headquarters, the Volunteer Hall; and two policemen were wounded when they attempted to break in.[47] As a result of this, Liam Mellows was deported to Leek in Staffordshire: while Thomas MacDonagh was reported by the industrious "Chalk" as telling a Volunteer meeting in Father Matthew Park on 22 March that "had the instructions given been carried out at Tullamore not one policeman would have crossed the door alive."[48]

This rather ominous remark was cancelled out by the report of an informer called "Granite" who told the G Division that the "members of the IRB section of the Irish Volunteers" — he did *not* mean the Military Council, then and thereafter a dead secret — were divided as to the wisdom of the Tullamore affair; and that "there is at present no fear of any rising by the Volunteers" since the majority of them was "practically unarmed and not sufficiently equipped."[49] This seems to have calmed all fears: so much so that when "Granite" mentioned by name those who had rifles and ammunition stored in their houses — among them Michael O'Hanrahan of 67 Connaught Street and Eamon de Valera of 33 Morehampton Terrace — no effort was made to find out if this was true.[50] The deliberately quietist policy of Dublin Castle and the Irish Office — "maximum inaction and minimum action" — thus prevailed until the Rising struck.

Chapter Thirteen

To the General Post Office: 9 April–24 April 1916

The news of the triangular negotiations between the Clan na Gael in New York, the Wilhelmstrasse in Berlin and the Military Council in Dublin came very belatedly to Sir Roger Casement, and, when it did come, came as a great blow.

He had long been neglected by his hosts. When they first announced his presence in Germany, on 20 November 1914,[1] he was something to crow about, an Irish Nationalist with an English knighthood. His usefulness was now over. He was sick, he seemed at times demented, and his genuine character of "well-known Irish Nationalist" was becoming, in their cynical eyes, less and less distinguishable from that of well-known English traitor. When it became clear as early as January 1915 that the Irish prisoners of war, moved for that purpose to Limburg, would have very little to do with an Irish Brigade; when the Germans refused to make an issue of Mr. Findlay; when his "Treaty" was not made public — then indeed Casement began to despair. He was an innocent idealist: he had fallen into the hands of men who cared little for such persons, and who did not bother to conceal their feelings. On 11 February he closed the first volume of his "German Diary" with the statement that he was being "played upon, fooled and used by a most selfish and unscrupulous government for its sole petty interest."[2]

Plunkett's treatment by Captain Nodolny only served to reinforce this "ever-growing want of faith in the German authorities": and when his visitor departed toward the end of June, "as I saw him off I thought the last link with hope was going from me."[3] Adler Christiansen, a trivial and faithless lover but still trusted, had left for the United States, probably not long before this;[4] and Casement now looked for friendship to Father Crotty of Limburg, St. John Gaffney the former American Consul-General in Munich, and the Irish-American Dr. Charles Curry and his family. Dr. Curry found him rooms at Riderau on the Amsee near Munich; and at Riderau Casement remained until his health broke down just after Christmas. Christiansen, before losing all credit with John Devoy, had at least brought Robert Monteith as far as Norway in November, and Monteith ("an invaluable man, loyal, brave, untiring and of great fidelity — what I should have done without him I know not")[5] was sent to Zossen to keep order among the unruly fifty-three who had now been "brigaded" there. He had become and remained one of Casement's staunchest admirers.

Dr. Curry and St. John Gaffney had procured Casement's admission to a sanatorium in Munich, and plans were made (with Casement's consent) to return him to America, when news arrived that a Rising was to take place on Holy Saturday and that the Germans proposed to support it with a shipload of twenty thousand rifles and a complement of ammunition and explosives. Casement was fully briefed on the shipload by representatives of the German General Staff on 16 March. "This," he told Curry in a long and desperate letter ten days later, "this was the final blow."

"I can't withdraw," he wrote. "They want to get rid of the whole thing at the cheapest cost to themselves — a tramp steamer, 20,000 old rifles" — actually Russian rifles captured by Hindenburg in 1914 — "4,000,000 cartridges and 10 machine guns. Monteith and the Irish Brigade and I go to our dooms — and the German Government washes its hands of all responsibility."[6]

In this letter he went on to rehearse the "crass stupidity" of the German Government in convincing the Irish prisoners of war at the very outset, through a set of clumsy questions, that Casement was a paid German agent; how when Joseph Plunkett urged him "imperatively" to try once more, pleading "no Irish Brigade, no Treaty," he found on arrival at Limburg on 10 May (12 May in Plunkett's Diary) that Captain Boehm of the General

Staff had issued yet another blundering questionnaire which ruined everything; and how he sent Plunkett home to Ireland with a photograph of the
Treaty hidden in a hollow walking stick and with instructions to urge
everyone on no account to rise. Then on 4 January 1916 the Germans withdrew their December promise to send his fifty-three recruits to the East "to
help drive England out of Egypt"; and at this "I broke down finally and
wished I were dead."

"At long last," he continued,

> when the sea is hermetically sealed and the British Government on the watch
> both at sea and in Ireland, this mad attempt is being made — and if I don't
> accompany it I shall be held a coward — and by going expose myself to the
> most dreadful fate . . . The British will not honour me with a High Trea-
> son trial. I am convinced of that. I should become a martyr or a Hero of
> revolutionary Ireland. They will rob Ireland of that and will charge me with
> something else — something baser than "high treason" — God knows what —
> and what chance of a trial will I have on any charge they choose to get up
> against me? . . . I go to far worse than death — death with the cause of
> Ireland to sustain me would be a joyful ending — but I go to a sham trial,
> to be wounded in my honour — to be defamed with no chance of defence
> probably and then a term of convict imprisonment that will end my days in
> jail — a convict. For I should not long support the indignities and miseries I
> should be exposed to.

Indeed the only hope was "to be killed at once . . . to perish in the
attempt."

He left his German diary — *"very confidential"* — in care of Dr. Curry,
together with the papers of "the poor forlorn little 'Irish Brigade.'" He
hoped these would one day be edited into a memoir by E. D. Morel and
Alice Stopford Green — it would at least save his reputation when he was
gone. And John Devoy — "had I lived I wanted to pay him back the sum of
at least $7,500": for the Clan na Gael had never ceased to finance him.

Since Article 6 of the Treaty could not possibly be implemented, Captain
Nodolny agreed that the Irish Brigade could be left behind. Casement seems
then to have tried, at least twice and in vain, to get messages through to Sir
Edward Grey, his old employer, saying that Germany was about to betray
Ireland.[7] He next insisted that he and Monteith should go to Ireland by
submarine: he was determined to stop the Rising if he could; if he could not,
then he would die in the fighting.

The trouble was that he and Monteith had not come into the negotiations at all. Devoy's agreement to a shipment of arms without troops (which both Casement and Monteith regarded as fatal) had been made without their knowledge. It was not until 6 or 7 April, in a message smuggled through from Count Plunkett in Berne, that he learned that Easter Sunday, 23 April, was the day fixed.[8] On 7 April, the German Foreign Office agreed to send him, Monteith, and a Sergeant Julian Bayley by submarine.[9] On 9 April the arms and ammunition ship, the *Aud,* disguised as a Norwegian freighter with a cargo of lumber, left Lubeck under the command of Captain Karl Spindler. She sailed off into a silence, for she had not been equipped to send or receive wireless messages.

The *Aud*'s journey has been told in full detail by Captain Spindler in his *Mystery of the Casement Ship.* His account of the critical night of 20 April has since been seriously questioned: but his voyage, regarded simply as a voyage, was a great success. Sailing between the east coast of Norway and the Shetlands, he turned around just south of the Arctic Sea, crept down between Iceland and the Faroes, and made a precise landfall on Thursday 20 April. First correctly at Innistookert, then perhaps incorrectly in Tralee Bay, Spindler waited in vain for the Irish pilot and for the submarine bringing Casement and his companions. There was no pilot boat; Fenit itself was dark and silent; the submarine was invisible.

Room 40 of the Admiralty still believed that the arms were to be landed on Saturday; but Captain Hall had, at least, seen to it that the west and south coasts of Ireland would be adequately patrolled all week. On Good Friday, 21 April, Spindler decided to cruise to and fro in Tralee Bay and then make for Lisbon under cover of darkness. He was hailed by one armed trawler and passed as a Norwegian; escaped another; and was at last intercepted by H.M. SS. *Zinnia* and *Bluebell* and compelled to follow *Bluebell* as she set a course for Queenstown. On the next morning, Saturday 22 April, as he trailed his captor into Queenstown harbor, Spindler suddenly ran up the German flag, he and his crew abandoned ship, and the *Aud,* with a charge of dynamite in her hold, blew up and sank to the bottom.

Casement, Monteith and Bayley left Wilhelmshafen in the Submarine U20 on 12 April and transferred into the U19 at Heligoland. The U19's captain had orders to transship his passengers into the *Aud* or, failing that, to put them ashore in a collapsible boat. Captain Weisbech reached the Thursday rendezvous on time; but the *Aud* had (presumably) put in at the wrong part of Tralee Bay. The U19, therefore, went on through the darkness to Ballyheigue Bay and set Casement and his companions ashore in the early morning of Good Friday. It was here on Banna Strand, on the bleak Kerry coast, that Casement experienced his first happiness in more than a year. He sent his companions on to Tralee to look for help and for Monteith to get a message through to Dublin, warning the leaders that the German arms shipment was a swindle. (Bayley was captured and at once prepared to tell all he knew; but Monteith did get a message through before he escaped — it fell into the hands of Connolly or Pearse and was suppressed.) Casement was soaking wet and exhausted because the boat had been swamped before they landed: he sat down among some bushes near an old fort; and

the sandhills were full of skylarks, rising in the dawn, the first I had heard for years . . . and all around were primroses and wild violets and the singing of skylarks in the air, and I was back in Ireland again.[10]

Later in the day, the police from Ardfort Barracks found him. He gave an English name and address, but at Tralee Barracks it was noticed that he resembled Sir Roger Casement's picture. On Saturday 22 April, still refusing to give his name, he was sent to the Dublin Detention Barracks and thence directly to London.[11]

I

The explanation of these mistakes is not just that they were part of a romantic Fenian muddle — although there were elements of that in them too. The explanation lies in the very character of the Rising itself — namely that it had taken on a symbolic, not a military purpose; that it was not expected to succeed; that it was expected only to happen.

To this the Revolutionary Directory of the Clan na Gael made a notable if involuntary contribution: it was composed of Irish-American politicans who were not equipped to handle or even to mishandle a delicate military operation. And in this the Directory was not alone. The Germans, now lukewarm about the whole affair, sent a load of barely serviceable rifles by a ship that could neither receive nor transmit wireless messages. The Military Council in Dublin, whose communications with New York were of necessity slow and awkward, made a most belated change of plans without considering the possible consequences.

On 14 April Miss Philomena Plunkett walked into the office of the *Gaelic American* in New York with an urgent message from the Military Council. Decoded, it read: "Arms must not be landed before the night of Sunday

23rd. This is vital." Having decided to begin the Rising on Easter Sunday, the Council did not wish a premature landing of arms to put the authorities on guard. Devoy carried this message to von Papen in Wall Street the next morning, and that evening it was wirelessed to Berlin.[12] On 19 April, the German Embassy sent out a final "very urgent" and barely rational message. "The landing of a body of troops, however small," it ended: "is urgently desired, and [the Irish] further suggest a strong demonstration of airships at sea."[13]

What the Germans thought of this has not been recorded, although a Zeppelin raid was made on East Anglia on 24 April and naval raids on Yarmouth and Lowestoft on 26 April. The simple fact remains that every armaments message sent after 9 April was sent into the void: on that day the deaf *Aud* had sailed and her orders could not be cancelled.

Meanwhile, on 18 April, the United States Secret Service raided an office at 60 Wall Street, New York City, where a German diplomat called Wolf von Igel pretended to be an advertising agent. Buried in his extensive files were copies of Devoy's messages to Berlin; and in time the United States District Attorney passed them on to the Department of Justice, which in turn relayed them to London. Since the United States Attorney General did not receive this information until 7 P.M. on 22 April, when Casement was already in custody and the *Aud* was under the sea, it cannot be said that Washington had anything to do with the misadventures of either.[14] As for the British, they gave, quite understandably, an emphasis to Casement and the *Aud* which was out of all proportion to the facts. They tended to assume that with the capture of the one and the loss of the other, no Rising would take place at all. In this roundabout way Casement's heroism — for hero he surely was — became of service to the very Rising he had hoped to prevent.

II

Eoin MacNeill's closest adviser was Bulmer Hobson, and Hobson was too old a hand not to see that something very odd was going on behind their backs.

As early as February, the two decided to summon the whole Headquarters Staff to MacNeill's house in Rathfarnham to hear and discuss a special Memorandum. Its burden was that Ireland was not a poetical abstraction — "there is no such person as Caitlin Ni Uallachain or Roisin Dubh or the Sean-bhean-Bhocht who is calling us to serve her" — but a concrete and visible reality. This Ireland was coming over to the Volunteers' side but not yet in the essential form of a deep and widespread popular discontent. There should be no insurrection, therefore, unless an attempt were made to disarm the Volunteers.[15] It was all to no avail — Pearse explicitly denied that he and his friends had any insurrection in mind. At a further meeting on 5 April, it was decided that all but routine orders should go out with MacNeill's signature: which meant only that the Military Council would now have to deceive him into giving it.[16] It was after this meeting that MacDonagh was co-opted into the Council.[17]

The first deception occurred on 8 April in the *Irish Volunteer,* where Pearse, with MacNeill's approval, called for general maneuvers throughout the country on Easter Sunday. What he proposed to do, however, and actually did, was to issue verbal orders to the various Brigade Commandants as to the areas in which they were to hold their exercises and the insurrectionary purpose these exercises were to serve.

The second deception was made on Tuesday in Holy Week when a paper was "planted" on MacNeill — nothing less than a "secret" Castle Document calling for the disarming of the Volunteers and the house arrest of the Archbishop of Dublin and the Lord Mayor. This document was the work of Joseph Plunkett and the printer of the defunct *Irish Review*.[18] Although no Government in its senses would have ordered the house arrest of the Archbishop of Dublin — here Plunkett's romantic imagination got the better of him — MacNeill took the matter seriously, and after two meetings with the Headquarters Staff put out a general order calling upon the Irish Volunteers to prepare themselves for resistance. This was on Wednesday 19 April.[19]

On Thursday, Bulmer Hobson discovered, through J. J. O'Connell and Eimar O'Duffy, that certain Volunteer Officers were being issued orders which could only be a part of some insurrectionary scheme. He and MacNeill then hastened to St. Enda's, got Pearse out of bed, and heard him declare bluntly that there was going to be an insurrection and that the Volunteers had not originated with MacNeill (which came as no surprise) but with "another body." MacNeill at once issued orders to Hobson (for Dublin and the Southeast) and J. J. O'Connell (for Cork and the Southwest): the Volunteers must be forbidden to take the initiative in any offensive action.[20]

On Good Friday morning Pearse, MacDiarmida and MacDonagh all came to MacNeill's house and told him, as a final argument, that a German ship bearing arms was expected to arrive on Sunday. MacNeill agreed at once that he would not interfere: he even signed a new circular for general distribution. It warned the Volunteers that suppression by the Government was now "inevitable."[21] To complete MacNeill's entrapment, it was arranged that Hobson should be kidnapped that afternoon in Phibsborough: and Hobson — a man of integrity and a key figure in Irish revolutionary history — was still in prison on the following Monday.[22]

Thus confusion was spreading in wide and ever wider circles. On Wednesday MacNeill issued a general order, warning the Volunteers to prepare themselves for resistance; on Thursday, Hobson and O'Connell put out orders to the opposite effect; on Friday MacNeill signed a circular which, to all intents and purposes, called for an insurrection in the near future. These directives, crossing and colliding with one another, knocked about the countryside with stupefying effect, although the stupefaction was by no means due to them alone.

On Saturday morning Joseph Plunkett called on MacNeill to arrange for a Volunteer proclamation: he had just been released from the hospital after an operation on his throat and was, in fact, a dying man. He had scarcely left when the newspapers arrived: they said that an unknown stranger, presumed to be Casement, had been arrested in Kerry. As MacNeill put it in a Memorandum written in 1917, this was decisive; and he prepared to take his part in the Rising because "we were entitled to protect ourselves."[23]

Yet it was now that the plans of the Military Council began to disintegrate. That evening The O'Rahilly and Sean Fitzgibbon, Director of Recruiting, came to MacNeill with dreadful news. Fitzgibbon had gone to Limerick with verbal orders concerning the arrival of German arms; he had been assured by Pearse that these orders came from MacNeill; he was told by The O'Rahilly and was now to learn from MacNeill that this was untrue. Worse still, Fitzgibbon reported that he had convincing proof that the "Castle Document" was a forgery. In short, no offensive movement by the Government had been intended; the only offensive had been planned by a group of faithless comrades, acting behind MacNeill's back and without his knowledge. With the sinking of the *Aud,* therefore, all reason for an insurrection had vanished.[24]

After a last meeting with Pearse, who told him brutally that they had used him all along and "we are done with you now," MacNeill hurried back to a temporary headquarters, chosen because it had a telephone, in Rathgar Road. Here between 9 P.M. and 1 A.M. came the messengers who would distribute his countermanding order: — "Volunteers have been completely deceived. All orders for action are hereby cancelled, and on no account will action be taken."[25]

Many of these messengers left that night for the country. Some were IRB men who, not knowing of the Military Council's existence, still supposed that MacNeill was entitled to give them orders. MacDiarmida, in any case — to him it was no more than a ruse of war — was already putting it about that the Chief of Staff was behind the Rising, which is why Clarke declared on Sunday that MacNeill was guilty "of the blackest treachery."[26]

MacNeill himself, meanwhile, had managed to get the following notice, dated Saturday 22 April, inserted in the Sunday *Independent:* — "Owing to the very critical situation all orders given to the Irish Volunteers for tomorrow, Easter Sunday, are hereby rescinded." He was further comforted by receiving a written assurance from Pearse and a confirming visit from Mac-Donagh, to the effect that the Rising was countermanded.

When all was over, MacDiarmida (for one) did his best for the man whose character he had so debased. A prisoner awaiting execution, he said that MacNeill was "one of Ireland's finest men," and among his last recorded sayings is a plea that no dishonor should rest on MacNeill's name.[27]

In the end, except among a few irreconcilables, the integrity of MacNeill's character was universally recognized and to the end he spoke without rancor of those who had deceived him.

III

In a city like Dublin, one might say in any city, all this could not have proceeded without making some stir. John Dillon, for example, had gone home for Holy Week and "Dublin is full of extraordinary rumors," he wrote to John Redmond on Easter Sunday, "and I have no doubt the Clan men are up to some devilish business — What it is I cannot make out — It may not come off — But you must not be surprised if something very unpleasant and mischievous — happens this week."[28]

Readers of such memoirs as Desmond Fitzgerald's realize how near the insurrection lay to the surface of daily life.[29] William O'Brien, the labor leader, actually asserts that Connolly had told him all the details on Palm Sunday — even that MacNeill was not acting with the insurrectionaries but that "it would be believed he was."[30] By Friday, O'Brien says, "the air was thick with rumors," and it is not surprising that Dillon should have been alarmed.

What is surprising is the relative complacency of Nathan and Birrell. They had, to be sure, already been fed to satiety on a daily diet of rumors and although Major Price, of Army Intelligence, had warned them that the Irish Volunteers were preparing to rise "if ever they got a good opportunity,"[31] where and whence, conscription apart, would the opportunity come? The economy was rather prosperous than otherwise, except for the urban consumer, and did not encourage rebellion. When Major General Friend at last, on 17 April, showed Nathan a guarded report from Brigadier General Stafford, who commanded in the eight southern counties, to the effect that arms were to be landed and a rising fixed "for Saturday," the Under Secretary was not upset. He conferred with Sir Neville Chamberlain, Inspector-General of the RIC and *"although we were doubtful there was any foundation to the rumor"* (he told Mr. Birrell) they agreed to alert the County Inspectors in the South and West and also Lieutenant Colonel Walter Edgeworth-Johnstone, Chief Commissioner of the Dublin Metropolitan Police.[32] With the news of Casement and the *Aud* this mood became even more relaxed. "The Irish Volunteers," Nathan wrote on Saturday, "are to have a mobilization and march out from Dublin tomorrow, but I see no indications of a 'rising.' "[33]

Upon Birrell in London the same news had an almost exhilarating effect. "At last," he replied on Sunday, "something has happened . . . But who can account for such a proceeding as the vessel's . . . Had the crew any grounds for a belief in a *Rising?* It seems that the Lunatic, being disgraced in Germany, was bound to make — this ridiculous effort. We seem to have been well served in the whole matter." "The march of the Volunteers," added this genial victim of Captain Hall, as a kind of afterthought, "will not be conducted in high spirits."[34]

Only Lord Wimborne was not reassured. He argued that a link had been established between Germany and the "Sinn Fein" leaders in Dublin and that they ought to be arrested and interned. For a brief while, on Sunday morning, Nathan seemed to agree: he had just learned that 250 pounds of gelignite had been brought to Liberty Hall.[35] But when the Viceroy pressed for *immediate* action, the Under Secretary retreated. A telegram must first be sent in cipher to Mr. Birrell, asking for his permission. This was done, but the request was not deciphered until the next day at noon; at the precise moment, in fact, when the Rising began.

At 10 P.M. Lord Wimborne made a final effort. He summoned everyone in authority to the Viceregal Lodge, everyone except Major General Friend, who had chosen this rather odd moment to go to London. Once again he urged immediate arrests: he was, he said, ready to issue the warrants on his own authority. At this the soldiers, the police and the Under-Secretary drew back in departmental alarm. And so it was at last agreed to do nothing but draw up a list of persons to be arrested and wait for a reply from Mr. Birrell.

IV

All that Sunday morning and on until 1 P.M. the Military Council sat in Liberty Hall deliberating what was to be done. In their public character as "Sinn Fein leaders" they were in grave danger: in their secret capacity, they were far from hopeless. The debate was not on whether but on when the Rising should take place. Overruling Clarke, who wanted it to happen that very evening, they at length decided to begin the next day at noon.[36] The various battalion commandants would be told to keep their men in readiness for further orders, and thus no violence would be done to MacNeill's cancellation, which had been for Sunday only.

The experience of Eamon de Valera, Commandant of the Third Battalion, is typical of the way in which the new Rising was disorganized.

This important man was born in New York City, on 14 October 1882, the son of a Spanish father and an Irish mother. On his father's death he was sent, still a very small boy, to live with his relatives near Bruree, County Limerick. Out of this bleak rural background he worked his way up to become Professor of Mathematics at a training college for women teachers at Blackrock. He was also a member of the Gaelic League and became Director of its Summer School at Tawin on Galway Bay, but had not been among those who tried to radicalize it in 1913. He was really converted to activism by the founding of the Irish National Volunteers in November of that year. Already happily married to his former instructress at the League, already the father of children, he found his decision to join the Volunteers a painful one since he assumed from the beginning that they would fight the English. Although he had a strong mystical feeling for the Irish past, he was not otherwise overly imaginative; the concept of a "Blood Sacrifice" would not have appealed to him; but, having made up his mind that a fight was necessary, he was prepared to die in it.

In this spirit he concentrated on Volunteer business, deserted the Redmondites after the split, rose to battalion commandant, and was sufficiently trusted by Pearse to attend a secret meeting in March 1915, when a possible Rising in December was discussed.[37] He was afterward sworn into the IRB by Thomas MacDonagh; reluctantly, because he had an orthodox Catholic dislike for oath-bound societies; and he stipulated that no secrets should be told him except those which applied to his immediate work, but added that he would always and without question obey MacDonagh's orders. This was one reason why MacDonagh had to be co-opted into the Military Council.

It was not until five o'clock on Sunday afternoon that de Valera — who had been deeply dismayed by MacNeill's countermand in the *Independent* — "learned with relief that the Rising was to take place at noon the next day, Easter Monday."[38]

He got into touch with as many of his Volunteers as he could, but when his Battalion assembled at Great Brunswick Street at 10 A.M., only a hundred and forty out of its five hundred men were there. How much of this absenteeism was due to the countermand and how much to second thoughts will never be known of course: but to de Valera's mathematical mind this loss of numbers was devastating. His post at Boland's Mill was one of the key posts in the city: it commanded the route by which troops from England might attempt to enter. For weeks he had reconnoitered it, for weeks he had planned to defend it with five hundred men. These plans were now in tatters; and he spent the whole week trying to put them together again.

V

When James Connolly stepped out of Liberty Hall just before noon on Easter Monday, he was smartly dressed in a uniform becoming his rank. The Headquarters Group, on the other hand, might have startled a conventional observer. There was a small detachment from the Irish Citizen Army, but its members were not all clothed in the Army's dark green uniform, far from it; nor were all or nearly all the Irish Volunteers in the Group wearing their heather green. Uniforms were always in short supply. Most men had merely done their best to put on a military appearance, with puttees, riding breeches, bandoliers, and brassards: and for arms they displayed a curious panoply — old German Mausers from Howth or rifles of a more ancient make or shotguns or pickaxes or pikes.[39] Such was the headquarters of a revolutionary army which set out to confront the British Empire.

Before he left Liberty Hall, Connolly stopped and spoke to William O'Brien. He told O'Brien to get on his bicycle and go home — he was needed as a labor organizer. Then he had something else to communicate. Lowering his voice, he said calmly: "We are going out to be slaughtered."[40]

These words throw a special light upon what is known of the Council's plans for the Rising.

All three known copies of the plans have disappeared and one cannot tell what modifications were made in the final hours: but roughly speaking they called for the drawing of a circle around the heart of the city. This circle, which the River Liffey bisected from east to west, was to be formed by occupying two posts north of the river (the General Post Office and the Four Courts of Justice) and four posts to the south of it (the South Dublin Union, Jacob's Biscuit Factory, St. Stephen's Green and Boland's Bakery). Two small groups were to occupy positions near Dublin Castle and in the Mendicity Institute, a building on the south bank of the Liffey almost opposite the Four Courts.

Except for the General Post Office on Sackville (O'Connell) Street, which acted as Headquarters, all the major positions with their outposts can be seen as concerned with the five military barracks outside the circle they so tenuously formed — the Royal and Marlborough Barracks on the north side of the river, and the Richmond, Portobello and Beggar's Bush Barracks on the south side. In the middle of the ring lay Dublin Castle. It was guarded, but very weakly, far more weakly than the rebels knew: just as nobody discovered (even de Valera who reconnoitered the surrounding district) that the Beggar's Bush Barracks was almost empty of soldiers.

The static nature of such a plan is very evident. Even in its original form, supposedly drawn up by Plunkett in 1915, its heroically frozen features could only have gratified a romantic mind. It is supposed to have been reworked by Connolly with Plunkett, after Connolly joined the Military Council: if so, although he lectured on street fighting, Connolly never proposed to introduce it here. The various detachments, in fact, were to act like besieged garrisons, ready to resist assault, prepared at most for sudden forays. All the Government forces had to do was to control the south bank of the Liffey from Kingsbridge Station on the west to Trinity College on the east, and thus break the spine of the rebellion. Even with twice their numbers the rebels never could have prevented this maneuver: with their numbers reduced through the countermand, it had already been virtually accomplished by Tuesday night, and completed with the surrender of the Mendicity Institute on Wednesday morning.

The symbolic character of the Easter Rising quietly emerges from these considerations. It is reinforced by the curious incident of the "attack" on Dublin Castle on Easter Monday. A detachment from the Citizen Army, under Captain Sean Connolly, had moved off toward the Castle not long before noon. At ten minutes past twelve, some of its members shot and killed an unarmed policeman who attempted to close the Castle gates in their faces. They then overpowered and bound six soldiers in the guardroom in the Upper Yard. After lying low for a while, however, they withdrew. They did not know that there were only two officers and twenty-five men in the barracks on the west side; that the Castle was theirs for the taking; that, indeed, they had already taken it.

Why did Captain Connolly make no attempt to seize the Castle? The problem has been the subject of an intricate debate; but it can be reduced to two contradictory statements. On the one hand, Pearse, on entering the Post Office, told Desmond Fitzgerald that the Castle was one of the buildings that had been seized. On the other hand O'Brien is very certain that "it was never intended to seize Dublin Castle. I had this from [James] Connolly himself. . . . What was intended, he said, was to take certain buildings commanding the entrance gates but not to take the Castle itself."[41]

Pearse's head may have been in the clouds once he had entered the Post Office; O'Brien could have been talking from hindsight. The fact that Sean Connolly was killed on the roof of the City Hall while endeavoring to establish a control of the Castle entrances is not therefore so conclusive as the nature of the plan itself. Even though our knowledge of it is incomplete, it cannot be seen as seriously considering so wanton a waste of human resources as pouring numbers of men into a structure too complicated to defend. The plan never called for such derring-do: it called for hanging on until the Rising had established its credentials.

Thus the 1st Battalion of the Dublin Brigade under Commandant Edward Daly in the Four Courts; the 2nd Battalion under Commandant Thomas MacDonagh in Jacob's Biscuit Factory; the 3rd Battalion under Commandant de Valera in Boland's Bakery; the 4th Battalion under Commandant Ceannt in the South Dublin Union; the Citizen Army under Michael Mallin in St. Stephen's Green and the College of Surgeons — all these obeyed their orders and stayed where they were until the end.

VI

According to Constable Calahan's routine report, the Headquarters Group left Beresford Place at 12:02 P.M.[42] At their head was Connolly; on his right was Padraic Pearse, President of the Provisional Republic and Commander-in-Chief of the Army of the Irish Republic; on his left was Joseph Plunkett, Chief of Staff, with his bandaged throat and pallid face, his bangles, his rings, his single spur. The column marched up Abbey Street and wheeled to the right into O'Connell Street, where Tom Clarke and the limping Mac-Diarmida had gone ahead and were waiting for them. "Somewhere in the rear lumbered two drays, packed with Howth Mausers, shotguns, miniature rifles, Sniders, Martinis, Lee-Enfields, pikes, explosives, boxes of rude bombs made of tin cans or lengths of piping."[43] And somewhere in the column was The O'Rahilly, who just returned from his Saturday mission to call off the (Sunday) maneuvers, and was very bitter because the leaders had never confided in him.[44] There were those in the column who still did not know where they were marching or what exactly they were marching for.[45] The people in the streets, like Constable Calahan at Beresford Place, assumed that they were seeing just another route march.

When he came opposite the General Post Office, the principal landmark of one of the finest streets in Europe, Connolly gave this order: "Left turn — the G.P.O. — Charge!"

The main body went through the main entrance under the portico, taking a few prisoners and hustling the public outside; a small detachment entered the Henry Street door and on into the upstairs premises; another group made for the roof. Very soon the unfamiliar Sinn Fein green, white and orange flag was run up on the north side of the great pediment and on the south side there fluttered a green flag with a gold harp. Across it in gold and white letters were the words IRISH REPUBLIC.

At 12:45, Padraic Perse came out on the steps of the Post Office and, standing on the lowest of them, read out to a small and seemingly indifferent group of bystanders, the Proclamation of the Republic, the joint work of himself and James Connolly.

POBLACHT NA h-EIREANN
THE PROVISIONAL GOVERNMENT
of the
IRISH REPUBLIC
TO THE PEOPLE OF IRELAND

Irishmen and Irishwomen: In the name of God and of the dead generations from which she receives her old tradition of nationhood, Ireland, through us, summons her children to her flag and strikes for her freedom.

Having organised and trained her manhood through her secret revolutionary organisation, the Irish Republican Brotherhood, and through her open military organisations, the Irish Volunteers and the Irish Citizen Army, having patiently perfected her discipline, having resolutely waited for the right moment to reveal itself, she now seizes that moment, and, supported by her exiled children in America and by gallant allies in Europe, but relying in the first upon her own strength, she strikes in full confidence of victory.

We declare the right of the people of Ireland to the ownership of Ireland, and to the unfettered control of Irish destinies, to be sovereign and indefeasible. The long usurpation of that right by a foreign people and government has not extinguished the right, nor can it ever be extinguished except by the destruction of the Irish people. In every generation the Irish people have asserted their right to national freedom and sovereignty; six times during the past three hundred years they have asserted it in arms. Standing on that fundamental right and again asserting it in arms in the face of the world, we hereby proclaim the Irish Republic as a Sovereign Independent State, and we pledge our lives and the lives of our comrades-in-arms to the cause of its freedom, of its welfare, and of its exaltation among the nations.

The Irish Republic is entitled to, and hereby claims, the allegiance of every Irishman and Irishwoman. The Republic guarantees religious and civil liberty, equal rights and equal opportunities to all its citizens and declares its resolve to pursue the happiness and prosperity of the whole nation and of all its parts, cherishing all the children of the nation equally, and oblivious of the differences, carefully fostered by an alien government, which have divided a minority from the majority in the past.

Until our arms have brought the opportune moment for the establishment of a permanent National Government, representative of the whole people of Ireland and elected by the suffrages of all her men and women, the Provisional Government, hereby constituted, will administer the civil and military affairs of the Republic in trust for the people.

We place the cause of the Irish Republic under the protection of the Most High God, Whose blessing we invoke upon our arms, and we pray that no one who serves that cause will dishonour it by cowardice, inhumanity, or rapine. In this supreme hour the Irish nation must, by its valour and discipline and by the readiness of its children to sacrifice themselves for the common good, prove itself worthy of the august destiny to which it is called.

Signed on behalf of the Provisional Government

THOMAS J. CLARKE

SEAN MacDIARMIDA	THOMAS MacDONAGH
P. H. PEARSE	EAMONN CEANNT
JAMES CONNOLLY	JOSEPH PLUNKETT

"Republic" has many meanings. The singular quality of the Proclamation lies in its hopeful compromise between the ideas of Pearse and those of Connolly, with a courteous but distant bow toward the conservative republicanism of the IRB. Pearse himself had shown a lively interest in and sympathy with the teachings of Young Ireland's Fintan Lalor, who decried a purely political rebellion since "those who own the land will make your laws, and command your liberties and your lives . . . The entire soil of a country belongs of right to the entire people of that country, and is the rightful property, not of any one class, but of the nation at large, in full effective possession." Then he relented — "Ireland, poor lady, had ever a soft heart and a grateful disposition . . . she may, if she please, in reward of allegiance, confer new titles or confirm the old."[46] In much the same manner, Pearse insisted in his final article "The Sovereign People" (which he finished at St. Enda's on 31 March 1916 with the prefatory words "For my part I have no more to say"), that "I do not disallow the right to private property; but I insist that all property is held subject to the national sanction."[47]

In the Proclamation all this appears as: "We declare the right of the people of Ireland to the ownership of Ireland . . . to be sovereign and indefeasible" — a statement broad enough for the ideas of Pearse and Connolly, of Lalor and Marx, to be deployed in it without collision. Connolly, after all, had already sacrificed much that was rigorous and systematic in his thinking to the cause of nationalism. At this moment, he may even have been content to differ from Pearse only "in resolving 'the people' into its component parts, and seeing the leading role of the working class within the class alliance."[48] His inmost mind had already appeared in the *Workers' Republic* for 18 December 1915, under the title of "Economic Conscription." Here he reminded his readers of the great strike of 1913, when "the misguided Irish people stood so callously by . . . Out of that experience is growing the feeling of identity between the forces of real nationalism and labour which we have long worked for and hoped for in Ireland." "We want and must have economic conscription in Ireland," he continued. "Not the conscription of men by hunger to compel them to fight for the power that denies them the right to govern their own country, but the conscription by an Irish nation of all the resources of the nation — its land, its railways, its canals, its workshops, its docks, its mines, its mountains, and rivers and streams, its factories and machinery, its horses, its cattle, *and* its men and women, all co-operating together under one common direction that Ireland may live and bear upon her fruitful bosom the greatest number of the freest people she has ever known."[49]

For Pearse the Proclamation was founded upon Young Ireland; for Connolly it was filled with echoes of the great strike. Connolly's ultimate objective was a socialist Workers' Republic, which he thought would come as a matter of historical necessity. Pearse's was an ideal Commonwealth, a political and social Tir na n'Og, a kind of eternity. Each believed that it must all begin with the shedding of blood: but they did so for very different reasons.

VII

There is a passage in Pearse's "Peace and the Gael," written in December 1915, which strikes one as impossibly morbid. "The last sixteen months," wrote Pearse, "have been the most glorious in the history of Europe. Heroism has come to earth. On whichever side the men who rule the peoples have marshalled them, whether with England to uphold the tyranny of the seas, or with Germany to break that tyranny, the people themselves have gone into battle because the old voice that speaks out of the soil of a nation has spoken anew . . . It is good for the world that such things should be done. The old heart of the earth needed to be warmed with the red wine of the battlefields. Such august homage was never before offered to God, the homage of millions of lives given gladly for love of country." "What peace [Ireland] has known these latter days," he wrote in the same article, "has been the devil's peace, peace with dishonour." The sin was the sin of submission to an alien and heretic rule: it could only be redeemed in blood.[50] Desmond Fitzgerald tells us that much of his conversation in the General Post Office during Easter Week was concerned with "the moral rectitude of what we had undertaken."[51]

Connolly was just as eager for a Rising; but his eagerness was fundamentally different. When he read Pearse's words about the "red wine of the battlefields," he said that it was great nonsense;[52] and if we find him, later on, in the *Workers' Republic,* using the Redemption as an example to be followed "in all humility and awe,"[53] he was employing a metaphor that came naturally to an Irish Catholic, without ceasing to think that revolution itself was redemption and that death might be a necessary step in a revolutionary process.

When the Proclamation referred to "our gallant allies" in Europe, it was a matter of small importance to him or to Pearse that the gallant allies had done little to help the Rising, that they did not formally even exist. What did matter was to establish Ireland's independence as a republic with "allies" in Europe, and to do so before Germany won the war. (This, too, was the reasoning behind Casement's "Treaty.") In the spring of 1916, in Ireland as elsewhere, many people did think that Germany was going to win the war. Not one of the leaders who sat in Liberty Hall on Sunday could have had, by that time, any idea of coming out of the Rising alive; not Clarke or Mac-Diarmida or Ceannt, physical force men who wanted only to get at the enemy; not Plunkett, a romantic revolutionary and a dying man, who saw the Rising as a perfect last adventure; not MacDonagh, who thought in terms of martyrdom; not Pearse, a second Cuchulainn; and least of all James Connolly.

DUBLIN ~ 1916

IRISH FORCES

▤ and ◉ Positions and outposts

◉▭ Battalion or equivalent defensive areas

BRITISH FORCES

▥ or ⊡ Barracks and positions

TROOP MOVEMENTS

•••◄••• Monday

◄━━━ Tuesday and Wednesday

━ ━ ━► Thursday, Friday and Saturday

0   1/2   1 MILE

0   400   800   1200   1600 METERS

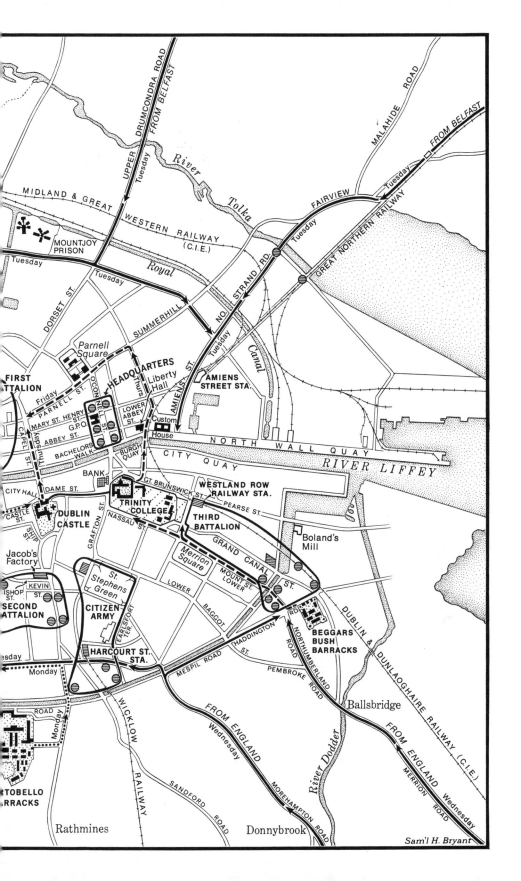

Chapter Fourteen

The Rising:
24 April–30 April 1916

I

If Captain Connolly had seized the Castle, he would have seized with it
Sir Matthew Nathan, the Under Secretary, and Major Ivor Price, the County
Carlow Inspector of the R.I.C. who, with a temporary commission, was head
of the Special Intelligence Branch at Army Headquarters.[1]

Sir Matthew had gone to work that fine morning with an uncomfortable
feeling that something was about to happen somewhere in Ireland. According to a telegram from the District Inspector at Tralee, received at 3:35 A.M.,
Sergeant Bayley had insisted that there was to be a general rising: and neither
the capture of Casement nor the sinking of the *Aud* appeared to him (on
second thoughts) to be altogether decisive.[2]

He was joined by Major Price, who had come to help him in drawing up a
list of suspects to be arrested and in arranging for security measures against

possible trouble in Southern Ireland. For this they needed the help of Mr. Norway, Secretary of the Post Office, in denying telephone and telegraph service to all but the Army and Navy. Norway, therefore, left the General Post Office and arrived at ten minutes to twelve. He had just finished making out an order for Nathan to sign, when there was a burst of rifle fire below the window. "That's the attack," said Nathan, jumping up and leaving the room. He was followed by Major Price. When Norway went downstairs a few minutes later, "at the foot of the staircase he found all the messengers huddled together. They were frightened out of their wits. They had just seen the policeman at the gate shot through the heart."[3]

It so happened that Michael King, who had been detailed to destroy the main telephone manhole outside the Telephone Exchange in Crown Alley, was unable to do so because the men who were to assist him did not turn up.[4] Thus the city's telephone system remained in working order, and Nathan was always in communication with the Vice-Regal Lodge and Major Price with the Army Headquarters at Parkgate, while the Chief Superintendent of the DMP was able from the start to instruct and be informed by his Superintendents in the city.

By two o'clock the main positions of the insurgents, with the exception of the South Dublin Union, were known to the Chief Superintendent in the Castle.[5] The Adjutant of the Dublin garrison, whose headquarters were also in the Castle, had already summoned to his assistance troops from each of the four main barracks — the so-called "inlying pickets" of one hundred officers and men which had been kept in readiness for some days — while General Friend's Adjutant General, Colonel Cowan, had (at 12:30 P.M.) telephoned to the Curragh for the 3rd Reserve Cavalry Brigade of sixteen hundred men and had sent trains from Kingsbridge Station to transport it. The first of these troops, traveling dismounted and commanded by Colonel Portal, are said to have reached Kingsbridge Station at 4:45 P.M.[6] The remainder came in at twenty minute intervals.[7]

Around 5:00 P.M. Nathan sent out a message to be telegraphed to the Chief Secretary. He was then able to inform him that the attack on the Castle had not been "pressed home." "Situation at present not satisfactory," the message ended, "but understand troops now beginning to arrive from Curragh."[8] His own position, apart from the fact that he could not leave the Castle without being sniped at, was also far from satisfactory. No one knew better than he that his career as Under Secretary was now at an end.

II

How many insurgents were there, in theory, available for a Rising on Easter Monday? The Irish Volunteers in Dublin numbered nearly three thousand. There were some members of the Fianna na hEireann, though how many is not known: they were given the task of blowing up the Magazine Fort in Phoenix Park at high noon, and would have done so if the officer in charge of the high explosives room had not gone off to the Fairy-house Races, prudently taking the key with him. There were fifty to seventy-five "exiles," Irishmen who had left England to avoid conscription and were now encamped on Plunkett property at Kimmage.

And there was the Citizen Army. Its roll books had been placed in the custody of Thomas Kain, Secretary of its Army Council, who hid them in a house in Castle Street, where they remained undiscovered until 1927. They give the total enrollment at 339 and state that 152 were out in the Rising with 7 uncertain.[9]

Cathal Brugha estimated the *actual* numbers of Volunteers involved at one thousand, Major Florence O'Donoghue at sixteen hundred. Since a large number came in after the fighting started, it would probably be safe to assume that there were less than one thousand at the beginning and at most sixteen hundred at the end,[10] by which time the troops opposed to them numbered around twelve thousand.[11]

At the beginning, the government troops available in Dublin numbered less than 2,500. Of these 386 were cavalrymen of the 5th and 7th Lancers, stationed in Marlborough Barracks; 403 were from the 3rd Battalion Royal Irish Regiment in Richmond Barracks; 467 were from the 10th Battalion Royal Dublin Fusiliers; and 671 were from the 3rd Battalion Royal Irish Rifles in Portobello Barracks.[12]

Like the warden of the high explosive room in the Magazine Fort, many of the officers commanding these troops had gone off to the Fairyhouse Races on Monday morning: but General Friend's inlying pickets were sufficient to secure Dublin Castle on the first day; and the troops who came in from the Curragh were in virtual control of the Kingsbridge Station–Trinity College line by the end of the second evening.

The first military casualties took place very early on Monday afternoon when a troop of cavalrymen appeared at the north end of O'Connell Street and began to move down toward the river. It seems that they were expecting to ride over the rebels in the open; and that the fire which came from the Post Office, killing four and forcing the rest to retreat, was a complete surprise. By taking to the houses and refusing to adopt what the irritated Lord Wimborne called "the ordinary tactics of revolutionaries," the Dublin rebels had at least made the use of mounted cavalry obsolete.[13]

The infantry pickets — with the exception of the severe resistance put up by Ceannt's men in the South Dublin Union — made their way cautiously to the Castle, brushing aside the rebel outposts and avoiding the snipers in Parliament Street and City Hall by using the Castle's western entrance in Ship Street. By two o'clock there were 150 reinforcements inside the Castle, with 100 more coming up. At 9:30 P.M. part of the last picket (Royal Irish Regiment) came in from its battle at the Union, and with it came Colonel Kennard, commander of the Castle garrison. The Castle had long been safe from attack; but it was midnight before any civilian was allowed to venture out.

The scene inside was anything but edifying. "The Yard," wrote Mr. Norway,

> was lit by torches and crowded with men and soldiers. Among them from time to time a woman was carried in, caught in the act of carrying ammunition to the rebels and fighting like trapped cats. It was a strange and awful scene. I turned to the Solicitor General [Mr. James O'Connor] and said, "This seems to be the death knell of Home Rule." Now he was a sane and moderate nationalist. But he said, "Upon my soul, I don't know are we fit for it after all."[14]

On Monday, Trinity College was held by a few O.T.C. men and a handful of Anzac and Canadian soldiers on leave: like Dublin Castle it could have been seized by the rebels, but was too complex a group of buildings to be defended. By Monday evening, too, the North Wall Quays, the Amiens Street Railway Station and the Customs House had been occupied by Government forces; and the sixty-five man detachment from the Second Irish Volunteer Battalion, covering the northeast approaches at Annesley Bridge, where the Tolka River runs by Fairview Park, was completely stranded and had to be withdrawn on Tuesday evening.

Brigadier General W. H. M. Lowe, next in seniority to Major General Friend in the Irish Command, arrived at Kingsbridge early on Tuesday morning: he came at much the same time as General Friend who, after a bad half hour with Lord French, left London on Monday. Lowe brought with him from the Curragh the 840 infantrymen of the 15th Irish Reserve Brigade;[15] General Friend brought only a damaged reputation. From now on it would appear that General Lowe was the leading strategist.

His problem at first could not have seemed too simple. The British Army had not fought inside a city since Lucknow and Delhi in the 1850s; "an enemy barricaded in defensive positions is notoriously hard to eject";[16] a German attack was even considered possible.

However, once he had realized that no Germans were coming and that the rebels intended to stay inside their strongholds, he had only to isolate the opposition south of the Liffey and concentrate upon the Headquarters. On Tuesday four eighteen-pounders came in from Athlone — two went to Trinity College, two stayed to blow away Commandant Daly's barricades at Cabra Road and the North Circular Road — an ominous event since it was artillery that destroyed the rebellion.

The rebels for their part always expected to be attacked head on, with rifle and bayonet. Thus Commandant Mallin's men, after they had arrived at St. Stephen's Green and mindlessly killed an inquisitive policeman, were set to work digging trenches under the supervision of the Countess Markievicz. At dawn they were surprised in their trenches by a party of one hundred men with a machine gun from Dublin Castle, who fired down on them from the roof of the Shelburne Hotel, and forced them to retreat to the Royal College of Surgeons, where they remained for the rest of the week, completely isolated.[17]

MacDonagh's men in Jacob's Biscuit Factory also had little or nothing to do all week. The second in command, John MacBride, begged his commandant to take to the streets, but MacDonagh stuck to the plan and stayed inside all week, eagerly awaiting the attack that never came.

All the leaders thought along the same lines. Commandant de Valera, for example, was obsessed by the belief that his post in Boland's Bakery would be overrun at any moment. The area for which he was responsible stretched from the slums of Ringsend to the Northumberland Road–Mount Street district. Through it ran the railroad from Kingstown (Dun Laoighre) by which troops arriving from England could ride into the city; its roads and bridges over the Grand Canal offered the most direct approach by foot; and across the Canal lay the Beggar's Bush Barracks which (he supposed) was full of troops. An important outpost had to be stationed at the Grand Canal Bridge to keep these nonexistent soldiers at bay; and yet another at the Mount

Street Bridge, where its exploits on Wednesday did indeed become famous.*
Rails had to be ripped up, walls loopholed, a gasworks and an electric supply
station dismantled — and how was all this to be accomplished with less than
half his battalion?[18] His tall gaunt figure, worried and sleepless, became
almost a menace: this was offset by his calmness under fire.

In fact, only de Valera's outposts on Wednesday and Ceannt's post on
Monday and Thursday experienced direct attacks: and all but one of these
was mounted through miscalculation and continued out of pride.

III

On Wednesday, after the Mendicity Institute under Sean Heuston had
been forced to surrender and the Royal Irish had been withdrawn from their
precarious foothold in the South Dublin Union, it seems that General Lowe
would have been quite content to leave the south side of the Liffey in
isolation. But then something went very wrong.

Lord French, on Monday, had directed that two brigades of the 59th
Division — the 176th and the 178th — were to move at once to Dublin. The
troops were mostly recruits, mere boys who had been trained in the barest
elements of trench warfare and who had never fired a shot in anger. Seasick
and bewildered (some of them thought they were in France) they disem-
barked at Kingstown and marched toward the city: because of the haste of
their departure they had neither hand grenades nor machine guns.

Their objective was the Royal Hospital in Kilmainham, far off to the
west: and two of their battalions, the 2/5 and 2/6 Sherwood Foresters,
moved to the left by way of Donnybrook, certainly the most practicable way
of getting there. The other two battalions, the 2/7 and 2/8 Sherwood Foresters, through some misunderstanding of their marching orders, were directed to cross the Grand Canal by the Mount Street Bridge.

The 2/7 Battalion, led by Lieutenant Colonel Cecil Fane, C.M.G., D.S.O.,
a cavalry officer and a veteran of Mons, moved up the Northumberland
Road straight into the fire of de Valera's outposts. Fane was a brave man and

---

* On Monday these outposts were approached by a holiday route march of the loyalist
Dublin and Rathmines Volunteer Corps — all middle-aged professional men whose armbands
bore the initials G.R (Georgius Rex), which earned them the nickname of Gorgeous Wrecks.
The outposts tragically killed six of these inoffensive gentlemen before it was realized that their
guns were unloaded and they carried no ammunition. If Nathan had had his way some of them
would have been guarding such important buildings as the General Post Office and the Telephone
Exchange on Monday: their arms would have been sticks and whistles. CSO RP 7974.

his raw troops fought with exemplary valor: but they had been led into a trap. De Valera's outposts consisted of seventeen men — two in No. 25 Northumberland Road on Fane's left; four in the Parochial Hall to his right; eleven across the Canal and commanding the bridge and its approaches.[19] Few as they were, they had every advantage.

The attack began at 12:30 P.M. and in Number 25 alone the two Volunteers, Lieutenant Michael Malone and section-commander James Grace, did fearful damage among their enemies. It was not until 5 P.M. that the door of Number 25 was blown in by bomb and machine gun reinforcements; and not until 6 P.M. that the house was rushed and the indomitable Malone killed. Grace somehow made his escape and was captured three days later.

Fane tried to outflank his tormentors, to the left by the Baggot Street Bridge, to the right toward Beggar's Bush Barracks: both efforts were driven back. Between 5 and 6 P.M. the Brigade Commander, Colonel Maconchy, got into touch with General Lowe and General Lowe bleakly announced that the Mount Street Bridge must be carried at all costs. It was not until eight o'clock that it all ended with Clanwilliam House, commanding the bridge, in flames and three of its stern defenders (George Reynolds, Patrick Doyle and Dick Murphy) dead. The Sherwood Foresters lost 230 men of all ranks killed and wounded in this almost medieval and most unnecessary engagement, the largest of the whole Rising.

De Valera had listened for hours in anguish to the battle on his right. He could not reinforce his outposts because he believed from minute to minute, from hour to hour, that his main position was to be assaulted: and he had not a man to spare. That night, watching the flames from Clanwilliam House and an ominous red glow from inner Dublin, he and his men waited for the English to mount their bayonet attack; and when Thursday morning came some of them had to be kicked awake at their posts.

On this day the battered 2/8 Sherwood Foresters, who had relieved the 2/7 halfway through the battle of Mount Street Bridge, were marched off toward their original objective, the Royal Hospital in Kilmainham: and their commander led them by the one route certain to bring them under the fire of Ceannt's men in the South Dublin Union. Some of the Battalion broke into the Union buildings; there was a fierce struggle which lasted until evening, after which the Battalion withdrew. It was here that Vice-Commandant Cathal Brugha, severely wounded, fought on with a ferocity that was one day to become proverbial.[20]

Otherwise very little more was done that day by the leaders on the south side of the Liffey. MacDonagh, idle in Jacob's Factory, sent some cyclists out to assist de Valera. De Valera, who was being shelled by the converted trawler *Helga* in the morning, diverted her fire from the glass roof of his Bakery by climbing the tower of a nearby distillery and planting a Republican flag there.[21] While the *Helga* pounded away at the tower, he contemplated a sortie toward Mallin and dissuaded himself or was dissuaded; while Mallin tried a foray toward Harcourt Street and was driven back. The chief problem for all of them now became a shortage of food, and the chief emotion one of helplessness.

Another onlooker was Augustine Birrell, who arrived on Thursday morning in the destroyer H.M.S. *Dove* and who, from the windows of the Vice-Regal Lodge, gazed down in tears, an anti-Nero, upon the flames for which he would soon be held responsible.[22]

IV

On Easter Monday, after the cavalry patrol had been driven away, the rebel Headquarters in the General Post Office was left in peace. The most disturbing event was the appearance of looters as the afternoon wore on. The uniformed police had been withdrawn from the streets after one constable had been killed at the Castle and another in St. Stephen's Green: and so, from the tenements in Gardner Street and Marlborough Street, and the rookeries in the back of Moore Street and Great Britain (Parnell) Street, the poorest of the poorest descended by the hundreds upon the treasures of Sackville (O'Connell) Street. Extreme poverty has a sweet tooth, and Noblett's the confectioners at the corner of North Earl Street was the first to be gutted; after that it was the turn of Dunn the hatter and the Saxone Shoe Shop; and so it went on, far into the night.

In his little four-page paper, *Irish War News*, which appeared for the first and last time on Tuesday and sold for a penny, Pearse endeavored to shame these looters by calling them "hangers-on of the British Army." Jim Larkin would not have put it that way, and in any case the looters did not read *Irish War News*. It was from the loiterers and the looters, the inquisitive and the destitute, alike oblivious to their danger, that most of the civilian casualties were drawn.

The looting had another consequence, indirect, but very sad: its story is an important part of the Easter Week canon.

On Tuesday the Chief Superintendent telephoned to Military Headquarters to say that "Sheehy-Skeffington has posted up placards calling for a meeting of the Women's Franchise Association at 5:00 P.M. this evening to establish a police force to stop the looting."[23]

Francis Sheehy-Skeffington was a great embracer of causes — he was a feminist, a vegetarian, a teetotaller, a pacifist, a socialist. Tobacco and vivisection had no greater enemy, Larkin and Connolly no better friend than he. His appearance was all of a piece with the rest of him. He was small and wiry, with a reddish-brown beard and keen serious eyes. He was usually dressed in tweeds, knickerbockers, long stockings, boots and a cloth cap. On his lapel there would be a large button with the words "Votes for Women."[24]

In Dublin he was known and highly regarded as a crank: since his views were barely respectable this did not prevent him from being often assaulted in one way or another. "After blows of fists, sticks or umbrellas," writes Professor Roger McHugh, "he would still have his way, and one Dublin snap-shot of memory catches Skeffington, clinging to a lamp-post from which he is being dragged by the police, and saying in his high-pitched voice 'one further point before I go.' "[25]

He had a brilliant mind which no one would accuse of being overburdened with humor. On the other hand, he was a gentle and lovable man, with a wife (she was Hanna Sheehy, the strong-minded daughter of a Nationalist M.P.) who shared to the full his passion for humanitarian causes and his disregard for the ordinary creature comforts. "There was a joyousness in their manner of living," a friend wrote after his death, "which more worldly and more outwardly comfortable people entirely miss." It is possible that he came as close as one can get to complete integrity.

On 31 May 1915 he was arrested under the Defence of the Realm Act for "making statements likely to be prejudicial to recruiting" — statements which he usually made in the columns of the *Irish Citizen* or from the steps of Liberty Hall. He was sentenced to six months at hard labor and a further six months if he did not produce £50 bail. "Any sentence you may pass on me," he said from the dock, "is a sentence upon British rule in Ireland."[26]

He was sent to Mountjoy Prison, where his wife had been gaoled in 1912 for breaking windows in Dublin Castle. After a six-day hunger strike and a four-day thirst strike, he was released under the "Cat and Mouse" of evil memory, the Act which permitted rearrest without trial. His son remembers him "a pale skeleton of his former self, being slowly helped by a cabbie up our garden path at 11 Grosvenor Place. Even his voice was almost gone as he tried to greet me: 'Hello laddie.' "[27] Public opinion was too strong and the Birrell-Nathan administration too sensible to permit his rearrest: and so, as soon as he had recovered his health, he was allowed to go to America to lecture to large and gratifying audiences on the topic of Irish freedom. He returned on 20 December 1915.

This, then, was the serious personage who, crossing Portobello Bridge on Tuesday evening on his way home from the antilooting conference, was arrested and taken to Portobello Barracks. "Are you in sympathy with the Sinn Feiners?" he was asked "Yes," he replied, "but I am not in favor of militarism." This was thought sufficient to detain him: but Captain Bowen-Colthurst, who came from a land-owning family in the South, and who had been shell-shocked at Mons, had further plans. He took Sheehy-Skeffington out, as a hostage, on a raiding tour of Rathmines, where he and his men killed a harmless boy outside the church, and seized two magazine editors — Mr. Dickson of the *Eye-Opener* and Mr. McIntyre of the *Searchlight* — whom he found in Alderman Kelly's bar. Both editors were loyalist, Redmondite writers. The next morning, Wednesday 26 April, he ordered Sheehy-Skeffington and the two editors out into the barracks yard at 10 A.M. and, without trial or warning, had them shot.[28] He had already committed four other murders, but the military would have left him alone if Major Sir Francis Vane — a protegé of Lord French whom Nathan, for some reason, described as a "ruffian"[29] — had not taken the matter up. Colthurst was sent to Broadmoor Prison for the criminally insane, released after twenty months, and settled in Canada on a military pension. Vane, for his efforts, was temporarily deprived of his command. "Some of us," said the ineffable Major Price, "think it a good thing that Sheehy-Skeffington was put out of the way anyhow."[30]

V

On this Wednesday, General Lowe began his concentration on the Headquarters in the General Post Office, which he proposed to isolate from Daly's Volunteers in the Four Courts and then reduce by artillery fire. In spite of Connolly's doctrinaire belief that no capitalist general would act in such a way, General Lowe did not hesitate to destroy valuable structures, public and private. He got into practice by turning two eighteen-pounders onto Liberty Hall which, though not a valuable structure, was a highly suggestive one: and its interior was completely burned out, although its walls remained standing. It was also artillery fire which, by hurling an incendiary shell into the *Irish Times* printing office in Lower Abbey Street, started a general conflagration in the heart of the city.

On Wednesday, troops began moving out of their assembly point at Trinity College and occupying the two quays east and west of O'Connell Bridge. Machine guns were placed on the roof of Trinity College, on the tower of Tara Street fire station, on Amiens Street railway station roof, on the Rotunda at the top of O'Connell Street (where the Irish Volunteer movement had been born in 1913).[31] In this way O'Connell Street and the adjacent streets to the east were swept by fire; while two eighteen-pounders opened up on the insurgent nest in Kelly's ammunition shop at the corner of Bachelor's Walk. The snipers here and in Hopkins's jewelry shop at the corner of Eden Quay[32] were withdrawn and brought into the Metropole Hotel, adjacent to the General Post Office; and Connolly was forced to reduce his outposts elsewhere in Lower O'Connell Street.

In spite of much evidence to the contrary, he still believed that the General Post Office was to be attacked by bayonet; and he seems also to have believed that this attack would first come from the south. He concentrated particularly, therefore, on the defenses of Lower Abbey Street, and when the detachment from the 2nd Volunteer Battalion came in on Tuesday, he placed it in the Imperial Hotel opposite the Headquarters.

By Wednesday afternoon, however, Lowe had already moved the 3rd Battalion of the Royal Irish Regiment across the top of Upper O'Connell Street on the north and as far west as Moore Street, where it could fire down upon the Headquarters' northern exits; and at almost the same time rifle and machine gun fire opened up from the roofs of Jervis Street to the west. In other words, the rebel Headquarters was now surrounded, if somewhat sketchily; and Connolly managed to improvise a new system of outposts, not for once abandoning his resolve to beat back an assault which was never intended and never came.

On Thursday, General Lowe's cordon grew tighter and tighter as more troops were available to him; while his machine-gun fire was doubled from new emplacements north and south of O'Connell Street. Connolly in turn became more and more active and daring in setting up barricades to the north, south and west of his position. He was wounded in the arm, had his wound dressed in secret, and went back to work. He had just mustered a party of 30 men to occupy the printing offices of Murphy's *Irish Independent,* and was standing at the curb to watch them as they dashed across, when he was struck by a bullet just above the ankle. He dragged himself back to Prince's Street, the little cul-de-sac beneath the southern wall of the Post Office, and was carried inside.[33]

It was a frightful wound and crippling in more senses than one, for Connolly had an outstanding gift for leadership, as Michael Collins, who fought in the Post Office, afterward attested. It came not long before General Lowe's incendiary shell hit the *Irish Times* printing office and set fire to its rolls of loyalist newsprint. The fire jumped to Wynn's Hotel; houses on both sides of Lower Abbey Street were soon in a blaze; the Volunteer detachment withdrew from the Imperial Hotel; and all the military needed to do was to wait in their encircling positions until the fire, spreading to the General Post Office by one means or another, forced the rebels out.

General Lowe's other concern on Thursday had been to draw a cordon around the Four Courts, thus making a new semicircular investment of the General Post Office. For this he used the 2/5 and 2/6 Sherwood Foresters, who had not taken part in the Mount Street or South Dublin Union battles, elements of the 5th Leinsters and Royal Irish Regiment, and a composite battalion from Belfast.[34] Daly's men kept up a steady fire from beneath the Dome of the Four Courts, but the Government troops got across the Liffey by way of Grattan Bridge and, moving along Capel Street with the help of a new contraption called the armored lorry, set up their barricades in Upper Abbey Street. The upshot of these maneuvers was to force the withdrawal of the very outposts which Connolly had set up just before he was wounded; and so the investment was complete.

VI

On Friday morning at 2 A.M. a new figure appeared upon this scene. The Government had decided that only a senior general in Ireland would satisfy Parliament, and Lord French had selected Lieutenant General Sir John Maxwell for this unenviable post.

Born in 1859 and commissioned in the 42nd Highlanders in 1879, General Maxwell had seen all his active service in Africa — the Egyptian War of 1882, the Nile Expedition of 1884–5, the Battle of Omdurman in 1898, the Boer War. He had then acted as Chief Staff Officer to the Duke of Connaught in Ireland and was afterward rewarded with the command of "what was known as The Force in Egypt."[35]

When the war broke out and the Turks came in, General Maxwell repulsed them at the Suez Canal, and he was preparing a cautious attack on the Senussi in the Wetsern Desert when the Gallipoli campaign ended, and the command was given to Sir Archibald Murray. Maxwell felt that he had been the victim of a political maneuver, and when he came to Dublin he was that quite dangerous person, a general with a grievance.

His fellow officers thought him good-natured, rather lazy, something of a wit. In appearance he was stocky and good-looking except for an oversized nose, which earned him the nickname of "Conky." "I hope Conky begins," wrote Sir Henry Wilson cheerfully, "by shooting Birrell." General Maxwell began by telling Mr. Birrell and the Viceroy that they were now under his control, news which they did not take with too good a grace. Martial law had been proclaimed for Dublin (on Tuesday) and for all of Ireland (on Wednesday), however, and they seemed to have no choice.

From his headquarters at the Royal Hospital, Maxwell placed the 2/4 Lincolnshires at Lowe's disposal, so as to form a cordon along the Grand Canal and block off any rebel retreat from the city's southern exits: otherwise Lowe was to continue doing just what he had done all week. From the end of Westmoreland Street, therefore, the gunners kept pounding away at the General Post Office, more often hitting the Metropole next door, but making it clear at last that the military was not going to stage a hand to hand attack At 4 P.M. on Friday "the roof [of the G.P.O.] half penetrated by an incendiary shell, caught fire";[36] and this was the end. There was a general confusion, and only The O'Rahilly, "who was something of an engineer and expert at doing things with his hands,"[37] seemed able to create any order; and even he admitted that the fire was winning.

The Military Council had never trusted The O'Rahilly, in spite of the intensity of his speeches against recruiting.[38] He would not join the IRB, he had supported The MacNeill; he had helped distribute the countermand. And yet, as early as Monday in the General Post Office, Clarke was heard to say that "of all men he admired O'Rahilly." In a famous poem O'Rahilly is made to tell Pearse and Connolly "because I helped to wind the clock, I came to hear it strike."[39] He joined the Rising, which he thought inopportune not wrong, because he was a fighting man (which is why he earned the admiration of Tom Clarke) and out of principle. Whether he said anything about a clock is doubtful, but he certainly told Desmond Fitzgerald "fancy missing this and then catching [one's death of] a cold running for a tram."[40]

The evacuation of the sixteen wounded men was made through holes tunnelled through the western walls into the Colosseum Music Hall. With the party went Desmond Fitzgerald in command and his two assistants, Michael O'Reilly and Willie Pearse; also Father Flanagan of the Pro-Cathedral, who had come in on Thursday and stayed to see it out; a very responsible prisoner, Lieutenant Mahony of the Royal Medical Corps; and twelve of the fourteen valiant Cummann na mBann and ICA women who had been in the Post Office all week. Connolly and Plunkett stayed with the main body, as did Nurses Elizabeth O'Farrell and Julia Grenan, Winifred Carney, Connolly's secretary, and Tom Clarke and Sean MacDiarmida, the two civilian members of the Provisional Government.[41]

The idea was to make a dash for it before the flames engulfed them and to establish a new headquarters in the Williams & Woods soap and sweets factory in Parnell Street. The advance party was led by The O'Rahilly, who was mortally wounded as he charged across the Sherwood Foresters' barricade at the top of Moore Street with both revolvers blazing. Propping himself up against a wall in Sackville Lane, he wrote a last note to his wife.[42]

The main party got as far as Cogan's grocery shop on Henry Place, where Pearse went back to see if the Post Office had been fully evacuated, and where it was joined by O'Reilly and Willie Pearse. It then moved on to Hanlon's Fish Shop at No. 16 Moore Street before being pinned down. Thus Hanlon's Fish Shop became the last headquarters of the Army of the Irish Republic.

General Maxwell, meanwhile, had called up the 2/5 and 2/6 South Staffords from Trinity College and sent them to complete General Lowe's cordon around the Four Courts: they were to link up in North King Street where Commandant Daly still had strong outposts, his key position being an empty public house or "Reilly's Fort."[43] This was so fiercely defended that the commander of the 2/6 Battalion decided to outflank it by tunnelling through the houses on either side, many of whose inhabitants had been too afraid to heed the military's warning and leave. The maneuver took place at night; the South Staffs, rough Black Country troops, were in a state of exasperation; and undoubtedly no very nice distinction was made between innocent civilians and Volunteers in civilian clothes. How many died in this "Massacre of North King Street" will never be known — the official count was only two, whose bodies were recovered on 10 May — and the fighting in that area, which did not end until Reilly's Fort fell at 9 A.M. on Saturday, has borne an evil reputation ever since.[44]

VII

On Saturday, a little after 12 noon, the Provisional Government members in Hanlon's decided that they no longer had any choice but to surrender. Elizabeth O'Farrell, the pretty nurse who had stayed through it all, was sent out with a white flag. After being subjected to some verbal indignities, she was brought before General Lowe, who "treated me in a very gentlemanly manner," but said that Pearse would have to surrender unconditionally.[45] It was not until 3:30 P.M. that Padraic Pearse, in his Volunteer's uniform with its slouch hat, handed his sword to General Lowe.

Pearse then wrote out the order for surrender as follows: — "29 April 3:45 P.M. In order to prevent the further slaughter of Dublin citizens, and in the hope of saving the lives of our followers now surrounded and hopelessly outnumbered, the members of the Provisional Government present at Headquarters have agreed to an unconditional surrender, and the Commandants of the various districts in the City and Country will order their commands to lay down arms. P. H. Pearse."

It was then countersigned by James Connolly in these terms: "I agree to these conditions for the men now under my command in the Moore Street District and for the men in the Stephen's Green command. James Connolly." In other words, he countersigned for the Irish Citizen Army.

To Miss O'Farrell was now given the distasteful and, indeed, dangerous assignment of carrying the message around to the various commands. Daly's men in the Four Courts surrendered on Saturday. The others could not be reached until Sunday. One and all, they were reluctant to give in. At the College of Surgeons, the Countess Markievicz, wearing her green breeches and service tunic and her slouch hat with feathers, could not resist a last touch of melodrama when she surrendered. Taking off her revolver, she kissed it before handing it to a Major Wheeler, and said "I am ready." The major prosaically offered her a ride to gaol, but she refused it and went off with Commandant Mallin at the head of the men and women who had been beleaguered with them. On the way, she and Mallin discussed the question of most immediate interest — whether they would be shot or hanged.[46]

De Valera, who did not know Miss O'Farrell, insisted that she should bring him MacDonagh's countersignature before he gave in. As he marched away, with a British officer on each side of him, with a white flag in front, at the head of the Boland's garrison, through lines of listless or actively hostile onlookers, he was heard to say, "If only you had come out with [hay]-forks."[47]

VIII

In a manifesto, written on Thursday and issued on Friday, in which he generously and justly acquitted Eoin MacNeill of bad faith ("both MacNeill and we have acted in the best interest of Ireland"), Padraic Pearse said: "We should have accomplished the task of enthroning, as well as proclaiming, the Irish Republic, had our arrangements for a simultaneous rising in the whole country, with a combined plan as sound as the Dublin plan has proved to be, been allowed to go through on Easter Sunday."[48]

Taking into account the exalted state of mind in which he wrote these words, with the Dublin plan as a military venture in ruins all around him, how much substance can we give them? What was the nature of that "simultaneous rising in the whole country" which was not "allowed to go through on Easter Sunday"?

Later on, in the summer, Mr. H. E. Duke (Mr. Birrell's successor) spent some time in the West — in Galway, Mayo, Limerick, Kerry and Cork. Here he consulted with public officials most concerned in suppressing the rebellion. He was told that the Irish Volunteers, while unpopular with "farmers of all classes," had been composed of farmers' sons and farm laborers in the rural districts and of clerks, shop-boys, sons of publicans and workmen in the towns; that they had been organized by emissaries from Dublin as well as by local agitators; that they had been armed with rifles, shotguns, and revolvers; and that the plans for their Rising had been made "with foresight and completeness," especially with regard to the landing of the "revolutionary arsenal" in the *Aud*. Indeed, Duke reported, "given the arms from Germany" the Rising would have been "formidable and even dangerous."[49] This concept of a well-planned provincial enterprise, foiled only by the loss of the *Aud*, received the official blessing and lingered on in the hospitable recesses of the official mind. But was it really the case?

As we have seen, the arrangements for a simultaneous Rising in Dublin and in the Provinces depended upon Pearse's issuance of two sets of orders for the Sunday "maneuvers" — one, the official orders approved by MacNeill and the whole Volunteer executive; the other, secret orders to selected commanders, defining the areas in which their revolutionary "maneuvers" were to be held. However, the word that a Rising would take place was not to go out until the last minute — that is to say, at the beginning of Holy Week — to special leaders and at different times; and the rank and file of the IRB were to be just as much in the dark as the rank and file of the Volunteers.

If MacNeill's two countermands, and especially the second, caused great confusion, therefore, the elements of confusion were already present before the countermands arrived. As the late Dr. Maureen Wall has suggested in her admirable recomposition of these events, the confusion may well have had a deeper cause. This would be found in Thomas Clarke's passionate conviction that one could profit from the lessons of history.

Irish national history is very persuasive; but, like other national histories, it is extremely doubtful if it can be said to teach lessons — such past lessons, that is to say, as will (if learned) provide the right solution to contemporary problems. Clarke and MacDiarmida had realized that elaborate secret societies, especially in Ireland, had been peculiarly subject to infiltration by informers — the rebellions of 1798 and 1867, under the United Irishmen and the Irish Republican Brotherhood respectively, gave signs enough of that. Chosen individuals therefore "were sworn into the I.R.B. if they passed the tests of acceptability demanded by Clarke and MacDiarmida. . . . In the last weeks before the Rising, officers of the Volunteers were taken into the I.R.B. — a seeming reversal of the secret society infiltration idea — and men were even sworn as members immediately before undertaking particular missions."[50]

This meant, in effect, a partial dismantling of those processes by which the orders of IRB leaders found their way swiftly down to the rank and file and were obeyed without demur.* It also meant that a good deal of improvisation entered into the general plan itself — or, at any rate, into such features of the general plan as have come to light. For example, Denis McCullogh, the President of the Supreme Council, puzzled by the curious uneasiness of Bulmer Hobson on Palm Sunday, came to Dublin on Monday to find out what was really going on. He was told that a Rising would take place on Sunday, and that he was to muster his 132 Belfast Volunteers at Coalisland, in order to join up with Liam Mellows "on the line of the Shannon."[51] Furthermore, he would be joined by Dr. Patrick McCartan's Tyrone Volunteers, several hundred strong, at Belcoo in County Fermanagh, from which point they were to march on together into Connaught. "It was apparently benignly assumed," writes Professor Martin, "that, despite the fighting in Dublin, the many R.I.C. barracks between Coalisland and Connaught would be passive spectators of the marching Volunteers."[52]

Dr. McCartan, a member of the IRB's Supreme Council, actually did not receive his orders until Wednesday or possibly Thursday. In any event, he and McCullogh consulted together and came to the conclusion that it would be quite impossible to obey such extraordinary commands at such short notice; and they made this decision before they knew anything about MacNeill's countermand.[53] It is not surprising that McCartan, on 28 April, when he was on the run in Tyrone, should have written a letter to Joseph McGar-

---

* The IRB was, ideally, organized into Circles. Each Circle was commanded by a Center (A), under each Center were nine Bs, under each B were nine Cs, under each C were nine Ds. The members of each group were aware only of their own fellow members and thus secrecy was supposed to be maintained and orders swiftly obeyed.

rity blaming the Dublin leaders for keeping him in the dark until it was too late.[54]

Michael Colivet of the IRB was the leader appointed for Limerick, Clare and West Tipperary; and he had made his plans for "holding the line of the Shannon" from Limerick to Killaloe, when he received a message from Pearse on Tuesday in Holy Week. Arms were going to be landed in Kerry, and he was to supervise their distribution in his own area and in Galway. This was his first intimation that the Rising was no longer a project but an actuality; and he rushed to Dublin, where Pearse told him that it was to begin on Sunday at 7 P.M.: but gave him no hint that Eoin MacNeill was still in the dark.[55]

On Saturday Colivet heard of the sinking of the gun-running ship, the capture of someone believed to be Casement, the arrest of Austin Stack, and he naturally cancelled all his arrangements for Easter Sunday. When The O'Rahilly arrived in Limerick on Sunday morning, with the MacNeill countermand, this was the first time that Colivet learned of the split at Volunteer Headquarters: but by then everything, as far as Kerry was concerned, was at an end and MacNeill cannot be blamed for it.

As for Austin Stack, who was very much in the secret, he kept his plans to himself: but the point is that the two men sent to assist him (Con Collins, a close friend of MacDiarmida, and William Partridge, one of Connolly's labor lieutenants, both men of unswerving loyalty) did not receive their instructions until Wednesday and Thursday respectively, and had little or no time to become acquainted with either the terrain or the Tralee Volunteers.[56]

These dreamy miscalculations in one area were offset, in another, by an equally unreal demand for exactness. In Galway, it has been claimed, the plans called for the Volunteers to assemble at Gort station on Sunday evening, there to receive a shipment of arms and be in the Rising. This could only mean that the *Aud* had to arrive on time; that Stack and his men had to unload the guns and get them to Tralee by narrow-gauge line, that at Tralee they had to be reloaded onto a train to Limerick, after which part of the arms were to be unshipped at Abbeyfayle and part sent on by the Ballysimon loop line to Gort.[57]

Even if all these maneuvers were carried out with inhuman precision, even if all interference at Fenit and Tralee and Limerick had been neutralized, how were the arms to be used at once by the Galway Volunteers? It took time and practice to accustom oneself to German weapons; and (although this extra dampener was not known) it would take more time and more practice if the guns were Russian.

In Galway, moreover, communications had already broken down long
before the sinking of the *Aud* or the arrival of MacNeill's final countermanding order. The orders outlined above were communicated to Eamonn Corbett by Padraic Pearse on Monday in Holy Week; and also to Liam
Mellows, who had made his escape from England with the help of Nora
Connally, and arrived at St. Enda's on Tuesday on his way west. Corbett
returned to Athenry on Tuesday and passed Pearse's commands on to Larry
Lardner, the Volunteer commander in that town. Lardner, like Corbett, was
an IRB man: but he was not in the secret and he refused to obey. On Friday
morning the first of MacNeill's messages after his break with Pearse arrived:
it seemed to call for a suspension of all activity; and a Volunteer meeting in
Galway City produced only division — some were for following Pearse, some
for obeying MacNeill. The countermand, arriving on Sunday, only made
things worse. In short, it was not until news arrived that a Rising had
actually begun, that Lardner went out with his men, to be joined by Mellows, who emerged from hiding and took command. But their plans, concerted at the last moment, produced only a skirmish; and one is not surprised to learn that before the week was over Mellows was in flight again.[58]
Obviously, the trouble in Galway had begun because some IRB men, such as
Corbett and Mellows, were more in the know than others, such as Lardner;
and the secretiveness of the Military Council was really as much to blame for
what happened as the countermand of MacNeill.

The Volunteer leaders in Cork — Terence McSwiney, Thomas MacCurtain, and Sean O'Sullivan, all IRB men — were similarly confused. They had
received their orders to march on Easter Sunday evening and link up with
the Kerry volunteers in a Rising; but they did not know that these orders
had been issued without the knowledge or consent of MacNeill. Bewildered
by contradictory orders on Thursday, Friday and Saturday, by the news of
the *Aud,* and by MacNeill's final countermand, which reached them on
Sunday, they recalled their march. Late on Easter Monday another message,
signed by Pearse and MacDiarmida, told them to go ahead with the Rising.
They were only too eager to obey; but night had fallen, the weather was
dirty; and when they woke on Tuesday they found that General Stafford
had invested the city with troops and artillery.[59]

In Tipperary, the Volunteer Commandant was Pierce McCann, probably
not an IRB man. His orders, which he believed to have come from MacNeill,
were to link up with the Volunteers in Limerick, and "hold the line of the
Shannon." He received the countermand from The O'Rahilly on Sunday,
and at once obeyed it: but when he was persuaded by two local IRB men to

take action on Tuesday, he found that the Limerick Volunteers — who in any case were neither numerous nor well-armed — had already been told by Colivet to do nothing at all. In Limerick and Tipperary, therefore, as throughout the West and Southwest except for a tentative rising in Galway, nothing occurred.[60]

In the Southeast a body of six hundred men — only two hundred of whom were armed — invaded Enniscorthy in County Wexford on Easter Thursday. They seized the Athenaeum, commandeered arms, motor cars and food, but made no attempt to attack the police barracks, and were passively opposed by townsfolk, priests, the Redmondite Volunteers for so long inactive, and also by the police who — throughout the country — still followed the Birrell-Nathan policy of nonprovocation. Their Rising dissolved without bloodshed when infantry, cavalry and an armored car arrived from Cork on 1 May.[61]

Only in Counties Dublin and Meath was there a small but really successful effort, when the Fifth Dublin Battalion, under Commandant Ashe, seized the Donabate, Swords, and Garristown police barracks; attacked the Ashbourne barracks; and ambushed and captured an RIC column coming in from Slane to Ashbourne's relief.[62] But Ashe's exploits had no effect on the Rising in Dublin.

What deductions could be made from these events? In the first place, although it added greatly to a confusion which already existed, MacNeill's final countermand cannot (except in Cork) be considered a "fatal" or decisive happening. In the second place, one can assert with some confidence that a Rising was first considered for Dublin alone; that it was then extended to include, at least, some plan to hold the line of the Shannon, either for an advance to Dublin or a retreat from it; and that by September 1915, when the Military Council first decided on Fenit, a success in the West and Southwest was predicated upon the landing of arms and men from Germany. Austin Stack must have known about the arms shipment well ahead of time: but there is no way of telling how many of the provincial leaders knew of it, or if any of them did, when the order for Easter "maneuvers" first came out in the *Irish Volunteer* on 8 April. If Michael Colivet's predicament (not to mention that of McCullogh and McCartan) is any criterion, nothing specific was issued until the beginning of Holy Week, and then *seriatim* to selected persons.

Clearly the Military Council depended upon a last-minute conversion of Eoin MacNeill; and when the "Secret Castle Document" failed to do this, they seem to have hoped that he would yield to a *fait accompli*. They therefore took the precaution of kidnapping Bulmer Hobson. They could not kidnap MacNeill, because his continued absence would have been too blatant and would have ruined everything. Indeed, this dependence on Mac-Neill makes a shambles out of another essential feature of their plans — their reliance upon the IRB men in the Volunteers to carry out their orders on the spur of the moment and to take the non-IRB men with them. As it turned out, the dislocation in the chain of command was such that many IRB men never learned that a split had taken place at Headquarters and continued to believe — even when the choice of MacNeill or Pearse was clearly before them — that they were under MacNeill's command.

This leads one to the final consideration. There was clearly a strong vein of fatalism in the thinking and planning of the Military Council. Could one not say, indeed, that the provinces had always been of secondary importance? That the provincial Volunteers were known to be far more poorly armed and far less tightly organized than their Dublin counterparts? That the loss of the *Aud,* the warnings of Monteith, the capture of Sir Roger Casement, were peripheral events? The evidence strongly suggests that the first and essential objective had always been a Rising in Dublin; and that, as time went on, considerations of this Rising's success or failure were swallowed up in the paramount question of its endurance. All one can say is that the Rising endured long enough to change the course of Irish history.

Chapter Fifteen

Terrible Beauty:
1 May–12 May 1916

O n Monday, 1 May, while an occasional sniper might still be seen or heard among the rooftops, the Rising had apparently vanished into the past, a dismal failure. It had failed as an armed *putsch,* and it had failed as a political gesture. It had conspicuously not aroused the sympathies of the city of Dublin, upon whom it had visited many discomforts, whose private and public buildings it had burned or been responsible for burning, to the tune of an estimated £2,500,000, and whose wayfarers and looters it had too often killed or wounded. In Dublin and indeed in the country as a whole it was, and for this there is abundant evidence, widely regarded as irresponsible and mischievous — as something calculated to provoke the government into making things more uncomfortable than they already were.[1]

The statistics of the Rising were, in their own way, evidence of ample provocation. According to the official English figures they were as follows: — 116 military killed and 368 wounded; 13 R.I.C. killed and 22 wounded; 3 D.M.P. killed and 7 wounded; 318 civilians and insurgents killed and 2,217 wounded.[2] The R.I.C. casualties occurred, of course, outside Dublin: otherwise that city was, as the Norsemen would have put it, "the place of slaughter."

The figures given in the *Sinn Fein Rebellion Handbook* are much lower for civilians and insurgents killed and wounded — 180 and 614 — but these were given out on 11 May, and were taken from the tally of persons who, according to the police and medical authorities, had already passed through the hospitals. "Beyond this," the *Handbook* says, "the casualties of the rebels were not ascertainable. Many of the rebels were not in uniform, and it was not possible to distinguish between them and the civilians, hence they are included in the last figures given. Since these figures were issued the deaths of wounded persons have increased the total death roll considerably."[3]

The number of insurgents killed has since been estimated as sixty-four, although the exact number of wounded has never come to light. The figures in the *Handbook,* however, are of importance because they give some idea of the state of mind which existed on 11 May. Something had occurred whose mere numerical size, while it could not be estimated or predicted, was evidently changing in a momentous fashion. And there was another change, of which the *Handbook* says nothing. On 1 May, the Rising was seen as a failure, either malevolent or squalid or both. On 11 May, it was still seen as a failure; but it was beginning to look heroic.

It has been suggested, and not in irony, that General Maxwell — as the man immediately responsible for suppressing the rebellion — ought to have proceeded on the principle that "the way to treat the insurrectionary leaders was to make them look ridiculous."[4] This is an odd suggestion on any terms: it is even odder when one considers the character and situation of General Maxwell.

He was not exactly a simple man, but he was a conventional soldier, to whom the insurrectionary leaders were nothing more nor less than subjects of His Majesty King George V, caught in the act of bearing arms against His Majesty, and therefore traitors and meet for death. He was also a general who believed that he had been mishandled by the politicians over the Egyptian command, and who was out to prove that he was a better man than the politicians thought him. In either case, he would not have treated the leaders as ridiculous because, to his way of thinking, they were not ridiculous at all. On this one point, at any rate, history is fully in agreement with General Maxwell.

I

Fourteen rebels were tried by court-martial, sentenced to death, and shot.
They were (with the date of execution) : —

  3 May—Padraic Pearse, Thomas MacDonagh, Thomas J. Clarke
  4 May—William Pearse, Joseph Plunkett, Edward Daly,
         Michael O'Hanrahan
  5 May—John MacBride
  8 May—Cornelius Colbert, Eamonn Ceannt, Michael Mallin,
         Sean Heuston
  12 May—James Connolly, Sean MacDiarmida.

And on 9 May Thomas Kent, of Coole near Fermoy, after a court-martial
in Cork, was executed in Cork Gaol for killing a policeman (Head Constable William Rowe) who attempted to search his house for arms.

General Maxwell had let it be known that "in view of the gravity of the
Rebellion and its connection with German intrigue and propaganda and in
view of the great loss of life and destruction of property resulting therefrom,
the General Officer Commanding in Chief, Irish Command, has found it
imperative to inflict the most severe sentences on the organisers of this
detestable Rising and on the Commanders who took an actual part in the
fighting which occurred."[5]

Willie Pearse had been with his brother in the G.P.O., and had boasted at
his court-martial that he had been privy to all the plans for Easter Week:
but such boasts are transparent. He had been neither a Commandant nor an
organizer. This was also true of John MacBride, the second in command at
Jacob's Factory. A water bailiff in the employment of the Dublin Corporation, MacBride was a member of the IRB, but was considered too heavy a
drinker to be entrusted with secrets. He had fought against the British in the
Boer War, which may have been the reason for his execution: when he heard
his sentence, he remarked contemptuously that he had looked down British
barrels before. Colbert had been what might be called a charter member of
the Countess Markievicz's militant Boy Scouts, as had Sean Heuston: but
Colbert had been neither a commander nor an organizer, whereas Heuston
had held out in the Mendicity Institute much longer than was expected. For
Michael O'Hanrahan's death no reason can be found.

Seventy-five others were sentenced to death by courts-martial before it was
all over, but their sentences were commuted to various terms of penal servitude, from life to three years.

General Maxwell was in London on 5 May, and "at the Prime Minister's request" — Asquith told the King — "gave the Cabinet an account of the present situation in Dublin & the rest of Ireland. He has commuted the sentence of death passed by the Court Martial on the Countess Markievitch [sic] to one of penal servitude for life."[6] The Countess told the bashful young officer who read the commutation order to her, "I wish you had had the decency to kill me."[7]

Eamon de Valera had his death sentence commuted to penal servitude for life on 11 May, either because he had been born in America or (as he himself believed) because of the unfortunate effect the executions were already having on public opinion. The fact that Thomas Ashe also escaped the firing squad on that day — and he was both a commander and an organizer — supports the latter view.[8]

Eoin MacNeill, toward the end of Easter Week, had written a letter to General Maxwell, asking for an interview with the object of preventing further bloodshed. He was thereupon arrested, confined in Arbor Hill Retention Barracks, and confronted with Major Price.[9] This confrontation took place on 4 May, according to Price; and in his statement Price emphatically denied that he had tried to get MacNeill to implicate John Dillon and Joseph Devlin — "such a suggestion was absolutely ridiculous" — but admitted that he had hoped (in vain) to get something on Laurence Ginnell, M.P. for Westmeath. MacNeill, according to Price, was threatened with death if he did not give at least some information about the men who were in touch with Germany, but this he refused to do.[10] The rumor that Price had tried to entangle Dillon and Devlin persisted until the end of October, when questions were still being asked in Parliament about it, and we have only his word that he did not do so.[11]

At his court-martial MacNeill testified that on Easter Sunday around 5 P.M. his efforts to stop the Rising had succeeded; but that his fellow-rebels had "probably" heard of the meeting in the Vice-Regal Lodge and of the decision to arrest them. Here, in his belief, was the cause of the Rising.[12] This shows how much in the dark he had been about the connection, such as it was, between Germany and the Rising, and how very much more in the dark about the existence of the Military Council: it also demonstrates how careful he was to say nothing that would hurt the leaders who had duped him. "They were men of honour," he told the Court. "They were truthful and honourable men."

On 29 May, it was announced that MacNeill had been sentenced to penal servitude for life, having been convicted on twelve counts — eight for attempting to cause disaffection among a civil population, and four for acting in a way likely to prejudice recruiting.[13]

II

Before any executions had taken place, John Redmond had told the House of Commons that "the overwhelming mass of the Irish people" looked upon the Rising "with feelings of detestation and horror."[14] This was undoubtedly true of conservative middle-class nationalism. In a public statement to the press on the next day, 28 April, he spoke of his "horror, discouragement, even despair [on hearing of] this insane movement." This was his honest belief. Honesty is the best policy, as we all know, although the annals of politics are not the most convincing witness to this. It would have been prudent, perhaps, in Redmond's case, if he had moderated his language until more was known of the feelings of the Irish people.

John Dillon had spent a dreadful Easter Week in his house on North Great George Street, too close to O'Connell Street for him to go outdoors in safety until Friday. On Sunday he wrote with some assurance to Redmond, advising him to urge "strongly" the "extreme unwisdom" of any wholesale executions, since the effects on public opinion would be disastrous. "I have no doubt if any of the well-known leaders are taken alive they will be shot — But except the leaders there should be no court-martial executions." Redmond had already written to him — their letters crossing — to say in strict confidence that Casement and the other "real ringleaders" should be dealt with in the severest manner possible; that the others should be treated "with the greatest leniency"; and that the Prime Minister had agreed with him.[15]

Dillon wrote two letters to his colleague on 2 May. In the first he urged the removal of Attorney-General Campbell, Lord Wimborne, Augustine Birrell and Sir Matthew Nathan — "Nathan has behaved splendidly . . . but I fear he can be useful to Ireland no more" — but actually suggested that Sir John Maxwell ("if he be a Home Ruler") should take Lord Wimborne's place! This letter was written before he had been in touch with General Maxwell. In his second letter he told Redmond that "English military officers are determined to have a battue on their own hook" and that Maxwell had said to him, "after I have finished with Dublin I propose to deal with the country."[16]

Dillon was naturally horrified: but at this point, before there had been any executions, he and Redmond believed that nothing could prevent the execution of the ringleaders; and Asquith, at least in Redmond's mind, had professed to agree that this would be sufficient. After the news of the executions of Pearse, MacDonagh and Clarke had been telegraphed to London, Asquith told Redmond that he was "shocked," but he would not promise — he would only hope — that this would be the end of it. On 4 May, he assured Redmond that there had been no more executions: on that morning, four more were shot.[17]

In the meantime, the *Irish Times,* in its issue of May 1-3, and not unmindful of its charred newsprint, had said that "the rapine and bloodshed of the past week must be punished with a severity which will make any repetition of them impossible for generations to come." The Protestant Archbishop, on 4 May, in what amounted to an *ex cathedra* pronouncement — a letter to the London *Times* — called for "punishment, swift and stern." The *Independent* of 5 May denounced the "insane and criminal rising of last week," and said that it cared little what happened to the leaders. Only the *Freeman's Journal,* an old enemy of the *Independent,* called for leniency: but the *Freeman's Journal* strained the quality of mercy with a reference to "the blind self-devoted victims of the Hun."

Dillon had been in consultation with the staff of the *Freeman's Journal* on 4 May: the leader writer may have been expressing Dillon's view, not his own. When he read the *Irish Times,* it is true, Dillon called its language "bloodthirsty and wicked,"[18] but his view of the rebel leaders was quite as unfavorable as Redmond's. To him Francis Sheehy-Skeffington was "a preposterous and mischievous creature," nor was he "personally concerned to save Connolly or Kent [Eamonn Ceannt]." Yet he had no doubt, he said, that Skeffington's was an absolute case of murder and he could not sufficiently condemn what he called "the policy of dribbling executions." Father Aloysius had told him that feeling among the working classes was growing very bitter, and rumors were already circulating that numbers were being shot without a trial.[19]

Redmond had not lost faith in the Prime Minister. He forwarded to Downing Street protesting cables from America; he spoke of denunciations in Parliament; he threatened to retire. He was answered with solemn assurances. He continued to accept them. On 7 May, he received a cable from Dillon, who had special permission from Assistant Under Secretary Sir Edward Farrell to send it, warning him that further executions were to be carried out the next day. It was Sunday; Asquith was in the country, impervious to the noises of the outside world. Redmond could only hope that his "urgent message" would get through the Prime Minister's defenses: and he therefore cabled back a presentiment that "no more executions will take place."[20] The result was the same. The executions duly took place on Monday; and on Tuesday Mr. Asquith was again assuring Redmond that he had sent a "strong telegram" to General Maxwell.[21]

It was the executions of 8 May which blew upon the embers of Dillon's revolutionary past. When he came over to London on 9 May, he was, if not exactly a new man, for he still condemned the Rising, at least a renewed one. On 11 May there was at last a debate in the Commons on the Irish crisis. The Irish Party was now unsure of its own survival and enraged by the secret trials, the hasty executions after trial, the deportations, the mobile columns sent into the countryside, searching and arresting in districts where no disturbance whatever had taken place.[22] It was in such an atmosphere, so laden with fear, so charged with historical enmities, that Dillon arose to make the speech of his lifetime.[23] It ranged over the whole Rebellion landscape, from Wexford to Mayo, from the draconic acts of the General and his troops in Dublin to the provocative language of the Home Secretary in London. It condemned the rebellion, but it now approved the rebels. "It is not murderers who are being executed," said Dillon, "it is insurgents who have fought a clean fight, a brave fight, however misguided, and it would be a damned good thing for you if your soldiers were able to put up as good a fight as did these men in Dublin."

Weeks later the Irish Attorney-General, Mr. Campbell, was still referring to Dillon's "deplorable speech" and wishing that it had been "censored in the press in England and certainly in Ireland."[24] Indeed, from that day onward Dillon was held to be an implacable enemy.

On the night of 11–12 May, with this speech still ringing in his ears, the Prime Minister left for Ireland. He left with the knowledge, which Maxwell had sent him on 9 May, that Connolly and MacDiarmida were to be shot that morning. Connolly's horrible wound, which had smashed his leg above the ankle, was now gangrened; he was so weak that he had to be carried to the place of execution and there tied to a chair; and it was noticed that at the last moment he raised himself with an effort so that he could meet his death defiantly, with his head lifted and sitting upright. These ghastly details were probably not told to Mr. Asquith.

On his return the Prime Minister submitted a report to the Cabinet which was divided into two parts: the first, "The Actual Situation," dated 19 May;

the second, "The Future," dated 21 May. Although both were marked "Most Secret," either could have been read by almost anyone without alarm to himself or danger to the realm.

The men and boys whom he had visited in Richmond Barracks, he said in "The Actual Situation," had mostly taken no part in the Dublin Rising but were merely "suspected by the local police of active membership in the Sinn Fein organization." He had ordered a comb-out to be started at once. Here and elsewhere, the police had sometimes acted with excessive zeal. The military were guilty of killing unarmed and even innocent persons — he was afraid this had happened in more than one house in North King Street — and such cases ("along with the Skeffington case, which, so far as I can judge, is the worst blot on the proceedings of the military") had aroused a good deal of public uneasiness and sympathy. Otherwise, to judge from the report, all was friendliness. In Dublin itself, and "in places where the normal political atmosphere is so widely different as Belfast and Cork," he had been greeted, not only without disrespect, but even with "remarkable warmth."[25]

What the Cabinet thought of this first document has not been recorded: but the opening sentence of the second, "The Future," must have occasioned a certain queasiness among that group of ex-enemies: —

For reasons, good or bad, with which my colleagues are familiar [it ran] and which it would serve no good purpose now to review, the British Government has allowed in recent years the formation and development in Ireland of a number of independent and irresponsible armed forces — the Ulster Volunteers, the National Volunteers, the Irish Volunteers, and the Citizen Army.

Mr. Asquith now went on to say that he had learned from the Lord Mayor of Belfast that, in the autumn of 1915, "a sort of atmospheric wave" had overspread Protestant Ulster. It was felt that Protestant Ulster had sent the best of its manhood to the front; that the Catholics of the South and West had contributed substantially less; and that if more Protestant Ulstermen were allowed to enlist, the Protestants would be left defenseless against a possible, and even probable, Nationalist invasion of the province. "From that day to this, recruiting in Protestant Ulster has practically ceased."

The leading employers of labor and other prominent citizens whom Mr. Asquith consulted, all of them Carsonites, while not themselves agreeing with this extravagant view, were satisfied that it was held by the vast majority of the Protestants in Belfast and industrial Ulster, "and that nothing could dislodge it from their minds."

"My own conclusion," said Mr. Asquith, "is that the arms question [i.e. the disarming of the Volunteers in Ulster and in the South] cannot be satisfactorily or effectively handled except as part of a general settlement . . . I am by no means sure that the Nationalists (except the O'Brienites)" — they had sent him a truculent deputation while he was in Cork — "would not now be disposed to prefer the total exclusion (for the time at any rate) of Ulster. It appears to me to be the immediate duty of the Government to do everything in their power to force a general settlement."

Force was not an Asquithian word. He turned at once to an examination of the sort of executive government which ought to be provided for Ireland until the general settlement arrived. He was convinced, he said, that the Viceroyalty had become — through no fault of Lord Wimborne — "a costly and futile anomaly." Its only function of any value had been a ceremonial one; this could be performed with far more success by royalty itself; and "I am glad to be able to say that His Majesty whole-heartedly accepts the necessity of the change, and is prepared and anxious to arrange for an annual residence of himself, the Queen and the Court in Ireland." With the Viceroy thus disposed of in this fanciful way, there would disappear what Mr. Asquith called "the fiction of a Chief Secretary." "There must," he concluded, "be a single Minister controlling and responsible for Irish administration."[26]

The response to all this was quite predictable. Lord Wimborne was very shortly restored to the Vice-Regal Lodge; a new Chief Secretary was found in the shape of H. E. Duke, a Unionist lawyer; and the old order, discredited but unabashed, remained until the curtain fell in 1922.

III

In the Chief Secretary's office in the Castle, there sat for the time being a gentleman called Sir Robert Chalmers, the permanent Secretary to the Treasury, for Sir Matthew Nathan had of course resigned, and so had Mr. Augustine Birrell: the former in a letter of great dignity;[27] the latter in a way which showed how hurt he was at the collapse of his administration. "I feel very sorry," he wrote, "for 'Nathan the Unwise,' who up to Ireland has always been successful everywhere." It was not characteristic of him to turn

on a colleague in this way. In this letter, too — he was writing on 30 April —
he described the rebels who were already surrendering as "a miserable lot"
and called their leaders "criminals to whom short shrift should be given."
This, again, was not in his style. Only at the end of the letter did he return to
something like his true form. "Of course I can't go on . . . I advised you to
pole-axe me some months ago. I have *refined* and *subtilized* thought too
much about Ireland."[28]

Later on, back in London, and standing in the Prime Minister's room in
the House of Commons, he said his goodbye to Mr. Asquith. These two
authentic Liberals had been colleagues who truly appreciated and cherished
each other's gifts and foibles: to Asquith, especially, Augustine Birrell — humane, witty, lovable and loyal — was an appalling loss. "Birrell," writes Dr.
Ó Broin, "was so upset that he could not remember what words were
spoken; the Prime Minister, jingling some coins in his pocket, just stood at
the window and wept."[29]

After Birrell had made his resignation speech in the Commons, he was
praised by John Redmond for the work he had done in Ireland, and the Irish
leader even took upon himself some of the blame for what had happened
because "for all I know, what I have said influenced him in his conduct and
in his management of Irish affairs." A few days later, Redmond took it all
back. He had, he said, never been consulted by Dublin Castle as to policy —
a statement which the facts hardly bear out. Redmond and Birrell had been
friends, insofar as friendship was possible between a Chief Secretary and a
chairman of the Parliamentary Party. Now the Rising stood between them
like a salt, estranging sea.[30]

Only Sir John Maxwell stood unmoved among all these changes. If it had
not been for his callous and vindictive attitude toward the killing of James
Connolly, he might be excused for his part in the executions. As Mr. Asquith
told the King, the Cabinet had agreed "to leave to his [Maxwell's] discretion
the dealing with particular cases, subject to a general instruction that death
should not be inflicted except upon ringleaders and proved murderers, and
that it is desirable to bring the executions to a close as quickly as possible."[31]
This instruction was far too general to be left to the discretion of such a
mind. To General Maxwell a sentence of death was no unjust act. He might
have said, like an eighteenth century proconsul on a very different occasion,
that considering his opportunities he was astonished at his moderation.
Would a German Commander, in similar circumstances, have behaved so
well? Indeed, he cannot be made to sustain the character of villain: he was
little more than the government's scapegoat. What scales did he have upon

which to weigh the delicacies of Anglo-Irish relations in an Empire at war? Mr. Asquith could and should have stopped all executions until the sentences had been examined and confirmed by the Cabinet. It is true that martial law had been declared in Dublin and all over the country, but as the Prime Minister was careful to point out to his colleagues, "all the trials and sentences have been conducted, passed and carried out under the Defence of the Realm Act."[32] And he had been amply warned: almost from the beginning, Redmond had dinned into his ears the disastrous effects of hasty executions.

But then, with all his great gifts, Mr. Asquith was not noticeably an imaginative man. To him Ireland was "this most perplexing and damnable country."* His Government was not, after all, a Liberal Government: it was a Coalition Government, made up in part from men who were the bitter enemies of Irish nationalism, whether moderate or extreme. In a Cabinet so constituted, the instructions given to General Maxwell may well have represented the farthest limit of leniency. Although the Liberal *Daily Chronicle* on 5 May criticized the four executions of 4 May, and the officially Liberal *Daily News* on 6 May called for "tempering with mercy the proper sternness of the first sentences," they did not dispute the justice of what had been done to Pearse, MacDonagh and Clarke. It is more than possible that without at least the executions of all the seven signers of the Proclamation, the Unionist Ministers, the Unionist press, the Tory back benchers and the public at large would have staged their own rebellion.

Behind all these considerations, and making them almost pointless, there looms the awful corroding presence of the Great War itself. The damage which this blood-letting had already done to the moral conscience is beyond all calculation. Where death had become a commonplace, if a hateful one, of what account were the deaths of a few rebels? And of rebels, moreover, who had struck at a nation and empire when they were already reeling from repeated defeats?

IV

Indeed, the only way to look at Easter Week is in terms, not of its injustices, but of its achievements: and the rest of this study will, in some measure, be devoted to that question.

---

* This marvelously Asquithian phrase, which suggested the title of this book, will be found in a letter he wrote to Margot Asquith from Dublin on 16 May 1916, having just returned from Belfast where, to his astonishment, he was cheered to the echo. J. A. Spender and Cyril Asquith, *The Life of Herbert Henry Asquith, Lord Oxford and Asquith* (2 vols. London: 1932) II, 217.

As Conor Cruise O'Brien has written of Padraic Pearse — "such men do not die in vain."[33] In Pearse's discourse one can, it must be admitted, always hear the protest of Ecclesiastes and its *vanitas vanitatum*. In his speech over the grave of O'Donovan Rossa, Pearse spoke of "Ireland as we would have her: but Gaelic as well; not Gaelic merely, but free as well." He died for such an Ireland, bilingual and unpartitioned; and such an Ireland has still to appear.

And Connolly, after his court-martial, when he was allowed to see his daughter Nora, asked her, "Have you seen any socialist papers?" She said she had not. "They will never understand why I am here," he went on. "They will all forget that I am an Irishman."[34] He believed, in other and lesser words, that Ireland had first to become a free nation before she could become socialist: he had not lost his faith in the emergence of a socialist Ireland. "In August 1916 the Trades Union Congress at Sligo declined to identify itself with Connolly's participation in the Easter Rising."[35] His name is ritually honored in Irish labor circles today: but the socialist Ireland, for which he died, has yet to appear.

Nonetheless, every student of the Rising, reluctantly or otherwise, has reached the conclusion that it was a cardinal event — a *cardo rerum,* a hinge or turning point of fortune, after which all recourse to Home Rule on the part of the English government became impossible. This did not dawn all at once. It appeared first as sympathy with the rebels; then as a martyrology; then as a growing rejection of the sober promises of constitutionalism. Had Home Rule been accepted by the Tories in 1912, this constitutional path would have led in the long run to independence without partition: but, as J. M. Keynes has reminded us, in the long run we are all dead. The great political effect of the Easter Rising was that it generated impatience in a living generation.

The process of turning the leaders into martyrs began very soon. There is the well-known story, a great favorite with T. P. O'Connor, of the little girl who wanted her mother to give her a hat, and when she was refused prayed silently to "Saint Pearse," whereupon her mother suddenly relented and bought her a hat. This insipid tale would not have gratified Pearse: a hat was not a tin whistle. Other stories were of greater authenticity or impact. It was soon known that Connolly, whom many had accused of atheism, had gone to his death with a Capuchin priest, Father Aloysius, at his side. It was known that Joseph Plunkett and Grace Gifford, ringed about by bayonets, had been married by candlelight on the night before his execution. It was told everywhere that, although rebels had been stationed in places like the

Four Courts, with famous and well-stocked cellars, or the Hotels Imperial and Metropole, where there was plenty of liquor, no rebel had taken a drink during the whole week. Broadcasts were made of court-martial speeches, whether actual or invented; songs were composed. Above all, there were memorial masses for the dead leaders, all attended by overflowing congregations, all ending with collections for their families at the church doors. No wonder the authorities in England soon realized that if the military had got out of control in dealing with the aftermath of the Rising, the aftermath of the Rising, in its turn, had got out of the control of the military.

And there was another result of the Rising, perhaps a foreseeable, certainly an essential one. It became the occasion for great art.

W. B. Yeats was in England, staying with the Rothensteins in Gloucestershire, when the Rising took place. On the whole, he seems to have believed that Irish Nationalists ought to cooperate with England in the War. Lady Gregory was strongly in favor of Irish participation. On the other hand, Yeats had acquired a pronounced distaste for the cruder side of English war propaganda. When the news came, he was at first startled; then fretful — he thought (of all things) that he should have been consulted; then deeply moved.

MacDonagh, whom he liked and who (he thought) was just "coming into his force," was the leader best known to him; but he was at least acquainted with Pearse and Plunkett; and Connolly carried him back in memory all the way to 1898, to Maud Gonne's house in Nassau Street.[36] Madame Markievicz's role in the Irish Citizen Army he had disapproved, if not detested. John MacBride he hated for having married Maud Gonne. The Rising was at first not a public occasion to him but a personal one: and he returned it to its status as a public occasion, not in a political form (he believed that "England may yet keep faith," which belied the politics of the Rising), but in the form of a tragedy.

On 8 May, he wrote to Lady Gregory of "the heroic, tragic lunacy of Sinn Fein"; and soon he was "trying to write a poem on the men executed — 'terrible beauty has been born again.'" As Donald Davie has pointed out, he did not justify the Rising on moral grounds.[37] In the poem in its final form, "Easter 1916," the refrain is "a terrible beauty is born," where "terrible" equals "tragic." He begins by writing of the players in it, whom he would pass in the street with a nod and make the subjects of a mocking tale to please a friend at the club, "being certain that they and I/ But lived where motley is worn."

The tragedy unfolds itself in three kinds of metamorphosis. In the lines about MacBride it is:

> *This other man I had dreamed*
> *A drunken, vainglorious lout.*
> *He had done most bitter wrong*
> *To some who are near my heart,*
> *Yet I number him in my song;*
> *He, too, has resigned his part*
> *In the casual comedy;*
> *He, too, has been changed in his turn,*
> *Transformed utterly:*
> *A terrible beauty is born.*

Then he goes on to the change which comes over those who are dedicated to death. "Hearts with one purpose alone/ Through summer and winter seem/ Enchanted to a stone/ To trouble the living stream." Everything else is changing: only this stony dedication stands motionless. And then as the poem ends, he transforms the stony heart back into something human, changing and mortal; and consciously echoes Pearse's words out of Colmcille, "If I die it shall be for the excess of love I bear the Gael."

> *We know their dream; enough*
> *To know they dreamed and are dead;*
> *And what if excess of love*
> *Bewildered them till they died?*
> *I write it out in a verse —*
> *MacDonagh and MacBride,*
> *And Connolly and Pearse,*
> *Now and in time to be,*
> *Wherever green is worn,*
> *Are changed, changed utterly:*
> *A terrible beauty is born.*[38]

Part Four

SECESSION:
May 1916–January 1919

Chapter Sixteen

Lloyd George Negotiates: 16 May–16 July 1916

After Mr. Asquith had completed his "combing-out" of prisoners during his brief stay in Dublin, the number of those who were interned in England was 1,841 out of a total of 3,343 arrested.[1] It may be remarked that 1,647 of these arrests had been made outside Dublin: the suppression had been very widespread and, in far too many instances, most unnecessary. In Dublin, for example, the senior military officers did not at first always distinguish between the Irish and the Redmondite Volunteers.[2] All in all, the system of arrests and internments, like the "dribbling executions," showed little knowledge and less forethought and produced only uneasiness, fear, and hostility.

As General Maxwell pointed out, in a studiously polite letter to Mr. Redmond, who had been bombarding him with demands for the release of prisoners, Section 14 B of the Defence of the Realm Act empowered him to detain persons without trial in Ireland, and recommend persons for internment in England: but release from internment was now in the hands of an Advisory Committee of the Home Office.[3] And the Home Office was in something of a dilemma. The Irish internees were legally British subjects; they had a right to trial by jury; and with some of them, at least, there was not enough evidence to secure a conviction. What would happen, asked the Home Secretary on 15 May, if a writ of *habeas corpus* were applied for in respect to such persons? For while it was true that the right to trial by jury had been suspended *in Ireland* by a proclamation, issued in accordance with Section 1(7) of the Defence of the Realm (Amendment) Act of 1915, it had not been and could not be suspended *in Great Britain*. One could, of course, take refuge in Section 14B of the Act, which permitted internment without trial in the case of "hostile association": but Section 14B had been under attack, and this attack would increase "if the procedure is now applied to a large body of persons, particularly since their connection with Germany is only indirect."[4]

This was only one of many difficulties facing the Government. Another was the attitude of the Catholic Church in Ireland. Although it can hardly be said to have favored an insurrection, it was now distinctly hostile: and Dr. O'Dwyer, the Bishop of Limerick, had gone so far as to publish in the press a letter to General Maxwell in which he said: "You took care that no plea for mercy should interpose on behalf of the poor young fellows who surrendered to you in Dublin. The first intimation that we got of their fate was the announcement that they had been shot in cold blood. Personally, I regard your action with horror, and I believe that it has outraged the conscience of the country."[5]

General Maxwell may have been proof against such attacks, but not the Government. Nor could it fail to be alarmed at the news coming in from America. On 19 May, for example, Sir Cecil Spring-Rice, the Ambassador in Washington, wrote a dispatch to Sir Edward Grey which began: "I have the honour to state that the events in Ireland are exciting a great deal of hostile comment in the American press." "It is true," continued Sir Cecil, "that the rebellion has miserably failed. But the military executions which have been its consequence have raised the victims to the status of martyrs . . . the sorrows of Ireland now fill the front page. Had the executions ceased in the first few days, the excitement would no doubt have died down. But their continuance has had a gradually exasperating effect . . . After the executions, the more important clergy expressed their horror. Cardinal Farley, of New York, has allowed his name to be placed on the committee for the organisation of Irish relief."[6]

Under such circumstances, it was all too clear that some composition would have to be attempted with the Irish: and it is one of the features of the

Rising's aftermath that one finds the Government making, year by year, more and more conciliatory offers, although it accompanied them (as time went on) with more and more coercive gestures. The first effort at conciliation was placed in the hands of David Lloyd George.

I

The Government had deluded itself into thinking that the time was favorable to such an effort;[7] and claims have since been made that it was, in fact, the last that had any chance of success. The documentation now available makes it clear that this was not the case, and suggests, indeed demonstrates, that from the very beginning success was quite impossible. The negotiations are not the less significant for that: they prove that no settlement, on the basis of the Home Rule of 1914, could ever succeed in post-Rising Ireland.

The task allotted to Mr. Lloyd George was "to bring about a permanent solution." This, it seemed at the time, could be done only in one way. The Government of Ireland (or Home Rule) Act, in the form in which it had been placed on the statute book in 1914, had to be brought into operation at once, or as soon as practicable: and the six northeastern counties of Ulster had to be excluded from its provisions. If the Unionists accepted Home Rule in this form, the question then remained: Upon what terms were the six counties to be excluded? Was the exclusion to be temporary or was it to be permanent? Anything less than a permanent exclusion would now be unacceptable to Sir Edward Carson and Captain Craig: anything more than a temporary exclusion would be immediately rejected by Messrs. Redmond, Dillon and Devlin.

Looking back on David Lloyd George's career as a negotiator, beginning with the railway negotiations in 1907, one is tempted to ask whether that statesman had ever quite distinguished between negotiation and sorcery. Relying upon a charm which was deservedly famous and upon an insight into the weaknesses of the human mind which was nearly inhuman, he had been known to coax both sides of a controversy into accepting results which had everything to recommend them but substance. A brief examination of his proceedings in May and June 1916 will demonstrate this, and will also perhaps reveal that strain of "inner purposelessness" which J. M. Keynes detected in his character and which — to do him justice — usually appeared only when his real purpose was not the one he was ostensibly pursuing.

When his plan for a permanent settlement was published as a white paper later in the year, under the title of "Headings of a Settlement as to the Government of Ireland," it was seen that Mr. Lloyd George had proposed that the six Ulster counties were to be excluded from Home Rule and administered by a Secretary of State, with the help of such officers and departments as might be needed; and that these officers and departments were not to be responsible to the new Irish Government in Dublin. He also proposed that the new Irish Parliament should be composed of the existing Irish M.P.s, less those who represented the excluded area, and that the Irish representation in the House of Commons should remain at 103 — something which Mr. Redmond found indispensable, since it would insure the temporary nature of the whole arangement. The plan — which was not presented to the Cabinet in printed form until 17 July — was relatively simple, leaving (as was only correct) the many technical details to be settled by experts. Only in its fourteenth and final article did it become vague. This article read as follows:

> The Bill [excluding the six counties] to remain in force during the continuance of the war, and a period of twelve months thereafter, but if Parliament has not by that time made further and permanent provision for the Government of Ireland, the period for which the Bill is to remain in force is to be extended by Order in Council for such time as may be necessary to enable Parliament to make such provision.[8]

Since the plan failed to mention whether the exclusion was to be temporary or permanent, one can only assume from the wording of article fourteen that Lloyd George intended to postpone this essential question until after the war and even then for "such time as may be necessary." Only a gift for deception of the highest order could make this hollow compromise acceptable to either side. Mr. Lloyd George, therefore, bargained separately with the Irish Nationalists (represented by Mr. Redmond, Mr. Dillon, Mr. Devlin and Mr. T. P. O'Connor) and the Ulster Unionists (represented by Sir Edward Carson and Captain Craig). Each side had to depend upon him (he hoped) for information about the attitude of the other: or, better still, for no information at all.

It is now possible to examine the events which preceded the emergence of Lloyd George's ambiguous plan. On 22 May the Prime Minister asked him to "take up Ireland, at any rate for a short time. It is a *unique* opportunity, and there is no one else who could do so much to bring about a permanent solution." The next day there came a note from Mrs. Asquith, its envelope coyly addressed to "The Right Hon. David Ll. George, next door." "If you want to please Henry & me," said its embarrassing contents, "settle Ireland. Everyone with a sense of humour must enjoy Ireland, trying as the Irish are."[9]

Why did Lloyd George accept the Prime Minister's offer of such a potentially dangerous and thankless assignment? On 24 May Mr. Asquith told Lady Scott (the widow of the Arctic explorer and a new *confidante*) that Lloyd George "was an ambitious man, he'd stand or fall by the success he made."[10] Possibly this was the case. But it so happened that on 23 May, Mr. Walter Long had written Lloyd George a letter in which he begged him to go to Ireland. If he did, said this fossilized but influential Unionist, now President of the Local Government Board, he would do a service to "Ireland, G. Britain & the Empire . . . the extent of which no man can measure." He could count upon Mr. Long's knowledge and experience "now extending over more than fifty years" and on his influence with his friends, if they would be of use.[11] Had Lloyd George persuaded himself that he had spells at his command which could captivate the unimpressionable Long?

Whatever the answer, Mr. Asquith's offer was accepted on 25 May. In order to take on this new negotiation, Lloyd George had to abandon a plan to accompany Lord Kitchener to Russia, where he was to have tackled the problem of Russian munitions. On 4 June Lord Kitchener left London. The following evening his ship was torpedoed off the Orkneys and all aboard were drowned. At this stage in his career, Lord Kitchener's tragic death did not greatly affect the course of events: had Lloyd George been with him, much history would have been changed.

II

David Lloyd George began his negotiations on 26 May by tackling Lord Midleton, one of the most powerful of the Southern Unionists. Lord Midleton replied the same day that a meeting of "Peers and Commons" connected with the three provinces outside Ulster had expressed itself as being "altogether averse" to any reopening of the Home Rule question without a general election.[12] Lloyd George then arranged a meeting between William O'Brien, the dissident Nationalist, and Sir Edward Carson, to take place on 30 May. The only outcome of this, so far as is known, was a memorandum from O'Brien, in which he suggested a federal solution for Ulster ("securing

Ulstermen substantially the same rights of imperial citizenship as English-men, Welshmen and Scotchmen"), and ended with the emphatic declaration that "to any scheme expressly or implicitly contemplating Partition in any form, my friends and I are unalterably opposed."[13]

No more time was spent with Mr. O'Brien: but on the advice of Walter Long, who said that Sir Edward Carson and Attorney-General Campbell — though "courageous and incorruptible and an immense force" — were not fully representative of Unionist opinion, Lloyd George had already laid his plans before Mr. George Stewart, a Dublin businessman and a former Governor of the Bank of Ireland, who was also an important land agent, and who had just come to London. Stewart told Long, who passed his letter on to Lloyd George, that he had discussed the proposals with Lord Barrymore, Chairman of the Irish Unionist Alliance; and had reached the conclusion that they were "unworkable, repugnant to all Unionist feelings, and would probably only satisfy the Unionists for a brief period." Moreover, said Mr. Stewart, as a final argument, they would simply "justify the recent Sinn Fein Rebellion."[14]

Lord Midleton, in the meantime, had not been idle. On 29 May he called on Lord Lansdowne with the news of his encounter with Lloyd George; whereupon Lord Lansdowne hastened to Lloyd George and "at once told him that the scheme was not one that I could accept." On 1 June, Lord Lansdowne and Mr. Long met with a small Cabinet Committee appointed by the Prime Minister and again stated their "emphatic" objections. This committee was composed of Mr. Asquith, Mr. Lloyd George, Lord Crewe, Lord Lansdowne, and Mr. Long. "In order that there might be no misapprehension," wrote Lord Lansdowne in a paper submitted to the Cabinet on 21 June, "I subsequently sent to the Prime Minister a memorandum explanatory of my views, which he circulated to the members of the Committee."[15]

In the memorandum, Lord Lansdowne said quite simply: "These [Lloyd George] proposals seem to me profoundly alarming . . . [and] will be deeply resented by many of those who now support the Coalition Government. . . . Is this the moment for imposing upon the country, in the guise of an interim arrangement, a bold and startling scheme, which at once conceded in principle all that the most extreme Nationalists have been demanding, viz., the disappearance of the Castle Government and the establishment of an Irish Parliament with an Irish executive responsible to it? The triumph of lawlessness and disloyalty would be complete."[16]

Lord Lansdowne had been given the novel title of "minister without portfolio" in the Coalition Cabinet; he was one of the greatest of Irish

landowners; he was the arch-leader of the Southern Unionists. It is doubtful
if the Government could have survived his resignation. His account was
supported by Mr. Walter Long, moreover, in a memorandum submitted to
the Cabinet on 23 June. Here Long stated that he had met Lloyd George, at
the latter's request, on 30 May; had been shown a rough outline of the
proposals; and had immediately objected that no Irish or English Unionist
would (in his belief) have anything to do with them. "He said I was wrong
and that he had shown the scheme to the leaders of the Unionist party in the
North and South and to the leaders of the Irish Nationalists, and that, on the
whole, with one exception" — Mr. William O'Brien? — "it did not meet with
an unfavourable reception. I still adhered to my views, and in one respect, at
all events, it has been proved that I was right, for Sir Edward Carson appears
to have insisted upon the exclusion of Ulster being made permanent."

It must be repeated that this was not presented to the full Cabinet until 23
June, when the character of Lloyd George's negotiations was just beginning
to come to light. Mr. Long went on to say that he met with Lord Lansdowne immediately upon leaving Mr. Lloyd George; that the three of them
conferred again that evening, when Landsowne and Long repeated their
objections; and that these objections were emphatically presented to the
Cabinet Committee on 1 June.

But just as, in 1911, Lloyd George had settled a railway strike by an appeal
for unity in the face of the Agadir crisis, so now, on this even more difficult
occasion, he resorted to the same expedient.

> Mr. Lloyd George [continued Walter Long] then for the first time, to my
> knowledge, mentioned the question of America and the necessity of an im-
> mediate settlement if we are to get munitions from that country. I at once
> emphatically dissented from that view . . .[17]

A lesser man might have thrown in the sponge after these discouraging
forays among the subgroups in Irish and Cabinet politics. But Mr. Lloyd
George refused to admit that there was an unbreakable link between the
Unionists in the Cabinet and such Southern leaders as Lords Midleton,
Bessborough, Barrymore, Kenmare and Desart and Messrs. Walter Guinness,
M.P., and J. R. Pretyman Newman, M.P. (an Irish landowner sitting for
Finchley in the House of Commons), all of whom had just formed a Com-
mittee to oppose any settlement whatsoever. Instead he turned — indeed had
already turned — to Sir Edward Carson, in whom he thought the key to his
problem was really to be found.

On 29 May, he wrote a brief note to Sir Edward: — "My dear Carson — I enclose Greer's draft propositions. [Sir Francis Greer was Parliamentary Draftsman in the Irish Office.] We must make it clear that at the end of the provisional period Ulster does not, whether she wills it or not, merge with the rest of Ireland."[18] Here then was the promise that the exclusion of the six counties would be permanent. On 6 June, Carson laid the draft terms before the Unionist Council in Belfast: and, against his own deepest wishes but with all the eloquence at his command, urged a permanent exclusion upon the Council. This meant that the Unionists in Donegal, Monaghan and Cavan would have to be left to their fate: but Sir Edward argued conclusively that if some agreement were not reached the flow of American munitions would fail. At a second meeting of the Council on 12 June, therefore, their delegates agreed; and so, while many members of that dour assembly shed tears at the very thought, the truncated Ulster of today began to take shape.[19]

The Prime Minister had appealed to all parties, and these included the Cabinet Committee, to refrain from any immediate discussion (by which he meant public discussion) of Irish affairs. The Ulster Unionist Council, accordingly, merely let it be known that it had accepted a "definite" settlement. On 14 June, Captain W. H. Owen — Lloyd George's liaison with John Dillon — reported that Dillon was not satisfied with the word "definite" but was pressing for an unequivocal statement concerning the temporary nature of the whole arrangement.[20]

And well he might; for Lloyd George had also made assurances to Messrs. Redmond, Dillon and Devlin. Like those he had made to Sir Edward Carson, they were apparently quite straightforward. At some time before the end of May, Mr. Redmond had persuaded his two colleagues to accept the exclusion of the six counties "for a brief period"; and Lloyd George had then solemnly declared that "he had placed his life upon the table and would stand or fall upon the agreement come to."[21] On 5 June, Devlin reported that *"everywhere* outside Belfast the proposed terms were rejected with contempt" but he was of a sanguine temperament, and he was convinced (he told John Dillon) that the forthcoming Nationalist Convention in Belfast would yield to his persuasions.[22]

Mr. Lloyd George had thus promised Sir Edward Carson that the exclusion of the six Ulster counties from Home Rule Ireland would be permanent and had also made, in terms explicit enough for ordinary mortals, a promise to Mr. Redmond and his colleagues that it would be only temporary. We may well ask ourselves what this most extraordinary man had in mind when he entered upon such a course of deception. Presumably he had nothing in mind beyond the hope that he could get his "headings of a Settlement" through the Cabinet over the objections of Lansdowne and Long and that he could then present both the Carsonites and the Redmond-ites with a *fait accompli*. Carson might well have accepted this, since the Ulster Unionist Council would no doubt believe his assurances that the provisional agreement was really permanent. But Redmond and his col-leagues were not as they had been in that world on the other side of the looking-glass, that already ancient, that abolished Liberal world when Great Britain and the Empire were still at peace. In post-Rising Ireland they could accept nothing less than a public promise that Ulster would be returned intact to the Home Rule Parliament, once the provisional period was over.

Meanwhile, during Mr. Asquith's imposed silence, all Lloyd George could do was to keep the two sides apart in the Micawber-like hope that something would turn up; for were they ever to meet across a conference table the whole negotiation would, within five minutes, have vanished into the thin air from whence it came.

The silence was very trying to the nerves of Mr. Redmond and his col-leagues. In Ireland the courts-martial were still proceeding, arrests and deten-tions and the searching of houses were still taking place, Maxwell was still in command, the ill-famed Major Price was still at his right hand: the atmo-sphere, therefore, was a potentially explosive mixture of fear and anger. In Dublin the situation was even considered critical and by 9 June T. P. O'Con-nor was pleading with Lloyd George to get Maxwell withdrawn and Lloyd George was writing to Dillon about the General's "stupid administration."[23] Dillon himself was wondering if Home Rule with a temporary exclusion, though he would do his best for it, would actually answer. "You have let Hell loose in Ireland," he wrote. "And I do not see how the country is to be governed."[24] In such a state of affairs, how exasperating it was to keep silence, and how easily this silence could be misconstrued!

Indeed, the smiling visage of Mr. Lloyd George's deception was, feature by feature, like some Cheshire Cat's, steadily becoming visible. He had already begged Mr. William Martin Murphy, whose *Independent* was the organ of the O'Brien-Healy dissidents, "not to make mischief in Ireland."[25] Mischief, however, from now on to the end of his career, was the one thing Murphy hoped to make: and it was not the less mischievous because he made it under the pretense (was it ever more than that?) of advocating an independent unpartitioned Ireland. On 14 June, two days after the decisive meeting of the Ulster Unionist Council, he had put the correct interpretation on the word "definite" and was writing, sarcastically and ominously, about the Ulster dove returning to the Ark, "having got all he ever asked for . . . a separate empire."[26] On 15 June, the Belfast *News Letter,* generally considered as Carson's mouthpiece, was maintaining that the exclusion was permanent.[27] At this point a marvelously ambiguous speech by Mr. Asquith at Ladybank on 14 June had a soothing effect upon the Belfast Nationalists: and on 18 June their Conference, meeting in secret, agreed to accept a temporary exclusion of the six Ulster counties.[28] As Devlin put it, the meeting had been a "magnificent success" in spite of the lying reports of Murphy's *Independent:* but he begged O'Connor to make sure that nothing was said about it in Parliament until the Ulster Nationalist Convention met the next week.[29]

On 23 June this presumably crucial conference opened at twelve noon in Belfast. It was to be attended by 170 priests, all of them said to be opposed to exclusion in any form, headed by a noted Home Ruler, Father McHugh of Derry.[30] But Devlin had been working day and night among the delegates; several leading Belfast clerics, including the Vicar General of the diocese, were canvassing for him; and he could count on 50 Belfast priests to offset the influence of Father McHugh.[31]

In spite of the pessimistic attitude of Redmond and Dillon, and the reported hostility of the Irish hierarchy,[32] Devlin was in tearing spirits. And he was right. Yielding to his eloquence and to a threat of resignation from Redmond, the convention voted to accept all the Lloyd George proposals, including the temporary exclusion of the Ulster counties.[33]

This was a great success: but, like everything else in these proceedings, it was pure delusion. It coincided with a statement in the *Irish Times* of 23 June, which declared categorically that Sir Edward Carson had received a promise of permanent exclusion from Mr. Lloyd George. On 23 June, also, the Cabinet was told by Irish Attorney-General Campbell: "While the Ulster Unionists are solemnly assured that the exclusion of the six counties is to be a clean cut and a permanent one, the official Nationalists are endeavoring to disarm suspicion by secret assurances to their followers that the exclusion is to be temporary and provisional only."[34] On 24 June, Murphy's *Independent* remarked that, while Mr. Redmond had called the statement in the *Irish Times* a lie, neither Mr. Lloyd George nor Sir Edward Carson had issued any denial.[35] And, on 24 June, Mr. Balfour circulated a formidable memorandum to the Unionist members of the Cabinet, in which he announced his support of the Lloyd George proposals because "were Lloyd George's scheme carried through, the six Ulster counties would have *permanently* secured to them — by consent and without bloodshed — their place in the United Kingdom."[36] The pressure upon Lloyd George's deception was now becoming so great that even he could not have saved either it or himself from exposure.

From this he was most ironically rescued, for his lifetime and far beyond —as late as 1965 an eminent historian was still saying that he "nearly succeeded"[37]—by the stubborn opposition of the Southern Unionists and their allies.

III

Mr. George Stewart, as has been shown, when first confronted with the Lloyd George proposals, had turned them down. But he was a moderate Dublin Unionist; he had been exposed to a famous charm; and he continued to flutter around that equivocal flame. It was partly through his influence that the Dublin Chamber of Commerce decided that it would accept "a temporary settlement . . . for imperial reasons."[38] Indeed, members of the Dublin Chamber of Commerce had been known to say that, rather than endure another bout of Castle rule, they would eventually accept Home Rule if Ulster were included.[39] They were businessmen; they needed Ulster for business reasons and because a Dublin Parliament without Ulster representation would be (they continued) hopelessly lopsided. Thus it will be seen that, unlike the Belfast Unionists, who would accept Home Rule only if six of the nine Ulster counties were permanently excluded, the Dublin Unionists would accept it only if all Ulster was permanently left inside. This, at least, was the contention of the Chamber's vice-president, Mr. R. W. Booth, and its secretary, Mr. R. King Irvine. Such moderate tones, however, were altogether lost among the more forcible utterances of the southern landowners, to whom at this moment *any* settlement was out of the question.

By 10 June, Mr. Lloyd George was all too well aware of this danger: he told John Dillon that the Southern Unionists were bringing "unwonted pressure" to bear upon the Unionists in the Cabinet. Did he hope that he could turn this to his own account, by using it to frighten the Irish Nationalists into accepting his proposals without raising any inconvenient questions about their temporary or permanent character? He went on to tell Dillon that he had kept the southerners' "most gruesome paragraphs" out of the papers; but that the *Morning Post,* which was out for Dillon's blood, could not be suppressed. The only hope for Home Rule, therefore, lay in a quick settlement. "If you and Carson succeed," wrote this bland deceiver, "there will be a deadly struggle in the Cabinet. Lansdowne has sent us a strong memorandum: I am certain he will go. Long is sulky: that is ominous, but I do not mind in the least. If these men withdraw, the Prime Minister and I standing together could compel them to surrender."[40]

But could they? On 11 June, Walter Long sent Lloyd George "a brief statement of [my] views on the Irish question." He had now had time to reconsider his position; things were far graver than when "we first discussed the question" in the Cabinet Committee; and he no longer thought it possible for him to give his assent to any agreement which included the adoption of Home Rule — the more so because he did not believe that the United States of America would interfere with the flow of ammunition and other supplies if the proposals were not carried out.[41] He had been saying this — if his memorandum of 23 June was correct — as early as 1 June: but Lloyd George affected intense surprise. He at once wrote a letter to Mr. Asquith — which he did not send — tendering his resignation, on the grounds that "without a united Government settlement is impossible and as I am so committed to both Irish sections [!] I could not assent to the withdrawal of the proffered terms."[42] He then wrote to Long to say what he had done, or rather had not done.

"It would have been fairer to a colleague who was undertaking a risky and thankless task," he wrote, "had you expressed the views now embodied in your Memo. at the time I was chosen to negotiate . . . Now things have gone so far that they cannot be put right except by my resignation, and in the face of your letter I have written to the PM withdrawing from the negotiation and the Government. The task is a difficult one — without loyal support it is impossible."[43]

Mr. Long's answer was one of shocked surprise. He said he had never been given more than a rough idea of what Mr. Lloyd George's proposals were; nor could he express a clear-cut opinion before consulting "those [the Southern Unionists] whom I am supposed to represent." He could not believe that Lloyd George intended to base his resignation on the excuse that his colleagues had been disloyal and "I need hardly say that I regret extremely that you should even contemplate leaving the Government of which you are so distinguished a member."[44] He had, in fact, been caught off his guard: such threats of resignation were supposed to come from the Unionists, not the Liberals in the Government.

Lloyd George also wrote to the Prime Minister, saying that he had tendered his resignation but had withdrawn the letter. The issue, he thought, was clearly based on a misunderstanding. Some ministers — Lord Selborne, for instance, the President of the Board of Agriculture, and Lord Robert

Cecil, the Minister of Blockade — had assumed that he had told the Irish leaders that his proposals had already been submitted to the Cabinet. He had of course done no such thing, he said: he had told the Irish leaders that his proposals had the Prime Minister's approval; that Lord Lansdowne had disapproved of them; that no other Cabinet minister, except Long, had seen them; and that it was quite on the cards that the Unionist members would reject them. In Ireland they were known, not as the Government proposals, but as "Lloyd George proposals," which did not mean, he hastened to add, that he would have to "stand by them at all hazards." He ended with these words by way of postscript: "If the nationalists & Carson with his Ulsterites support the settlement Selborne and Cecil will rail in vain."[45]

This letter is full of interest: but more for what it concealed than for what it revealed. Lloyd George did not tell the Prime Minister that he had assured Mr. Dillon of their ability to carry his proposals through the Cabinet; he did not confess that he had told Mr. Long that the Nationalists and the Carsonites were very nearly in agreement, which — as we know now — they assuredly were not. Having informed the Prime Minister that he had no intention of standing by his proposals "at all hazards," he wrote at once to John Dillon to say that he was "absolutely committed" to them.[46] It was like a juggling act, immensely skillful and quite meaningless: an act, moreover, which was about to collapse. Even while he was telling Dillon of his absolute commitment, he was obliged to inform him in the same letter that, according to Bonar Law, "the Southern Unionists were moving heaven and the other place" to thwart a settlement; that the Catholic bishops in Ulster were of a like mind; and that Home Rule might yet be defeated by combination of its open and secret enemies.

Five days later, on 17 June, he told the same correspondent that the Unionist members were in a state of mutiny:[47] and this was, in fact, the beginning of the end. The Milnerite Lord Selborne had already threatened resignation on 16 June,[48] a loss which might have been borne with equanimity: but on 20 June "they are all in it," Lloyd George told John Dillon, "except Balfour, Bonar Law and F. E. [Smith]. Long has behaved in a specially treacherous manner. He has actually been engaged clandestinely in trying to undermine the influence of Carson in Ulster by representing to the Ulster leaders that they were induced to assent to the agreement by false pretenses. . . . It is quite on the cards that the Government will go to pieces on the question."[49]

On 21 June Lord Lansdowne reminded the Cabinet that Mr. Asquith, on his return from Ireland, had stated explicitly: "The Home Rule Act, however amended, cannot come into operation until the end of the war." If, in spite of this explicit statement, it *were* to come into operation (said Lansdowne), a government headed by Mr. Redmond could not be relied upon to deal with "what every sensible and well-informed Irishman anticipates . . . a recrudescence of the recent troubles." As for the exclusion of Ulster, in any form, had not the Buckingham Palace Conference of 1914 already proved that this was impracticable?[50]

These words produced a critical situation in the Cabinet. Two days later, it is true, the Ulster Nationalist Convention accepted the Lloyd George proposals on a temporary basis; and on 26 June the Governing Body of the United Irish League and the Irish Parliamentary Party followed suit.[51] But these were mere castles in the air, ideal habitations summoned out of nowhere: the solid material power lay with Lord Lansdowne and the Southern Unionists. On 22 June Austen Chamberlain and Lord Robert Cecil wrote angry letters to the Prime Minister, complaining that Lloyd George had exceeded his instructions:[52] and on 26 June, Cecil followed this up with a stern memorandum to the Cabinet. Had not their friends and supporters in Ulster been told that because of "serious American and colonial complications" the Cabinet had resolved to give Redmond Home Rule at once? And was it not for this "wholly specious reason" that Carson and his followers had assented to the proposals? Was not Redmond, though "loyal," without administrative experience? Was not Dillon "a convinced enemy of this country?" Had not Devlin promised that the first act of such a Government would be to grant amnesty to all the rebel prisoners? On and on he went, until he reached this forbidding conclusion: If Home Rule must come — "and Sir Edward Carson tells us that to withdraw the proposals would throw Ulster into a ferment and convert the rest of Ireland into 'hell' " — then let it come in this form. Let the Amending Bill, always supposing it could be passed, stipulate that the Home Rule Parliament should meet forthwith, elect a Speaker, and then adjourn until the end of the war. "Until then [the end of the war] the present system of government under Sir John Maxwell would continue."[53] If this represented Unionist thinking, what hope was there for an understanding?

Of the Cabinet which met on the afternoon and evening of the next day, and from which Lord Selborne had just resigned, Mr. Asquith wrote an unusually long account to the King. From this it appears that Lord Lansdowne and Mr. Long were ready to leave the Government, Lord Lansdowne saying that he could not assent to the proposals *"though now concurred in by Sir E. Carson and Mr. Redmond"* and that Lord Robert Cecil, Mr. Austen Chamberlain (Secretary for India) and Lord Curzon (Lord Privy

Seal) were not far behind. The strongest supporters of the proposals, on the other hand, were Mr. Balfour (First Lord of the Admiralty) and the Foreign Secretary, Sir Edward Grey. Mr. Bonar Law took an odd position: he (who had once preached Unionist treason from so many Orange platforms) was now prepared to accept these Home Rule proposals, and would recommend their ratification to his party the next day; but he was understood to add that unless he received a large vote in their favor, "his position in the Government would be impossible." It seemed, indeed, as if the Government were breaking up, when Mr. Lloyd George intervened with a felicitous or at any rate a facile suggestion.

"If the resignation of the Unionist members of the Cabinet could be averted," he said, "by a further consideration of possible safeguards for the maintenance of Imperial Military & Naval control in Ireland . . . a small committee of the Cabinet (of 4 or 5 members) should at once be appointed to discuss its terms." The Prime Minister then told his colleagues that "in his opinion at this critical conjuncture of the War, a series of resignations and the possible dissolution of the Government would be not only a national calamity but a national crime." He therefore proposed that a committee consisting of himself, Lloyd George, Lord Robert Cecil and Sir F. E. Smith "should at once proceed to consider & to formulate such additions as seemed to them to be necessary for this purpose *to the arrangements already agreed upon between the Irish leaders.*" At this "all the Ministers who had threatened resignation (including with much personal reluctance Mr. Long) agreed to retain in the meantime their offices."[54]

It must be admitted that this Cabinet was singularly forgetful, for no discussion whatever was made on the essential question: Was the exclusion of the Ulster counties to be temporary or permanent? And this was not all. Lord Lansdowne seems to have believed, and all the Ministers, including the Prime Minister, to have concurred with him, that the Nationalist and Unionist leaders had come to an agreement between themselves, when all they had really done was to come to separate and contradictory agreements with Mr. Lloyd George.

IV

In one sense, and in one sense only, Mr. Lloyd George might be said to have "nearly succeeded": the Cabinet was still discussing his proposals. True, the Unionist members had threatened a dissolution of Government because of them, and had only been prevented by the formation of a face-saving committee. True, the fraudulent character of Lloyd George's commitments to the Carsonite and Nationalist leaders was on the verge of exposure. But Lloyd George continued, presumably in the hope that the Unionist obstinacy, precisely because it was incorrigible, could somehow or other be turned to his account.

Messrs. Redmond and Dillon were now summoned to London at Lloyd George's insistence. "I have to go into this Committee," he said, "with not a single guiding light from the Irish leaders."[55] Redmond was willing enough to go; but Dillon balked. Even a telegram from Mr. Maurice Bonham Carter, the Prime Minister's private secretary, failed to impress him — it was the first communication (he grumbled), direct or indirect, which Mr. Asquith had sent them since the negotiations began, and its purpose was only to extract some large concession. Besides, he had never trusted Lloyd George: "You know that ever since the P.M. shouldered us onto L.G. and cut off all *direct* communication with us, I have all along suspected treachery."[56] Nonetheless, he felt he had to go.

On 5 July they were presented with the committee's findings on the safeguarding of British military and naval rights in Ireland for the duration of the war: these were accepted by Redmond, as also (in a separate conference) by Lansdowne and Long, who put off their resignations while "awaiting the form which [the settlement] might ultimately take."[57] On 7 July the meeting of the Unionist Party, which had been postponed until the committee had completed its work, was held at the Carlton Club. Bonar Law, it will be remembered, had told the Cabinet that he would have to resign if the vote was unfavorable. He now pleaded that "if we go back on these negotiations as a party, we shall make a terrible mistake." The reponse was so hostile that he dared not put the question to a vote, and in this way he retained his seat in the Cabinet.[58]

It was on 11 July that Lord Lansdowne at last put an end to these unseemly and unreal proceedings. In the course of a long speech to the House of Lords, he said that any legislation arising from the Lloyd George proposals would have to be such as to make them "permanent and enduring"; and, as if to give this statement an extra degree of explicitness, he went on to express a perfect confidence in the administration of General Maxwell, now backed by forty thousand troops.[59] In a memorandum circulated to the Cabinet on 18 July, he made a most peculiar admission. He said that the "permanent and enduring" part of his speech had been made *after full discussion with the Prime Minister and Lord Crewe* [Lord President of the

Council and Leader of the House of Lords]." *"I have, of course,"* he continued, *"no doubt as to the Prime Minister's intentions":* but the wording of the
draft bill which the Cabinet had just received "is such as to leave it open to
Mr. Redmond or to anyone else to contend that the whole of the provisions of
the Bill, including that under which the six counties are to be permanently
excluded, are of the nature of temporary modifications . . . I cannot state
too clearly that I consented to remain in the Government in the belief that
the exclusion of the six counties was permanent, in the sense that it would
continue until the Ulster loyalists desired to terminate the arrangement."[60]
In other words, until the crack of doom, or thereabouts.

It was in vain that John Redmond denounced Lord Lansdowne's speech as
"a gross insult to Ireland." It was in vain that he insisted that "the Bill to
carry out the agreements to come must and will, of course, be in all its details
strictly provisional and temporary." It was in vain that he took the unusual
course of publishing a memorandum he had submitted to Asquith and
Lloyd George, in which he declared the agreement to be at an end unless its
provisional and temporary nature was accepted.[61]

Lloyd George should have resigned when he read Lord Lansdowne's
memorandum. But he had already (6 July) been given the War Office, in
place of the late Lord Kitchener. Power was in his grasp. He would not
sacrifice it to those solemn promises which, "laying his life upon the table," he
had made to the Irish leaders far back in May. Summoning Mr. Redmond to
the War Office, he and Herbert Samuel, the Home Secretary, told the Irish
leader that the Cabinet had decided the day before to treat the settlement as
permanent. It had therefore cancelled that clause in the Lloyd George proposals under which the Irish representation in the Commons was to remain
unchanged. Now, at last, John Redmond realized that Lloyd George and Mr.
Asquith had abandoned him to his enemies; he wrote at once to the Prime
Minister to say that any bill framed on such permanent lines would receive
"the vehement opposition in all its stages of the Irish Party."[62] Two days
after his meeting at the War Office, on 24 July, in a speech full of bitterness,
he told the House of Commons that all faith in constitutional methods had
been shattered, that all agreement was over, and that the consequences would
be a national agitation in full sympathy with the Easter Rising.[63]

The words he spoke that day are memorable indeed. "Some tragic fatal-
ity," he said, "seems to dog the footsteps of the Government in all their
dealings with Ireland. . . . They have disregarded every advice we tendd
them, and now, in the end, having got us to induce our people to make a
tremendous sacrifice and to agree to a temporary exclusion of these Ulster

counties, they throw this agreement to the winds." They had also thrown
Mr. Redmond's reputation to the winds: whether that honest man knew it
or not, and he probably knew it, his power had been extinguished and his
day was done.

There remained a singular and rather sorry coda to all this deception and
disharmony.

On 28 July the Prime Minister wrote a letter to Mr. Redmond, marked
"Strictly Personal. This is for you alone." "(1) I am more afflicted than
I can say," it ran, "(in the midst of my other troubles and worries) by
the breakdown of the negotiations. I say nothing as to the responsibility of
this person or that. (2) I think it is of the greatest importance to keep the
'negotiating spirit alive.'" (3) [Here he said he was sure a compromise could
be reached on the number of Irish M.P.s to be retained at Westminster.]
"(4) The real point is the future of the excluded area. Carson (naturally)
wants safeguards against the possibility of 'automatic inclusion.' You (with
equal reason) desire to keep open, & effectively open, the possibility of revision & review — at an early date. (5) I hope and believe that point (4) which
is the crux of the whole matter can be got right."[64]

It is hard to understand how so gifted a man could have brought himself
to write this letter. The answer can only be found in the depths of Asquithian history. The Prime Minister had been a Liberal Imperialist when he
succeeded Sir Henry Campbell-Bannerman; he was still a Liberal Imperialist
when he introduced the Home Rule Bill in 1912. His imagination had never
crossed the sea from one island to another. He had yielded to the *force
majeure* of Tory-Orangeism before World War I; he yielded to it now when
it appeared as a Southern Unionist pressure in the Cabinet. Even if there had
been no Lloyd George subterfuges and stratagems to make the proposals
impossible, the Southern Unionists were from the beginning determined that
no settlement should be accepted unless it was guaranteed to be unacceptable
to their opponents. The Southern Unionists had captured the Conservative
Party meeting at the Carlton on 7 July; they had triumphed in the Cabinet
on 21 July; their spokesmen to Mr. Redmond had been — it was the final
irony — two Liberal ministers, Mr. Lloyd George and Mr. Herbert Samuel.
The victory lay with Lord Lansdowne and Mr. Walter Long, men who,
when the landed interest of southern and western Ireland entered their
minds, invariably stopped thinking, and who had the Easter Rising as a
further impediment to thought. With such a Cabinet, headed by such a
Prime Minister, any agreement with Irish Nationalism in the summer of
1916 was impossible from the start.

How can one account for Lloyd George's part in all this? It was not a simple one: nothing in that great man's career was ever that. A letter he wrote to R. J. Lynn, editor of the *Northern Whig,* may offer some partial explanation. He wrote this letter on 5 June, and in it he said that he had always been sympathetic to the claims of Ulster and that, as a Protestant Nonconformist, he had a "thorough appreciation of Ulster's anxieties as regarded Home Rule."[65] This was the predictable small talk of negotiation, and yet — could there have been a note of genuine feeling in it?

From the Budget of 1909 onward he had never been really straightforward in his dealings with Irish nationalism. In this, of course, he was not singular: the same might be said of all his Liberal colleagues. But there were those who thought that, as a Celt, he would be more sympathetic to the Irish than were the rest of his colleagues. Even John Dillon had once flirted with this idea. Whatever his religious beliefs may have been, however, Lloyd George's cultural background was deeply suffused with Welsh Nonconformity, and Baptist Nonconformity at that. Such a man might be expected to be an enemy to landlords, aristocrats, brewers, publicans, generals and the Anglican Establishment: but would he, *could* he ever be a friend to Catholic Ireland? "Sometimes these cogitations still amaze. . . ."

Then again, and this is more to the point, the whole character of the negotiation had been subtly changed by the death of Lord Kitchener and the consequent vacancy at the War Office. On 11 June it was decided between Bonar Law and Lloyd George, meeting at Lord Beaverbrook's country house, that Lloyd George should take Kitchener's place.[66] True, this was no longer what it had been: Lord Kitchener had been stripped of many of his powers, including the power of appointment to the higher commands, and these had passed to the Chief of the Imperial General Staff, Sir William Robertson, who was expected to cling to them like a limpet.

Nonetheless, in spite of the usual disclaimers and one refusal, Lloyd George wanted the War Office. His work as Minister of Munitions, to which patriotic task he had brought all his powers of imagination, originality and resourcefulness, was complete: any competent administrator could now take over. Even if he failed to get the better of Robertson, the War Office would be a positive step toward his next goal. That was not the Premiership — he wanted Mr. Asquith to stay there. It was, rather, the chairmanship of some new small War Council, which would take from the Prime Minister all his powers of directing the course of battle: for he was convinced, and rightly convinced, that under Mr. Asquith's nerveless hand the war would soon be lost.

From 11 June onward, one cannot help thinking, his intention was not merely to keep the Irish negotiation from ignominious collapse but also to keep it in suspension until some adversary — a Long or a Lansdowne — would take all further responsibility from his shoulders by smashing it without any more ado. Success, on the other hand — if by some utter miracle he *had* succeeded — would not have served his purpose: those Unionists whose support he would now need for his War Council scheme regarded *any* Home Rule arrangement as a surrender to rebellion.

On 27 June, he saved the Asquith Government with his suggestion of a committee on military and naval defense in Ireland; on 28 June he was — for the second time — offered the War Office. On 6 July he became Secretary of State for War. On 7 July the Unionist M.P.s declared their hostility to any Irish negotiation. On 11 July, after consultation (he said) with Mr. Asquith and Lord Crewe,* Lord Lansdowne made his destructive speech in the Lords, the Southern Unionists triumphed, and Lloyd George was spared any further embarrassment.

His abuse of Lord Lansdowne's speech was said to have been unmeasured: and why not? It was the only way in which he could show his gratitude.

---

* Lord Lansdowne was never very reliable on Irish affairs. In a letter to Lord Crewe on 12 July, Mr. Asquith called the Lansdowne speech "tactless and inaccurate and totally uncalled for." J. A. Spender and Cyril Asquith, *The Life of Herbert Henry Asquith, Lord Asquith and Oxford* (2 vols. London: 1932) II, 222. Mr. Asquith might be given the benefit of the doubt, except that, as his latest biographer concedes (Roy Jenkins, *Asquith: Portrait of a Man and an Era* (New York: 1964), 402), "it was indeed even probable that he . . . had by this time become anxious to escape from any arrangement."

Chapter Seventeen

The Rise of Sinn Fein: August 1916– November 1917

On 3 August 1916, Sir Roger Casement was hanged for treason, thus fulfilling what — as he had told Dr. Curry — were his last and dearest hopes.

He was tried under a statute of 1351, known as 25 Edward III, Cap 2: and his chief counsel, A. M. Sullivan, K.C., second Serjeant of the Irish Bar, ingeniously showed that under the wording of this statute, which was certainly susceptible to two interpretations, a man could not be tried for treason if his offense had been committed outside the realm. It is not to be supposed that the judges would or could have released Sir Roger on a medieval technicality: while Sullivan's second line of defense — as Brian Inglis has shown in his masterly and very beautiful account of Casement's last great days — broke down because he saw that it would get him into deep trouble with the English bar. Sullivan had hoped to have his cake and eat it: to put up a great defense, but not offend the higher authorities. He had wished to make a comparison between the treasonable utterances of the Unionist leaders before the War and those of Casement after it: "but here, in court, was Sir Frederick Smith, Attorney-General, a member of the Government. He would not be at all pleased to be reminded of what he had said, before the war. Nor would Lord Reading [the Lord Chief Justice]. He had been a supporter of Home Rule under the Liberal Government; but now, he was concerned with the war effort, and he would not welcome the dredging up of the embarrassing past."[1]

The Attorney-General went on to make a very deadly attack upon Sir Roger. "The prisoner, blinded by a hatred of this country as malignant in quality as it was sudden in its origin, has played a desperate hazard. He has played it and he has lost it. Today the forfeit is claimed." Almost everybody agreed that an Attorney-General had a right to say these words; but many believed that Sir Frederick should not have been that Attorney-General. Had he not once — and not so long ago — incited the youth of England to take up arms against an Act of Parliament?

The Government had hoped to rid themselves of the incubus of one more execution by having Casement declared insane. His diaries for 1903, 1910 and 1911 and an account book for 1911 had been found in a trunk taken from his former lodgings in Ebury Street, apparently late in 1914: they showed, in a most explicit manner, that he was an active and ardent homosexual. A great deal of literature has appeared concerning these documents, and much ingenious argument has been used to prove them forgeries: but the weight of evidence is altogether against such an interpretation. Today, Casement's homosexuality seems irrelevant to the question of his guilt or innocence: it was not so then. When the Government found that the defense refused to have the diaries admitted in evidence at the trial, it turned to baser devices — devices which had in a way been predicted in Casement's letter to Dr. Curry. Copies of the more telling passages were circulated where they would do most harm, the clubs, the Commons, the press, the palace: and many a prominent philistine, including the King, shuddered with loathing at what he read. Casement had become a monster: what he had done was less unintelligible than what he was.

Casement was particularly hated in official circles, no doubt because he had once moved there with some distinction. Sir Ernley Blackwell, legal adviser to the Home Office, was especially bent on his destruction: a memorandum of Blackwell's, written while a reprieve was still possible, is particularly striking. "So far as I can judge," it ends, "it would be far wiser from every point of view to allow the law to take its course, *and by judicious means to use these diaries to prevent Casement attaining martyrdom.*" His colleague, Sir Edward Troup, who also submitted a memorandum, was less vicious. "If

Casement, a Protestant, an ex-official, and a member of the 'ascendency' class in Ireland," he wrote, "is let off the extreme penalty, while mere Catholic Nationalists like Pearse and MacDonagh were executed out of hand, although their guilt was really less deep than his, a bad impression will certainly be made in Ireland."[2]

Troup's appeal to Irish opinion was of more weight on 18 July, when it was circulated to the Cabinet, than it would have been after 24 July, when Redmond's bitter denunciation in Parliament pronounced the end of the Lloyd George negotiations. There was now no hope for Home Rule; and the Government was concerned with a different problem: — How would an execution affect America on the one hand? How would a reprieve affect England on the other? During the Cabinet discussions on the Lloyd George proposals, there had been a real division between those ministers who thought that the influence of Anglo-Irish politics upon American opinion was overrated and those who thought that it was not. Lord Robert Cecil headed the former group, Sir Edward Grey and Mr. Balfour the latter: the result was a less concerted sensitivity at the top. On 19 July, moreover, an "American Press Résumé" contrived to convey the suggestion — undoubtedly wrong — that there was no great transatlantic concern with Casement's fate.[3]

The evidence pouring in, of course, was too great not to give the Cabinet grave anxiety: and one can still be permitted to wonder what would have happened if a Senate resolution of 29 July, supporting a Casement reprieve without naming Casement, and mysteriously delayed in the State Department, had arrived at the Foreign Office in time.[4] According to Grey, to be sure, it would have very little effect:[5] and, in any event, one cannot resist the conclusion that English public opinion was the deciding factor.

The War was going badly in every theater; the much vaunted offensive on the Somme was grinding to a bloody halt; the battle of Jutland, at first hailed as a great naval victory, was far too inconclusive "for British opinion, educated in the legend of Nelson and Trafalgar."[6] There had been Townshend's surrender to the Turks at Kut; there had been Zeppelin raids on London. On 27 July, it was reported that the captain of a British merchant ship had been executed by the Germans for attempting to ram a U-boat:[7] and the new wave of hatred boded ill for a man whose paradoxical relations with Germany had never been and never could have been understood. A reprieve at such a time, and in such a state of public nerves, would have been rather more than injudicious. As the Home Secretary told his wife, it "would be bitterly resented by the great mass of the people in Great Britain and by the whole of the army."[8]

There were people in high places who interested themselves in Casement's reprieve: the Archbishop of Canterbury; the Vatican's Cardinal Secretary of State. He also enjoyed for a while the courageous support of George Bernard Shaw, whose place at the time, to be sure, was not exactly high. Elsewhere a petition was circulated by Casement's old friend, Alice Stopford Green; his great-hearted niece, Gertrude Bannister, braved the astringent Sir Ernley Blackwell in his den at the Home Office; Eva Gore-Booth (who denied that she was attached to Sinn Fein) wrote to the Prime Minister and the Foreign Secretary to insist that Casement had come to Ireland to stop, not to start a Rising, and that the prospect of his execution was regarded in Ireland "with hopeless despair and bitterness."[9] High or lowly, such efforts met with no response.

Casement had sought admission to the Roman Catholic Church during his imprisonment. He made his first confession on the evening before his execution, and his first and last Communion the next morning. "He marched to the scaffold with the dignity of a prince," wrote Father Carey, who ministered to him in his last days at Pentonville, "and towered over us all."[10]

Time has erased the work of Sir Ernley Blackwell. Casement is remembered now almost as much for his labors in the Congo and the Putumayo as for anything else. In his latter days, he was a vain, tormented idealist, certainly deluded at times, just as certainly heroic, never entirely wrong. As the prison bell began tolling to announce his execution, Brian Inglis writes, "a small crowd gathered in the street outside raised a derisory cheer . . . 'It is a cruel thing to die,' he had written in his last letter to his sister Nina, 'with all men misunderstanding.' But now it no longer mattered. He had followed Swift, where cruel rage could tear the heart no more."[11]

I

The Government had already lost interest in the middle class Nationalism of Mr. Redmond and his party, but it had as yet barely begun to realize that a less manageable politics would arise to take its place. The Home Secretary now circulated a report from the Inspector General of the RIC which said that "the raising of the Home Rule question immediately after the Rebellion has been regarded as a victory for the Sinn Feiners, and has thrown into their ranks many who had previously shown no sympathy for them."[12] This was on 2 August: it merely confirmed a report which General Maxwell had submitted to the Cabinet more than a month before; and on the front page of which one minister had noted, "H. H. A[squith] must surely have had some twinges of conscience when he read the report he now circulates." "It is impossible," the General wrote, "to conceive a more inflammable or dangerous condition than Ireland has been allowed to drift into" — he was referring, of course, to the late administration of Mr. Augustine Birrell. Of the Government's post-Rising policy, he felt obliged to say that "clemency has not been attended with the best results." But then there came a peculiar and interesting change. The General began confessing to perplexity — always a sign of grace.[13]

"What appears to be wanting," he wrote, "is a strong hand with full powers to insist on the laws being carried out [and] to rectify such grievances which undoubtedly exist and have 'fair play, no favour' for all alike." Economic conditions were favorable, he said "[but] the social conditions of the cities in the South are deplorable, especially Dublin City; whether this is due to the incompetence of the municipality or to economic reasons, I am not in a position to say; but as long as the labour questions, the incidence of wages, the housing of the poor, remain as they are, rioting and disorder can be expected on the least provocation. Under the circumstances I have tried to depict things cannot remain as they are." In September, when the question of conscription in Ireland was once again coming to the fore, he ventured, in another report, to ask whether it was not now too late. There were some one hundred thousand men available; perhaps they might be offered special concessions with regard to acquiring farmlands after the war. But he would need at least another division with full transport if the Irish conscripts were to be armed in Ireland, for that might well lead to "a bloody rebellion on a large scale." It was a discouraged and discouraging report.[14]

On 19 October, Mr. Asquith told the King that "it was thought desirable that a command should if possible be found elsewhere for Sir John Maxwell of such a kind as to show that the Government fully appreciated his services."[15] In November he was offered the Northern Command, a domestic employment which scarcely showed such appreciation. He accepted with reluctance, and so retired from a country where he had earned a hatred which his superiors had deserved far more than he.

II

Maxwell was certainly not alone in criticizing the administration of Augustine Birrell; almost everyone had had a fling at the late Chief Secretary. Captain Reginald Hall, possibly, deep in Room 40 of the Admiralty, may have permitted himself a twinge of uneasiness. If he had allowed Mr. Birrell and Sir Matthew Nathan to know what he knew, and by what means he had come to know it, things might have gone differently. But Captain Hall, even if he had wished to speak, was obliged for security reasons to remain silent. And so the Birrell administration was thrown to the wolves — that is to say, to the three members of the Royal Commission on the Rebellion in Ireland, Lord Hardinge, Mr. Justice Shearman and Sir Mackenzie Chalmers.

They were mild wolves, but deceptively so — one gets the impression that it was out of sheer hostility that they refrained from asking or pursuing the right questions when Mr. Birrell gave his evidence on 19 and 22 May 1916. Mr. Birrell, to be sure, was not a good witness: he hesitated, he appeared to be ignorant, he lost himself in the clouds. What might have been a very significant series of questions, for example, went as follows:

636. (Mr. Justice Shearman) I take it from what you have said . . . that no effort was made . . . to try and get a general disarmament of volunteers before the outbreak? — (Mr. Birrell) No.

637. (Shearman) This is the thing that puzzles me. One of your advisers thought that it was dangerous and indeed you did yourself? — (Mr. Birrell) Yes. . . .

639. (Shearman) But meanwhile, the Germans might have landed — ? — (Birrell) It is not easy.

640. (Shearman) Well, there was a possibility — disloyal people were allowed to drill, and to drill with arms in their hands. Why? Was not that an overt act which could have been suppressed wherever it was, in whatever part of Ireland? — (Mr. Birrell) We thought it would have been difficult to prove that the arming and drilling of these people was in any way associated with the enemy.

646. (Shearman) . . . I am only saying what puzzles me — what everybody knew — your Under-Secretary said so quite frankly — that these people were known to be disloyal? — (Birrell) Yes, undoubtedly disloyal.

647. (Shearman) And they were known to be having sham fights and training people for warfare in the field, including ladies in ambulance work, and

yet they were allowed to go on doing it? (Birrell) I quite agree it seems almost ridiculous, but on the other hand the alternative would have been to have employed the soldiers. The police could not have done it. You would have had to attack these people, and disarm them, and whether that was done north, south, east or west, it would have resulted in bloodshed.[16]

Here, in these halting answers, we have the essence of Birrell's administration. It was humane, peace-loving, and civilized; possibly it had not been able to adapt itself to the exigencies of an Empire at war. But then again, as Birrell can be heard to say if we examine these answers with any sympathy, once the War had broken out, whether you practiced coercion or whether you practiced conciliation, would not the end be the same? Why then shed innocent blood? "It seems almost ridiculous," said this sensitive man, uttering in vain, and for the last time in history, the seductive voice of Liberal England. The Commission, however, took his words at the foot of the letter. In its report it laid the blame squarely upon Augustine Birrell.

III

It has been claimed in a distinguished book that a vast majority of the Irish nationalists wanted nothing more than Home Rule for all Ireland: and this may well have been true.[17] The evidence shows with overwhelming force that the Rising and its aftermath had aroused a latent nationalism in Ireland; but there is no evidence to prove that a majority of Irishmen wanted to achieve its nationalist aims (as opposed to its no-conscription aims) by further violence, now or at any later time. The point is that when the concept of Home Rule for all of Ireland vanished, as it did with the collapse of the Lloyd George negotiations, Nationalist Ireland drifted, slowly but by perceptible degrees, into a position where only republican and revolutionary leadership became possible. If this was a drift, it was as irreversible as anything can be in an uncertain world.

And now there came a change which was, to many minds, long overdue, and which carried its own special portent for Anglo-Irish relations: on 7 December David Lloyd George succeeded Mr. Asquith as Prime Minister. The issue was, for many reasons, in doubt almost to the end: one of the reasons was that Mr. Asquith brought more ferocity and more skill to the retention of his power than he ever had to running the war. Even now, after his fall, he is said to have lain in waiting "like a crocodile in the shallows, ready to pounce upon Ministers at the first opportunity."[18] It never came, at least in any form where Mr. Asquith, a more and more torpid crocodile, could hope to exploit it.

Lloyd George was not a good party man. He had little respect for tradition and none for loyalty. Where Mr. Asquith had seen Coalition as a lamentable necessity, Mr. Lloyd George (as in 1910, so now) welcomed it as the only solution to the nation's distress. His new War Cabinet, composed of five members, only one of whom had departmental duties, occupied a position (one historian has written) of "uncontrolled and centralized power, only rivalled in modern English history by Cromwell and Chatham."[19] This was true, and more than true, on the civilian side of affairs, where five new ministries — of shipping, labor, food, national service and food production — sprang almost at once into being and constituted a species of "war socialism."[20] It was not true on the service side. Mr. Lloyd George had hoped to become master of the First Lord of the Admiralty (Sir Edward Carson) and the Secretary of War (The Earl of Derby) precisely because they were no longer in the War Cabinet and had to come to it for their orders. As A. J. P. Taylor has pointed out, the opposite was really the case. Carson became the anxious servant of his professional advisers; Derby the puppet of General Sir William Robertson, a soldier who looked upon the War Cabinet as a whole and Lloyd George in particular with profound suspicion.[21]

Lloyd George intended, of course, that the War Cabinet should be an instrument for enforcing his will as Prime Minister. As Prime Minister, however, he had no "department or expert advisers of his own, since his office became virtually divorced from the treasury in the course of the nineteenth century."[22] He introduced a new device, a Cabinet secretariat. Its secretary prepared the agenda; kept minutes which were afterwards shown to and if necessary altered by the Cabinet and its conferees, except for particularly private occasions; and saw that the Cabinet's decisions were carried out by the departments concerned. The Secretary, Sir Maurice Hankey, had been Secretary to the Committee of Imperial Defence; he was a man of great ability, modest demeanor, and (as his diary reveals) unbounded pride. In time, and no lengthy time at that, he became a maker of proposals on his own: and this was true, to a lesser extent, of his principal Assistant Secretary, the more devious Mr. Thomas Jones. No doubt, they exceeded their functions: but, considering their opportunities, and the reliance which was placed upon them, they would have been barely human if they had not.

The Prime Minister also assembled his own private staff, which did its work in huts in St. James's Park and was known and deeply mistrusted as "the Garden Suburb." Upon this staff he came more and more to rely for information and ideas, but it was not an adequate substitute for a staff of expert advisers. The result was that the War Cabinet was full of imperfections. Its original members were Andrew Bonar Law, Chancellor of the Exchequer and Unionist leader; Arthur Henderson, who represented Labour; Lord Milner, who "carried great weight with the Tory intelligentsia and Die Hards (by no means identical groups)";[23] Lord Curzon, a practiced fence-sitter and competent administrator; and the new Prime Minister. Under the weight and variety of business constantly bearing it down, it became in certain respects, though by no means in all, as inefficient as its predecessor, but with this immense difference: Whereas Mr. Asquith had little to offer but official prestige and imperturbable torpor, Lloyd George's famous mastery of men and events, though disreputable and prone to error, never deserted him or his country until the war was over.

One of Lloyd George's first acts was to summon John Redmond to an interview. The Nationalist whom he had so recently betrayed, and who had lost all faith in his betrayer, listened with very mixed feelings when he was told that while the Irishmen interned in England without trial would be released and martial law revoked, there would be no change in the personnel of the Irish Government.[24]

Redmond had recently recovered some of his spirits when a follower of his, in mid-November, won a closely fought by-election at West Cork, the two defeated candidates being a brother of Tim Healy's and a Sinn Feiner who disavowed physical force. Whether this contest in West Cork could be called a local feud or a typical election or neither, it was at any rate the last but one that the Parliamentary Party was ever to win in Southern Ireland. It was undoubtedly one of the reasons why Redmond was summoned to this early interview with the new Prime Minister and offered a new bargain; and one of the reasons, too, why he denounced this bargain with renewed confidence. If any proposal were made to impose conscription on Ireland, said Lloyd George, he would ask for immediate and unpartitioned Home Rule. Redmond replied, with contempt, that he would never accept conscription as a condition of Home Rule.[25]

From now on, conscription became one of the great issues — perhaps *the* issue — which gave spirit and momentum to the new nationalism arising from the Easter Rebellion. Its appearance is all too easy to explain. The Lloyd George Government came into being as a necessary reaction to a series of disasters and difficulties: the Dardanelles, Mesopotamia, Jutland, the Somme; food prices and war profiteering; the "comb-out" in industry; the U-boats. This last problem was particularly awful. The average amount of tonnage sunk monthly from October to December 1916 was 300,000; while the decline in mercantile shipbuilding, whether from inertia or from prior naval requirements, had been even more dismaying.[26] One can well imagine with what irritation the new Government found itself engaged, amidst all these terrible distractions, in a wrestling match with Irish Conscription. The problem could not be avoided altogether; public opinion in England would not permit that: at best it could only be postponed. It involved the most delicate imperial and American relations, and it was greatly out of proportion to the number of men concerned. In October 1916, Mr. Duke, the new Chief Secretary, told the Asquith Cabinet that there were 160,000 Irishmen actually available for service, and that (like Sir John Maxwell) he was much opposed to the idea of conscripting them — it would, he argued, "produce grave and widespread disturbances."[27] Even the old Redmondite (or National) Volunteer leaders, men like J. J. Donovan and T. M. Kettle, were now saying — so Duke reported — that the National Volunteers might have to be called out at a moment's notice in order to resist conscription. They even proposed to increase this potential resistance by distributing Volunteer recruiting posters throughout the country.[28]

The new Prime Minister's response to this problem was quite in character. First, he endeavored to prove that his recent negotiations had been abortive because they had been conducted in, as he put it, "a quagmire of distrust which clogged the footsteps and made progress impossible."[29] (He did not add that if there had been a quagmire he had been its *ignis fatuus,* leading men deeper and deeper into the morass.) When this argument failed to convince the Irish, he resorted to threats. In January 1917 he invited T. P. O'Connor to dinner at the National Liberal Club; the talk turned to conscription for Ireland; and Lloyd George told his guest of a great sensation in the Cabinet when Sir William Robertson, the Chief of the Imperial General Staff, reported that Irish recruiting had dropped to eighty a week. He went so far as to say that the feeling in the country was so strong that he could well be beaten in the House on the conscription issue; in which case, he assured O'Connor, a purely Tory Government would follow.[30]

In the meantime, as a gesture of conciliation, the six hundred or so political prisoners interned in England had been released in time to get home for Christmas: among them were Michael Collins, who had fought in the Post Office, and Arthur Griffith, whose reputation the Government had saved at the last minute by locking him up. Their reception was not particularly impressive, and they had no concerted program; but, combined with and enhanced by the conscription issue, their power began almost at once to show itself.

In January there died the old Parnellite and veteran of the land war, J. J. O'Kelly, M.P.; and the candidates nominated to fill his vacant seat at North Roscommon were an official Remondite, Mr. Devine; an Independent Nationalist, Jasper Tully; and Count Plunkett, the father of the dead hero Joseph Plunkett. Two more of the Count's sons had taken part in the Rising and were now lying in English prisons under a sentence of ten years penal servitude. The Count himself had been one of the internees released before Christmas: and his election address, which the censor suppressed, though he could not suppress his speeches, was full of tales of police brutality after the Rising.[31]

Michael Collins and Arthur Griffith both worked hard for Plunkett; Laurence Ginnell (M.P. for Westmeath) came over and denounced Redmond and the Irish Party as traitors and job hunters; and the notorious Father Michael O'Flanagan was there to stump the constituency. The historian first encounters Father O'Flanagan in August 1915 when, as curate in charge of Claffoney in County Sligo, he fell foul of the Congested Districts Board by urging his parishioners to cut turf on the Board's land. O'Flanagan was transferred to another curacy in October, whereupon his parishioners took the unusual step of locking the church against the new curate and would not give up the key until Christmas Day.[32] There was clearly something rather special about this priest, and it would have been a poor compliment to him if the police had not put him on their list of seditious preachers. He was now the curate of Crossna in County Roscommon, and was proclaiming, as a final argument for Count Plunkett, that the heroes of Easter Week had saved the young men of Ireland from being conscripted into the army of "the only enemy Ireland has had for the past one thousand years."

On 4 February 1917, Count Plunkett was elected with 3022 votes against 1702 for Devine and 687 for Tully. Somewhat against his will, he bowed to the wishes of his constituents and followed the Sinn Fein plan by refusing to take his seat in Westminster. Thereafter his speeches became more and more spirited.

The unrest which came to the surface in the Roscommon election was repeated in a more formidable manner at South Longford, where another by-election was pending. Here the newly formed Sinn Fein National Council of 19 April 1917, whose program denied the right of any foreign parliament to make laws for Ireland and demanded a seat for the nation at the Peace Conference,[33] decided to put up a new kind of candidate. He was Joseph

MacGuiness, who was serving three years in Lewes Gaol for his part in the Rising and who, as an IRB man, was most unwilling to play a part in conventional politics. He was nominated nonetheless; Michael Collins and Arthur Griffith, in spite of some outstanding differences, joined in the campaign; and, as Robert Kee has reminded us, MacGuiness actually received the endorsement of Dr. W. J. Walsh, Archbishop of Dublin — an endorsement which the candidate would certainly have repudiated, had he been given the chance, but which was almost as certainly decisive.[34]

The Irish Parliamentary Party organizers had been, with the single exception of John Dillon, confident of victory; South Longford was one of their strongholds; and when the poll was declared on 10 May, and it was found that the Sinn Fein candidate had won by 37 votes, their consternation was acute, and many spoke of resigning in a body.[35] In the RIC report, Count Plunkett was said to have declared that the first blow for separation from the United Kingdom had been struck in Easter Week; the second in North Roscommon; the third in South Longford.[36]

IV

All this was being followed with dismay by political observers in Great Britain. On 6 April, the United States entered the war; and on the next day the *Daily Mail* said: "There is only one obstacle to the undiluted outpouring of American sentiment in favor of the allies. That obstacle is Ireland." The *Daily Mail,* a Northcliffe paper, had supported Lloyd George in his ascent to the premiership; it could not be disregarded; but did not the *Daily Mail* know that everything had been attempted?

On 16 April the War Cabinet confessed to itself that

(1) The Home Rule Act is, in certain respects, out of date, and, in any circumstances and by common consent, must be amended before it can come into operation.

(2) The Government have announced in Parliament their intention of endeavouring to find a settlement.

(3) The Irish Nationalist Party decline to enter into any negotiations for a settlement.

(4) The permanent partition of Ireland has no friends, but, on the other hand, any attempt to include Ulster in a scheme of Home Rule at the present time must end in failure.[37]

As a way out of this apparent impasse it now proposed that an Amending Bill should be introduced, allowing each of the six Ulster counties to vote itself out of Home Rule by a 55 percent majority of electors voting — which meant that two of the six counties would certainly remain in — and providing for a very unwieldy Council of Ireland, composed of Ulster M.P.s and an equal delegation from the Home Rule Parliament, to consider questions affecting both the Home Rule and the excluded areas. It also proposed that this singular bill, between its second reading and its committee stages, should be referred to a Speaker's Conference, not necessarily composed of M.P.s or peers. If the Amending Bill survived such stern treatment, the Government was then to announce its intention of enforcing the original Home Rule Act unless the bill was agreed upon and accepted before a certain date. These were desperate expedients; and they were none the less desperate because Sir Edward Carson, who had been summoned from the Admiralty to attend this Cabinet, said that he was totally opposed to them.[38]

As A. M. Gollin has explained, Sir Edward, although a member of the Government, was now mounting a massive opposition to Lloyd George; it consisted of fusing the naval and the Irish problems into one issue.[39] The naval question had become almost overwhelming. "In the first ten days alone [of April] 250,000 tons had been sunk"; at the end of the month the loss amounted to 850,000; and in official circles 1 November was given as the furthest limit of British endurance.[40] To David Lloyd George the answer to such an appalling state of affairs had long been the institution of a convoy system: to this the leading admirals, with the full support of Carson, stubbornly opposed their own arguments, bristling with a multitude of technical objections. The Prime Minister at length secured the support of Lord Milner (one of Carson's closest friends) and, thus fortified, took the unusual step of storming the Admiralty in person: as a result, in due time, on 20 May, the first convoy reached England in safety. Carson was soon removed from the Admiralty by the simple device of pushing him up into the War Cabinet: here, it was believed, his promotion would appease the Unionists and his negativism would actually do less harm.

The Irish problem, meanwhile, received another and temporary solution. At the Cabinet of 16 April, Carson's opposition to the proposed Amending Bill, combined with his still current battle over the convoy system, had put the administration in genuine danger. For a whole month the crisis continued. But it so happened that one of the inhabitants of the Garden Suburb, Professor W. S. G. Adams, had already presented a plan for an All-Ireland Convention, which should work out some agreement between the north and south:[41] and now — whether by judicious planting or sheer coincidence — the plan reappeared in the mind of Mr. Redmond.

On 15 May, at a banquet given for General Smuts, Redmond was seated next to the Marquess of Crewe, Mr. Asquith's close friend. To Lord Crewe he now confided his belief that a Convention of Irishmen might work out their own ideas and offer them to the Government as a recommended settlement. Lord Crewe (so he told Mr. Asquith) hastened to Number 10 Downing Street as soon as the banquet broke up; Mr. Lloyd George was all compliance; Mr. Bonar Law was called in from next door; and it was agreed that every encouragement should be given to Mr. Redmond.[42]

After the "quagmire" speech, however, Mr. Redmond — and not for the first time — refused to have anything to do with Mr. Lloyd George; and a good deal of diplomacy was required before he would allow Lord Crewe so much as to approach him. Lord Crewe then worked out a scheme of his own, which he presented to the Prime Minister and the Prime Minister presented to the War Cabinet, and which offered Mr. Redmond a new and even more complicated version of the Irish Council proposal on the one hand, and, on the other, as a kind of afterthought, an Irish Convention. Even Sir Edward Carson, who had been summoned to the Cabinet on 16 May, could find no objection to this; a letter was at once dispatched;[43] and Mr. Redmond, while contemptuously dismissing the Irish Council, consented to accept the Convention which he had himself suggested to Lord Crewe.

The Convention, which began its meetings at the Regent House of Trinity College on 25 July, has been given a brilliant treatment by Professor J. B. MacDowell: but to those who, like the present writer, believe that Home Rule in any form was finished when the Lloyd George negotiations came to an end in July 1916, it has only the charm (admittedly a considerable one) that attaches itself to the irrelevant and the foredoomed. As an example of the varieties of Irishmen, lay and clerical, which could be got together for such an occasion, and of the varieties of argument they could invent, it is certainly instructive. But since Sinn Fein refused to appear and Labor was virtually unrepresented, might it not be hinted, with due modesty, that the Convention was extinct from the start?

Any hope of an agreement between the Southern Unionists, (now, rather than face a partitioned Ireland, willing to accept a modified Home Rule),[44] the constitutional Nationalists and the Ulster Unionists was quashed by an unfortunate and almost predictable difference between those Nationalists who demanded fiscal autonomy and with it an unpartitioned Ireland and those Unionists, all from Ulster, to whom fiscal autonomy was detestable and who would accept nothing less than partition. Moreover, John Dillon had decided that he could not in conscience attend: and although Joseph Devlin brought his sanguine temperament to those debates and John Redmond fought nobly on until he died, the loss of Dillon was not only severe but also symbolic. It showed that the Irish Party was rapidly dissolving, that it had, indeed, dissolved. Although it still had some nuisance value in the Commons, and could still win two by-elections in the Catholic districts of Ulster, and one at Waterford, its political consequence in Ireland was nearly at an end.

To the Prime Minister, of course, the Convention was an unmixed blessing. In November, he wrote to Redmond, who had been prophesying "violence and bloodshed all over Ireland" if the Convention broke up: "I know too well what the consequences of the failure of the Convention would mean to Ireland. The alternative to that failure I, with my record of opposition to anything in the nature of Coercion in Ireland, would regard with perfect horror."[45] In the light of what we now know about the Prime Minister's subsequent maneuvers, these words have a meaning all their own. The Convention was nothing more to Lloyd George than a most respectable and plausible way of marking time for months on end: and the coercion he dreaded had nothing to do with the imposition of Home Rule or the suppression of Sinn Fein. The coercion he dreaded was the enforcement of conscription.

Lloyd George's language was often, more often than usual even in politics, quite at variance with his actions. It was because he seemed to be threatening Ulster with coercion that Sir Edward Carson resigned from the War Cabinet in January 1918.[46] Carson's influence was on the wane; it was time for him to go; and within a month the Prime Minister was writing to him to say how dissatisfied he was with Dublin Castle's failure to "suppress those Bolsheviks [Sinn Fein]" and to ask "how would Robertson do for Ireland?"[47] Sir William Robertson, Carson's close friend, Lloyd George's enemy, had just been ousted as C.I.G.S.: if *he* had gone to Ireland, it could only have meant suppression. As the Milnerite F. S. Oliver said: "[Lloyd George] is always changing his mind"; as Lady Carson put it: "He seems to be acting very slyly." They were writing about a mind which flickered and shimmered like a trout in the shallows; but which moved on upstream magically, indomitably, against all obstacles. The Convention had revealed the differences between the Southern Unionists and the Ulster Unionists and it had managed to linger on until 9 April 1918. No more had ever been expected of it, at least by David Lloyd George.

V

In order to get the Convention off to a good start, the War Cabinet had agreed to release all the Irish rebels who — sometimes with life sentences — were still imprisoned in England. This was first mooted on 22 May 1917; two days later the Chief Secretary agreed; and the Home Secretary's report of a "slight mutiny" among the Irish prisoners in Lewes Prison rather hastened than delayed the Cabinet's resolve.[48]

The final decision was made on 14 June: and Mr. Balfour and Mr. Walter Long, now Colonial Secretary, who had been summoned to the War Cabinet because both had been Chief Secretaries in their day, listened with attention while the Prime Minister pointed out that refusal of amnesty had become a flag around which the extremists were able to rally public opinion. As an example, he offered the pro-amnesty meeting at Dublin on 10 July, which had resulted in the death of Inspector Mills of the DMP. After this, Mr. Balfour agreed that the Cabinet should recommend amnesty to the King, and Sir Edward Carson unwillingly supported him: only Mr. Long dissented.[49] The announcement was made the next day, and the prisoners returned by the morning and evening boats on 18 June.

When the first batch arrived, with Eamon de Valera at their head, they were received by a group of Aldermen at Westland Station and "in the streets of Dublin all work was suspended and all traffic sidetracked while the prisoners were driven in cars between ranks of people cheering and shouting their welcome and delight."[50] By the evening boat, into the same tumult, came the Countess Markievicz, the "virago" of St. Stephen's Green who, in Aylesbury's Prison for Women, had suffered many indignities and borne them without a murmur, in the spirit of John O'Leary. All the returning prisoners, although they had heard rumor of an "awakening," were astonished at their reception: they remembered the jeering or sullen crowds which had seen them off.

Considering the by-elections at North Roscommon and South Longford, and their hostile implications, the Government had made a most conciliatory move. The result might have been expected. There was to be a by-election at East Clare, the constituency of Major Willie Redmond, John Redmond's brother and dearest friend, a brave, kind and popular man, who had been killed in action at Messines on 7 June. The Sinn Fein nominee was Eamon de Valera, now famous for his part in the Easter Rising. By his side on the platforms stood Eoin MacNeill, to whom — in Dartmoor Prison — de Valera had done an immense service by insisting that he should be treated as a Volunteer in good standing. If the police reports are to be believed, de Valera's speeches were nothing if not uncompromising: on 1 July, "We are not at war with Germany . . . You have no enemy but England"; on 5 July, "It is my wish that the British Empire will be blown into ruins."[51]

On 12 July the result was announced: de Valera, 5,110; Patrick Lynch, K.C. (a well-known and popular figure, especially handpicked by the Parliamentary Party), 2,035. It was another stupefying defeat for constitutionalism.

Again, in August, the death of Paddy O'Brien, the Party's Chief Whip and almost the last of Redmond's intimate friends, brought on a by-election in Kilkenny. The Sinn Fein candidate was William Cosgrave, who had fought in the Easter Rising, and whose sentence of death had been commuted to one of penal servitude for life: on 14 August he defeated his Redmondite opponent by 772 to 392. This event called forth many speeches even more violent than those delivered at East Clare, some of them so violent as to produce a sentence of imprisonment: one was by Thomas Ashe of County Dublin fame. In Mountjoy Prison, Ashe and his companions demanded, somewhat unreasonably, to be treated as prisoners of war. There followed a riot and a hunger strike; and Ashe died on 25 September after repeated and brutal subjections to the feeding tube by an incompetent doctor. His funeral, stage-managed by the Wolfe Tone Executive Committee (*alias* the IRB), was the focus for a huge public demonstration.[52]

All this took place against a background of increasing disaffection. On 3 July, Lord Wimborne, Mr. H. E. Duke, Sir Brian Mahon (Maxwell's successor in the Irish Command) and Brigadier-General J. A. Byrne of the RIC attended the War Cabinet, which sat without a break from 3:15 to 7:30 P.M., to report on the condition of Ireland. General Mahon said that he had thirty-four thousand troops of fighting strength under him, enough to deal with an immediate emergency: but he thought that there would be a serious rising if the Convention failed. At this the Prime Minister pointedly congratulated the soldiers and police on having acted with great discretion:[53] and Mr. Duke, "speaking like a man overworked and overwrought and on the verge of breakdown," took the Prime Minister's remarks to be a "ramp" against his own administration.[54]

On 14 July the Chief Secretary once again attended the War Cabinet and warned it that de Valera and a small group of Sinn Feiners had now advanced from claiming a representation at the Peace Conference to an "avowed advocacy of physical force"; that, emigration having ceased because of the war, the young men of Ireland were increasing in numbers and disaffection; and that he was convinced Sinn Fein would resort to direct military force, as in Dublin in 1916. Even without arms, he said, it would overwhelm the police barracks and government offices by mere weight of numbers.[55]

If there was a note of hysteria in this, and there certainly was, the War Cabinet disregarded it, for Chief Secretaries were hard to come by. It authorized Mr. Duke to stop, by police action, all marching or drilling in military formation or Volunteer uniforms; to enforce the regulation which required special permission for processions; to seize seditious presses; to take possession of premises used for drill halls; but not to prosecute speakers for seditious language which did not actually incite to violence. Was there not still a hope, said the Prime Minister, who had no such hope himself, that the Convention would bring into existence "a new central party of moderate men?"[56]

Thus there began "the policy of pin-pricks" — the words were Sir Edward Carson's — which (though it scarcely offered the *mot juste* for the medical murder of Thomas Ashe) generally prevailed so long as Lord Wimborne and Mr. H. E. Duke headed the Irish Government. Such a policy may only have served to embitter feelings, extremist and moderate alike: and it certainly had no effect on disaffection. Yet what else could the Government do?

VI

In July 1917 Eamon de Valera was given a place on the Sinn Fein National Council and in the provisional executive of the Irish Volunteers.[57] This led to the concept, honored in the police reports and expressed by de Valera himself at Ruane on 6 October, that the Sinn Fein clubs were the political arm and the Volunteers the military arm of the separatist movement. It also temporarily reconciled the orthodox Sinn Feiners and the revolutionary Volunteers; and it represented de Valera's own synthesis, which he offered at Kilkenny on 5 August — namely that the Irish should first battle England with votes and then, if that failed, with rifles.[58] De Valera also ended his relationship with the Irish Republican Brotherhood: like Cathal Brugha, the hero of the South Dublin Union in the Rising, he wanted the movement to stay out in the open. Had he not experienced at first hand the bewildering character of a bicephalous leadership, where the powerless head was visible and the powerful head was not? It is true that men like Harry

Boland and Austin Stack, now openly boasting of his part at Tralee, or Michael Collins (who had formed an IRB circle in the internment camp at Frongoch), did not at all share this point of view; and that it was the beginning of a fateful division between Collins and Brugha: but at the time it was not of the first importance.

The central problem still was how to make a permanent reconciliation between Sinn Fein and the Irish Volunteers. On 26 October, the tenth Sinn Fein Convention, or *Ard-fheis,* was to meet: it was expected to ratify a new Constitution — an extremely delicate undertaking, for Arthur Griffith would not pledge himself to a Republican form of government and Cathal Brugha would settle for nothing less. In the committee appointed to prepare a draft Constitution, de Valera endeavored to avoid this clash of ideas by suggesting an ingenious definition of the aims of Sinn Fein.

Sinn Fein aims at securing the international recognition of Ireland as an independent Irish republic. Having achieved that status the Irish people may by Referendum freely choose their own form of Government.[59]

This was accepted unanimously by the Provisional Executive Committee and became part of the preamble to the Constitution brought before the Convention. The fact that it was accepted unanimously, although it was very nearly if not quite a contradiction in terms, shows how anxious the Irish leadership was to reach a composition.

De Valera also made it clear that he expected to succeed Griffith as the Sinn Fein President; to this Griffith assented; and when the Convention opened at Dublin's Mansion House his speech laid special emphasis on the need to subordinate all differences to the great issues lying ahead. The Constitution was then moved by Cathal Brugha, seconded by John Milroy, and accepted unanimously by the seventeen hundred delegates. After this it was explained, once more, that Sinn Fein was to be a political organization and the Irish Volunteers a military one.[60]

In the elections, held on 27 October, de Valera was unanimously made President; the two Vice-Presidents were Arthur Griffith and Father O'Flanagan, with Count Plunkett running third; while the two Treasurers (W. T. Cosgrave and Laurence Ginnell) and the two Secretaries (Austin Stack and Darrell Figgis) were elected without opposition. The only real difficulty seems to have arisen in the election of members for the Executive Committee: here the Countess Markievicz bitterly objected to the candidacy of Eoin MacNeill. But de Valera overruled her. "I know what happened," he said, "and I believe I am the only man who knows what happened . . . and I am perfectly convinced that Eoin MacNeill did not act otherwise than as a good Irishman. Had I the slightest doubt of that, I would not have had him on my platform at Ennis [in the East Clare election]."[61]

As it turned out, MacNeill came in at the head of the polls with 888 votes over (for example) Cathal Brugha with 688 and the Countess with 617. Well down the list of the 24 elected were Mrs. Tom Clarke (402), Mrs. Joseph Plunkett (345) and — at the very bottom — Ernest Blythe and Michael Collins with 340 apiece.[62] Thus Sinn Fein, a small group which had played no part in the Easter Rising, became the Rising's political heir, with a somewhat equivocal dedication to republicanism and — if MacNeill's appearance at the head of the poll meant anything — to moderation as well.

If this was so, it was offset by de Valera's presidential address, which police reported as being openly rebellious. Speaking as a Catholic, he went after the "theologians" of the Redmondite *Freeman's Journal* and the Unionist *Irish Times,* who "tell us that rebellion is not justified . . . I say to these people who start as theologians with a glass of grog by their side, with their feet planked up on the mantelpiece of the editorial room — and it is there they write many of the anonymous letters — I say in theology . . . of all subjects 'a little learning is a dangerous thing.' May God grant the day when we will be able to get rid of [this Government] by physical force."[63]

In the preamble to the Sinn Fein Constitution there appeared the declaration that Sinn Fein should "make use of any and every means available to render impotent the power of England to hold Ireland in subjection to military force or otherwise." To this a priest had offered the amendment that, after the word "available," there should be added this careful qualification — "which in the judgment of the National Council are deemed legitimate and effective." He did not, he said, want Sinn Fein sullied by "any crime or outrage."[64]

Though this amendment was tactfully disposed of, and the Constitution passed unanimously, a very large area of disagreement had been opened. There is no evidence that the majority of the Irish people wanted another insurrection or wished to move beyond the methods of orthodox Sinn Feinism — passive resistance, abstention from Westminster, self-reliance.[65] On the other hand, as men like Thomas Ashe and the Mountjoy prisoners or, for that matter, the rhetoric of Roscommon and Longford and East Clare had amply demonstrated, there was a minority which wanted a good deal more.

This minority was represented by the Irish Volunteers who, the day after the Sinn Fein *Ard-Fheis,* held their own Convention on the GAA's grounds. Here de Valera was elected President, Cathal Brugha Chief of Staff, Diarmid Lynch Director of Communications, and Sean McGarry General Secretary. The Volunteers were so basically Republican that it was unnecessary to incorporate the Republic into their Constitution. The objectives of 1914 remained unchanged: "1. To secure and maintain the rights and liberties common to all the people of Ireland. 2. To train, discipline and equip for this purpose an Irish Volunteer Force. 3. To unite in the service of Ireland Irishmen of every creed and every party and class." The Director of Communications and the General Secretary — two key posts — were in the hands of IRB men; and in the executive appeared the name of Michael Collins: it is not to be supposed that the IRB presence escaped the attention of de Valera.

In his address, as reported to the Castle, he said:

By proper organisation and recruiting they could have 500,000 fighting volunteers in Ireland. That would be a big army, but, without the opportunity and the means of fighting, it could only be used as a menace. There had been already too much bloodshed without success, and he would never advocate another rebellion without hopeful chances of success . . . When the war was over, England would be tottering. The Allies could not win. All nations at the Peace Conference would claim their right to the Freedom of the Seas, and Ireland was of such international importance in that respect that her claim must be admitted. They wanted an army to back up that claim.[66]

To bring in the delusive concept of the Freedom of the Seas was, now as always, to use the language of moderation: and de Valera was trying to achieve a balance by uttering extremist doctrine in the moderate camp and moderate doctrine among the extremists. He was a stern republican: but he was, at this stage in his career, developing a flexibility in maneuver which made him unique among the Irish leaders. The equilibrium he was trying to maintain was a very unstable one, and there were signs at the end of 1917 and the beginning of 1918 that the activists were growing impatient of control. At this critical moment, however, there loomed up a horrendous but absolutely reliable means of reconciling dissident thoughts and incompatible philosophies — and that was the Great War upon its Western Front.

Chapter Eighteen

Conscription and Vindication: January 1918—January 1919

When David Lloyd George formed his Coalition in December 1916, one of the conditions imposed upon him by the Conservatives was that he should keep Sir Douglas Haig in command in France.[1] Sir Douglas was an odd combination of cavalier and roundhead, a society general with a strong sense of personal righteousness, and a well-developed gift for intrigue. At his back stood the massive form of Sir William Robertson, Chief of the Imperial General Staff, an officer who had risen from the ranks and who concealed, behind the mask of plaint blunt soldier, the keen features of a politician. He had already secured an Order in Council which made him, in effect, the Cabinet's sole military adviser. Haig's and Robertson's relations with the Press, and with important and exalted people in and out of politics, made them difficult men to circumvent. Then they had another characteristic, which they seemed to share with most officers of high rank in that terrible war. They were noticeably lacking in compassion and humility — qualities, no doubt, not very serviceable to military commanders in a time of crisis, but for the want of which they often seem to transform themselves into figures of quite monstrous aspect. To send thousands upon thousands of men to death or mutilation in Western offensives, "more because my instinct prompts me to stick to it [the words are General Robertson's] than because of any good argument by which I can support it," is no great sign of genius or even resolution, whatever it may have seemed at the time.

Of such commanders J. M. Keynes wrote: "They slept well, they ate well — *nothing* could upset them." This was an exaggeration. General Robertson, hearing in February 1917 that the British armies were to be put under the command of General Nivelle, said that this had given him his first sleepless night since the beginning of the war. It was not until February 1918 that Lloyd George managed to get rid of General Robertson, and Haig he could never dismiss. In those days the truism that war is too serious a thing to be left to the generals was not widely current; there certainly would have been a dreadful fuss in Parliament if Haig had gone.

Haig and Robertson were tried professional soldiers, to whom trench warfare was a mystery, and innovation an enemy: they cannot be blamed for that; only for their fixation on slaughter in the West. Under their direction, the fearful Passchendaele campaign was allowed to take place in spite of repeated warnings that artillery bombardment would so weaken the system of drainage that the battlefield would be turned into a sea of mud. To this the generals paid no heed at all. The result was a campaign which, though less costly than the Somme had been in 1916, three hundred thousand to four hundred thousand, was regarded by "all the combatants on either side as the culmination of horror."[2]

It is the impact of all this upon Anglo-Irish relations which has now to be examined. Since the Prime Minister, who liked to have his hand upon as many levers as possible, was absorbed from day to day in problems of the most critical description, it was only natural that he should try to give Ireland, over which he had exercised his gifts in vain, as little attention as he possibly could. But it was all to no avail. Huddled away in its geographical corner, overshadowed by so many past or impending disasters, almost lost in the shuffle of intrigue and jealousy, yet all the while of great potential consequence, the Irish problem stubbornly refused to disappear.

I

After the Sinn Fein and Irish Volunteer Conventions, which amounted to a regrouping of nationalist forces, there was a "continued prevalence of political unrest and the open defiance of Government authority characteristic of the Sinn Fein movement."[3] The movement was trading upon a growing irritation at the prolonged suspension of land purchase, particularly in Galway, Roscommon, Sligo and Clare, where grazing farms abounded, and where agitators like Laurence Ginnell called for a renewal of cattle driving. Counties Galway and Clare were also, in the eyes of the Inspector General, the scenes of a new form of Ribbonism: they were "largely controlled by Secret Society gangs," most of them members of the Irish Volunteers and all anxious to "exploit the land hunger of the people and their greed for the possession of firearms."[4]

The total number of Sinn Fein Clubs was now said to be 1080 with a membership of 69,000, 3,000 new members having joined in January. Whether this could be called a significant increase or not the Inspector General confessed himself unable to decide: for a while, on the one hand, Sinn Fein appeared to be merely holding its own, on the other there was a spirit of lawlessness and turbulence which was giving increasing embarrassment to the authorities. Even the South Armagh by-election, which (on 1 February) resulted in a victory of the Redmondite over the Sinn Fein candidate (Dr. Pat McCartan, then in America) by 2324 to 1305, gave the police but cold comfort. They pointed out that at least one-third of the Unionists (or some 560) voted for the Redmondite, that many Nationalists were known to have abstained, and that the influence of Cardinal Logue, Archbishop of Armagh, prevented the Sinn Fein sympathizers among the younger clergy from taking an active part.[5]

Moreover, the two other by-elections which the Redmondites won in the winter and spring of 1918 were not very consoling. On 4 April, in East Tyrone, the Redmondite candidate won by 1802 to 1222: but it was well known that Sinn Fein contested this seat only at the last moment and merely to test the strength of opinion there. And some three weeks before, in his father's faithful constituency of Waterford, Captain William Redmond defeated the Sinn Fein candidate by 1242 to 764 votes. This was expected: it was the proper tribute to John Redmond, who had died on 6 March.

When this good and honorable man died, the Irish Convention was already marked for destruction. It was being slowly dismembered by the opposition of Orange Ulster and the intransigence of Fiscal Autonomy. In the War Cabinet of 13 February 1918, both Mr. Bonar Law and Lord Milner "expressed the view that the shadow was more formidable than the substance and that, provided treaty-making power was not conceded, Customs might conceivably be left to the Irish Parliament." Lord Southborough and

Mr. Long, who had been summoned for this meeting, at once protested. "Any offer at this stage by the Government of the Customs," they said . . . "would make the position of the Unionists almost, if not quite, impossible."[6] In the end, as in the beginning, Orange Ulster never combined with Southern Unionism except to create mischief, while any combination of Southern Unionism with Redmond produced only division among Redmond's followers.

In January, for example, John Redmond had, for himself if not for his party, agreed to accept Lord Midleton's proposal that Ireland should be given the control of excise but not of customs. On 14 January, he discovered that his amendment to this effect could not even be presented to the Convention, so great was the resistance within his own ranks — specifically of Joseph Devlin and of the three Catholic bishops of Ross, Down and Connor, and Raphoe: and he told the Convention that he felt he could be of no further service. In private, he wrote to Lloyd George to say that if the Government would agree to fight the Ulster Unionists on this point, he thought he could swing his forces behind the Midleton proposal. In a second communication, he demanded that the Prime Minister should call for an immediate adjournment of the Convention, so that the leading men of all sections could come to London to confer with the Cabinet.[7]

Lloyd George's reply took the form of a draft letter to Sir Horace Plunkett, then in London, who brought it to Dublin on 21 January. It read as follows:

> No 10 Downing Street
> 21 January 1918.

Dear Sir Horace Plunkett:

In our conversation on Saturday you told me that the situation in the Convention has now reached a very critical stage. The issues are so grave that I feel the Convention should not come to a definite break without the Government having the opportunity of full consultation with the leaders of different sections. If and when, therefore, a point is reached at which the convention finds that it can make no further progress towards an agreed settlement, I would ask that representatives should be sent to confer with the Cabinet. The Government are agreed and determined that a solution should be found. But they are firmly convinced that the best hope of a settlement lies within the Convention and they are prepared to do anything in their power to assist the Convention finally to reach a basis of agreement, which would enable a new Irish Constitution to come into operation with the consent of all parties.[8]

When this letter was read to the War Cabinet on Monday 21 January, it drove Sir Edward Carson out of the Government. To him, it suggested the coercion of Ulster: and in his letter of resignation he said that, whatever its outcome, the Convention was bound to lead to a Government decision on grave matters of policy in Ireland, and that he thought it would be best if it discussed this policy without his further presence. Lloyd George accepted "with the deepest and most unfeigned regret" the departure of a gentleman who, said Sir Maurice Hankey, would not be missed.[9]

When the same letter was shown to Redmond, on the same day, in Dublin, his reaction was quite different. He was convinced that its ambiguous language was a sign of weakness; and he wrote to the Prime Minister suggesting a stronger form of words for him to use; just after midnight on 23 January he received Lloyd George's telegraphed refusal to do so. This was effectually the end of Mr. Redmond. That day, lying in bed at the Gresham Hotel, he wrote to Sir Horace to say that he was "suffering a good deal of pain and cannot eat anything," and that he would not be able to take part in the Convention.[10] He "funked," said the ineffable eighth Earl of Granard; but this was not the case: he was simply dying. The end came on 6 March, in London, after a serious operation which in his exhausted and despondent condition he could not sustain. With him died the Irish Parliamentary Party. On 9 April, after approving a report which revealed only its incurable differences, the Convention also passed into history.

II

The time was now fast approaching when a decision of another and more desperate nature would have to be faced. Should compulsory military service be extended to Ireland or should it not? The question was not a new one; it had been raised over and over again; but never so urgently as now. In February and March, as if to acknowledge its imminence, the state of the country became more and more restless. In February this was especially visible in Sligo, Roscommon, Leitrim, Galway, Clare, Mayo, Limerick, King's County (Leix), Queen's County (Offaly) and Westmeath, where large bodies of men with ploughs and bands and Sinn Fein flags marched to the grazing farms and, if the owners did not submit to their demands, took forcible possession of as much land as they required. It was to be let to laborers and farmers having ten acres or less, in the name of the Irish republic, and at £4 an acre, the rent to be paid over to the owners of the land.

The cattle drives in these counties — cattle drives had become the special interest of Laurence Ginnell — amounted to one hundred and forty. In Clare the situation was so grave that "it could not be much worse," and the county was declared a "special military area": which meant that special permits were needed either to enter or to leave it or to move along its roads; that fairs and markets were prohibited, a burdensome economic sanction; and that public houses were strictly regulated, to the manifest discomfort of all.[11]

Among the speakers whom the RIC particularly singled out were Laurence Ginnell and Eamon de Valera. Ginnell, who had gone as far east as Lusk in County Dublin, was advising everyone to join the Sinn Fein Clubs, or the Irish Volunteers or the Transport Workers' Union, which was becoming once again as radical as it had been in the days of the Great Strike, and he called for cattle driving unless the neighboring lands were distributed to the landless before St. Patrick's Day. De Valera, growing steadily more militant, was active in Roscommon and Donegal: he called on his hearers — whom the police described as "half-educated shop assistants and excitable young rustics" — to join the Sinn Fein Clubs and the Volunteers in order to fight conscription and divide the land. Physical force, he said at Castlefin, had defeated the tithe laws and wrested the Land Acts from England; and at Ballybofey he spoke of a national army of Volunteers, drilled and armed so as to strike when the opportunity came, as it would soon.

Thus it would seem that the Volunteers (or IRA) were being organized to fight on two fronts: for land redistribution and against conscription. The former battle was greatly enlivened by the suspicion that food was being recklessly exported by the English Food Comptroller; the latter by the thought that England's manpower was running out — or as de Valera was reported to have put it at Raphoe — that "France is being bled white and please God England will soon be bled white too."[12]

In March it was reported that "the republican and mischievous doctrine publicly preached by Sinn Fein and disseminated by its journals" was having a great influence upon the younger generation. "Mere boys now defy the Police, and when charged in Court declare themselves citizens of the Irish Republic or soldiers of the Irish Republican Army and refuse to acknowledge the jurisdiction of the Magistrates." Recruiting had dropped to 579 for Army and Navy. The Sinn Fein clubs had been increased to 1025 Clubs and 81,200 members. The Irish Volunteers, although a distinct body under separate control, were recruited from the Sinn Fein clubs, each club being supposed to contain a company: this made it extremely difficult to estimate their numbers. By the end of the month, they could probably muster double the fifteen thousand actually observed — "a force immensely greater than that which was in existence at the time of the outbreak in 1916."[13]

III

During March the British Army in the west was getting ready to defend itself against a blow which, its General Headquarters well knew, the Germans were about to deliver. The Army was in grave need for manpower. Five divisions had gone to Italy. The losses of 1917 — which amounted to 760,000 in France alone — had been only partially replaced. "Divisions had been reduced from twelve to nine battalions. This reduction seriously interfered with the existing organization of every division, and with the tactical handling of every brigade, while the breaking up of battalions was often bitterly resented by officers and men and tended to lower morale."[14] At the most optimistic calculation, the Army faced Ludendorff's onslaught with 100,000 men less than it had deployed at the same date a year ago.[15]

At 4:30 on the morning of 21 March, six thousand guns started the great bombardment; at 9:45, in a thick fog, the German infantry came over. The first attack was launched between Arras and St. Quentin; and its greatest success was on the British right flank. Here Ludendorff, by massing his reserves until the last days very far behind the front and in so central a position that they could be used as readily against the French as the British, achieved an effect more potent even than surprise. He exploited the known differences, suspicions and hostilities that existed between the British and the French command. General Philippe Pétain, whom nobody has accused of Anglophilia, was so convinced that the Germans were about to attack him that he refused to send help to the embattled British Fifth Army on his left. Its commander, General Sir Hubert Gough (of the Curragh incident) was therefore obliged to withdraw his right wing behind the Crozat Canal in such haste and disorder that many bridges were left undamaged. The next day, believing the false news that the Canal had been forced, Gough ordered a retreat behind the Somme, which a long drought had rendered fordable at many places. The retreat was precipitous and confused and became a rout; wounded, stores, matériel — all were abandoned; and its effect was to open a critical gap between Gough's left and the right of the Third Army, under General Byng. Through this gap drove the German Second Army. On 24 March, a French army-group took over the line south of the Somme (including Gough's disintegrating Army), but edged away to the southwest, opening the gap still wider. For a moment it seemed to Ludendorff that the great railway junction of Amiens itself would fall into his hands: with it he would have severed all connections between the British and the French.[16]

On 26 March, at the town of Doullens, with tanks at the eastern exits in case the German cavalry should break in, there took place the dramatic meeting between Lord Milner, Field Marshal Haig, and Sir Henry Wilson, the new C.I.G.S., on the one side, and Premier Georges Clemenceau, General Foch and General Pétain, on the other, in the course of which Foch was appointed coordinator of "the operations of the Allies on the whole Western Front." *"C'est aujourd'hui une journée historique,"* said Clemenceau to Milner when they met that day. *"Le sort de la guerre va se fixer."* But how and upon what side? The energetic spirit of Foch needed time to make itself felt. His powers were not exactly defined until 3 April and it was not until 24 April that he was given the title of Commander-in-Chief.[17] The day of the Doullens meeting, Byng's army was securely pinned upon the Ancre but was in danger of having its northern flank turned; on 27 March the Germans on the south reached Montdidier, the great French detraining center, only forty miles from Paris, but were restrained by a scratch British force from moving up to Amiens; on 28 March that vital center was secured for the time being by the valiant stand of Byng's Army. On that day, although the situation was too confused for anyone to grasp it, Ludendorff's first attack had come to a stop.

IV

The effect of these events upon the Government can be traced, as well as anywhere, in the response of Sir Maurice Hankey, Secretary to the War Cabinet. On 22 March he wrote in his diary that "during the day the news became worse. The Fifth Army was obviously giving way, and the situation was menacing." On 23 March "we could not fear a *débacle*." On Sunday 24 March, he was summoned to London where "the news was about as bad as it could be," with Haig reporting that the situation was "serious" and with Churchill (Minister of Munitions) and Sir Henry Wilson "bombarding the P.M. with demands for a *levée en masse*." On 25 March the news was "terrible" and the War Cabinet (as well it might) held "an anxious meeting."[18]

At this meeting it was decided that "advantage should be taken of the present desperate military situation" to obtain from Parliament powers to increase the military age limit from forty-two to fifty or even fifty-five years old, and at the same time to extend the Military Service Act to Ireland. Lord French, who was summoned to attend, had made a three-day tour of Ireland earlier in the month. He flattered himself that, coming from an Ascendency family long domiciled in that country, he had a special insight into the Irish character; and he had reported to the Prime Minister that he had found the people "like nothing so much as a lot of frightened children who dread being thrashed" and that with a little careful handling the Prime Minister would see law and order completely restored within a few weeks.[19] He now insisted (in that mercurial fashion which those who knew him had learned to dread) that the Military Service Act could be applied without disorder, and with only a moderate increase in the troops in garrison there. But even if this were the case, how many men would they obtain?

Sir Auckland Geddes, Minister for National Service, estimated that within the present limits of military age one hundred fifty thousand men could be recruited. Here he was about ten thousand under the figures compiled by the Irish Department of Agriculture in October 1915, figures which had not since been revised.[20] He thought that if the age limit were raised to forty-five, he could get another twenty-five thousand; and yet another twenty-five thousand if it were raised to 55.[21]

Thus, at this most critical moment, the question of Ireland — unwanted, imperative, and punctual — moved once again into the foreground.

Between 25 March and 5 April, when the Military Service Bill was introduced into Parliament, the War Cabinet was obliged to spend many hours on this perplexing and dangerous subject. So straitened were its resources that it was forced to place great hope on the expiring Irish Convention. On 26 March, for example, when Major General F. B. Maurice, Director of Military Operations, informed it that the situation would become "desperate" if Byng's Army was forced back from the Ancre, the decision was made to wait for the Convention's Report before taking steps towards further conscription.[22] On the next day there came a report from General Sir Brian Mahon, now Commanding in Chief in Ireland, that "conscription can be enforced but with the greatest difficulty . . . The present time is the worst for it since I have been in Ireland . . . I would suggest that the first thing is to get all known leaders out of the way at once, extra troops should be on the spot immediately, and everyone irrespective of who he is arrested on the first sign of giving trouble."[23] The Prime Minister called this report "on the whole, in favor of conscription" — such as it was, it was certainly one of the most favorable the Cabinet ever got: but he could not say as much for the reports of Chief Secretary Duke or Brigadier General Byrne, Inspector General of the RIC, which were submitted the same day. These were blankly pessimistic.[24] On 28 March even Sir Edward Carson — "with great regret" — said that conscription would cause too much bloodshed to be worth contemplating.[25]

This then was the dilemma now faced by the Government. On the one hand, Home Rule, in any form in which Parliament would consent to pass it, would almost certainly be rejected by Unionist Ulster and Nationalist Ireland alike: in short, would have to be not only passed but *enforced* as well. On the other hand, responsible opinion — North as well as South — agreed that conscription would be a perilous and even a disastrous undertaking. And yet the undermanned divisions at the Front, reeling in bloody disarray under the shock of Ludendorff's attack, seemed to demand that it must be attempted. How could the Government ask the people of Great Britain for one more supreme effort which (Sir Auckland Geddes calculated) would produce 555,000 men and boys, if 150,000 Irishmen were allowed to stand idly by?

We can now be fairly sure, judging by his maneuvers from this time on, that Lloyd George intended to solve this dilemma by offering Home Rule as a *quid pro quo* for conscription, and then seeing to it that both were indefinitely postponed. This was not a policy, it was improvisation of a masterly kind. To his way of thinking, the manpower problem, while desperate, was not quite so desperate as Irish conscription. He had already discovered that Lord Derby, quite at sea in the War Office, had somehow overlooked the fact that eighty-eight thousand men were home on leave: going over Lord Derby's head, he got the men back within a week.[26] He told the Cabinet of 29 March that one American division had been in the line when Ludendorff attacked; that two more were in reserve; and that he was urging President Wilson to send one hundred thousand men a month for the next three months.[27] On 30 March word came back that America would send one hundred thousand a month for four months instead of the requested three. "This is a good Easter egg," Sir Maurice Hankey wrote in his diary for 31 March, ". . . Nevertheless I doubt not that the future has many terrible things in store for us."[28]

No doubt: but crisis, specific crisis, was something upon which Lloyd George fed and flourished. On 30 March, in a secret message to the Dominion Prime Ministers, he set forth in measured language the gallantry of the troops and the gravity of the situation. "The whole military situation depends upon our being able to maintain and refit our armies," he said. "Our losses up to the present time

> in only a week's fighting are about 120,000 men, and all trained and partially trained men in this country will be used in making this good. We are, therefore, taking immediate action to raise fresh troops by raising the military age to 50 and taking boys of 18, and making another large comb-out of industry, which will cause the greatest dislocation and hardship to our industries. We are also prepared to face trouble in Ireland because we feel that it is vital to prove ourselves stronger than the Germans this summer.[29]

"All the dominions and yours among them," the message said in conclusion, "have done splendidly in this battle, but assuming that we can stay the enemy's present effort the issue will depend upon whether the Germans or the Allies are the first in making good their losses . . . We have no time to lose." It will be noticed that the reference to Ireland was extremely vague.

The Prime Minister now left England for a critical conference at Beauvais, and on his return held a meeting of all the ministers in order, as Hankey put it, "to have an opportunity of explaining the military situation, the manpower bill, and the Irish policy, i.e. gilding the conscription bill with the Home Rule Bill."[30] This meeting, on 6 April, was of the greatest importance: it would be firsthand news from the front, given by a narrator whose courage was equal to his convictions, and whose convictions had never favored the military establishment. Not counting the forty-eight thousand Americans (of whom thirteen thousand were in the battle) or the Belgians or the Portuguese, the British and French (said the Prime Minister) were approximately equal in number to the Germans: and yet, at the point of attack the Germans were overwhelmingly superior. This was due to a misconception on the part of Haig and Pétain — quite a natural one, but a misconception nonetheless and one that caused a great delay in bringing up reserves. They had thought the attack was going to be three-pronged, and it was not. Then again, Pétain had held back his reserves too long, much to the Germans' advantage. The weather, too, like the generalship of Haig and Pétain, was in the Germans' favor. In short, "they got in between our lines. There was great confusion. I cannot tell you what happened, nor can General [Sir Henry] Wilson tell me nor Field Marshal Haig. I went over to France to find out and came back knowing little more than when I went."

This was a masterly introduction to his first point — the dangers to strategy, tactics and communication which attend a divided command at the Front. "I hope at least that evil has been cured," he told the ministers. And, indeed, Foch's position as Generalissimo had been greatly strengthened at Beauvais.

Lloyd George could now turn to manpower. Field Marshal Haig had put the British losses at one hundred thirty thousand, including casualties of all kinds: but he himself was convinced, from a careful analysis of the German reports, that he had not nearly given the' full toll. "Ministers will remember that we gave a pledge that only in a grave emergency would we send overseas boys under nineteen. We feel that the emergency has arisen and have decided to send boys of eighteen and a half to France."

And boys alone would not be sufficient to appease this Moloch in Flanders: "We must draw on the Americans." He confessed that the failure of the Americans to come up on time had had a serious effect. America had promised seventeen and a half divisions in France by March: she had produced four divisions and two "displacement divisions for draft"; she had only one division ("I am told that they fought well") in the line. President Wilson had agreed to send more troops but they "will be exhausted by August because the fighting will be continuous and heavy . . . We ought therefore to be able to put our men in, hundreds of thousands of men more than we contemplated, so as to hold on until the Germans say they have had enough. I refuse to contemplate the other contingency."

He had now prepared the way for "a highly controversial question which has caused great perplexity in the Cabinet — the question whether conscription should be extended to Ireland." He began on a belligerent note. "I do not believe it possible in this country to tear up single businesses, to take fathers of 45 and upwards to fight the battle of a Catholic nationality on the Continent without deep resentment at the spectacle of sturdy young Catholics in Ireland spending their time in increasing the difficulties of this country by drilling and compelling us to keep troops in Ireland . . ."

He next turned to Home Rule as a necessary adjunct to conscription, trying to persuade his Unionist colleagues that Orange Ulster would accept a Home Rule measure based on the Report of the Irish Convention, which had just been approved in Dublin by a vote of 44 to 29. He did not say that the report was little more than a narrative of proceedings, that it had been accompanied by two minority reports and five dissenting "notes," and that in the minority there stood in unbending opposition all the Ulster Unionists. He called the result "a remarkable result," the report "a moderate report," and he drew upon his imagination to add that Sinn Fein, which was not present, would have accepted it, if only Ireland had been conceded complete fiscal autonomy.

Under pressure, however, he was forced to admit that the Convention's report, however remarkable and moderate, had not in fact been passed by a substantial majority, and that he would have to substitute a bill based on a letter he had been authorized to send to Sir Horace Plunkett in February. In this letter he had proposed (i) that for the duration of the war and for two years thereafter Irish customs and excise should be reserved for the Imperial Parliament, and that a Royal Commission should be set up at the end of the war to examine this whole question of Irish fiscal autonomy; (ii) that there should be an all-Ireland Parliament, having within it an Ulster Committee with power to modify or exclude from application to Ulster all legislation "not consonant with the interests of Ulster"; and (iii) that the Ulster and Southern Unionists should have an extra representation in a Parliament which might properly meet in alternate sessions in Dublin and Belfast.[31]

Since it was improbable that the fiscal autonomists could bring themselves to accept (i), barely possible that the Nationalists would agree to (ii) and unlikely that the Ulster Unionists would have anything to do with (iii), a bill based on the Plunkett letter does not seem a very hopeful project. Nonetheless, the Prime Minister told the assembled ministers that the War Cabinet expected to bring in a new Military Service Bill "which will provide for the application of conscription [to Ireland] by Order in Council. We propose to bring in simultaneously our Home Rule Bill, put it through Parliament, and then immediately apply the Military Service Act [to Great Britain] . . . It will take time to put conscription into force in Ireland. We have not the machinery. We will have to provide a register, with the aid of the police."

This was not really "gilding the conscription bill with Home Rule" — something which the Unionists would never accept. Actually, it was pure evasion. It would take some weeks to pass the suggested Home Rule Bill through Parliament, always supposing it could be passed at all. On the other hand, to bring in a new Military Service Bill but extend it to Ireland only by Order in Council: what danger was there in that? The bill could be enacted and the Order delayed: as, in the event, delayed it was, and forever.

In the ensuing discussion, it became clear that Mr. Barnes — who spoke not only for Labour but also (it was believed) for a substantial Liberal section — would not accept Irish conscription unless the Home Rule Bill could be presented as a definite *quid pro quo*. The Unionist Ministers, on the other hand, insisted that the two bills should not be contingent: why bribe the Irish to do what (the Unionists considered) was no more than their duty? Since the bill was in any case so unpalatable, it was not surprising that Bonar Law should have protested against ministers being asked to commit themselves to it; or that Winston Churchill (Minister for Munitions), who with Lord Milner had been so far the most resolute for Irish conscription, should have wound up this spellbound and irresolute discussion with a characteristic statement: "I have not met one soldier in France who does not think we shall get good material from Ireland. I think the decision of the War Cabinet is a battlefield decision, but a wise one."[32]

Three days later, General J. C. Smuts, who had joined the War Cabinet in June, wrote the Prime Minister an impassioned letter: For the sake of the country and the British Empire, he said, Parliament should not be asked to waste its time on Home Rule, and conscription "in the present temper of Ireland" should not be enforced.[33]

But in truth the ministers had not been asked to commit themselves to anything, and the War Cabinet had made no decision at all.

Sir Maurice Hankey recorded this debate with less than his usual reticence. He had been listening outside the Cabinet to "sound and sensible" proposals, whereby Home Rule would be linked, not with conscription, but with a new scheme designed to produce fifty thousand to eighty thousand volunteers for the old Irish regiments, or for an Irish army composed of Irish divisions, or (strangest of all) through enlistment in the American army.[34] He was not in sympathy with the Prime Minister. When Lloyd George introduced the new manpower bill on 9 April, a bill which included compulsory service for Ireland, but postponed it until the issuance of an Order in Council, Hankey was present in the official gallery. He thought the speech too long and involved, and the House sullen and unresponsive, except for the Irish Party which was loud in "declamation." The Prime Minister also announced that he intended to "invite Parliament to pass a measure of self-government for Ireland": but he now successfully flouted Labour and Liberal opinion by taking the Unionist line. "Both questions," he said, "will not hang together. Each must be taken on its own merits."[35] John Dillon, who moved an amendment excluding Ireland, fought back in an angry speech. The British would not get a single soldier from such a bill; on the contrary, "all Ireland as one man will rise against you."[36] The bill went rapidly through all its stages, and was passed on 16 April.

All this took place against a dreadful background. On the day of the bill's introduction, 9 April, Ludendorff mounted a new attack in Flanders, aimed at Hazelbrouck, the junction of five railway lines, the key to the Channel ports. In three days it surged forward eleven miles until it was halted by one of those stubborn defenses for which the British Army was famous. Nonetheless, the situation was so critical that orders were given for the evacuation of Calais, for its demolition, for the flooding of all the country west of Dunkirk.[37] On 13 April, Field Marshall Haig issued his stern General Order: "Every position must be held to the last man: there must be no retirement. With our backs to the wall and believing in the justice of our cause, each one of us must fight on to the end." It was not until 19 April, after many mutual recriminations, that Foch surrendered to British pleas his motto of "No reliefs during a battle" and sent up some French troops to the assistance of Haig; and it was not until 29 April that this murderous battle died away.

Coming on the heels of the attack of 21 March, promising (as it assuredly did) fresh assaults to follow, costing the British 305,000 in casualties, the battle of 9 to 29 April gave its own meaning to the Military Service Bill which the Commons passed on 16 April. But it would be wrong to suppose that it increased the Prime Minister's interest in Irish conscription. It was, as regards Ireland, a bill for deferred conscription. At the same time, his allusion to the accompanying Home Rule Bill was cloudy in the extreme. Historically his words have become quite empty. As long as the war was on, he never asked for an Order in Council; until the war was over, he never introduced a Home Rule Bill.

His verbal abuse of the Irish in private was, it is true, almost unmeasured and his threats against them, again in private, were quite fearful. Hankey says that Sir Mark Sykes — a Conservative Home Ruler and a member of the secretariat — was convinced that "the Curragh crowd" (Lord Milner and Sir Henry Wilson) had captured him and "screwed him up to a pogrom." Hankey confessed that "he seemed to contemplate massacre with equanimity." Tom Jones told Hankey that his Irish policy was "mad."[38]

Hankey and Jones were both urging a conciliatory policy; and they can be excused for not realizing something about the Prime Minister which can only be seen in retrospect. As Shakespeare's Fluellen said of Pistol, Lloyd George had been uttering "prave words at the pridge": his language merely relieved his feelings. Hankey, for example, had not perceived that a genuine Irish conciliation was a thing of the past, and substantial Irish recruiting an impossibility. No one in the Government was well informed on Irish matters: but Lloyd George's acute and subtle instincts had warned him, if his subsequent actions are anything to go by, that the best one could do was to play for time; that the only sound procedure was to improvise; that the best policy was not to have one.

Here one must remove from consideration all questions of principle. Lloyd

George had never cared much for Home Rule; he cared even less for it now. As for conscription, he was not a bloodthirsty man. He did not see it (as some of his colleagues tended to do) not only as a necessary measure but also as a punitive one. To him it was quite a pragmatic policy: true, if it could be made to work; false, if it could not. On these terms, it was demonstrably false. Chief Secretary Duke, Chief Inspector Byrne, Commissioner Edgeworth-Johnstone of the DMP — all were opposed. Sir Brian Mahon had barely concealed a high alarm; Lord Chief Justice Campbell and Sir Edward Carson had spoken of bloodshed, north as well as south; Lord Wimborne had predicted an "explosion"; Lord MacDonnell from his sickbed had prophesied disaster; General Smuts, in the name of the Empire, had begged for postponement. All this added up to one question: with the armies in France locked in desperate battle, how could one take the awful risk of starting another Irish rebellion?

And in Ireland itself, new events were adding to these perplexities.

V

Before the Commons passed the Military Service Bill on 16 April, John Dillon had led his party out of the House: the postponement implied by the reference to an Order in Council meant nothing to him or his followers. They had barely arrived in Ireland when, at the suggestion of the Lord Mayor, Laurence O'Neill, a meeting was held at the Mansion House "to arrange for a united opposition to conscription and to arrange for an all-Ireland Convention on the subject." De Valera and Griffith were asked to attend on behalf on Sinn Fein; after some hesitation, they accepted. With them at the meeting were John Dillon and Joseph Devlin, William O'Brien, Tim Healy and various labor leaders, including the other William O'Brien. "Not even in his most strenuous labours for an Irish settlement had Lloyd George ever come near producing such uniformity of views amongst so diverse a group of Irishmen."[39]

It was settled at once that a fund should be started to finance their efforts. It was agreed, without dispute, that all Irishmen should be asked to take a pledge. "Defying the right of the Government," it read, "to enforce compulsory service in this country, we pledge ourselves solemnly to one another to resist conscription by the most effective means at our disposal." One thing more was needed. Mr. Dillon, Mr. Healy, Mr. de Valera headed a deputation which made for Maynooth College, where the Catholic bishops were holding their own conclave. Since it was well known that the word "republic" was a red rag to Cardinal Logue, his reception of Mr. de Valera — or, at any rate, of Mr. de Valera's arguments — was thought to be doubtful. But de Valera, as his biographers remind us, was an ex–collegiate lecturer and quite at home in an ecclesiastical atmosphere. He said that passive resistance was a fantasy; it must lead to physical resistance if conscription were applied. He argued that the morality of physical force was in direct proportion to the immorality of the effort to conscript the Irish nation. John Dillon added his persuasions: the constitutionalist Irish Party, he said, would resist conscription by all the means in their power. Step by step, the Cardinal was brought to agree.[40]

The result was all that could be wished for. The bishops ordered the pledge to be read at every mass in every parish on the following Sunday, when subscriptions for a defense fund might be taken up outside the churches.[41] They also issued an uncompromising manifesto: "We consider that conscription forced in this way upon Ireland is an oppressive and inhuman law which the Irish people have a right to resist by every means consonant with the law of God." At this, Mr. de Valera took what was, for him, the decisive step: on 26 April he presented the Executive of the Irish Volunteers with a written pledge of resistance: each member must sign it, or show good reason why he should not. All signed. In the meantime the Trades Union Congress in Dublin had decided to protest conscription with a twenty-four-hour general strike: and on 23 April, everywhere except in Belfast, there was a complete shutdown. Shops, factories, trains, trams, even hackney-cars — all came to a standstill.[42] Public houses were closed, newspapers silenced. Only at the Punchestown horse races was there any action; and to these one made one's way on foot.

All this was, in fact if not in form, a secession from the Union. As compared to Lloyd George's statement to the War Cabinet, that Irishmen had the same rights as Englishmen, it said that Irishmen had different rights. The next and final step was the extinction of what little life remained in the Irish Party. It had, oddly enough, paved the way by walking out of the Commons, for this seemed merely to justify the Sinn Fein policy of abstention. Its subsequent withdrawal from the by-election in North King's County on 19 April, leaving the field clear for Sinn Fein's Dr. McCartan, was taken for a defeat. Dillon had suggested that all vacancies should be filled by the party in possession (usually his own, since there had been no General Election since 1910); when this was turned down, he asked that only neutral candidates should be nominated. At last, standing beside de Valera on an anticonscription platform on 5 May, he called for party unity:

de Valera replied with devastating promptness that unity was not amalgamation. This point was driven home by Sinn Fein's nominee for a by-election in Cavan at the end of the month. It was none other than Arthur Griffith, whom Dillon had called "the most offensive and scurrilous critic of the Irish Party." "There never was in the history of the world," said Dillon bitterly, "any country or people quite the equal of our people."[43]

The British public, no doubt, would have agreed with John Dillon. The defense fund, the pledge, the bishops' manifesto, the general strike: all these had taken place while the British armies were locked in a deadly and perhaps disastrous battle with the Germans. The War Cabinet was warned that there were no more than twenty-five thousand troops in Ireland, and that these consisted of twenty-three "training battalions" — untrained men who had just left civilian life — together with a trained mobile division of five thousand cyclists. It was most undesirable that these innocents should be used to repress rebellion, since news from all over the country, including Belfast, indicated that *"even given adequate* military support, it would be almost impossible to enforce conscription."[44]

If the Prime Minister had not already lost interest in conscription, the recent events in Ireland would have lost it for him. On 23 April, after the War Cabinet had been told that a general stoppage had begun, he made a most significant statement. He said that the Irish situation had raised the biggest constitutional issue "on which Parliament had been divided" of the past thirty or forty years — namely, the real supremacy of the Imperial Parliament. The Irish were now challenging its right to impose upon them an act which they disliked. "Whether the Cabinet had been right in raising the issue at this time was questionable. It was important, therefore, to make the situation as favourable as possible for the Cabinet to engage on such a conflict . . . *Until Home Rule was carried through Parliament the Cabinet would not be in a strategical position for enforcing the Military Service Act in Ireland.*" Mr. Balfour, who was present, "fully concurred with this view," which was anything but a bold one. He had recently observed that it would be "a greater weakness to do something in Ireland than to do nothing."[45]

The word "enforcing" shows that Lloyd George had not returned to the idea of "gilding the conscription bill with Home Rule." On the contrary, more conscious than ever of his magical powers, he had already come forward with an ingenious device. After the Cabinet of 9 April he had proposed that Mr. Walter Long should preside over a Committee to draft an acceptable Home Rule Bill. The other members were men of widely varying opinions: Lord Curzon, Mr. Barnes and General Jan Smuts of the War Cabinet; Mr.

Duke the Chief Secretary; Dr. Addison (Minister of Reconstruction); Sir George Cave (Home Secretary); Sir Gordon Hewart (Solicitor General); and Mr. H. A. L. Fisher (President of the Board of Education).

The Committee first met on 15 April; the next day Mr. Long complained that it was composed of so many members, all holding important duties, that it simply could not meet as often as he would wish. It was thereupon agreed that he should draw up a bill himself and consult with the Committee on points of difference only.[46] Here two considerations present themselves: if Mr. Long were left to draw up a bill on his own, merely consulting the Committee on matters of difference which were bound to be either acute or contentious, he would take some time to do it; and, since he had not lost his taste for Federalism (*alias* Devolution),[47] the bill that he did draw up — supposing that he was allowed to draw one up at all — would in all probability be of so odious a nature that the Cabinet would be justified in laying it aside. In short, Mr. Lloyd George, when he assured the Cabinet on 23 April that conscription could not be applied to Ireland until a Home Rule Bill had been passed through Parliament, had done his best to see that it never got there.

As if to justify this course of inaction, on 27 April a letter was circulated to the War Cabinet which had been sent to the Chief Secretary by Sir Henry Robinson, Vice-President of the Irish Local Government Board. Sir Henry was a blank Tory, with a great deal of charm and even greater prestige. His letter was as follows:

> Local Government Board, Dublin
> 26 April, 1918.
>
> Dear Mr. Duke:
>
> You may perhaps remember my giving you my opinion[48] that the opposition of Ulster to Home Rule would not be intractable, long lived, or a serious danger.
>
> In case you do remember it I want to say that I withdraw that opinion now as the situation has entirely changed.
>
> The linking up of the R.C. Hierarchy with the Sinn Fein Rebels and their joint refusal to allow the Irish Catholics to help us win the war by agreeing to conscription has had such an effect on the Protestants of the North and of Belfast, that they seem to have gone mad.

They are beside themselves at the idea of being placed under such a Parliament — a Popish and Rebel Parliament as they call it — and I truly believe that as matters stand the introduction of a Home Rule Parliament would be accompanied by serious religious riots in the North which would react on the Protestants in the South, and that shipbuilding and munitions work in Belfast would be to a very serious extent shut down.

Over here the consensus of opinion seems to be to let things cool down, and drop both Conscription and Home Rule till after the war.[49]

Although this letter was based on the belief that the Government intended to introduce a Home Rule Bill very soon, its conclusion was most acceptable to the Prime Minister.

One further encouragement to inaction was the state of American opinion. America's entry into the war had had a quietening effect upon hyphenist activity — upon the Irish-Americans and the German-Americans. Even extremists such as the Clan na Gael and the Friends of Irish Freedom now spoke of Irish independence as something to be demanded at the peace table and not before. Yet the fear of Irish-America remained.[50] There was always a chance that an adverse situation in Ireland would enliven this group and even stir up the Anglophobia still latent in American minds. President Wilson, a sturdy anti-hyphenist, had himself warned the British Government in April 1917 that "the only circumstance which now seems to stand in the way of an absolutely cordial cooperation is the failure to find a satisfactory method of self-government in Ireland." The Irish Convention had been able to divert such inconvenient thoughts as these; and it was still doubtfully alive on 1 April when the War Cabinet agreed that Mr. Balfour, as Foreign Secretary, should ask the British Ambassador in Washington (Lord Reading) to sound out Colonel House on the possible effects of an Irish conscription. Mr. Balfour was to point out in his telegram to Lord Reading the measures which the War Cabinet had in contemplation for dealing "simultaneously" with Home Rule and conscription.[51] "I feel certain," was House's reply, dictated by President Wilson on 3 April, "that [conscription] will accentuate the whole Irish and Catholic intrigue which has gone hand in hand in some quarters with the German intrigue."[52] This would have been a greater blow if Sir William Wiseman, a young baronet of pleasing manners who occupied a semi-diplomatic position in the American capital, and was supposed to be a shrewd observer of the American scene, had not had quite a different reaction to the House reply when he was shown it. He at once cabled Sir Eric Drummond, Mr. Balfour's secretary: "America's view will depend largely on how the case is presented to the Press, and I do not believe that the possibility of bad effects here should influence your decision."[53] But the case proved too difficult for a favorable presentation. The Report of the Irish Convention with its attending disclaimers cannot have helped if (as was generally supposed) it was to provide the basis for an acceptable Home Rule; the Irish pledge and the bishops' Manifesto made everything worse; and early in May an "Irish Progressive League" meeting in New York's Madison Square Garden, attended by 15,000 people, denounced conscription as genocide and called for Irish self-determination.[54] When the American armies were fully engaged on the Western Front, this kind of thing would perhaps die down: but in the meantime, as far as the American war effort was concerned, it was all too evident that the less that was done in either direction, the better it would be.

VI

The state of Ireland itself, however, was already calling for action, but action of quite another kind.

On 13 April, Mr. Duke circulated a memorandum to the War Cabinet in which he said that a crisis was imminent, and that there were only two ways of meeting it: wide-spread preventive arrests or Home Rule in return for conscription. He preferred the latter course, and, should the Government choose the former, he begged them to appoint a new Chief Secretary.[55] Three days later, he submitted a more desperate paper: there was a possibility, he said, of the Irish Party and the "revolutionists" setting up a Provisional Government, and, if it was not immediately made clear that no conscription would take place until Parliament had thoroughly examined Home Rule, "I desire I may forthwith be relieved of responsibility with regard to Irish affairs."[56]

If Mr. Duke found his responsibilities too heavy, Lord Wimborne found his not heavy enough. He complained that he was never consulted, that Mahon and Byrne left for London without his knowledge, that his office was being transformed into a "dangerous anomaly," and that he did not know what useful function there was left him to perform.[57] A month later, on 28 April, he was informed by his brother, Captain Frederick Guest, who was Lloyd George's Chief Whip, that the Prime Minister thought it would be helpful if he resigned: and accordingly he did so. But he had been steadily growing in stature since the Easter Rising. When the Prime Minister thanked him on 6 May for his "ready and generous willingness to facilitate the new arrangement . . . a policy which the Government is assured will meet with approval and success," he retorted bitterly that he did not acquiesce in something which "foreshadowed a military regime" and would convert the British Army into "a coercive press-gang."[58] With him went the more complaisant Mr. Duke.

What was the "new arrangement" which so disturbed Lord Wimborne? On 5 May, the Lord Lieutenancy had been offered to Field Marshal Lord French, who accepted with alacrity. He quite understood, he said in his letter of acceptance, that the Government's intention was not to proceed with Home Rule or Conscription until its authority had been re-established; and that for this reason it was proposed to set up "a quasi-military government in Ireland with a Soldier for a Lord Lieutenant."[59]

With Lord French as Lord Lieutenant came Edward Shortt, K.C., as Chief Secretary. Mr. Shortt was an Asquithian Liberal, who opposed conscription, and who had asked Mr. Asquith's permission before accepting office.[60] He was presumably selected as a counterpoise to French. He would come to Ireland bearing a Liberal olive branch, while his military Viceroy brandished a thunderbolt. For Lord French no longer thought, as he had in March, that the Irish were a lot of frightened children. He had returned in April, and had come back calling for forty more airplanes, armed with bombs and machine guns, "to put the fear of God into these playful young Sinn Feiners." The troops in Ireland now numbered twenty-five thousand; he managed to "scrape up" twelve thousand more; talked of martial law; and told the Prime Minister that any and every contingency could be met "if only we act promptly and decisively." "But I may also add," said this ponderous flatterer, "that with you at the helm I have no fear."[61]

The second part of the "new arrangement" begins to appear in a letter to the Prime Minister from Mr. Arthur W. Samuels, the Irish Attorney-General in Dublin Castle. It was written on 2 May, and it still excites one's curiosity. He said that the country was "on the verge of civil war," and civil war of a religious nature, civil war stirred up by priests who, ever since the hierarchy's manifesto, had been openly preaching rebellion and justifying the assassination of soldiers or police if they tried to enforce conscription. It was useless, continued Mr. Samuels, to try these "treason mongers" if the Sinn Fein leaders were allowed to go scot free — indeed, the people were saying that the Government was afraid of them. It was equally futile to proceed with Home Rule, since the Irish Party had now been "captured" by Sinn Fein and would simply flout the government.

There was, moreover (Mr. Samuels continued), no doubt about the existence of a "German intrigue"; the War Cabinet had only to ask Admiral Hall of Naval Intelligence. The people in Ireland were hoarding silver — it was almost impossible to get change anywhere — because they were told that English paper money would be worthless when the Germans won. He enclosed a secret report from Major Ivor Price, still head of the Special Intelligence Branch at Army Headquarters in Dublin.

The Price report concerned a Corporal Robert J. Dowling, of the 2nd Connaught Rangers, who had been captured on 12 April as he landed in a small canvas canoe on Crabb Island off the coast of Clare. He confessed that he had been one of Casement's three lieutenants; and that he had been sent from Germany in a U-boat with instructions to get in touch with the Sinn Fein leaders, find out the state of affairs, and return to Germany by way of Norway. A German "expedition" would set out three weeks after his return. The Sinn Fein leaders did not know of his coming and had not requested it: he had merely been told to seek them out. He was now in the Tower.

Aside from this sad adventure — which, incidentally, had been circulated to an unperturbed War Cabinet four days after Dowling's capture[62] — Major Price had nothing to offer except some vague but "reliable reports" of expected arms landings in Mayo and Galway; information given by a defecting Irish Volunteer, a "respectable Limerick farmer," who said he had received imported German arms; and a story about the Cotter brothers ("one being a brother-in-law of Eamon de Valera") who had been found in a sailing boat at 3:50 a.m. near Kingstown Pier. A German submarine had been seen near the Kish Lightship the previous evening; and calculations of wind and tide made it possible that the Cotters had arranged a rendezvous.[63]

It is odd, to say the least, that an Irish Attorney-General, presumably well acquainted with the nature of evidence, should have presented the Government with such straws as these; unless, of course, someone higher up had already intimated that he was prepared to clutch them. However this may have been, Mr. Samuels submitted a futile report, this time to the War Cabinet. It said that the RIC could no longer be trusted to carry out arrests of priests or to enforce conscription: County Inspector Power of Kilkenny and Inspector-General Byrne had both assured him that the result would be disastrous and might break up the force altogether. If, on the other hand, priests were arrested by the military, no jury would dare convict them. Ireland was in a "dangerous and seditious condition"; and the Sinn Fein organization should be proclaimed under the Criminal Law and Procedure (Ireland) Act of 1887. Only this would teach the peasantry that the Government meant to govern. This and one thing more: the Sinn Fein leaders should be at once deported and interned; for there was "abundant evidence of hostile association with the Germans" and they were daily "organizing effectively and concocting rebellion." Mr. Samuels ended with the customary plea, backed by a letter from Mr. Justice James O'Connor, for the postponement of conscription and Home Rule: and thus the "new arrangement" had emerged as a whole.[64]

On the day this report was presented, Mr. Walter Long was gratified by being empowered to act on the Cabinet's behalf in all Irish matters not requiring special attention: he now readily agreed that Home Rule and conscription should be postponed for the time being; and he swallowed with barely a murmur the evidence presented by Major Price and the recommendations of Mr. Samuels. "A stern hand was needed," he said, "to put down the Irish-German conspiracy which appeared to be widespread in Germany"; he did not add, in Ireland. As for the arrest of the leaders, it would drive a wedge "between the extreme Sinn Feiners, on the one hand, and the Catholic hierarchy and the moderate nationalists, on the other." He even proposed the issuance of a Proclamation by the Lord Lieutenant which should (a) justify the arrests of the leaders and (b) offer the Irish one more chance to enlist as volunteers.[65]

Thus conscription for Ireland was postponed again. The compulsionists among the War Cabinet and the attendant Ministers were very uneasy: would not this be a sign of weakness? The Prime Minister, who now saw his own ideas gradually but steadily coming into view, agreed that it would be more fitting to issue the justification first, and keep back the volunteering offer until after law and order had been restored. (He had just learned that there were now ninety thousand Americans behind the lines.)[66] On 15 May, however, on an urgent representation from Lord French, this decision was reversed; justification and offer must go hand in hand; "the facts of the situation as laid before the Cabinet," said Lord Curzon, had made this necessary.[67] On 16 May Lloyd George told Lord Milner and Sir Henry Wilson in secret that he had been informed that an insurrection might take place in a fortnight, that it would be a guerilla affair, away from the towns, and that the Sinn Feiners had plenty of rifles for such a purpose.[68]

On the night of 17–18 May the arrests were made.

VII

One cannot read Mr. Samuels's two missives without sensing the fear which underlay every paragraph: the fear that a rebellion might break out, regardless of conscription. The fighting had died down at the end of April, without the loss of Amiens or Ypres; but it had been very close; and all authorities agreed that Ludendorff would try again. If an Irish rebellion were timed to break out when the weary British armies were once more battling for their lives, it would have to be suppressed by the harshest methods, methods of sheer terrorism. As Conor Cruise O'Brien has suggested, in a brilliant excursion into the might-have-been, the Irish troops on the Western Front were not in sympathy with anti-conscription or rebellion: but terrorism applied to their towns and villages could not have been kept very long from them, and might well have produced desertions and mutinies. In those war-worn armies, where morale was low and "uniform more conspicuous than nationality," an Irish mutiny could have spread to the British and from the British to the French and so — who knows? — to the Germans: and something which Governments feared even more than defeat, a revolution on Bolshevik lines, might have fastened its grip on Europe.[69]

No one has suggested that such speculations were entertained by David Lloyd George or any other member of his Government: but they are by no means fanciful. Little as it believed its own story of an Irish-German conspiracy, the Government was now being fed with daily rumors of an impending rebellion: and in these rumors it *did* believe.

Michael Collins, meanwhile, already a master in the art of gathering information, had learned from Detective Kavanagh of the DMP that arrests were to take place; he had warned the principal leaders; they had all agreed that their cause would be better served if they went to prison. Before it was over seventy-three persons had been deported to England and others followed later: among the first deportees were Eamon de Valera, Arthur Griffith, Count Plunkett, William Cosgrave, Madame Markievicz, Madame Maud Gonne MacBride and Mrs. Tom Clarke. Some of the senior officers of the Volunteers and of the Sinn Fein Executive were also seized: they were imprisoned without trial under the Defence of the Realm Act. But Michael Collins escaped.[70]

The next day, Lord French issued his Proclamation. "Whereas it has come to our knowledge that certain subjects of His Majesty the King, domiciled in Ireland, have conspired to enter into, and have entered into, treasonable communication with the German enemy," it began. And it ended, in accordance with the War Cabinet's decision of 15 May, with a promise that steps would be taken "to facilitate and encourage voluntary enlistment in Ireland, in His Majesty's forces in the hope that, without resort to compulsion, the contribution of Ireland to these forces may be brought up to its proper strength."

The Cabinet, of course, was bound to make some further justification for what had been done and on 22 May there was a most embarrassing and embarrassed meeting. To this Mr. Shortt was summoned, and here he read "a mass of evidence [to show that] the Sinn Feiners were preparing for another rising [and] that they considered it essential for the success of their next rising to have German assistance."

This mass of evidence, as summarized (with further comments by the Prime Minister) in the Cabinet minutes, bears a singular resemblance to *Documents Relative to the Sinn Fein Movement,* a parliamentary paper issued in 1921, during the last stages of the Anglo-Irish war. The *Documents* showed the connection between the Clan-na-Gael and Ambassador von Bernstorff in America and the German Foreign Office in Berlin in the days of the Easter Rising: but failed to implicate any of the deportees of May 1918. After von Bernstorff's departure with America's entry into the war, the *Documents* declined into incompetence: they dealt at length with the Irish message to the Stockholm Conference of 1917; with the disloyal speeches of St. John Gaffney's German-Irish Society in Berlin; with mysterious passages between the German Foreign Office in Berlin and its embassy in Madrid. Corporal Dowling appears, also the Cotter brothers, and with them a "local Sinn Fein leader," called James Duane, who was arrested at Kittimagh, County Mayo, in December. In Duane's possession were two pamphlets, of a perfectly startling irrelevance, except that they were printed in German, with the German impress *Kriegs-Anschluss der Deutschen Industrie, Berlin.*

It is small wonder that the Prime Minister, after hearing Mr. Shortt, rather wistfully said: "He would like to know what evidence did exist of the complicity of the Sinn Feiners and the Germans subsequent to January 1917 . . . it would be a strong moral support of the War Cabinet to know of its existence." Admiral Hall, of Naval Intelligence, was thereupon called in. Laying "the utmost stress on the secrecy of his information," he exhibited a series of intercepted messages between Berlin and German agents abroad, relating to the establishment of systems of communication by confidential agents with Ireland. Even this, strange to say, did not satisfy the Cabinet. "Lord Curzon pointed out that Admiral Hall's statement provided ample evidence of German designs, but not of Sinn Fein complicity."[71]

Mr. Shortt's statement for the press was then revised by the War Cabinet. In its final shape it covered two and a half pages of close print and was in two parts. The first successfully revealed the activities of Devoy, von Bernstorff, Casement and the *Aud;* the second failed to conceal the absence of any conspiracy after America's entry into the war. It then expressed the belief that Irish rebellion would be timed so as to coincide with a fresh German assault in the West. "In these circumstances," it concluded, "no other course was open to the Government, if useless bloodshed was to be avoided, and its duties to its allies fulfilled, but to intern the 'authors and abettors of this criminal intrigue.' "[72]

Only desperate times and the genuine belief that a rebellion was imminent could have justified such a puerile concoction as this. But the belief, though quite mistaken, was genuine enough; and the times were certainly desperate. On 27 May, the storm broke. The Germans attacked on a forty mile front between Soissons and Fismes and, advancing thirteen miles, had crossed the Ailette, the Aisne and the Vesle before the day was over. It was the longest advance since trench warfare had begun. By 30 May, after forty-five months, the Germans were again upon the Marne, and Paris was only thirty-seven miles away.[73] Surely no more critical situation had existed since the days before the First Battle of the Marne — so critical, indeed, that Sir Henry Wilson confided to his diary that "there is a possibility, indeed a probability, of the French army being beaten. What would this mean? The destruction of our army in France?"[74] On 2 June, Ludendorff came to a halt. Although he was still capable of an orderly retreat, this was to be his last successful attack. Among the favorable omens was the fierce, successful and continuous fighting of the Americans in their first major engagement at Belleau Wood near Chateau-Thierry. But authorities and experts still believed that the Germans would try again. It was to avert the possible coincidence of a rebellion in Ireland with a new German attack, not to prepare the Irish for conscription, that the Sinn Fein leaders had been deported to English prisons. Even on 30 May, when Sir Henry Wilson informed them (wrongly) of the capture of Reims, the exhausted War Cabinet agreed, not only to refrain from specifying fifty thousand or twenty thousand or indeed any definite number for the volunteers they would expect from the Irish in return for abandoning compulsory service, but also to postpone until 1 October the terminal date for voluntary recruitment.[75] With their world tottering about their ears, their solution for the Irish conscription problem was to follow Lloyd George's "new management" and shelve it; although there was further conscription talk both before and during October, that solution prevailed until the end.

Indeed, to the student of the Easter Rising and its aftermath in English history, one of the most significant events is the War Cabinet held on 19 June. To this Cabinet there was presented the Interim Report on the Government of Ireland (Home Rule) Bill, which had been under the consideration of Mr. Long and his committee since 15 April.[76] The committee had almost broken up on 4 June, when Sir George Cave asked to be excused from further attendance because they were "ploughing the sands," Lord Curzon suggested a three to six months' postponement, and General Smuts remarked that it was "tomfoolery to go on drafting."[77] Two days later, however, it was agreed to submit at least a report, and here it was: it offered no more than a Unionist modification of the Home Rule Act of 1914. Lord Curzon then asked what he was to tell the House of Lords — were conscription and Home Rule temporarily in abeyance, or had the Government decided to drop them indefinitely? Mr. Balfour at once took the line of Lloyd George's "new arrangement": the Government's first duty was to restore law and order in Ireland and until that was done "it was undesirable to outline any programme for the future." Mr. Long, not unnaturally irritated at this drowsy conclusion to his labors, reminded the War Cabinet of its decision — which the Prime Minister had certainly endorsed on 16 April[78] — that the Government would either pass a Home Rule Bill or resign.

Lloyd George now had the game in his hands. Once upon a time, he said, there had been sufficient agreement — "although in some quarters it was no more than a sullen assent" — to carry a Home Rule measure: but times had changed. There had been "the discovery of a grave Sinn Fein conspiracy"; there had been the Catholic hierarchy's challenge to the Imperial supremacy. It was impossible to ignore these two facts, for between them they destroyed the one essential condition of wartime legislation, and that was substantial agreement between "the two main parties in the State." Three months ago, Liberals would have warmly welcomed a Home Rule Bill and many Unionists would have tolerated it as a war measure; but the two facts had made such a difference in the political climate that it could not be carried now.

Mr. Long then asked what were the Government's intentions if voluntary recruiting failed in Ireland. Many Unionists maintained, he said, that one of the serious defects of the Irish policy was that it kept the Irish in suspense as to what the policy really was. Since this is exactly where the Prime Minister intended the Irish to be kept and where (with the unwitting assistance of Lord French) he believed that he was keeping them, his answer was a masterpiece of evasion: "If he were directly challenged as to whether the

Government stood by their dual policy [of conscription and Home Rule] he would reply in the affirmative, but would add that the time and the method of giving effect to it must be judged by the War Cabinet."

Thus Home Rule and conscription were conjured out of sight. When Mr. Long's Home Rule report appeared again before the Cabinet on 29 June, the Prime Minister remarked that he was so preoccupied with the crisis on the Western Front that he had had no time to read it. In the Cabinet of 19 June, he had said all that he had to say.

There is a brief sequel to this. On 17 July, Ludendorff finally lost all initiative. On 8 August, Sir Douglas Haig sent his army forward in Flanders and toward the Hindenburg line. After two years of failure, he had now hit upon the right way to manage an attack, and was prepared to exploit it with every means at his disposal. Though the civilians did not realize this — as late as 23 September Lord Milner was predicting another Passchendaele — Haig was entirely successful. Sir Henry Wilson had already promised Clemenceau that conscription was coming to Ireland; on 1 October he was saying that the Prime Minister would have an Order in Council ready when Parliament met on 15 October.[79] On 5 October, the 3rd and 4th British armies, the left wing of the allied offensive, broke clear through the Hindenburg Line and came out into the open country. Here they paused to regroup. Although the Germans had put out armistice feelers, it was still believed in England that the war would be prolonged into the next year: and Sir Henry, with his almost pathological hatred for non-Orange Ireland, which ended only when he was shot down by Irish bullets at the door of his London house in 1922, called all the more urgently for Irish conscripts. At last, on 23 October, at a dinner with Lord French, Mr. Churchill and Mr. Lloyd George, now Sir Henry was faced with the truth — French was still urging conscription, but Churchill and Lloyd George maintained that it would be simply "suicidal." The Prime Minister explained that his reasoning and Churchill's was not a matter of principle but of "practical expediency."[80] It was his very last word on the subject: his first, in its elusive way, had been much the same.

VIII

The Irish conscription problem illustrates, in a singularly eloquent fashion, the dread which post-Rising Ireland was able to inspire in a subtle and responsive mind, and the paramount importance which, in spite of many disclaimers,[81] this Ireland had begun to assume in the Government's deliberations. The Unionists did not always distinguish between conscription and coercion; but Lloyd George never made that mistake. He knew that the consequences of conscription would be disastrous, and he risked alienating public opinion in order to keep it in a state of suspension. The mistake he made was to assume, and to carry the Cabinet with him, that the Irish leaders were preparing a rebellion, and to insist on deporting them before they could begin it. He did not realize, indeed he had no evidence upon which to make such a judgment, that in deporting such Sinn Fein leaders as de Valera, Griffith, and Cosgrave, he had sent away the moderates of the Irish revolution, men who would certainly have called for resistance to conscription by force, but would otherwise much prefer to gain their ends by peaceful means. Only their rhetoric was rebellious. Their minds were fixed on Irish representation at the peace table; and their chief hopes were placed (how vainly they had yet to learn) on President Wilson and the principle of self-determination. It says a great deal for the fear in which Ireland was held, not only for herself but for her influence in America and the Empire, that a desperate German "plot" had to be invented in order to get these men out of the way.

In fact, by deporting them, the Government had handed the control of affairs over to the physical force men: men like Michael Collins, Harry Boland and Cathal Brugha. They, too, had no intention of starting a rebellion unless conscription was reintroduced: what had now begun was an intensive reorganization of the revolution's military wing. During Easter Week, boxed up in the post office, Collins had begun to see the Rising in perspective. He had afterwards been interned at Frongoch, a fertile breeding ground of Irish revolutionaries. Here he had started his reconstruction of the IRB, and here he had plenty of time in which to think and talk about what had gone wrong. The lack of any working coordination between the rebels in the provinces and the Rising in Dublin; the static character of the Rising itself; the poor training and poorer equipment of the provincials; the waste of men, the neglect of opportunity which this implied — it had all come home to that supremely practical mind. Collins kept the Sinn Fein clubs and the Irish Volunteers apart; as Volunteer Director of Organization, he hoped to reshape the latter through a hard inner core of IRB men. This was made the easier for him since Cathal Brugha, who had no use for the IRB, had left secretly for England, where he is said to have occupied himself in planning the assassination of the War Cabinet, should it be so imprudent as to decide on conscription.[82]

The acting head of the Sinn Fein executive was Father Michael O'Flanagan, who was so extremely visible and vocal that his bishop deprived him of his curacy in Roscommon.[83] In this way, all unwittingly, he acted as a screen for Collins and his intensive work with the Volunteers. From June onward, the police reports become more and more vague and puzzled about the Volunteers — authentic particulars could not be obtained; it could only be assumed, incorrectly, that the younger members of the Sinn Fein clubs were Volunteers as well.[84] For the Sinn Fein clubs had remained visible; their numbers could roughly be counted — 108,000, it was thought, in July: but the Volunteers had gone underground.

Michael Collins had made himself a reputation when he returned from Frongoch because, as Secretary to the Irish National Aid Association, he traveled throughout the country dispensing needed funds. He was a large and magnetic personage. With his full cheeks and his bee-stung lips he looked like a Renaissance *amorino,* an appearance which his character strenuously belied. He was a man of great energy, of sudden unaccountable rages, often harsh and tactless, but all in all a natural leader. Since his return in 1916, he had been steadily building his intelligence network, which remains to this day one of the curiosities of Irish history, a network so widespread and efficient that (even when on the run, his usual condition) he was able to go anywhere in broad daylight, untouched and seemingly invisible.

He was a composition of opposing qualities: a hero, a desperado; a high patriot, a ruthless killer. He was also, unlike so many Fenians, a Fenian with a hold on reality. He was a fine administrator; and given the time and experience he would have become an able statesman. But he was not given the time: at the end of his short life, in 1922, during the Irish Civil War, he was killed in ambush, and by the side which afterward got the higher marks in popular history.

In 1918, he was one of those who believed that the Volunteers should abandon their more romantic pastimes — the marches with guns, rook-rifles and pikes — for a more severe and quite secret discipline. Here Lord French's variation upon "Thorough" had been more helpful than otherwise: the Viceroy had told the police that they were to use the secret service funds to reward informers; close likely drill halls or places used for the exhibition of subversive cinema performances; hunt out and seize the printing presses of seditious journals; and proceed against night drilling with the cooperation of the military, of whom there should be no lack if he could help it. (And, as will be seen, there never was.) Even if the police had been less demoralized, all this would have been an incentive to the sort of underground training which Collins had in mind.

Although the internment of their leaders had not been followed by the enforcement of conscription, it had not made the anti-conscriptionists much quieter. On 15 June the cities of Cork and Limerick and the counties of Cork, Limerick, Clare, Galway, Kerry, King's County, Longford, Mayo, Queen's County, Sligo, Tipperary, and Westmeath were made "proclaimed" districts under the Coercion Act of 1885. On 18 June, counties Limerick and Tipperary were made "Special Military Areas," with the usual accompaniment of special entrance and exit permits, banned fairs, and regulated public houses. On 3 July the Lord Lieutenant, acting under section 6 of the 1885 Act, declared the following associations to be dangerous and persons attending them to be liable to prosecution: the Sinn Fein organization, the Sinn Fein clubs, the Irish Volunteers, and the Cummann na mBann. (By a singular oversight, he did not ban the Gaelic Athletic Association, the nursery of physical force; and games of hurley and football multiplied accordingly.) On 4 July, acting under section 9 AA of the Defence of the Realm Act, the Commander-in-Chief prohibited all meetings, processions, and assemblies throughout Ireland unless authorized by special written permits from the Inspector-General of the RIC or the Commissioner of the DMP. On 12 July, the Orange Anniversary, there were Orange meetings throughout Ulster, their promoters having obtained the required permission; and at Finaghy Sir Edward Carson regaled fourteen thousand persons with his own brand of particularism. It was remarked that on the Nationalist side there was a noticeable "reluctance" to ask for permits: they considered it a matter of national honor not to do so.[85]

The Commander-in-Chief in Ireland was now Sir Frederick Shaw, formerly Lord French's Chief of Staff in the Home Defense, who replaced Sir Brian Mahon. Sir Brian had (like General Jan Smuts) become completely anti-conscriptionist in April. He even began to recommend the use of the shamrock (always suspect in the War Office) as a recruiting device in June. With his departure, Lord French might flatter himself that he was beginning to get the sort of government he wanted: and it might be of interest to inquire what sort of government this was.

Later in the year, in October, Lord French told the Prime Minister that, considering his Anglo-Irish background and Mr. Shortt's "inexperience," he had always taken it for granted that he was to exercise the "full functions of a Governor General *de facto* and *de jure.*"[86] Already, on 13 July, when his program was substantially complete, he had informed King George V that his "proclamation" of Sinn Fein was merely a means to an end: his end was the complete removal of useless and idle young men, between the ages of eighteen and twenty-five, through the enforcement of conscription.[87] His "Thorough" was intended to prepare the Irish for conscription, much as Napoleon's artillery used to prepare the enemy's ranks for a final assault. He had lost all faith in voluntary enlistment, he told Lloyd George in September: there was not the slightest chance that Ireland would meet the quotas necessary to save her from compulsory service.[88] In the same letter he said that he and Mr. Shortt were quite agreed that the Prime Minister's policy was to enforce conscription and simultaneously "force" Home Rule on the whole country, excluding Ulster, but setting up a general council under French himself, to determine what legislation should be applied to Ireland as a whole.[89] He claimed to have got this idea originally from a conversation in Downing Street on 25 July.

In September, indeed, Lord French had persuaded himself that the condition of the country showed a great improvement; boycotting, intimidation, secret drilling, seizures of arms were (he was sure) on their way out. In October he told the Prime Minister that there had developed a serious disagreement between him and his Chief Secretary. The Viceroy still insisted that Ireland was ready for conscription but not for self-government, and Mr. Shortt, while pretending to agree with him, was secretly spreading the opposite point of view through his assistant Under Secretary, Mr. James MacMahon, a rigid Catholic (said French) and the mouthpiece of the hierarchy. But even the Viceroy's notions of "readiness for conscription" were beginning to waver; he now warned the Prime Minister that the Irish, congenitally disloyal, as always, "nourish secret sedition and are in a condition of veiled insurrection."[90]

The disagreements between French and Shortt, the vacillations of French himself, are historically important only to the extent that they can be seen to assist the Prime Minister. What the conversation in Downing Street on 25 July actually was we do not know; but it is possible to guess. The Milnerite L. S. Amery said that England was governed by two men, Lloyd George and the last person he spoke to. This was true of his words: here he was as volatile as French, if a good deal more interesting. It was not true of his actions, examined over any respectable period of time. He was perfectly capable of telling the Viceroy what, in his opinion, the Viceroy most wanted to hear, and even of meaning what he said. Once Lord French's back was turned, however, the Prime Minister continued with those immensely cunning postponements which, beginning with the Irish Convention, he had always favored and always practiced and of which, in the midst of all his distractions, he never lost control. Under Lord French's repressive military government, things could be allowed to remain in a state of barely manageable disorder: that was all that one could hope for — that, and the British public's continued willingness to accept an Irish conscription Act without an Irish conscription.

IX

In June there had been a most significant by-election in East Cavan: the candidates were John F. O'Hanlon, of the Irish Party, and Arthur Griffith. To the end, John Dillon believed that his man had an outside chance: but Griffith had the better platform, an English gaol. On 21 June, the result was announced: Griffith 3,785; O'Hanlon, 2,581. According to Dillon, there was "great rejoicing all over the country." This he attributed first to the priests — "their conduct was outrageous . . . the most violent spiritual intimidation" — and then to "the cry — who wants the blood of Griffith — and the desperate hatred of L. G. and the Government."[91] He had convinced himself that the Prime Minister's prescription for governing Ireland consisted of a certain amount of coercion mixed with "a firmer control of Dublin Castle by 'the Orange ascendancy party' than at any time since Catholic Emancipation." He had also encouraged Sinn Fein up to a point "sufficient to kill the parliamentary party and identify Irish nationalism with S. F. and pro-Germanism in the eyes of the world, especially of America. And he had played his game with immense skill and superb audacity."[92] Dillon believed this to have been the result of a preconceived and malignant plot. This gives the Prime Minister a degree of careful forethought he had never shown or been able to show. He had not been a plotter; he had been a conjurer. Whether conjuring can be called immensely skillful and superbly audacious is another question: perhaps it can.

In such a climate as the one described by Dillon, voluntary recruiting had little chance. On 4 July, French had asked for fifty thousand volunteers. On 12 August he had divided Ireland into ten districts, assigned each district a quota, and promised any district exemption from compulsory service if it filled its quota by the first of October. There had also been promises, not too clearly defined, of grants of land. By 12 September it was announced that the number of new recruits had reached 5,749;[93] and by the middle of October these figures had risen to around 9,000;[94] not an inconsiderable number, but one that could never have reached 50,000 if the war had gone on forever. French himself said in Derry on 21 August that "the law must be obeyed. The citizens of this country must take their share of the sacrifice this war has entailed."[95] This was, of course, taken to mean that he had little or no faith in his own recruiting scheme; nor had he.

On the other hand, his military government could boast 101,000 troops in early June, or so Walter Long reported to the War Cabinet.[96] This drew a comment from the Prime Minister that such a number was surely unnecessary after the Proclamation and the postponement. It was probably not only unnecessary but also exaggerated: even then, it had been an astonishing advance on the garrison of 25,000 estimated for the War Cabinet at the end of March. In October the United States Military Attaché told the State Department that, according to his information, the number of British troops in Ireland was around 87,500.[97]

The situation was somewhat eased by an August decision which turned men's minds toward the future: the decision to hold a General Election in December. According to Lord Esher, the object of this Election was to give Lloyd George "a mandate to finish the war and get the country on the road to peace."[98] The Irish register had to be revised in accordance with the 1918 Representation of the People Act, which extended the vote to virtually all males over twenty-one and all women over thirty; this was expected to triple the Irish vote, and the accession of women was thought to be very much in favor of Sinn Fein. When the news of a December election reached Ireland, therefore, the Sinn Fein organization became very busy. Its county executives began selecting candidates; it was present at all the Register Revision Sessions; and it was confidently expecting to win by a huge majority — an expectation in which the police concurred.[99]

Although there was always some doubt until the Armistice of 11 November that the Government meant what it said and that the elections would actually be held in Ireland, both the Irish Party and the Sinn Fein organization issued manifestos in mid-October. The Irish Party more than hinted at Dominion Home Rule; Sinn Fein called for the establishment of an Irish Republic and also of a constituent assembly as "the supreme national authority."[100] With the coming of the Armistice, the campaign increased in intensity: and here the Government did its best for Sinn Fein. On 12 November, Lloyd George, at a meeting at No. 10 Downing Street, made a speech so radical and so idealistic, in terms of peace and reconstruction, that it was hailed with delight on both sides of the Atlantic. The Coalition Government's manifesto of 22 November repeated some of these ideas, in a less passionate form, and then saw fit to say this:

> Ireland is unhappily rent by contending forces, and the main body of Irish opinion has seldom been more inflamed or less disposed to compromise than it is at the present moment. . . . But there are two paths that are closed — the one leading to a complete severance of Ireland from the British Empire, and the other to the forcible submission of Ulster to a Home Rule Parliament against their will.[101]

This contrived to flout both Sinn Fein and moderate nationalism, and thus to bring them closer together. It was not that the majority of nationalist Ireland, at this point, could be described as being in a revolutionary state of mind; and no historian has ever suggested that it was. The nationalist majority had simply lost all faith in the Irish Parliamentary Party because the party had been so conspicuously unable to cope with the Liberal Government and the two succeeding Coalitions; and it had learned to fear and even to detest the methods of the Lloyd George Coalition. Sinn Fein may not have been altogether intelligible to the moderate nationalist; its call for an Irish Republic may not have been taken literally; but at least it offered a more active, vigorous and exciting program. Moderate nationalism was, after all, in comparison to what it had been in 1914, relatively immoderate; the Easter Rising and its aftermath had stirred up something very old and unappeasable; and Anti-Conscription had created a bitterness all its own.

But it was not with the majority that the immediate future lay. All that was required from the majority was acquiescence. The immediate future might already have been discerned, by someone unusually gifted with second sight, in an article printed in the October 1918 issue of *An t-Oglach,* the privately printed organ of the Irish Volunteers. It was written by Ernest Blythe, who somehow got it smuggled out of prison. It contained this paragraph:

> If England decides on this atrocity [conscription] then we, on our part, must decide that in our resistance we shall acknowledge no limit and no scruple. We must recognize that anyone, civilian or soldier, who assists directly or by connivance in this crime against us, merits no more consideration than a wild beast and should be killed without hesitation as opportunity offers . . .[102]

This conveys a mood of cold savagery which, as Professor Lyons reminds us, "more than almost anything else written at this time marked out the distance Ireland had travelled since 1916."[103]

Here, indeed, one begins to part company, not so much with the spirit of the Easter Rising as with its idioms. It is to these words in *An t-Oglach*; to Michael Collins and the IRB as they reorganize the Irish Volunteers; to the Sinn Fein representatives at the Revision Sessions — it is to such phenomena that one must look for the meaning as well as the inner force of the December elections. The elections were filled with a promise of change for the Irish people, and that is all that their sense of nationality demanded: but the managers of the elections were men who wanted, not change but revolution.

While Lloyd George's own campaign descended, in almost vertiginous fashion, from the heights of his 12 November speech to the depths of "Hang the Kaiser," the campaign in Ireland destroyed nearly everyone who had ever been connected with him. Since a great part of the country was under military government, the censorship was still active, and by now more than a hundred of its leaders were in jail, it must be admitted that Sinn Fein was working under difficulties not usually experienced in democratic elections. It was, even now, officially a banned organization; its press had been driven underground; the election machinery and the post office were under hostile control. Its director of elections was arrested and hustled off to England late in November; airplanes scattered horrific warnings against voting for the Republican party; the police broke up meetings and tore down election posters. And yet — such was the anomalous character of the times — Sinn Fein candidates could present themselves for election and a Sinn Fein Manifesto, though mangled by the censor, could still be circulated publicly.

For the first time in English history, elections were to be held on the same day: this day was 14 December. When the results were declared on 28 December it was found that the Irish Parliamentary Party had secured only six out of the 105 Irish seats; that the Unionists had won 26; and that the other 73 had gone to Sinn Fein. Although there had been intimidation and personation on all sides, and although the victorious cause was managed by men to whom the niceties of political democracy meant very little, the elections, while far from exemplary, were not altogether undemocratic. It is true that the Government had mismanaged the soldier vote, so that only a small percentage of the Irish soldiers on leave or away from their units received their postal voting papers, and the Irish soldiers would in all probability have voted against Sinn Fein as pro-German. It is true that about 27 percent of the voters did not vote, and of those who did only 47 percent voted for Sinn Fein. The fact that in twenty-five constituencies the Sinn Fein candidate was returned unopposed might also imply that the other side had been virtually disfranchised. But it has been well and succinctly pointed out by Robert Kee that the percentage of the voters (73 percent) was about average for Irish General Elections; that unopposed returns were quite usual in such elections; and that "in short, Sinn Fein had taken over the Irish Parliamentary Party's place."[104]

In eight border constituencies, Sinn Fein and the Irish Party had agreed to divide the seats among themselves so as to keep the Unionists out — four of the six Party victories took place in this way. In Ulster as a whole, Ulster of the nine counties, the Unionists had a popular majority only in four; and in the six northeast counties the Nationalist minority was far larger in comparison with the Unionist majority than the Unionist majority was in comparison with the rest of Ireland. On the whole, therefore, it might be said of the 1918 elections that they made out a poor case for the exclusion of the six counties.

Of the two contested victories for the Irish Party, one was in faithful Waterford, where Captain Willie Redmond was returned for John Redmond's old seat; the other was in faithful West Belfast, where Joe Devlin defeated Eamon de Valera by 8,488 to 3,245. De Valera was also selected for South Down, where he withdrew in favor of Jeremiah McVeagh, East Clare (the seat he won in 1917) and East Mayo. East Mayo, where John Dillon had sat for thirty years, unopposed and invincible, gave the final answer: de Valera, 8,843; Dillon, 4,451: and the old warrior retired into the shades. De Valera, on the other hand, in prison in Lincoln Gaol, contemptuously refused even to issue an election address, since it would certainly have been censored. Forty-seven of the other Sinn Fein candidates were in jail. It remained only to fulfill the two most accessible of the Sinn Fein objectives — withdraw from Westminster and establish a constituent assembly in Dublin.

Meeting at the Dublin Mansion House, therefore, on 7 January, the twenty-six elected Sinn Fein representatives who were not in jail arranged to convene the Dail Eireann (or Assembly of Ireland). They appointed a committee to prepare for the public opening and to draw up a provisional Constitution; and Count Plunkett, their Chairman, wrote a letter to "all persons elected by the existing Irish constituencies" to attend as members of the Dail Eireann. Only Sinn Fein members appeared on 21 January, when the first Dail, with Cathal Brugha in the chair, was called to order at 3:30 P.M. Of the seventy-three who should have been there, twenty-seven were actually present, eight were absent for other reasons, and as the clerks called the roll the words "Fe ghlas ag Gallaibh" (imprisoned by the foreign enemy) were answered thirty-four times.[105]

The Provisional Constitution of the Dail was read and then, all standing, the deputies listened to Ireland's Declaration of Independence. It began:

> Whereas the Irish people is by right a free people: And whereas for seven hundred years the Irish people has never ceased to repudiate and has repeatedly protested in arms against foreign usurpation: And whereas English rule in this country is, and always has been based upon force and fraud and maintained by military occupation against the declared will of the people: And whereas the Irish Republic was proclaimed in Dublin on Easter Monday, 1916, by the Irish Republican Army, acting on behalf of the Irish people . . . Now, therefore, we, the elected Representatives of the ancient Irish people in National Parliament assembled, do, in the name of the Irish nation, ratify the establishment of the Irish Republic and pledge ourselves and our people to make this declaration effective by every means at our command . . .

It has been pointed out, and should certainly be emphasized, that this was not presented as a new departure but as the reaffirmation of an ancient right to which the Easter Rising itself had given a special sanction.[106]

There followed, on the same day, a message to the free nations of the world, claiming their recognition and support, and "demanding to be confronted publicly with England at the Congress of the Nations, that the civilized world having judged between English wrong and Irish right may guarantee to Ireland its permanent support for the maintenance of her national independence."[107]

And on that day there was read, and the Dail unanimously adopted, the "Democratic Program of Dail Eireann." This deserves a special attention:

> We declare in the words of the Irish Republican proclamation the right of the people of Ireland to the ownership of Ireland and to the unfettered control of Irish destinies to be indefeasible, and in the language of our first President, Padraic Pearse, we declare that the nation's sovereignty extends not only to all men and women of the nation, but to all its material possessions; the nation's soil and all its resources, all the wealth and wealth-producing processes within the nation and with him we re-affirm that all the rights to private property must be subordinated to the public right and welfare.

It now becomes more specific:

> It shall be the first duty of the Government of the Republic to make provision for the physical, mental and spiritual well-being of the children, to secure

that no child shall suffer hunger or cold from lack of food or clothing or
shelter, but that all shall be provided with the means and facilities requisite
for their proper education and training as citizens of a free and Gaelic Ireland.

The Irish Republic fully realizes the necessity of abolishing the present odious, degrading and foreign poor law system, substituting therefor a sympathetic native scheme for the nation's aged and infirm, who shall no longer
be regarded as a burden, but rather entitled to the nation's gratitude and consideration. Likewise it shall be the duty of the Republic to take measures that
will safeguard the health of the people and ensure the physical as well as the
moral well-being of the nation.

It shall be our duty to promote the nation's resources, to increase the pro-
ductivity of the soil, to exploit its mineral deposits, peat bogs and fisheries, its
waterways and harbours, in the interest and for the benefit of the Irish people.

It shall be the duty of the Republic to adopt all measures necessary for the
re-creation and re-invigoration of our industries, and to ensure their being
developed on the most beneficial and progressive co-operative lines . . .
[and] while undertaking the organization of the nation's trade, import and
export, it shall be the duty of the Republic to prevent the shipment from
Ireland of food and other necessaries until the wants of the Irish people are
fully satisfied and the future provided for.

It shall devolve upon the national government to seek the co-operation of
other countries in determining a standard of social and industrial improve-
ments in the conditions under which the working classes live and labour.[108]

Looking back from today, this seems like the formulation of some Tir na
nOg, a Land of Youth, a Never Never Land. To Pearse it would have
seemed the epitome of good sense. Connolly, no doubt, would have asked for
much more and, though the least vain of men, might then have wished to
see his name there: as it probably would have been if the original version
had passed inspection. Originally it had been given to the labor leaders,
Thomas Johnson and William O'Brien, and their version leaned more toward a doctrinaire socialism. It is said that Michael Collins and his IRB
colleagues took the traditional IRB stance when they read it — first drive the
English out, then discuss controversial matters: and it was accordingly
watered down by Sean T. O'Kelly, before being presented to the Dail. Collins even wanted the whole thing suppressed. What matters is that here in

the "Democratic Program" the promises and deeds of Easter Week received their recognition, and in words — are words negligible? — their fulfillment: and here a study of the Easter Rebellion properly turns toward a different kind of revolution. One might add that if Easter Week was a prime agent in changing the shape of things to come — forcing the British Government into offers which it was astonished and humiliated at having to make — arousing a new impatience in the people — it was not responsible for the actual shape into which things changed. "The people have voted for Sinn Fein," said Father Michael O'Flanagan. "What we have to do now is to explain to them what Sinn Fein is." But that neither he, nor anyone who came after him, could ever exactly do.

Part Five

THE UNFINISHED REVOLUTION: February 1919— December 1921

I

Apart from the Act of Union which, from its remote command post at the opening of the nineteenth century, managed the whole train of events, the obvious precipitant of the Easter Rising was the decision of the Unionists to fight the Home Rule Bill of 1912. How often in history does the irrational decision command our interest! As Lord Esher, who aspired to perceptiveness and often attained it, confided to a relative in 1912, the Tories would be "infernal asses" if they turned the bill down. Mr. Gladstone had maintained that the future peace of the Empire was involved in Home Rule; and while it has become impossible to imagine the House of Lords heeding either Mr. Gladstone in 1893 or Mr. Asquith in 1912, it is now possible to see that Ulster was in no shape to resist Home Rule if it had gone through Parliament in the latter year. From then onward the irrational took over, afflicting Lord Milner a little more violently than Mr. Bonar Law, and Professor Dicey only less conspicuously than General Wilson: and so on, up and down the Conservative ranks. As Mr. Bonar Law boasted, without Tory support in England the Orange extremists would not have got very far.

The Liberals, who represented reason and common sense, and who refrained from extraparliamentary action until it was too late to be of use, might have "proclaimed" the Ulster Volunteers in mid-1913, when they were manifestly rebellious and before they were properly armed: with the coming of the Irish National Volunteers at the end of the year, an event of the first importance, this became impossible. In any case, to suppress the Ulster Volunteers would have made the Liberals seem as irrational as their opponents; nor were they truly involved in the promotion of Irish self-government. Mr. Redmond and his colleagues, who suffered most from this English dementia, could have refused to accept the principle of exclusion when it was presented to them, turned the Government out, and aroused every town and village in Ireland with the tale of English treachery. This would have made them, in turn, as irrational as their Tory enemies, since it would have lost them Home Rule for the time being; it was indeed entirely out of character: but it would have given constitutional nationalism a vigor it had not known since the days of Parnell.

As it was, the Irish Party, with its huge majority in southern and western Ireland and its large minority in the north, drifted into World War I as a friend of the Empire; and, when the Rising struck, was among the most helpless of its victims, a stranded whale. In the end, in December 1921, Great Britain was compelled to offer Ireland terms which would have been unthinkable in 1912 or 1914; the Unionists never publicly confessed the sins they had committed; the Liberals did not admit their indecisions; and Mr. Redmond had already died, still clutching the shade of Home Rule, an honest, indeed a tragic martyr to constitutional propriety.

Thus the "integrity" of Irish history — the term is Winston Churchill's — permits us to see the Northeast Ireland of today as the last and saddest victim of the Act of Union; and to hear the voice of the past uttering as usual, and as usual in vain, its solemn warnings.

II

The Sinn Fein Dail Eireann had been elected in 1918 with a constituency, as often as not, of moderate nationalists. These moderates were not interested in a republic but they wanted something better than the Home Rule which had been enacted in 1914. So much the Rising and its troubled and rebellious aftermath had taught them and the lesson was never forgotten.

First the Rising had to be vindicated by demanding for Ireland that "place at the peace table" which Connolly had seen as the first fruits of his revolution. Alderman Sean T. O'Kelly, the Dail's Speaker (An Eann Comhairle), was sent to Paris, where he knocked persistently upon many doors, but was never admitted to the Peace Conference. He was later joined by George Gavan Duffy, but two heads were no better than one. In the first place, the great victorious powers were pledged not to interfere with one another's internal affairs, and Ireland was still by international law an internal affair of Great Britain's: in short, it was "upon the minorities of *defeated* powers" that the Conference was ready to bestow the blessing of self-determination.[1] In the second place, if this situation could be reversed in Ireland's favor, it could only be reversed with the help of the United States, and President Wilson (himself a descendant of Ulster Presbyterians) angrily resisted the pressure of the Friends of Irish Freedom, the Irish Race Convention and the House of Representatives. His private conscience was more difficult: he admitted to Frank P. Walsh, a Race Convention delegate, that Ireland was "an outstanding case of a small nationality." He solved this dilemma by allowing his conscience to plague him as an individual but not as President: indeed, as President, he would have intervened only at the cost of disrupting the Conference.

Except for allowing the Race Convention delegates their passports to Ireland, where they did what damage they could, the Lloyd George government was unwilling to make any concessions to the Irish. Thirty-four of the sixty-nine members of the Dail were in prison, without trial, under DORA 14 B; protests were coming in from every quarter; but the War Cabinet in early February refused to release them, since — it was a curious argument but by no means an unsound one — this would be taken as a sign of weakness by the industrial agitators in England and Scotland.[2] It was not until March, after a plea from the new Chief Secretary (Mr. Ian Macpherson, a Gaelic-speaking Scot) that the Government gave way: and then only when the new Home Secretary (Mr. Shortt) had bargained for the unconditional release of Captain Bowen-Colthurst from Broadmoor, and the Cabinet had been alarmed by the rumor that the "Spanish influenza" had invaded the prisons.[3] The decision was announced to the Commons on 6 March.

De Valera had been dramatically rescued from Lincoln Gaol with the help of Michael Collins on 3 February; he had lingered in hiding in England for many days; and then, on 20 February, arrived secretly in Dublin. When the rest of the prisoners were released, he was back in England, waiting for a possible journey to America; and it was not until 20 March that it was thought safe for him to return to Dublin. On 1 April he was unanimously elected President of the Republic. His Ministers were: Arthur Griffith (Home Affairs), Cathal Brugha (Defense), Michael Collins (Finance), Count Plunkett (Foreign Affairs), W. T. Cosgrave (Local Government), Countess Markievicz (Labour), Eoin MacNeill (Industry), Robert Barton (Agriculture), Laurence Ginnell (Propaganda) and, a little later, Ernest Blythe (Trade and Commerce).

The Dail, it has been pointed out by Professor Lyons, was composed chiefly of young men, men who had little connection with their constituents, and little experience of local government, men who were largely Dubliners by adoption. Sixty percent had some secondary education, twenty-five percent had had a university or professional training, only ten percent were farmers, the majority of the professional men were either journalists or teachers, and the commercial representatives were usually shopkeepers and employees. In fact, like the Irish Volunteers, they might be described as coming from the lower section of the middle class.

In the Ministry, President de Valera himself was a politician, a republican who wanted room for maneuver and did not wish to pin himself down at once to unqualified republicanism; Arthur Griffith was not exactly an extremist: but de Valera, Cosgrave and the Countess had all been condemned to death for their part in the Rising; Cathal Brugha, the hero of the South Dublin Union, had given up the post of Chief of Staff to the Irish Volunteers in order to become Minister of Defence; Blythe had been an IRB organizer for the Volunteers; and Collins (Minister of Finance), who fought in the Post Office, was not only a member of the Supreme Council of the IRB, he was also the Volunteers' Adjutant-General, Director of Organization and Director of Intelligence. Although their differences were acute, Cathal Brugha and Michael Collins were physical force men of the first order.

Collins was a member of the Sinn Fein executive as well; but because he was a physical activist he came to represent a dominant Fenian minority within Sinn Fein; and this minority was not, at least in 1919, representative of the movement as a whole. The movement's ideals came to the surface in a very different manner. They appear as an attempt to substitute British justice with a system of "Dail Courts": the first of these were the so-called "arbitration courts" set up in West Clare; they were followed by special land courts under the Minister of Agriculture (Robert Barton) with a special police force to execute their decrees. In June 1920, the Dail decreed that land claims could not be brought into court except by license of the Ministry of Home Affairs. This in turn introduced system into the administration of the law: and before the autumn of that year there were weekly "parish courts"; monthly "district courts"; four special sessions of the district courts presided over by four circuit judges three times a year; and a Supreme Court in Dublin. Civil and criminal cases, according to their importance, were dealt with in this hierarchy of courts; or were appealed up from one court to another. The law practiced here was the law as it existed in January 1919, together with certain esoteric amendments by the Dail, and although it was declared illegal by the government, the system was still in existence when the truce was declared in July 1921.[4]

In another way, the Sinn Fein ideal of a viable infrastructure of government was brought into being by the patient work of Cosgrave and Kevin O'Higgins at the Ministry of Local Government. They did their best to maintain a liaison with the local bodies all over the country: and although they could not expect to do much in the northeast, the results of the municipal elections of January 1920 were revealing enough. Since proportional representation prevailed, one can get a fairly good idea of the vote. Out of 1806 members elected to municipal bodies, 550 were Sinn Fein, 394 were Labour, 355 were Unionist, 238 were Nationalist (old style), 108 were Ratepayers' Association and 161 were Independent. This put the Sinn Feiners in a minority but the police, on the assumption that Labour would vote with them, conceded them a majority everywhere in the twenty-eight nationalist counties. It was noted, too, that — with the exception of Belfast and Derry City — all the elected mayors were Sinn Fein.[5] In fact, when it came to the Sinn Feiners' ideal of peaceable self-determination, it could safely be assumed that the Nationalists as well as Labour would vote with them to bring it about. And in the County Council elections of May 1920, twenty-eight out of thirty-three County Councils (Tipperary had two) were dominated by Sinn Fein, although here the voting conditions were far less democratic.[6] In the Dail courts, the municipal and County Council elections — here, if anywhere, men were to learn the meaning of Sinn Fein.

Even then, it was not too clear. The Sinn Fein courts were distinctly inclined toward an accommodation with the landlord interest, and this, though admirable in terms of equity, was simply baffling in terms of revolution. Nor were its intermittent relations with an increasingly radical labor force ever fraternal: the Revolution would have taken on an extra dimension if this had been the case.

III

The Sinn Fein system of law and local government was, of course, quite unacceptable to a Government and Parliament now dominated by Unionists: indeed, the only hope it had was to prevail by the very means it whole-heartedly wished to avoid — that is, by the use of force. When the Dail was declared illegal in September 1919, when Sinn Fein, the Irish Volunteers, the Gaelic League and the Cummann na mBann were "suppressed" by proclamation at the end of September,[7] these were the expected responses to a state of war (or what the Irish Volunteers considered to be a state of war) between the forces of republicanism and "the soldiers and policemen of the English usurper."[8]

On 21 January 1919, two policemen, escorting a cartload of gelignite to a nearby quarry, were ambushed by a group of Irish Volunteers at Solehead-beg in County Tipperary and both were killed. Among the killers was Dan Breen, a demobilized soldier and sudden convert, who was soon to become a notorious, indeed a legendary figure in the records of guerilla warfare. Such deeds were, to official England, savage and squalid, and these characteristics they always retained: only to those who believed *An t-Oglach,* the Volunteer paper, when it said (on 31 January) that a state of war existed, were they necessary. The majority of the people, and most of the hierarchy and priest-hood, denounced them: they were aimed against policemen who, whatever their occupational shortcomings, were Irishmen, co-religionists and neighbors.

Here again the English Government came to the republicans' rescue by sending fresh soldiers into the country, more as an occupying than a militant body, it is true, but one that paraded the streets in trench helmets and with fixed bayonets, and occasionally helped the police in their raids. Its presence alone was enough to shift the people's sympathy toward the republicans. But it was on the police, for the first year, that the republican attack was concentrated. In the Dail, in April, President de Valera said: "They must be shown and made to feel how base are the functions they perform and how vile is the position they occupy." This was harsh language and — although there was no causal connection, for de Valera was speaking of boycotts not bullets — by the end of the year the number of policemen killed had risen to twenty-one.

De Valera left for the United States in June: he hoped to influence the two great American parties in favor of Irish self-determination, to persuade the

American government to recognize the Irish Republic, and to raise money to support the fighting at home. For more than a year he struggled with the mysterious passions of the Irish-American leadership, which not only feuded with itself, the government, and Mr. de Valera, but was as usual more interested in hurting the British than in freeing the Irish. In American politics he was a neophyte and remained one. Only as a fund raiser and a favorite with the rank and file of Irish-America was he a success: but here his success was spectacular.

His departure left the field more open than ever before to the champions and exponents of physical force, and now the leadership passed more and more into the hands of Michael Collins. Collins was naturally suspect to a man like Cathal Brugha, the Minister of Defence, as ardent a republican as he but a far simpler human being. As a Volunteer, Collins was Brugha's subordinate, since Brugha was Minister of Defence; but he was his equal as Minister of Finance, in which capacity he raised (not always by the gentler forms of persuasion) a loan of over £350,000. Moreover, as a member of the Supreme Council of the IRB he moved in a secret and powerful world which Brugha detested; and his three posts in the Irish Volunteers (Adjutant-General, Director of Intelligence, Director of Organisation) gave him the virtual leadership of that body. Neither Richard Mulcahy, the Volunteers' Chief of Staff, nor the Minister of Defence, though important and vigorous men, ever came close to Collins, with his administrative genius, his enormous energy, his warm-blooded presence, his cold and concentrated purpose. It was in vain that Brugha endeavored and at length managed to bind the Volunteers to the Dail with an oath of allegiance: the binding was loose and possibly not even constitutional; and the Volunteers were a fluid body, not really susceptible to civil control. They remained what they always had been, the military and revolutionary arm of Sinn Fein. By the beginning of the year 1920 even the police were calling them "the Irish Republican Army," and in September *An t-Oglach* accepted this as the proper term.[9]

By the end of the year, Collins had perfected his system of intelligence, which, like the military Council in 1916, was a spectacular reversal of the usual condition of Fenianism. Under his control the Republic was no longer infiltrated by government informers. It was he who did the infiltrating, he who had friends everywhere — in the G Division of the DMP, the Castle, the post office, even among the officers of the British Army. He was so well protected that he could move freely from place to place, although officially a hunted man. The assassination of two of the ten senior detectives of the G Division, and the serious wounding of a third, had already been accomplished by his special "Execution Squad,"[10] when something rather more dramatic was attempted. This was an attack upon the Viceroy himself after he had alighted from his special train at Ashtown on 19 December and after his motorcade had just begun to move away from the station. Several shots were fired and several hand grenades were thrown at Lord French from behind a hedge and a dung heap near Bartholomew Kelly's public house; the viceregal car was struck, but not penetrated, in four places; and one assailant, Martin Savage, a grocer's assistant, was killed by the Viceroy's guard. There were at least five other suspects; but no witness could be induced to give evidence against them.[11]

IV

Apart from their policy of military occupation, which turned the moderates more and more against them, the Government had done very little in 1919. The reason for this is not that the British were flushed with victory and filled with arrogance after the defeat of the Central Powers: in fact, insofar as Great Britain was concerned, the Government was administering the affairs of an undernourished, sick and devitalized country. Even a postwar economic boom could not disguise that. Nor was it due to the fact that Lloyd George was preoccupied with peace-making. If nothing was done in Ireland, it was for a very different reason. The Government which met Parliament after the December 1918 elections, the elections which swept away the independent Liberals, was a Coalition Government, now depending for its very existence upon Unionist goodwill. Lloyd George was no longer the master in his own house; he was more like a court magician; he must either produce an acceptable repertoire, or be cast out; and his production schedule, in Unionist eyes, did not include Ireland. As late as 7 October 1919 it was still being suggested in the Cabinet that circumstances were unfavorable to an Irish settlement of any kind, and that it was a mistake to adopt a policy merely in response to popular clamor.[12]

Pressure, nonetheless, was mounting, and much of this was coming from America. On 4 October, for example, Viscount Grey, who had just arrived as temporary Ambassador, cabled from Washington that "one comes on the Irish difficulty everywhere. It poisons the atmosphere." A statement of policy on "self-government lines" was, he thought, becoming more and more desirable.[13] Two papers on American opinion, circulated by the War Office on 13 October, supported this view: it was generally believed that Ireland was not getting "a fair show"; that she was, in fact, suffering gross oppression; and that de Valera, who had completed his first triumphant tour, was the acknowledged representative of *all* Irish nationalists. The Irish revolutionary press, led by "that master of calumny, John Devoy" in the *Gaelic American,* was rabid in its hatred and misrepresentation; the Hearst press, with its influential chain of newspapers from coast to coast, was little better; the "more reputable radical press," such as the *New Republic* and *Nation,* held Britain up to obloquy for its oppression of Ireland, India and Egypt; the San Francisco *Chronicle* was calling for dominion status. And so it went on through the newspapers, from the St. Louis *Globe Democrat* to the Chicago *Daily News,* from the Chicago *Daily News* to the Chicago *Tribune,* from the Chicago *Tribune* to those usual Anglophiles, the New York *Tribune* and the New York *World.* All were turning against England on the Irish question: only the *Christian Science Monitor* was still holding out.[14]

The War Cabinet expired in October 1919, but the new Cabinet, with its full complement of departmental ministers, and with its proceedings formally recorded as "Conclusions" instead of "Minutes," did not seem very conclusive, at least as regards the Irish settlement. It proposed, after four reports from its Committee on the Situation in Ireland, in which the Unionist influence was prominent and hostile, that there should be two Irish Parliaments, one for the six northeast Ulster counties, one for the rest of Ireland. It also proposed to institute a Council of Ireland, containing twenty representatives from each parliament, which could be converted into an all-Ireland Parliament without reference to Westminster, if the two parties so wished. Apart from the Council, which gave a distant nod to the concept of a united Ireland, the bill which embodied these proposals was weighted in favor of Northern Ireland. The two parliaments were to exist on terms scarcely differing from those to be found in the Home Rule Act of 1914.[15] A more unlikely piece of legislation or one more unacceptable to nationalist Ireland could not have been devised: but Lloyd George duly presented it to the Commons on 22 December 1919. All through 1920 this Government of Ireland bill dragged its way through an indifferent Parliament, and received the royal assent on 23 December 1920. It was to come into force in May 1921.

Only the Ulster Protestants, who saw that with six rather than nine counties under their rule they could manage to keep their Catholics in order, would have anything to say to it. Anti-Catholic riots in Belfast and Derry in May, June and July 1920[16] had already given the Ulster Catholics some idea of what order meant. In September 1920, Captain Craig (or rather Sir James

Craig, for in 1918 he had been created a baronet) was asking for an armed Special Constabulary — two thousand would be sufficient to begin with — to assist in keeping an anti-Catholic peace. He also asked for a Special Reserve Constabulary to be formed, should the need arise, out of the Ulster Volunteers: and this too was conceded him.[17] (Such was the origin of the "B Specials" with their sorry history.)

V

A new and more deadly war, meanwhile, had broken out between the Irish Republican Army and the British Government: in a technical sense, it began on 4 April 1920 with a raid on the tax offices and a destruction of their records all over Ireland, a raid so successfully carried out that the administration was reduced to customs and excise for its revenues. At the same time more than three hundred empty police barracks were destroyed, severely hampering the military occupation of Cork, Kerry and Limerick.[18]

Between January and April, however, the murders of policemen and the consequent and indiscriminate reprisals, which included the gunning down at his bedroom door of Thomas MacCurtain, Lord Mayor of Cork, had already become so serious that a new force was recruited in England to act as a section of the Royal Irish Constabulary. The RIC had been greatly discouraged before the War by the thought that, with Home Rule, they would be on their way out; and their experiences during and since the War had been, to say the least, demoralizing. The new force that came to assist them was equally demoralized but in a different way. These "Black and Tans" — when they first arrived they could not be fitted out with the full RIC uniform, but were dressed in khaki coats with bottle-green RIC trousers and caps — were not, as was once claimed, the sweepings of the English prisons. They were demobilized soldiers, carefully screened but, alas, invisibly mutilated, victims of the horrible battlefields in which they had fought. They began arriving between 25 March and 15 April, by which date they amounted to four hundred. By midsummer this number was tripled.

In April Lord French asked the Prime Minister and Mr. Bonar Law whether the Government should take measures of war — that is, should round up the rebels as in the Boer War and put them in concentration camps — or whether it should call for a truce and summon both sides to a conference table. The Prime Minister replied offhandedly that one does not declare war on rebels, that a truce would be an admission of defeat, and that all that was needed was more troops.[19] But new troops were not easy to come by. On 19 May, the War Office agreed to hold eight battalions in readiness to proceed to Ireland if necessary; this would leave only twenty-nine battalions as "the central reserve of the Empire." The Secretary for War, Mr. Winston Churchill, then promised the Cabinet to submit a scheme for raising what he called a "Special Emergency Gendarmerie," which should become a branch of the RIC[20] — the first one hears of the Auxiliary Division, which was activated in July and sent its original five hundred to Ireland in September. The Auxiliaries were ex-officers, distinguished from the Black and Tans by their uniform and their pay. They were dressed in dark blue uniforms and glengarry caps; and they were paid twice as much — £1 a day, compared to 10/ a day for the Black and Tans. Their behavior was also, if possible, twice as brutal, although this has been disputed.

The cruelty of these assistant police has never been denied, still less (except officially) condoned: but it only serves to emphasize the fact that cruelty is inseparable from guerilla warfare; and that the invading or occupying force is, in this respect, merely more extreme than the indigenous one. The IRA used methods of terrorism all over the country during the bleak years of 1920 and 1921; but, given a choice of terrorists, the Irish preferred their own, supported them, hid them, and suffered both from and for them. "Suffered" is no exaggeration, for when it came to reprisals, the invading forces always exacted the greater price. Sniped at and bombed by an IRA in civilian clothes, which, having done its worst, melted back into the landscape, they tended to believe that all civilians were enemies. Moreover, Irish rebels were — were they not? — citizens of the United Kingdom of Great Britain and Ireland. The idea that their tormentors and killers actually represented a nation in arms was as alien to these Englishmen as it was to the Government that sent them. All this has become, with time, a peculiarly bitter example of the lack of imaginative intercourse which lay at the roots of Anglo-Irish history.

The IRA, since January 1920, according to a document found upon a suspect by the Dublin police, developed a plan of campaign which they called their "Active Defensive Strategy," as opposed to the passive defense which had prevailed in Easter Week. The theory behind it was that it was impossible to outgun and outman the enemy; that to concentrate large bodies of Volunteers for the purpose of attacking enemy strongholds could only lead to defeat; and that every training lecture "drives us to the one conclusion, namely that no matter what strategy we may adopt, we will eventually be beaten in a military sense, and . . . that the Offensive Defensive would be the best one for us to adopt."[21] From this there arose the "flying columns" which, composed of thirty to thirty-five men on full-time service, aided by part-time fighters who otherwise lived their ordinary lives, became the IRA's response to the discrepancy in guns and personnel.

Looking back over the year 1920, the observer traverses a bleak landscape, littered with corpses, disfigured with burned buildings — from Ascendency mansions to humble creameries — a silent witness to the bankruptcy of Unionism. In Ulster, said one police report, there were "feelings of bitterness which years will scarcely dispel"; in Munster and Connaught "there was little semblance of government control except in the immediate neighborhood of police and troops." The Dublin Metropolitan Police force was almost useless. The RIC was in sorry condition: its constables were boycotted, forced to commandeer food, housed in cramped quarters with no proper air or light, with every man's hand against them, and under constant pressure from their families to resign.[22]

Mr. Churchill, in July, had spoken to a conference in Downing Street of raising a force of thirty thousand men in Ulster and sending seven battalions of them into the South — a lethal suggestion, fortunately not acted upon.[23] On 10 November, he asked another Conference, "a very 'hush-hush' meeting," said Sir Maurice Hankey, for *authorized* reprisals: if there was drunkenness and gross disorder among the troops, he said, if there was looting, thieving, and clumsy and indiscriminate destruction, that was because the soldiers "goaded in the most brutal manner and finding no address" took action on their own account. He called for a policy of reprisals "within strict limits and under strict control"; but the Conference could not bring itself to authorize this kind of *lex talionis,* which invariably involved the innocent: it was decided that "the moment was not opportune."[24] Authorized reprisals, nonetheless, soon became a standard operating procedure in areas under martial law.

In Dublin, eleven days later, Michael Collins sent his Execution Squad into action against officers of the British Army who were believed to be active in intelligence work. Eleven were killed in their houses or hotels, two in front of their wives. Four more were wounded. That afternoon, in revenge, the RIC and Auxiliaries opened fire on a crowd that was watching a football match in Croke Park between Dublin and Tipperary: twelve people were killed and sixty wounded. That night in Dublin Castle two of Collins's best men in the Dublin Brigade, who had been captured twenty-four hours before, were killed by Auxiliaries "while attempting to escape." This was Bloody Sunday of 21 November: it produced something "not far short of panic in London."[25]

Bloody Sunday is only one of many horrors. One can but add to it a train of events which took place between 9 and 11 December. On 9 December a flying column under Tom Barry, Commandant of Cork's No. 3 Brigade, and one of the most ruthless and successful of all the guerilla leaders, ambushed two lorry loads of Auxiliaries, and wiped them out in circumstances of unusual savagery. On 10 December, martial law was proclaimed in Cork. On 11 December, there was another attack on the Auxiliaries. That night Auxiliaries and Black and Tans invaded Cork, looting, wrecking and burning, with the result that the center of the city was destroyed, with an estimated damage of £3,000,000. Major General Edward Strickland, commanding in the area, set up his own Court of Enquiry of three officers. Its report was so unfavorable to the Auxiliaries that a ministerial conference of 29 December decided that "to publish it while Parliament was sitting would be disastrous to the Government's whole policy in Ireland."[26] Indeed, the report was apparently so harsh that, after two special conferences in February 1921, it was determined never to publish it or reveal its contents to Parliament.[27]

VI

The Government had rearranged its Irish administration early in 1920. Major General Sir Nevil Macready, who had settled down as London's Commissioner of Police, was made Commander in Chief. Unlike many senior officers, who favored the Ulster loyalists, General Macready was quite impartial: he disliked both sides. After him, in April 1920, came Sir Hamar Greenwood, the new Chief Secretary, a Canadian and (like his two predecessors, Mr. Shortt and Mr. Ian MacPherson) a Home Ruler: his mission was to improve upon Mr. MacPherson, who had been thorough but not thorough enough: either that, or resign. It was not long before Sir Hamar showed every inclination to improve upon Mr. MacPherson. Major General H. H. Tudor, who took Sir Joseph Byrne's place at the head of the RIC, was of a like mind with Sir Hamar Greenwood. (Later on in the year they were joined by Brigadier General F. P. Crozier, as Commander of the Auxiliary Brigade. Crozier, a reformed alcoholic, had been an Orange firebrand before the War, a gentleman who far out-Carsoned Carson in the extremity of his views. In February 1921, however, he created a sensation by resigning his command — "I never could understand why Tudor took him on," said the disgusted Macready[28] — and thereafter, in speech and writing became more and more friendly to the Nationalists.)

Behind this policy can be discerned the prominent and unchanging figure of Sir Henry Wilson, now a Field Marshal and Chief of the Imperial General Staff. He told the Prime Minister in September that, if there had to be murder, the Government should do the murdering. Such language was at least candid: too candid for Lloyd George who "danced at all this" — they were discussing authorized reprisals — "and said that no Government could possibly take this responsibility."[29] The Government's "Restoration of Order in Ireland Act," however, which received the royal assent on 9 August, was quite in line with Sir Henry's Draconian thinking: it gave the military authorities "extraordinary immunities and extensive powers," such as the power to intern anyone, without charge or trial, for an indefinite period, and the power to try any prisoner by court-martial, and without legal advice, except in cases requiring the death penalty.[30] As late as October, the Prime Minister was saying that he was "a Gladstonian Home Ruler and wished to keep Ireland as an integral part of the United Kingdom."[31] This language, to which even a Gladstonian Home Ruler would not have assented, was simply an admission of bondage in some Unionist Egypt: but it would be a poor compliment to the Prime Minister to suppose that he was not keenly aware of the efforts being made to bring about his exodus.

Sir Maurice Hankey, the Cabinet's Secretary, had been converted to the view that "terror must be met by greater terror": he noticed, a little ruefully, that he was "no longer completely in the P.M.'s confidence about Ireland."[32] That place was being taken by Tom Jones, the Cabinet's Principal Assistant Secretary, a man with an ambiguous reputation in history, but one who, until late in 1921, consistently advocated a generous and candid approach to the Irish problem. Jones was hand in glove with A. W. Cope, Assistant Under-Secretary in Dublin Castle, a tactless but enlightened and humane official; and Cope was unremitting in his efforts at negotiation. In July, Tom Jones submitted a paper to the Prime Minister, setting forth the case for Dominion Home Rule:[33] and in August the Prime Minister conceded that a negotiation might take place, but only if the Irish would agree to terms in advance.[34]

Cope was not alone in his negotiations, although he was the official most often in touch with Sinn Fein and even with the IRA; nor was Jones singular in his belief that Dominion Home Rule (or a status roughly equivalent to that of Canada or Australia) was the proper solution for Ireland. On 15 July, Sir John Anderson, the Under-Secretary in Dublin Castle, wrote to the Chief Secretary to say that he was of the same mind—nothing but Dominion Home Rule would do. Three days later he noted that the *Freeman's Journal,* hitherto staunchly Republican, had come round to this milder solution; and that the Catholic hierarchy and a great majority of professed Sinn Feiners were thought to be of the same mind.[35] On 4 August a deputation of Cork businessmen, both Nationalist and Unionist, headed by the industrialist Sir Stanley Harrington, told Lloyd George the same story: *nobody* in southern Ireland (said Mr. Richard Beamish, head of the brewing firm of Beamish and Crawford) wanted the Home Rule Bill presently before Parliament; all were for Dominion Home Rule. The Prime Minister was polite but evasive.[36]

Indeed Lloyd George's *public* position was that he would consider only the Home Rule Bill; that he would even suspend the bill's third reading if Ireland did not come to her senses; that he would have "no truce with murder." And on 29 July the Cabinet Committee on the Situation in Ireland, meeting for the fifth time, first recommended unanimously the reactivation of the Ulster Volunteer Force as a measure of self-defence against the Catholic minority! It then declared that no person employed in the Irish Government—A. W. Cope was clearly indicated—should have any communication whatsoever with Sinn Fein.[37]

Negotiations continued nonetheless, although they actually did not come to the surface until 21 October, when Brigadier-General George Cockerill, M.P. for Reigate, who had written to the *Times* (8 October) calling for a conference without any restrictive terms, was visited by a mysterious envoy. He was probably the Patrick Moylett mentioned by Dorothy Macardle:[38] he told Cockerill that he was a merchant, that he had come from Arthur Griffith, and that he was empowered to suggest a negotiation on Cockerill's lines.[39] He got only as far as H. A. L. Fisher, a Liberal member of the Cabinet's Irish Committee: but he returned with a vague offer, which seemed to imply a partial recognition of the Dail.[40] This was promising; and on 2 November Under-Secretary Sir John Anderson received two visitors at Dublin Castle—he gave their names as "Dr. Crofton" and "General O'Gorman." They represented moderate Sinn Fein opinion and were empowered to offer negotiations if the ban on the Dail were lifted. These gentlemen actually did see Lloyd George, Bonar Law and Greenwood: and "it looked more like reality," Law wrote to Anderson, "than anything I had heard before."[41]

Nothing concrete came of this: but when Arthur Griffith was arrested on 20 November by the overzealous G.O.C. Dublin, Major General Sir Gerald Boyd, and when Archbishop Clune of Perth (Australia) was given permission to visit him in prison on 3 December and to confer with Michael Collins the next day, both were willing to agree to a truce without a surrender of arms. The good Archbishop hastened back to London in triumph, but found the Prime Minister adamant on the arms question — all must be surrendered. The same reply was given on 9 December to peace offers from Father O'Flanagan, Vice-President of Sinn Fein, acting entirely on his own, and from a rump session of the Galway County Council.[42] Lloyd George constructed a whole brick out of these straws: he declared at Carnarvon on 9 December that he "had murder by the throat:" and on 10 December Lord French issued a Proclamation placing Cork, Tipperary, Kerry and Limerick under martial law.[43] Since a truce conditioned upon arms surrender was quite unacceptable, it can be seen that Lloyd George, besides listening to intimates such as Tom Jones or agents of good will such as Archbishop Clune, was acting as a kind of devil's advocate for the Unionists. The Proclamation of 10 December only reinforces this assumption. "Blessed donkies [*sic*]" wrote T. M. Healy to Lord Beaverbrook, "this is worthy of Gallipoli and Antwerp."[44]

Nonetheless, negotiation without an arms surrender was very much in the air as the year closed: indeed, it received a most serious discussion in a Cabinet meeting of 29 December.[45]

VII

The Restoration of Order to Ireland Act had given the coercionists, in December and January, some hope that they were gaining the day.[46] In February, however, things began to deteriorate at an even faster pace: the only hope seemed to be that the IRA would break down under the weight of men and arms mobilized against it. The police were said to number 11,056, including Black and Tans and Auxiliaries in 1920, and 14,174 in 1921.[47] In December 1921, the Cabinet was told that there were 6,000 police and 7,000 Black and Tans in round figures.[48] This would put the Auxiliaries at about 1,400 at that time. The only certain figures for the military are those for 21

March. On that day, so General Macready reported to the Secretary of the Military Council,[49] the position was:—

Present Strength (Cavalry, Artillery, Infantry)	39,579
Numbers on courses, sick, absent	5,715
To be discharged March 31	5,335
Total strength	39,961
Provisional Establishment	47,810

He was fully aware, he told the Secretary, of the obligations which the Army Council had to meet, not only in England, but all over the world. Nonetheless, his command, now 7,849 under strength, must be reinforced: either that, or be dangerously reduced in health and efficiency. It was chiefly composed of young soldiers; their nights in bed varied from one to four; the strain, particularly in the cities of Dublin and Cork, was very great, and with the approach of finer weather would be greater still. One partial alleviation might be the removal of internees to England: it took five battalions to guard the internment camps. But even with this alleviation and even if he *were* reinforced, he could not promise that this would mean the total suppression of the rebels.*

The IRA had long been considered "an oath-bound secret society, scarcely distinguishable from the IRB."[50] It was, therefore, difficult if not impossible to estimate the numbers of those who actually pitted their wits and guns and lives against these forces of the Crown. Michael Collins said that their number in the field at any given time rarely exceeded three thousand; and their total number may never have been more than fifteen thousand.[51] The question appeared to be: Who would give out first? The IRA, oppressed by numbers and matériel? Or the Cabinet, from the force of domestic and imperial opinion? An Imperial Conference was to be held in London in June — an event of considerable embarrassment to a Government bogged down in an Irish war. As Field Marshal Jan Christian Smuts of South Africa put it, in a letter to the Prime Minister — "The present situation is an unmeasured calamity; it is a negation of all the principles of Government

---

* In an interview with Carl W. Ackerman of the Philadelphia *Public Ledger*, he refused to admit that anyone was *imprisoned* without a hearing. The men in the internment camps, he said, were not imprisoned — they were IRA officers, who were being detained while their cases were carefully investigated. If they were found to have played an active part in rebellion, they were tried by court-martial; if not, they were released. Whether this distinction satisfied the readers of the *Public Ledger* is not known. (PRO CO 904/188/(2):4 April, 1921.)

which we have professed as the basis of Empire, and it must more and more tend to poison both our Empire relations and our foreign relations."[52]

Under the Better Government of Ireland Act of 23 December 1920, elections were to take place in May. If the Parliament for Southern Ireland refused to perform its statutory duty, if more than 50 percent of the members declined to attend, then the twenty-six counties were to be reduced to the status of a Crown Colony. It was quite understood that it would take more than General Macready's thirty-nine thousand soldiers or General Tudor's police and auxiliaries to maintain even the semblance of control in that event.

In the middle of this, Eamon de Valera returned to Ireland. His work in America was done; events were becoming too critical for him to stay away any longer; indeed, he had been away too long. He was smuggled aboard the S.S. *Celtic* and arrived in Dublin on 23 December.

The Government had originally decided that he was never to be allowed to return, on the plea that he was not a citizen of the United Kingdom: but, once they learned of his arrival, they thought it wiser not to arrest him. The forces of the Crown, however, were to seize other accused persons, at public or private meetings, whether de Valera was present or not.[53] The possibility that such arrests — made in his very presence, while he himself went immune — might have laid de Valera open to the most odious imputations, cannot have escaped the Cabinet. Their attitude toward the returning President was ambivalent in the extreme: but it is certain that they saw in him a possible avenue toward truce and negotiation.

He faced an awkward situation in his own domain. With the arrest of Griffith, Collins had become Acting Provisional President: it was rumored that the IRB wanted him to remain at the head of affairs, even after de Valera's return. Though de Valera admired Collins, and could never be brought to criticize him in later years, a coolness between the two leaders began at this point. De Valera, of course, remained as President, but he must always have been conscious of the IRB behind the scenes . . . the IRB, which considered its Supreme Council to be the true government of the Irish republic, until the English were driven out.

The Dail met secretly on 21 January and again on 25 January: the President and his ministers were present at the second meeting; and here de Valera stated that their task was to "stick on," but at the same time "lighten the burden" on the people.[54] As for negotiations, his attitude was quite simply this — let the British Government come out openly and make an offer.

De Valera's efforts to lighten the people's burden proved ineffective; he had no real control over the IRA. On 25 May, for example, a company of the IRA seized the Customs House and — while fighting off the Auxiliaries at the cost of six IRA dead and most of the rest captured or wounded — set it afire. Thus the records of the Irish Local Government Board, and of Customs and Inland Revenue were lost in a revolutionary bonfire which, besides destroying Dublin's loveliest building, had made the administration of government almost impossible.

The police were, of course, by now hopelessly discouraged and their reports must be examined with that in mind: but they cannot be overlooked, and they indicate a condition of near anarchy, increasing month by month until the truce of July. By the end of May in Donegal, for example, all semblance of control had vanished and the Dungloe District, about one-sixth of the county, had become "a miniature republic."[55] This could be repeated, in less dramatic form, for many another county in the west and southwest, and not there alone. It was admitted that the Dublin Metropolitan Police, who should have kept crime off the City's Black-and-Tan-ridden streets, were (as General Macready had put it the year before), "past redemption." And in April it was noted that Waterford, usually the least disturbed county, was in a fearful condition.[56] In Cork's West Riding, in June, the situation was "desperate . . . damnable," and this was echoed everywhere.[57] It throws a somewhat questioning light upon Collins's later and now well-known contention that the IRA had almost reached the end of its tether when the truce was announced. Here and there, to be sure, a resolute voice could be heard: County Inspector G. Ross of King's County still maintained that only a stern determination to restore order in "this blood-sodden country" would win through. "These continuous peace rumors," he wrote, "hearten the ill-disposed and give them encouragement."[58] But the peace rumors could not be checked.

The Cabinet's indecision as it oscillated between a policy of coercion (headed by Mr. Balfour) and of conciliation (headed by Lord Curzon) with Mr. Churchill and Lord Birkenhead the most notable of the waverers between one side and the other, reflects this growing collapse of government in Ireland. So too does the friendly correspondence which Sir John Anderson maintained with Sir Nevil Macready, an important dialogue between Dublin Castle and Military Headquarters in Parkgate, and one of great interest. For the Black and Tans and the Auxiliaries Macready had a soldierly contempt: and in February 1921, one finds him telling Anderson — it is a truly frightening remark — that "they treat the martial law areas as a special game preserve for their amusement." In March Anderson told Macready that "there might be rising" in the West — rising is not a word that any official used lightly; and in April Macready told Anderson that the IRA were "running the [western] country" and particularly the network of roads which led from Mallow into Kerry and Limerick. Both the civilian and the soldier disapproved of General Tudor, the head of the RIC: and they seemed to differ chiefly on whether or not the Sinn Fein boycott on Belfast goods — instituted in September 1920 as a protest against the brutal expulsion of five thousand Catholic workers from the Belfast shipyards — should be suppressed or not. Macready thought that suppression was the only answer: Anderson thought it would be useless and wrong. On the whole no correspondence could have reflected more faithfully, in its cool way, a belief that the Irish situation was now beyond control.[59]

Lord Midleton told the Cabinet on 8 March that if resistance in July 1920 could be indicated by 100, it could now be put at 300: the situation was, in fact, "appalling."[60] On 22 April, travelling incognito as "Mr. Edwards," and wearing a pair of horn-rimmed glasses as his single concession to camouflage, the burly Lord Derby arrived in Dublin — a courageous but inadequate negotiator — for some fruitless discussions with de Valera. On 5 May Sir James Craig made the dangerous journey to Dublin and de Valera met him at a house in the Howth Road. Each believed that the other wished to see him; each had been deceived by A. W. Cope, who thought that something might come of it if only they could be persuaded to confer. But nothing did.[61] The Prime Minister professed to be very annoyed by this Castle interference, and Sir Hamar Greenwood vaingloriously said, "I have put my foot down on that." But the tireless Cope continued to keep the channels of communication open; Anderson was peaceful by disposition; Macready pointed out that, while coercion must be relentless if the soldiers and police were to be sustained, even then it could not succeed.[62] And at the Prime Minister's elbow stood Thomas Jones, still conciliatory, still in touch with Cope. If Lloyd George held out, this was not due to obstinacy but to politics. His powerful Cabinet Committee on the Situation in Ireland, dominated by Unionists, was calling for martial law. As late as 12 May, when the matter of a truce in Ireland came to a vote in a Cabinet discussion, he and Shortt were the only Liberals in the majority against it.[63]

However, with the Imperial Conference about to open, great pressure was building up for some peaceful gesture. Lord French had even been replaced in May by Lord FitzAlan, a civilian and a Catholic. It was true that Lord FitzAlan, as Lord Edmund Talbot, had been Unionist Chief Whip in 1919;

and Cardinal Logue was supposed to have said that he would just as soon have a Catholic hangman: but FitzAlan in place of French was a significant exchange for all that.[64]

In May there came the new elections under the Government of Ireland Act of 1920. They were held on 19 May for the 26 counties and on 24 May for the six counties. The results were quite predictable. In the six counties, where "B Specials" were used (at least in Belfast) to "keep order,"[65] the Nationalists and Republicans won only twelve of the fifty-two seats in the new Northern Parliament: and thus, on that fateful day, for fateful indeed it was, the Government of Northern Ireland came into being, with Sir James Craig as its first Prime Minister. This was not what the Ulster Unionists desired; what the Ulster Unionists desired was the *status quo;* but, as Captain Craig (Sir James's brother) had told the Commons in March, it would at least allow them to remain inside the United Kingdom.[66] As far as they were concerned, the partition of Ireland was now an accomplished fact.*

In the twenty-six county area, intimidation was such that there was no election at all: the Sinn Fein candidates were returned unopposed — "they are practically all gunmen," said Macready, "higher officials of the IRA" — and the four Trinity College Unionists were unopposed also. Since the Sinn Fein candidates had no intention of abiding by the Act of 1920, but considered themselves the members of a Second Dail Eireann, Southern Ireland, according to the Act, would be reduced to the status of a Crown Colony on 14 July. It was universally admitted that if such a reduction occurred, Macready would need every soldier they could send him to keep the peace.

Fourteen July was the date set for a proclamation of martial law all over the twenty-six counties; this was determined by the Cabinet of 2 June on the advice of the Committee on the Situation in Ireland.[67] Reinforcements were said to be "pouring" into Ireland, although they never amounted to more than ten thousand, and in Dublin it was rumored that Macready was to be replaced by a more Cromwellian general: but even then it was admitted that FitzAlan was seeking a settlement.[68] In fact, the Cabinet of 2 June represented the last rally of the Diehards: and twelve days later, under a long accumulation of pressures, from inside and from outside Ireland, the dam suddenly and dramatically broke. On 14 June, Sir Edward Grigg, private secretary to Lloyd George but in fact one of his close advisers, told the Prime Minister that the King's speech at the opening of the Northern Parliament

---

* It was after this that Sir Edward Carson, to whom partition was fundamentally distasteful (although he accepted it as a lesser evil), received a life peerage and ascended to the relative obscurity of a Lordship of Appeal.

on 22 June would be the real opportunity — "my nose tells me" — for an appeal for peace.[69] General Smuts, who had come for the Imperial Conference, was of the same mind; and Lord Stamfordham had already written to Lord FitzAlan to this effect. Only Sir Hamar Greenwood held out; he said that no move could be made without the consent of Craig; whereupon Grigg went to the Cabinet's Irish committee and insisted that the King should not be made "the mouthpiece of the Ulster Government."[70] He was emphatically supported by A. J. Balfour, hitherto the most irreconcilable of Ministers, and Greenwood at once gave in. While George V was making his genuine and moving plea for peace in Belfast on 22 June, de Valera, through a military blunder, was arrested in his house in Blackrock; all his papers were seized:[71] but he himself, much to his surprise and even embarrassment, was released after a few hours. On 25 June, Lloyd George wrote him a letter, saying that the time had come for a conference in London with him and Sir James Craig, "to explore to the utmost the possibility of a settlement."[72] The urgency of this language was perfectly genuine. There were dangerous signs of a breakup in the Coalition Government. A plot to oust the Prime Minister had begun within a few weeks of Bonar Law's resignation in March — whether from ill health or from policy is to this day uncertain — and the consequent accession of Austen Chamberlain to the Conservative leadership. Its leaders were Lord Birkenhead and Winston Churchill, the latter (already a crypto-Conservative) angry at not being given the Exchequer in Chamberlain's place, the former in the mistaken belief that he could lead any government that succeeded Lloyd George's. Behind them was Lord Beaverbrook, a busy but on the whole an imperfect conspirator.[73] The whole plot came to light in the *Manchester Guardian* on 23 June: but it lingered on until October, when the Prime Minister defused it by bringing both the plotters into the Anglo-Irish conference as delegates, a position neither could resist.

De Valera had a way of saying that he was "not a doctrinaire republican"; it was now rumored that he would abandon the idea of a republic. He was supposed to have admitted as much to the Deputy Lord Mayor of Cork;[74] and General Smuts, who went to Dublin in July and irritated the Irish leaders by comparing their situation to that of the Boers in 1902, came away with the impression — which happened to be wrong — that de Valera would accept Dominion status.[75]

De Valera was, however, willing to meet Lloyd George in London, so long as Sir James Craig was *not* present: but he insisted that there would have to be a truce before he left. The truce came into being on 11 July: it was welcomed by both sides, although for the IRA it meant a truce to fighting, and not to drilling and reorganization. On 14 July de Valera had the first of four meetings with Lloyd George. He was accompanied on this momentous journey by Arthur Griffith and Austin Stack, a moderate and an extremist, and by two cousins, Robert Barton and Erskine Childers, both products of English public schools, who had served with the British armed forces during the War and had then been converted to a stern republicanism. For Childers, the hero of the Howth gunrunning, Griffith had conceived an intense dislike. He called him "that Englishman," although as de Valera's Director of Publicity he had already revealed — it was surely most un-English of him — an "unequalled knowledge of the mentality to which Ireland's advocates had to appeal."[76]

When de Valera went to Downing Street, Art O'Brien, the quasi-official Irish representative in London, came along to make the introductions and hold the ring.[77] The Irish leader had been warned often enough — even by Sir James Craig, even by Lord Midleton — that it was dangerous to meet the Prime Minister alone; and Lloyd George certainly put forth all his charm and something more. On the wall of the Cabinet room he had hung a map of the world; it was rather too liberally splashed with the red of the British Empire. It was intended to impress Mr. de Valera, but "his schoolmaster's eye noted that it was based on Mercator's projection, which exaggerated the red markings"; and in any case to him these blots of color represented greed and aggrandizement, not power and glory.[78]

Lloyd George then pointed out that the chairs around the table were set for the Imperial Conference, already in session: only one had always been empty. When de Valera refused to play up, he said, after a pause: "That chair is waiting for Ireland." Lord Midleton had warned him that de Valera was "an uncompromising fanatic," that he would require "inexhaustible patience";[79] but Lloyd George's impressions were of a different kind. In a note dictated immediately after this interview, he said that de Valera was more inclined to listen than he had expected and "listened well"; but that he did not seem to grasp the issues clearly. Indeed, said Lloyd George, he felt he had been dealing with "a second-rate mind."[80] Later on, the Prime Minister revised these first impressions. He admitted that arguing with de Valera was like trying to pick up mercury with a fork: to which de Valera is said to have replied, "Why doesn't he use a spoon?"[81] Neither, in fact, was prepared to open his whole mind to the other.

Indeed, the Irish leader had not yet got his own ideas in order. On the eve of their fourth meeting, 20 July, he received the Prime Minister's proposals: they offered the twenty-six counties a qualified Dominion status. On the next day, after conferring with his colleagues, de Valera turned the proposals down. Lloyd George had already warned the Cabinet that he found it difficult to say "exactly where the Irish leader stood." He wanted a republic, but refused to admit that a republic was inconsistent with the Monarchy![82] On this note they parted.

It was on 27 July that de Valera arrived at the proper answer to the Lloyd George proposals: it came to him as he was bending down to tie his bootlaces before breakfast, when the word "external" dropped into his mind.[83] Fully developed, and presented to the Dail Cabinet, this became "external association"; it meant that Ireland was to be associated with the British Commonwealth but not a member of it: and in its final form, largely the work of Erskine Childers, the proposal went to London on 10 August. The Cabinet of 13 August agreed that this was "an attempt — even though a clumsy attempt — to keep open the discussion and that the document was intended merely as a step in a prolonged discussion."[84] The ensuing discussion was certainly prolonged: but the proposal was, and remained, de Valera's last word.

As a preliminary to the meeting of the new Dail in August, the Government announced that it would release all its members still lying in English prisons, with the exception of Sean McKeown, the chivalrous "blacksmith of Ballinglae," known for his mercy to the enemy wounded, but now under sentence of death for a successful ambush of Auxiliaries. It was at once informed that "the top fighting men in Dublin" had received this telephone message from the provincial IRB centers: — the truce would end if McKeown were not released.[85] The order for his release was issued, with a surprising and significant promptness, on 8 August.[86]

The new Dail met and at once elected de Valera President of the Irish Republic, to which he and the deputies swore to "bear true faith and allegiance." This, from an English point of view, was scarcely a felicitous beginning. De Valera then nominated his Cabinet: Griffith (Foreign Affairs), Stack (Home Affairs), Brugha (Defence), Collins (Finance), Cosgrave (Local Government) and Barton (Economic Affairs). Madame Markievicz and Count Plunkett were given portfolios which did not carry a seat in the Cabinet.

For a moment around 17 August, the Government contemplated a new and severe military operation: but at last allowed itself to enter a long, classical and — in retrospect at least — beguiling correspondence, in which one side tried to entice the other into the Empire and the other refused to be trapped. There was a time, in the third week in September, when the whole negotiation seemed about to collapse and the Cabinet with it. The IRA at once got ready for more fighting; while General Tudor of the RIC and his aides, on their side, talked of the necessity of killing freely, began once again to stigmatise Catholicism "a form of ju-ju worship" and in general behaved like the lower kind of seventeenth century bigot.[87] But the Irish leaders desired only to come to the conference without being tied down in advance. "It is precisely because neither side accepts the position of the other," wrote de Valera on 19 September, "that there is a dispute at all and that a Conference is necessary." In the end it was agreed to accept Lloyd George's formula and meet "with a view to ascertaining how the association of Ireland with the community of nations known as the British Empire can best be reconciled with Irish national aspirations." But the formula turned out to be more tactful than correct. Whether "external association" could be reconciled with British imperial aspirations — that was the question.

The Conference opened on 11 October 1921.

VIII

The Irish delegates were Arthur Griffith, Michael Collins, Robert Barton, E. J. Duggan, and George Gavan Duffy. Their head secretary was Erskine Childers.

Collins had not wanted to go: he was a Fenian and a very tough one, but he was also a realist: he did not believe that a republic could be wrested from the English, and he saw nothing ahead of him but personal disaster. Arthur Griffith did not altogether believe in republics. Barton was an economist who, as a Rugbeian, was supposed to have some insight into the workings of the English mind: this may have been so, but to Lloyd George, whose mind was not English, he was always "that pipsqueak." Duggan, a Dublin solicitor, and Duffy, Sinn Fein's representative in Rome, were selected because they were lawyers. Duggan would follow Collins; Duffy sided with Barton and Childers.

They came as plenipotentiaries; but they were plenipotentiaries in swaddling clothes. They could sign no treaty on their own; the draft must first be submitted to Dublin. It was for this reason that de Valera did not join the delegation: he saw Dublin as the command post from which to direct proceedings with a freedom, a lack of direct responsibility, which he could not possibly enjoy in London. For this reason and one other: Austin Stack and Cathal Brugha, republican extremists both, had refused to leave Dublin. They could hardly be trusted to run the Cabinet in de Valera's absence.

Confronting the delegation, with its awkward political background, its mixed feelings, its lack of full powers, were Lloyd George, Winston Churchill, Lord Birkenhead, Austen Chamberlain, Sir Laming Worthington-Evans, Sir Hamar Greenwood and Sir Gordon Hewart. Lloyd George, and the two ex-plotters, Birkenhead and Churchill, constituted a formidable and brilliant trio, equal to any debate; and Hewart, the Attorney-General, was known for his incisive mind. The Irish were mere tyros by comparison; but, even if they had not been, could they have done much more than they did?

The negotiations turned upon two vital questions — Unity and Status. Was Ireland to be partitioned or was she not? What was to be the nature of her association with the Crown and Commonwealth? To most Irishmen, the former was the more important question; to most Englishmen, the latter. The classical approach to the history of this conference is to say that the Irish should have made concessions on the Crown and taken their stand on unity. They were prepared to offer the six Ulster counties a qualified but generous and reasonable autonomy, so long as this autonomy was exercised under the aegis of a Dublin not a Westminster Parliament. English opinion, Empire opinion, would not have called this an untenable position. That is why they had been instructed to "lay the blame on Ulster," and, if they had to break off the negotiation, to do so on Unity.

As we now know, Lloyd George had long feared this approach: he told the King, in September, that if they could raise the problem of Ulster in a conference, they could maneuver their British opposites on to less favorable ground, and this would have a bad effect, "not on the Irish settlement only, but on India and elsewhere."[88] From the beginning, therefore, the English negotiators tried to make unity and status exchangeable. The Irish delegates had been instructed to accept "Free State" for "Republic" and, instead of allegiance to the Crown, to "recognize" the King as head of the Commonwealth . . . that Commonwealth with which they were to live in a happy state of external association. Lloyd George, in turn, promised them unity, if they would accept allegiance . . . allegiance, which transformed "external" into "internal" and association into membership.

He could not keep his promise because the Irish delegates stood firmly together against allegiance to the Crown and Ulster's Craig was no less firm in his refusal to submit to Unity. Lloyd George's efforts to overcome these difficulties are extremely complex: but they can be brought within a manageable compass.

His chief adviser at this point was Thomas Jones who, as Principal Secretary to the English delegation, played an active and rather too devious role in its backstairs negotiations. When Sir Maurice Hankey left England on 2 November, moreover, in order to run the British secretariat at the Washington Arms Conference, Jones automatically became Acting Principal Secretary to the Cabinet — a position of considerable power. From now on, in fact, he was the Prime Minister's co-adjutor, the *éminence grise* of the negotiations.

The first question was — could the Irish be made to weaken on the Crown? Lloyd George had decided to challenge the Conservative opposition to his Irish policy with a debate and a division (i.e., a vote) in the House of Commons on Monday 31 October: and Jones persuaded him to use this coming debate as a means of wringing from Arthur Griffith some private documentary assurance that the Irish would not be unreasonable. Griffith agreed; the first draft of his letter was quite accommodating; and Sir Laming Worthington-Evans announced after reading it, "I like this . . . They will presently say — O King."[89] It was not only accommodating, it was also quite unnecessary, since the Prime Minister received a vote of confidence in the House by a large if restless majority of 439–43.

The Griffith letter, however, had now taken on a life of its own; two more drafts were needed before the Irish delegation could be brought to accept it. In its final form, as received on 4 November, it was nothing more nor less than External Association, with a cautious nod toward Naval Defense (or the right of English warships to make use of certain Irish harbors), and a firm refusal to retreat from "the essential unity of Ireland."[90]

According to the diary of one of his secretaries, Frances Stevenson, Lloyd George read an Irish willingness to accept the Crown into this cool response. The Stevenson diary is important because Miss Stevenson was not only Lloyd George's secretary, she was also his mistress; and her diary gives us a unique picture of a Prime Minister in (as it were) carpet slippers. According to the Thomas Jones diary — which supplements the official "Conclusions" with eye-witness reports of Cabinet proceedings — the Prime Minister made a similar assurance to the important Cabinet meeting of 10 November, the first full Cabinet on Ireland since the negotiations began. He asserted that the Irish "had pulled down the Republican flag and adopted the flag of Empire."[91] It was, needless to say, all illusion.

He had already turned to Sir James Craig. On 5 November, closeted with Craig in private, he reminded him that Ulster would pay a much lower income tax if she came in under an All-Ireland Parliament than if her finances continued to be regulated on United Kingdom terms — which, of course, they would be under the Act of 1920. There was also, he added slyly, the little matter of an excess profits tax to be avoided. He had already told Miss Stevenson that you could always get at a Presbyterian through his pocketbook: and it certainly seems as if Craig, on 5 November, had shown a willingness to come to terms. On 7 November, however, he reversed his position: under no circumstances, he said, would he allow his government to subordinate itself to an all-Ireland Parliament.[92]

Perhaps Lloyd George's knowledge of the Presbyterian mind was insufficient, or perhaps this change of attitude, if it was a change, was due to the influence of Bonar Law, who had come back from his rest cure in the South of France, and was now contemplating a return to public life. Although he still considered himself a friend and colleague of Lloyd George's, he was ready to lead a Conservative opposition to any effort to tamper with Ulster, and was even squinting at the Premiership itself.[93]

Craig, at any rate, on 11 November, not only refused the Prime Minister's offer to sit at the conference table but also, flying in the face of Ulster's desire to rejoin the Union, suggested that the six counties should be given a separate Dominion status. This would deprive Ulster of her representation in the Imperial Parliament, but would release her from the burden of United Kingdom taxes; and Arthur Griffith, when he heard of it, professed to see "the cloven hoof of Ulster's sordidness."[94] The suggestion was not sordid, however, it was not even serious; it was merely stubborn. Besides being perfectly impractical, it would have compromised beyond repair Craig's leadership of the Ulster extremists.

With Craig's intransigence now blocking the way to Unity, Lloyd George turned back to a plan which he had concocted as early as 7 November. Tom Jones was to make the following suggestion to Arthur Griffith and Michael Collins: — If an acceptable Treaty could be made, let Ulster be included in it, but let her Parliament have the right to contract out of this Treaty within a year of its final ratification. If the Ulster Parliament exercised this right, however, it would have to accept a Boundary Commission, appointed to determine the proper line between Ulster and the rest of Ireland in accordance with the wishes of the inhabitants and the rational demands of geography and economics.

On such a basis, it was to be rather more than hinted, a Boundary Commission would have to give large parts of Tyrone and Fermanagh, and smaller but important sections of Down, Derry and Armagh to Southern Ireland. What was left of Ulster would then become entirely too small for political or economic survival, and would fall like a ripe fruit into the lap of the Dublin Parliament.

It was thought that Griffith and Collins would approve of this scheme: but when it was offered to them by Jones on 8 November, under the cautious pretense that it was entirely his own idea, they did not much care for it. Griffith preferred a plebiscite; Collins said that it sacrificed Unity. "I agreed," Jones wrote in his Diary, "but what was the alternative? Chaos, Crown Colony Government, Civil War. We were bound to try every device to avert that."[95]

"Every device" has a somewhat sinister ring today. On 12 November, the Boundary Commission scheme had become a trap, and the victim was Arthur Griffith. At Sir Philip Sassoon's house, that day, alone with Lloyd George, Griffith was told that Bonar Law was threatening a revolt on Irish policy when the Conservative Party Conference met at Liverpool on 17 November. He was told that Lord Birkenhead and Austen Chamberlain were to quell this revolt by persuading Sir Archibald Salvidge, the powerful Conservative boss, to present the Boundary Commission idea to the Conference. He was told that they could hardly expect Sir Archibald (no friend to nationalist Ireland) to perform this distasteful task, if they did not have Griffith's assurance that he would not obstruct their efforts by repudiating the Commission.

Griffith agreed; the idea was not his, he said; it was Lloyd George's: but he did not wish to be obstructive. This was at once reported to Lord Birkenhead and Austen Chamberlain; "I do not think that I have seen D. [Lloyd George] so excited about anything before," Miss Stevenson recorded;[96] and the next day the wily Jones brought Griffith the Boundary Commission idea in the form of a memorandum in the handwriting of Austen Chamberlain.[97] Lloyd George and Jones had marked their quarry and run him down. They knew that Griffith was the most moderate of the delegates; they had been told that he was a man of the strictest probity.

Griffith read the memorandum; and while it is doubtful that he initialed it (it has since disappeared) he certainly assented to it. He then forgot the whole thing: to him it had been simply a matter of not making trouble between the Prime Minister and the Conservatives. Once again, English party politics had become the undoing of an Irish leader. Griffith did not realize that he had tacitly accepted the Partition of Ireland; or, to put it more bluntly, that Lloyd George and Tom Jones, men whose probity was by no means so strict as his own, could now use the memorandum against him.

At Liverpool, a diehard rebellion was easily snuffed out. Indeed it is quite apparent today that the Conservatives wished the negotiations to go on under the Prime Minister's direction. The last thing they wanted was to have the Irish problem dumped into their laps. Little as they cared for the Prime Minister, they believed that his skill and his alone could get the Irish off their backs. After he had done that, it would be time to consider when and how to get rid of him.

Yet even the Prime Minister's gifts, it soon appeared, peculiar and powerful as they were, might prove insufficient: by 22 November the negotiations showed every sign of breaking down. On 25 November Griffith, Barton and Collins crossed over to Ireland: when they returned they made it clear that they could have nothing to do with an oath of allegiance to the Crown.

Lloyd George had promised to tell Sir James Craig what the final agreement was or was not to be no later than 6 December: this, for some reason, such was the strange influence of Ulster, was accepted as a terminal date. The Irish delegation and Childers went back to Dublin for a final conference with the Dail Cabinet on 2 December. They were already divided against themselves — Griffith, Collins and Duggan against Barton, Duffy and Childers. Griffith brought with him the ultimate British proposals: — Full Dominion status, with certain modifications concerning naval and military defenses; a united Ireland, subject to Ulster's right to contract out and accept a Boundary Commission instead; an oath of allegiance to the Crown. De Valera now joined Brugha and Stack in opposing any concessions: they would not compromise with the formula to which they had consented on 25 November:

> Ireland shall agree to be associated with the British Commonwealth for purposes of common concern such as defense, peace and war; and she shall recognize the British Crown as head of the association; and that, as token of that recognition, she shall vote an annual sum to the King's Civil List. Her legislative and executive authority shall be derived exclusively from her elected representatives.[98]

The delegates were instructed to return and stand upon this formula. If they had to break with the British, they should endeavor to "lay the blame on Ulster." Although he had no unshakeable objection to an oath of allegiance to the King, Griffith himself agreed that he would sign no document prescribing it until that document had been brought back to Dublin. All this was decided by men who were tired, overwrought and in a hurry: it left the delegates little or no room for maneuver.

When they returned to London on 4 December, Collins — according to the British report — was so "fed up" that he "sent Mr. Barton and Mr. Duffy to see if the Prime Minister could convert them." A meeting accordingly took place in Downing Street at 4 P.M., and Griffith, Barton and Duffy presented Lloyd George, Chamberlain, Birkenhead and Sir Robert Horne with the reply they had been instructed to give to the British proposals. These "Amendments" made no reference whatsoever to Ulster or partition.[99] The English conferees at once retired, but stayed away for only two minutes. Coming back into the room, they declared the Irish counterproposals to be quite inadmissible. "I cannot understand," said the Prime Minister, "what is your difficulty in accepting Clauses I, II, and III of our proposals." (Clauses I, II, and III in the proposed Articles of Agreement dealt with the grant of Dominion status; and the presence of the Crown in Ireland was implicit in every clause.) "Our difficulty," answered Duffy, with great simplicity, *"is to come into the Empire,* looking at what has happened in the past." "In that case it is war," was the reply; and with that the meeting broke up.[100]

Great pressure was now brought to bear on Griffith. Tom Jones was with him at midnight and, if Jones' diary is correct, Griffith admitted that he and Collins would agree to Dominion status if Lloyd George could wring from Sir James Craig "a conditional recognition, however shadowy," of the concept of a united Ireland.[101] Griffith then talked Collins into meeting alone with Lloyd George at 9 the next morning; and here the Prime Minister, who played with consummate artistry on the theme of a Boundary Commission and its fatal consequences for Ulster,[102] persuaded Collins to return for another conference at 3 P.M.

At noon, the Prime Minister told his Cabinet that Griffith and Collins were "greatly disappointed" at their colleagues' refusal to accept the British proposals, and that Collins seemed "not unwilling" to give way on the first three Articles (or "clauses" or "paragraphs" as they were variously called). It was at once agreed that if the Irish could be brought to accept these three clauses, together with those on naval defense and on customs, "it might be possible to try to meet them on the Oath of Allegiance (Article IV)."

The Cabinet, therefore, agreed upon this form of words:

"I . . . do solemnly swear true faith and allegiance to the Constitution of the Irish Free State as by law established and that I will be faithful to H.M.

King George V, his heirs and successors at law in virtue of the common citizenship of Ireland with Great Britain and her adherence to and membership of the group of nations known as the British Commonwealth."[103]

This was not exactly allegiance; but then it was not external association either. It kept Ireland inside the Empire, and the Crown inside Ireland.

At the 3 P.M. meeting Griffith, Collins and Barton were faced with Lloyd George, Birkenhead, Churchill and Chamberlain. Griffith, faithful to his instructions, at once brought up the question of unity. "I repeat," he said, "that I will accept inclusion in the Empire if Ulster comes in [to a united Ireland]." But he said that he and Collins both wanted to know what Craig's reaction would be. Lloyd George, who had been waiting for this for many days, now pounced upon his victim. This was not what Griffith had said before. Had he not agreed to accept the alternative proposal — that Ulster could stay out of the Free State if she agreed to a Boundary Commission? And had he not agreed to accept it without any conditions? At this the fatal document of 13 November was produced, like a rabbit from a hat, and "shown to Mr. Griffith and Mr. Collins." Collins had never heard of it, and Griffith, if he remembered it at all, never dreamed that it would be used in this manner. "I said I would not let you down," was all that he could answer, "and I won't." It was no longer possible for him to break on Ulster.[104]

Lloyd George celebrated this sorcerous victory with a substantial concession. He said that "provisionally both parties should be left free to do what they liked in the matter of customs"; and, a little later, as a final objective, removed the word "provisionally." Thus Ireland was to have complete fiscal autonomy, something which Mr. Redmond had merely dreamed of far back in 1912. The Prime Minister then asked again if the delegation was prepared to stand by the Articles of Agreement, as now amended, Oath and all. Only Griffith promised that he would.

The Prime Minister, of course, needed more than this: all must sign. If they did not, he solemnly promised that he would not even give them time to lay the matter before the Dail: it would be "war within three days," and war more terrible by far than any they had yet experienced. At 7:45 P.M., the meeting broke up. Griffith had agreed to sign; Collins appeared to hesitate only over the Oath; Barton, who came to this meeting as a sort of *hostis curiae,* had not committed himself at all.

Lloyd George knew all too well that liberal British opinion, let alone that of the Empire and the United States, would have rebelled against any further bloodshed in Ireland. What he put forward on 5 December was a gigantic bluff: if the Irish were taken in by it, he would retain his power; if they were not, he would have to go.

And the Irish were taken in. To Griffith, of course, as an orthodox Sinn Feiner, a dual monarchy was not a repugnant concept. Collins, simply as a practical man, and even more simply as a very tired one, did not think that the IRA could sustain or that the Irish people should endure another armed invasion. Then again, he had believed the Prime Minister's assurances, in their morning conference of 5 December, that a Boundary Commission would make a political impossibility out of the Northern government. He saw the Treaty, oath and all, as a first step out of the Empire, indeed a first stride. But he was a Fenian leader: he detested the oath and he did not deceive himself as to the character of the extremist element in the Irish Resistance. He afterwards said that, when he signed the Treaty, he had signed his own death warrant.

Duggan would naturally follow Collins, and Duffy and Barton were persuaded to follow Duggan — so they afterwards told the Dail Cabinet — by Lloyd George's threat of instant war.

The final version of the British offer was brought to them in their headquarters in Hans Place at 9 P.M. At 11:15 Griffith, Collins and Barton called at No. 10 Downing Street; discussed the offer; spoke "quietly" of a few small adjustments; waited for a final retyping; and, at last, at 2:10 A.M. on 6 December, signed the Articles of Agreement. (Duffy and Duggan signed later.) Then, and then only, did the two delegations exchange their first handshake, the British "expressing their hope that [they] might together have laid the foundations for a permanent understanding and lasting friendship between the two peoples."[105]

IX

Why had not the Irish, at the very least, telephoned Dublin before signing this agreement? Presumably because they knew in advance that the Cabinet's answer would be negative. They were five patriots who, in one way or another, risked their reputations so that the Dail — in full session — might consider the Treaty and make its own decision. As for Lloyd George, he may have bluffed and deceived the Irish delegates: but, from his point of view, and that of his colleagues, the agreement was generous and constructive.

Indeed, it was, on the whole, from the imperial and moderate point of view, a good Treaty: of all Lloyd George's negotiations, this was the most substantial. A majority in Ireland would almost certainly have accepted it. It is true that if it gave Ireland the same status as the Dominion of Canada, it did so with two important and limiting differences: — (1) In recognition of Ireland's propinquity, her coastal defenses were to be undertaken by "His Majesty's Imperial Forces" until an arrangement should be made for her to undertake them on her own. (Article VI.) (2) The Government of the Irish-Free State was to afford His Majesty's Imperial Forces certain stated harbor and other facilities (at Brerehaven, Cobh, Belfast Lough and Lough Swilly) and, in time of war or of strained relations with a foreign power, such other facilities as the British Government might require. (Article VII, [a] and [b].) These, with the Oath, swearing faithfulness to the King (Article IV), were the Articles which seemed, to the revolutionary mind, to be a specific betrayal of Ireland's hopes.

Article IX, by its silence, bestowed fiscal autonomy on Ireland. Article XII recognized Partition in the form of a Boundary Commission, should Ulster contract out of the Free State within *one month* of the Treaty's ratification. Article VIII (another limitation) allowed Ireland a "military defence force" bearing the same numerical proportion to the "military establishments maintained in Great Britain" as the population of Ireland bore to the British population. Proper safeguards would be provided Northern Ireland, and its "local militia" and defense force, if it did not contract out of the Free State. (Article XV.)[106]

All in all, this would be seen to be a limited, but viable Dominion status — always supposing one knew what Dominion status really was. At the end of a long memorandum, circulated to the Irish Delegation in October, Lionel Curtis (the British delegation's second secretary and editor of the Milnerite *Round Table*) summed it all up in this way:

The Dominions and Britain are now once and for all on a footing of formal equality in external as well as domestic affairs . . . In matters common to all the Empire must speak with one voice and the Foreign Office in Whitehall is the mouthpiece through which the voice is heard . . . Each Government is free to take any action it chooses, but each is expected to consult the others before taking action which affects the unity of the Commonwealth as a whole. And if the Imperial Conference is of the opinion that the action proposed would affect that unity, the Government proposing it is expected to ⌐bstain. This is actually how the system works. It depends entirely on the willingness of each to refrain from doing what it is free to do, but which, if done, would limit the freedom of all the rest.[107]

This was Milnerite metaphysics, quite charming and perfectly baffling to all but true believers. In 1931, under the Statute of Westminster, no miracle of precision and designedly so, the Crown was left as the only uniting link, and the Imperial Parliament ceased to be sovereign over the Dominions. But in 1921 nobody could have predicted the arrival of this statute, still less the manner in which — as de Valera showed in 1932 — an Irish statesman could use it to initiate, precisely, a state of "external association." In 1921 Lionel Curtis's language would have seemed to an Irish revolutionary merely another example of the old net — now refined into a sophisticated and clinging web — which the English had always thrown over the struggles of militant Ireland.

X

When the Coalition Cabinet met on 6 December, it did so in a state of jubilee. It celebrated, in Lloyd George's words, "the greatest day in the history of the British Empire"; it hinted (this was the Prime Minister again) "that it has been represented that a Boundary Commission would give Ulster more than she would lose"; it congratulated the Chief Secretary on "the rough treatment to which the extremists had been subjected"; it praised the Prime Minister for his "skill, wisdom and foresight"; it agreed that all prisoners interned without a trial in Ireland — they were said to number around four thousand — should be released without even waiting for the Dail to approve the Articles of Agreement.[108] In this orgy of relief and congratulation the press (with the exception of the incorrigible *Morning Post*) thankfully joined. Parliament approved the Articles on 16 December.

Yet when the Prime Minister, hoping to profit by this popular success, suggested in late December that a General Election would be in order, he was turned down by the Conservative Party leadership. He was turned down again in February 1922. The Conservative back benchers, for arcane reasons not unconnected with a traditional obtuseness, were determined to punish him for solving a huge Irish problem by coming to terms with the Irish — in other words, as the *Morning Post* of 8 December 1921 had put it, with an almost guileless candor, for his "abandonment and betrayal of British powers and British friends in Ireland."

XI

In British imperial history, the Treaty of 6 December 1921 is and deserves to be considered as a success; and so it is in the history of Anglo-Irish relations. In Irish history, or that existentialist side of Irish history which is governed by an unappeasable past, it is a failure. It produced a tragic division which lacked only the tragic element of necessity. It is true, of course, that when a nationalist movement, somewhat against its will, is being led into extremist courses by a revolutionary minority, that minority is very vulnerable. The well-known "fissiparous" quality of Irish politics, at any rate, now asserted itself: and differences, maladjustments and resentments, more or less under control while the war was being fought, now became visible.

De Valera first read a summary of the Treaty, with horror, in the Tuesday (7 December) *Evening Mail:* then came Duggan carrying the Articles of Agreement in full. A Cabinet was called for 8 December, and for five hours the seven members, together with Duffy and Childers, fought the matter out. Barton said that he and Duffy had signed because of the threat of war; Collins spoke of the "duress of facts"; Griffith maintained that the Treaty could stand on its own merits. When the matter came to a vote, Barton voted for the Treaty simply because he had signed it; Griffith because he believed in it; Cosgrave came over to the side of Collins; and de Valera, Brugha, and Stack were thus left in a minority of three to four.

That evening de Valera issued a Proclamation in which he said that the terms of the Articles of Agreement were in violent conflict with the wishes of the majority "as expressed freely in successive elections during the past three years." "I feel it my duty," he ended "to inform you immediately that I cannot recommend the acceptance of this Treaty either to Dail Eireann or to the country. In this attitude, I am supported by the Ministers for Home Affairs and Defence." On the next day, Griffith issued his own statement. "I believe that this treaty will lay the foundations of peace and friendship between the two nations. What I have signed I will stand by in the belief that the end of the conflict is at hand."[109]

The Dail had been summoned to meet on 14 December. From then on, until 6 January — with a break for Christmas with its peaceful influence — it debated the proposed Articles, and on 7 January, by a vote of 64–57, the Articles were approved. The pro-Treaty forces were well represented by Griffith and Collins; and perhaps best of all by Collins, backed (as President of its Supreme Council) by the powerful influence of the IRB. Nobody (although Brugha made an ill-advised attempt) could accuse Collins of truckling to the English; he was the least pusillanimous of men. His was quite possibly a classical exposition of the gradualist approach: the Treaty, he said, gave "not the ultimate freedom that all nations aspire and develop to, but the freedom to achieve it."

On the anti-Treaty side, there were two main arguments. De Valera himself took his stand on these words: "You have an oath to the Irish Constitution which will have the King of Great Britain as Head of Ireland. You will swear allegiance to that Constitution and to that King." By the Treaty, he argued, British authority would remain the master in Ireland.

Erskine Childers, as became a convert, was far more uncompromising. He condemned the cession of the ports — which the Dail Cabinet's "Amendments" of 4 December had at least accepted for five years[110] — as "the most humiliating condition that can be inflicted on any nation claiming to be free." The Treaty was basically vicious — "it places Ireland definitely and irrevocably under British authority and the British Crown." In this he was echoed by Austin Stack, who said he would fight the Articles even if the Oath were taken out.[111] Here one must remark that the English Cabinet itself concurred with Stack: the first three Articles, it agreed in its noonday meeting of 5 December 1921, involved the presence of the King in Ireland, since all writs would run in His Majesty's name. The Oath (Article IV) had to be insisted upon, not because it was essential, but only to avoid all misunderstanding.[112]

Among the most unyielding in the anti-Treaty ranks were those who had most reason to be locked into the past: Mrs. Pearse, the mother of Padraic and Willie; Mrs. O'Callaghan, widow of the murdered Mayor of Limerick; Mrs. Clarke, widow of Tom Clarke; Miss Mary McSwiney, the sister of Terence McSwiney, who died in 1920 after seventy-four days of political hunger strike, watched in anguish by the whole civilized world. To these devoted women, and those who thought like them, the past could only be redeemed by leaving the Empire at all costs.

The English delegation during the Treaty negotiations had not really taken this kind of thinking into account; still less had they tried to imagine themselves into the mind of a man like de Valera, waiting and watching behind the scenes in Dublin. When Field Marshal Smuts, for example, went to Dublin in July 1921, he reported in some distaste that de Valera "spoke continuously of oppression and seemed to live in a world of dreams, visions and shadows."[113] This was existential Irish history, the living past, openly at work in the mind of one of its devotees. It was irritating, it was indeed incomprehensible to the Boer Field Marshal: but it made an oath of "faith-fulness" to an English King detestable to de Valera.

There was, however, quite another side to Eamon de Valera. This can be found in his proposed alternative to the Articles of Agreement — Document No. 2 as it came to be called (the Articles being Document No. 1). Presented to the Dail in secret session on 15 and 16 December 1921, it reappeared in a modified form on 4 January 1922, as an amendment to the motion to approve the Articles. It was less stirring but more statesmanlike than the pronouncements of Childers and Stack. It accepted a five years' occupation of the treaty ports; it offered safeguards to Ulster in a brief addendum. But it stood firmly on "External Association," there was no doubt about that. One has only to examine its two fundamental declarations. (1) "The legislative, executive, and judicial authority of Ireland shall be derived solely from the people of Ireland." (2) "For the purposes of Association, Ireland shall recognize His Britannic Majesty as head of the Association."[114] Although the English negotiators had declared on 4 December that they would not accept this formula, Document No. 2 was nothing more nor less than an appeal to moderation and common sense.

If the Dail Cabinet had been united behind some such document it is fairly safe to assume that the anti-Treaty purists, even Erskine Childers, the most sternly logical of them all, would have gone along. When it was all over, the redoubtable Mary McSwiney agreed that they would have been ready to die for the difference between the Articles and Document No. 2.[115] At Cork, in February, Cathal Brugha called the Document "a supreme effort by the Captain of the ship to pull it off the rocks."[116] It was withdrawn on 4 January on a technicality, and three days later the Articles were approved.

After the approval de Valera resigned as President and the motion to re-elect him was lost by two votes. He and his followers then withdrew, while the rump Dail elected Arthur Griffith in his place. Thus began the fission which developed into a nine months' civil war — from July 1922 to April 1923 — the wounds of which have not yet been healed. The IRB's leadership followed Collins and the Treaty; the IRA's was divided; the rank and file of both bodies could be found on either side. It was an uglier conflict than even the Anglo-Irish War because the Irish Revolution was now forced to devour its own children — a grim feast which, one cannot help thinking, might well have been averted.

In other words, what would have happened if the Irish delegates had obeyed their instructions and — defying Lloyd George's threat of war — had "broken" with the English on 5–6 December, using Ulster for their reason? Since the Lloyd George bluff was called more than once in the Dail debates, this is not just a conjecture in the writer's mind. It deserves a brief excursion into that other world which runs its affairs in the conditional mood.

A revolutionary minority does not consult the will of the people — (it is a matter of historical consensus that the majority of the Irish laity and clergy approved the Articles) — it consults only what it believes the will of the people ought to be. If the delegates had come back in December with the Articles unsigned, if the Cabinet and the Dail had then remained true to its revolutionary origins, it is as certain as anything can be that there would have been no war.

Lloyd George himself confessed in private that he would have resigned rather than fire another shot: the diaries of Lord Riddell, Thomas Jones, and (somewhat less conclusively) C. P. Scott attest to this.[117] Since he habitually resorted to threats of resignation, however, and under circumstances far less exacting than these, the evidence of the diaries is somewhat less persuasive than the evidence of the circumstances themselves. This is solid enough. Headed by the *Times* and the *Daily Mail,* the press of whatever persuasion (such diehards as the *Morning Post* excepted) had for months been opposed to the Anglo-Irish war. Domestic opinion, Empire opinion, world opinion — all had condemned it: in America, where an important Arms Conference was now taking place, it had always been greatly to England's disadvantage; and its effect upon such highly sensitive areas as India had been, if not calamitous, at any rate a matter of grave concern. What would the case be if it were now renewed?

The Prime Minister was not a man of blood or even of iron: his was a more subtle composition. Other things being equal, he greatly preferred peace to war; or if war, then a war that men could respect: and his Irish policy, so relentless in public, was stimulated less by a desire to punish the Irish than by a need to appease the Unionists — in short, by his lust for power. His underlying plan, however, had long been to convert the Coalition into an anti-Socialist Centre Party, one which would attract the moderate Labourite and the progressive Conservative. This plan had been compromised by his Irish war and would have been ruined once and for all by its renewal. To resign in the name of peace — this was the least desperate course for him if the Irish had defied his threats and turned the Articles down.

It is almost inconceivable that a Conservative government, with such a leader as Bonar Law or as Austen Chamberlain, or indeed with any leader, would seriously have considered doing what the great Welshman had not dared to do. To put the Conservative position in its proper context, however, one must consider not merely opinion, powerful as that was, but something rather more concrete — an organized labor movement to which, in those early postwar years and particularly in Conservative minds, very sinister and subversive motives were attributed.

The British Trade Union Congress, in July 1920, at its Scarborough conference, had called for a withdrawal of all British military and para-military forces from Ireland; organized Irish labor had gone along with it; and opposition on this important front had stiffened ever since.[118] Moreover, it was during the last months of 1921 that the English economy began its precipitous slide into a deep and stultifying depression. This was hardly the time, therefore, or the growing pool of unemployed workers quite the place, in which to recruit (or conscript) the thousands upon thousands of fresh soldiers needed to renew this unpopular "capitalist" war. For it could not be renewed on the former frustrating scale of semi-coercion: something more "thorough" — in the old cruel seventeenth century meaning of that term — would undoubtedly be needed.

There remained only economic blockade, which, besides being cruel to the point of sheer inhumanity, would also have a very unhappy effect upon England's fainting economy — a serious consideration in that bad year. A new war itself would hardly have been less tolerable or have provoked a more dangerous opposition.

What then would have been left? The *Daily Chronicle,* Lloyd George's semi-official organ, had suggested on 6 December (writing before the news of the signing broke) that the Prime Minister should adjourn his negotiations for several weeks if no agreement could be reached.[119] If he had followed this advice; or followed it after winning a General Election; or, as seems altogether more probable, in the light of his war threat, he had resigned and left the problem up to the Conservatives — there remained one great resource. The English mind has always been fertile in the art of political compromise — it used to be one of the keys to an understanding of the English polity — and now, with their backs to the wall (for this was the *moral* position to which the IRA had strangely pushed them) what other resort would Lloyd George or his successors have had except a resort to compromise?

Here Document No. 2, which in substance would have been offered them as an alternative to the Articles, is of great importance. It is a very careful document; it could have given little satisfaction to that small minority within the Revolution which was still passionately devoted to the Workers'

Republic of James Connolly;[120] it reflected the social conservatism which lay behind this nationalist revolution. Would the Conservative leaders, in this impasse, have made the same mistake which those demented Unionists made in 1912–1914? Would they not have realized, despite their own back benchers and their more troglodyte constituents, that the Irish Revolution, once its political appetites had been appeased, would become moderately respectable and reasonably safe? As respectable and safe, in fact if not in appearance, as John Redmond and his colleagues? And would they not then have offered External Association and Irish Unity in return for a friendly attitude toward Naval Defense — something which would have stood them in good stead in the years to come?

In his Addendum to Document No. 2 de Valera, "while refusing to admit the right of any part of Ireland to be excluded from the Supreme Authority of Parliament," nonetheless says that he is willing to grant Ulster "privileges and safeguards no less substantial than those provided in the Articles of Agreement." Whether this was a stand on Unity or a nod to the Boundary Commission, in the belief that it would settle Ulster's hash, we cannot tell: for the Ulster problem, strange so say, was barely mentioned in the Dail debates. Once Lloyd George's bluff had been called, however, no one can doubt that Unity would have returned with all its old insistence.

Outside the Orange lodges Irish Unity was not considered at all an unreasonable proposition in those days; and those were desperate times in Anglo-Irish history, almost as desperate as "1798." But they were times which did not permit the brutal coercive methods of that distant year. To allow the Protestant northeast to fight it out in a religious war with the Catholic south and west and northwest would have been the negation of all responsibility: a very different thing from letting the Irish Revolution wear itself down in a civil war among the twenty-six counties. Where then could the English leadership have turned except to a compromise on such terms as those suggested in the Addendum?

And yet how could Craig and his following be induced to accept this reasonable arrangement? They could not be coerced by force of arms; nor could the people of Ulster be subjected to an economic blockade: no English leader could have survived if he had insisted upon such terms as those. Only one expedient remained — scarcely less desperate but still just within the pale — and that was to withdraw from the Ulster government the means of governing. Almost all the Ulster revenues came from reserved taxes which were imposed and collected at uniform rates throughout the United Kingdom: of these Ulster's proportion was calculated by a Joint Exchequer

Board, under the Treasury thumb. A withdrawal of these revenues, even a threat of withdrawal, might not this have been sufficient to bring Ulster in?

At this stage there was still a viable opposition to Sir James Craig. As James Lichfield, a responsible civil servant in the northeast, told Thomas Jones early in 1922, the Belfast business leaders were all in favor of coming to terms with the South.[121] Ulster had not yet hardened into the Ulster of today. These businesslike Unionists had realized for some time that the hooligan Orange vendetta against Ulster's Catholic minority, carried out by the "B Specials" and their like under the accommodating shadow of the Anglo-Irish war, was doing immense harm. When Bonar Law's opposition, for example, collapsed at the Conservative Conference at Liverpool in November, it is not the rout of the diehards that matters. What really matters is the report of Sir George Younger, the Conservative Party chairman, to the effect that hundreds of Conservatives were complaining bitterly of Ulster's intransigence.[122] They had no intention of coercing her, they said, but . . .

With all the important revolutionary factions united behind External Association, with Unity a reasonable proposition in all but Orange eyes and the eyes of such English fanatics as Colonel John Gretton, Rupert Gwynne, and Sir Henry Wilson, where would the pressure have been put? On the twenty-six counties or on the six?

Thus the possibility of a privileged, safeguarded Ulster coming in under an All-Ireland Parliament, with all the happy consequences which this would have had for the Ulster and the Ireland of today, flits for a moment before one's mind. And so, in a more substantial form, does the thought that, if the Articles had been rejected, no matter what the retaliation, there would have been no civil war: and the civil war is one of the greatest tragedies in Irish history.

Coda

It is time to return to the actual world in which the Treaty was signed and accepted and its friends and enemies began to take sides.

Even now, looking back at the Irish Revolution after the January split, one is astonished at its vitality. It made possible a Coalition pact between de Valera and Collins on 23 May 1922 — a pact to rig the 18 June elections with a revolutionary disregard for the demands of political democracy. It persuaded Collins and his legal advisers to produce in early June a constitution for the new Free State so very republican as to outrage the English who read it. The Pact was broken by Collins at the last moment, the constitution was rewritten in more submissive terms — but only under intense English pressure and at the cost of giving the June elections (with their large pro-Treaty majority) a dubious reputation to this very day. After Rory O'Connor, the engineer commander of Dublin's IRA Brigade, had occupied the Four Courts with some anti-Treaty comrades in April, hoping to bring popularity to his cause by forcing the English Army to drive him out, it was the English who compelled the reluctant Collins to do the job for them at the end of June.

This was the beginning of the Civil War, in which the pro-Treaty side gained the day, and the anti-Treaty side the laurels. The memory of Michael Collins, a folk hero if ever a man was born to be one, has been tragically flawed because, as he predicted, he lost his life in halting a nationalist revolution which a majority of nationalists did not really want. As so often before in this irrational world, it was the defeat that won the laurels.

What happened to the chief events and actors? Arthur Griffith died on 12 August 1922 of a heart attack brought on (it was thought) by overwork and sheer grief. Michael Collins was killed in an anti-Treaty ambush ten days later. The Treaty which brought such praise to Lloyd George in December 1921 became a factor in his downfall in October 1922. The Ulster Parliament "contracted out" of the Treaty at the first opportunity the following December. The Boundary Commission came to nothing in 1925. De Valera, after signing (on the grounds that it had no meaning) the very oath he had once so execrated, reentered the Dail in 1927. Under the External Association Act of 1936 and the *de facto* Republic of 1937, the Crown was bundled out of the twenty-six counties and the twenty-six counties out of the Empire. One is tempted to say, with Shakespeare's Feste, "Thus the whirligig of time brings in his revenges."

And yet "the whirligig of time," the seductive concept of a circular history, is only a fiction: events do not return in different disguises over and over again. All revolutions of course have some similarities: each is nonetheless unique. In thinking of this one in particular, it is best to usher the Inevitable out of the front door and bring the Contingent in through the basement entrance: for it was not through the workings of some malign destiny but through the humbler, more poignant and more mysterious agencies of human nature that it took the course it did.

"The peace of the past" is a form of awareness in which the commonplaces of the moral judgment are suspended; and where the attention is focussed upon the strangeness and variety of the human condition, which is the stuff of history. In the long struggle between the two cultures, Protestant English and Catholic Irish, Gall and Gael, invader and invaded, alien and indigene, the blame is easily assigned. Yet this same struggle can be seen as a profoundly human confrontation, one which finally gave to Irish history, in the Easter Rising, one of its most heroic symbols and to British imperial history, in the Anglo-Irish War and Treaty, one of its saddest yet most illuminating chapters. It is in this kind of peace, the peace of the past, that the Irish Revolution may one day come to rest.

ABBREVIATIONS,
REFERENCES,
BIBLIOGRAPHY

Abbreviations

BLP	Bonar Law Papers
CAB	Cabinet Papers
CO	Colonial Office Papers
CSO RP	Chief Secretary's Office, Registered Papers
DMP	Dublin Metropolitan Police
IRA	Irish Republican Army
IRB	Irish Republican Brotherhood
LGP	Lloyd George Papers
NLI MSS	National Library of Ireland, Manuscript Division
PRO	Public Record Office, London
RIC	Royal Irish Constabulary
SPO	State Paper Office, Dublin
UVF	Ulster Volunteer Force

References

PART ONE: CHAPTER ONE (Pages 3–14)

1. F. S. L. Lyons, *Ireland Since The Famine* (London: 1971), 368.
2. E. L. Woodward, *The Age of Reform* (Oxford: 1936), 447.
3. Ibid., 333.
4. Anthony Trollope, *Autobiography* (London: 1950), 65.
5. Nicholas Mansergh, *The Irish Question* (Toronto: 1965), 22.
6. Woodward, 321.
7. Hansard, 3 ser. XXII, 1204–6.
8. Emmet Larkin, "The Devotional Revolution in Ireland, 1850–75," *American Historical Review*, LXXII, No. 3 (June 1973) 625–652.
9. Maire & Conor Cruise O'Brien, *The Story of Ireland* (New York: 1972), 106.
10. Cecil Woodham-Smith, *The Great Hunger* (New York: 1962), 405.
11. J. C. Beckett, *The Making of Modern Ireland* (New York: 1966), 350.
12. Woodham-Smith, 407.

PART ONE: CHAPTER TWO (Pages 15–27)

1. Barbara Solow, *The Land Question and Irish Economy* (Cambridge, Mass.: 1971), 55.
2. C. E. Pomfret, *The Struggle for Land in Ireland* (New York: 1969 reissue), 50.
3. Patrick O'Farrell, *Ireland's English Question* (New York: 1971).
4. Sir Philip Magnus, *Gladstone* (New York: 1954), 196.
5. W. F. Monypenny and G. E. Buckle, *The Life of Benjamin Disraeli* (6 vols., New York: 1916–1920), V, 120.
6. Solow, 127–28.
7. Robert Kee, *The Green Flag* (New York: 1972), 373.
8. John Devoy, *Recollections of an Irish Rebel* (Shannon: 1969 ed.), 284.
9. R. Barry O'Brien, *The Life of Charles Stewart Parnell* (London: 1899), I, 129.
10. Ibid., I, 249.
11. Conor Cruise O'Brien, *Parnell and his Party* (Oxford: 1957), 230.
12. Ibid., 233–34.
13. Redmond to O'Brien, 22 August 1902: National Library of Ireland, MSS 15,212 (9).

14. Lyons, *John Dillon: A Biography* (London: 1968), 232.
15. Ibid.: cit *Parliamentary Debates*, HC, 4 ser., CXXI, 1300–13.
16. Dillon to Redmond, 2 October 1903; O'Brien to Redmond, 11 September, 4 November 1903: NLI MSS 15, 212 (11).

PART ONE: CHAPTER THREE (Pages 28–43)

1. Lyons, *Ireland Since the Famine*, 197.
2. Lyons, "Decline and Fall of the Nationalist Party" in Edwards & Pyle eds. *1916*, 58.
3. Nicholas Mansergh, *The Irish Question* (Toronto: 1965), 223.
4. W. B. Yeats, *Autobiography* (New York: 1938), 63.
5. Marcus Bourke, *John O'Leary* (Tralee: 1967), 181–82.
6. Yeats, *Autobiography*, 180.
7. Donald T. Torchiana, *W. B. Yeats and Georgian Ireland* (Evanston: 1966), 5.
8. Yeats, *Autobiography*, 189.
9. Parliamentary Papers, 1916, *Royal Commission on the Rebellion in Ireland*, xi Cd8311 21.
10. Lyons, *Ireland*, 223.
11. Ernest A. Boyd, *Ireland's Literary Renaissance* (New York: 1916), 73.
12. Frank O'Connor, *A Short History of Irish Literature* (New York: 1967), 189.
13. Brian Ó Cuív, "Gaelic Cultural Movements and the New Nationalism" in Kevin B. Nowlan, ed., *The Making of 1916* (Dublin: 1969), 14.
14. Lyons, *Ireland*, 80.
15. David Greene in Conor Cruise O'Brien, ed., *The Shaping of Modern Ireland* (London: 1960), 153.
16. Lyons, *Ireland*, 248.
17. Dudley Edwards, "Ireland" in Edwards, Evans, Rhys and MacDiarmid eds., *Celtic Nationalism* (London: 1968), 130.
18. Donal McCartney, "The Sinn Fein Movement" in Nowlan, ed., *Making of 1916*, 32.
19. Lyons, *Ireland*, 248.
20. McCartney, loc. cit., 35.
21. McCartney, 36.
22. McCartney, 24.
23. Brian Inglis, "Moran and Ryan" in O'Brien, ed., *Shaping of Modern Ireland*.
24. J. J. Byrne, "AE and Sir Horace Plunkett," ibid. 53.

PART TWO: CHAPTER FOUR (Pages 47–55)

1. Kenneth O. Morgan, *The Age of Lloyd George* (London: 1971), 8.
2. Peter Stansky, *Ambitions and Strategies* (Oxford: 1964), 297–98.
3. Martin Gilbert, ed., *Lloyd George* (Englewood Cliffs: 1968), 1.
4. A. J. P. Taylor, ed., *Lloyd George, A Diary by Frances Stevenson* (London: 1972), 77.
5. J. M. Keynes, *Essays in Biography* (London: 1929), 35–36.
6. A. M. Gollin, *Proconsul in Politics* (New York: 1964), 386.
7. As Lloyd George had predicted to T. P. O'Connor: T. P. O'Connor to Redmond, 4 June, 6 June 8 June, 1910: NLI MSS 15,125 (1).
8. A. M. Gollin, *The Observer and J. L. Garvin* (London: 1960), 204–32.
9. Inaugurated 12 July 1908: NLI MSS 15,212 (12).
10. Asquith to Redmond, 29 October 1909: NLI MSS 15,165 (1).
11. Devlin to Redmond, 2 January 1907; Redmond to Birrell, 25 April 1907: NLI MSS 15,181 (2) and 15,159 (1).
12. Birrell to Campbell-Bannerman, 24 March 1907: Leon Ó Broín, *The Chief Secretary* (London: 1969), 15.
13. Birrell to Redmond, 1 December 1909: NLI MSS 15,169 (2); Redmond to Morley, 6(?) December 1909: Asquith Papers, 36, fol.1.
14. Robert Kee, *The Green Flag* (New York: 1972), 472.

PART TWO: CHAPTER FIVE (Pages 56–65)

1. R. B. McDowell, *The Irish Administration, 1801–1914* (Dublin: 1964), 29–40, 54–61.
2. Leon Ó Broin, *The Chief Secretary* (London: 1969), 31.
3. Roy Jenkins, *Asquith* (London: 1964), 43.
4. Samuel Hynes, *The Edwardian Turn of Mind* (Princeton: 1968), 78–80.
5. Jenkins, *Asquith*, 277.
6. *Parliamentary Debates*, HC 5, XXXVI 1425.
7. Ibid., 1452, 2330.
8. Birrell to Redmond, n.d. NLI MSS 15,169 (3).
9. Redmond to Birrell, private, 20 November 1912. Birrell to Redmond, confidential, 21 November 1912: NLI MSS 15,169 (3).
10. F. S. L. Lyons, *John Dillon* (London: 1968), 336.
11. *Report of the Primrose Committee, Parliamentary Papers*, 1912–13, Cd. 6153 XXIV vii, p. 7.
12. Ibid., p. 16.
13. Dillon to Redmond, 14 January 1912: NLI MSS 15,182 (19).
14. Redmond, Memorandum n.d. NLI MSS 15,169 (3).
15. See David W. Miller's admirable discussion in *Church, State and Nation* (Pittsburgh: 1973), Chapter 13.

PART TWO: CHAPTER SIX (Pages 66–74)

1. R. McNeill, *Ulster's Stand for Union* (London: 1922), 53.
2. Nicholas Mansergh, *The Irish Question* (Toronto: 1965), 184.
3. E. Strauss, *Irish Nationalism and British Democracy* (London: 1957), 231–32.
4. McNeill, 49–51.
5. A. M. Gollin in Donald Southgate, ed., *The Conservative Leadership 1832–1932* (London: 1974), 170.
6. Monypenny and Buckle, *Life of Benjamin Disraeli* (6 vols. New York: 1916–1920), II, 401.
7. *Parliamentary Debates*, HC 5, XXXVI, 1425.
8. A. J. P. Taylor, *Beaverbrook* (London: 1972), 46.
9. Idem.
10. Dennis R. Gwynn, *The Life of John Redmond* (London: 1932), 206–08.

PART TWO: CHAPTER SEVEN (Pages 75–90)

1. A. T. Q. Stewart, *The Ulster Crisis* (London: 1967), 57.
2. George Dangerfield, *The Strange Death of Liberal England* (New York: 1935), 106.
3. Robert Blake, *The Unknown Prime Minister* (London: 1955), 133.
4. Bonar Law's Memorandum of "September 1912": Bonar Law Papers, 39/1/6.
5. Dicey to Strachey, 9 February 1913; Strachey to Dicey, 19 February 1913. St. Loe Strachey Papers, S/5/6/8.
6. Blake, as *supra*.
7. Jenkins, *Asquith*, 283 ff.
8. Lord Lansdowne's Memorandum of 9 September 1913. Bonar Law Papers, 39/1/7. See also Oliver Viscount Esher, ed., *Journals and Letters of Reginald Viscount Esher*, (3 vols., London: 1938), III, 130–31.
9. Jenkins, *Asquith*, 295.
10. Blake, 170.
11. Redmond's Memorandum of 2 February 1914: NLI MSS 15, 165 (1).
12. Idem.
13. Reported in Lewis Coward to Ailwyn Fellowes, 5 December 1913. Bonar Law Papers, 31/1/7.

14. Bonar Law to Lansdowne, 30 January 1914. Bonar Law Papers, 34/1/25. Lansdowne to Bonar Law, 1 February 1914; Lord Hugh Cecil to Bonar Law, 3 February 1914, Bonar Law Papers, 31/3/1,3,7.
15. Dicey to Bonar Law, 18 February 1914. Bonar Law Papers, 31/3/32.
16. Randolph Churchill, *Churchill*, I, 474.
17. Stewart, 107.
18. Jenkins, *Asquith*, 301.
19. Stewart, 141; Colvin, Carson, II, 298.
20. Public Record Office. CAB 37/115/25. Memorandum of 15 April, 1913.
21. Stewart, 102.
22. Jenkins, *Asquith*, 306.
23. Breandán Mac Giolla Choille, ed., *Intelligence Notes, 1913–16* (Dublin: 1966), 34.
24. Stewart, 126.
25. *Intelligence Notes*, 35–36.
26. Churchill, *Churchill*, I, 474.
27. Jenkins, *Asquith*, 306.
28. Sir James Fergusson, *The Curragh Incident* (London: 1964), 46–7 and Appendix A, 219–221.
29. H. A. Gwynne's (Editor, *Morning Post*) Memorandum of 22 April 1914. Bonar Law Papers, 39/2/25.
30. Fergusson, *Curragh Incident*, 67–69.
31. Ibid., 123.
32. Ibid., 67.
33. Ibid., 152. See also L. S. Amery to Bonar Law, passing on a report from General Wilson, 23 March 1919, Bonar Law Papers, 32/1/46.
34. Major General Sir C. E. Callwell, *Field Marshal Sir Henry Wilson* (2 vols., London: 1927).
35. A. M. Gollin, *Proconsul in Politics* (New York: 1964), 188.
36. Callwell, I, 144.
37. Fergusson, 126.
38. Stewart, 151 cit. *Parliamentary Debates*, HC. 5, LIX 2271 ff.
39. Walter Long's Memorandum "Very Secret" 28 March 1914. Bonar Law Papers 39/2/22. See also Long to Bonar Law, 20 March, Bonar Law Papers 32/1/6.
40. Carson to Bonar Law, 20 March 1914. Bonar Law Papers, 32/1/36.
41. Gollin, *Proconsul*, 206.
42. Blake, 162.
43. Jenkins, *Asquith*, 290–291.

PART THREE: CHAPTER EIGHT (Pages 93–109)

1. Lyons, *Ireland Since the Famine*, 316.
2. Hobson, *Ireland Yesterday and Tomorrow* (Tralee: 1968), 31–39.
3. Thomas J. Clarke, *Glimpses of an Irish Felon's Prison Life* (Dublin: 1922), 8–9.
4. Ibid., xiii.
5. R. H. West, unpublished dissertation.
6. Hobson, 43.
7. F. X. Martin, ed., *The Irish Volunteers, 1913–1915* (Dublin: 1963), 57ff.
8. Ibid., 72.
9. Ibid., 29ff.
10. Emmet Larkin, *James Larkin* (Cambridge: 1965), 11.
11. Larkin, 42. Mansergh, *Irish Question*, 236. *Parliamentary Papers* 1913 Cd. 6663 & cxviii 22 and 1914 Cd. 7273 xix 61.
12. Joseph Hone, *W. B. Yeats* (New York: 1943), 283.
13. Conor Cruise O'Brien, "Passion and Cunning, an Essay on the Politics of W. B. Yeats" in Norman Jeffares and K.G.W. Cross, eds., *In Excited Reverie*, 232–36.
14. *Parliamentary Papers*, 1914, Cd. 7421 & xliv 247.
15. Desmond Ryan, ed., *The Workers' Republic* (Dublin: 1951), 3–5.

---

16. C. D. Greaves, *The Life and Times of James Connolly* (Dublin: 1964), 133.
17. F. S. L. Lyons, *John Dillon* (Chicago: 1968), 335.
18. Conor Cruise O'Brien, *States of Ireland* (New York: 1972), 92.
19. Jacqueline Van Voris, *Constance de Markievicz* (Amherst: 1967), 121.
20. W. B. Yeats, "Anima Mundi" in *Essays* (New York: 1924), 533–34.
21. Sean O'Casey, *The Story of the Citizen Army* (Dublin: 1919), 10.
22. R. M. Henry, *The Evolution of Sinn Fein* (Dublin: 1920), 193.
23. NLI MSS 15,653 (1).

PART THREE: CHAPTER NINE *(Pages 110–123)*

1. Sir Nevil Macready, *Annals of an Active Life*, I, 182. Carson, he said, reminded him of the Dalai Lama.
2. A. T. Q. Stewart, *Ulster Crisis*, 153, 175.
3. Ibid., 139.
4. Ibid., 215.
5. *Parliamentary Debates*, H.C., 5, LXI, 1751.
6. Leon Ó Broin, *Chief Secretary*, 99–102.
7. Brian Inglis, *Roger Casement* (London: 1973), 53.
8. A. J. P. Taylor, *The Trouble Makers* (London: 1970), 108–109.
9. Casement, "Why I Came to Germany" (pencil draft), 16 December 1915: NLI MSS 13,085 (2).
10. MacNeill to Devlin, 13 May 1914: NLI MSS 15,204.
11. Redmond to MacNeill, 16 May; MacNeill to Redmond, 19 May; Redmond to MacNeill, 29 May 1914: NLI MSS 15,204.
12. MacNeill to Stephen Gwynn, 20 May 1914: NLI MSS 15,204.
13. Gwynn, *Redmond*, 335.
14. Hobson, *Ireland*, 49.
15. John Gore to Redmond, 26 June 1914: NLI MSS 15,527.
16. The list is in NLI MSS 15,527.
17. Dicey to St. Loe Strachey, 21 May 1913: Strachey Papers 5/5/6/11.
18. Gollin, *Proconsul*, 198.
19. Callwell, *Wilson*, I, 148.
20. Macready, *Annals*, I, 181, 190–192.
21. T. P. O'Connor to Redmond, 10 July 1914: NLI MSS 15,215. Bonar Law "Memorandum" 17 July 1914. Bonar Law Papers 39/4/43. These two for preliminaries to Redmond's "digging in" in Gwynn *Redmond*, 335.
22. Jenkins, *Asquith*, 322.
23. Redmond, "Private Note": NLI MSS 15,527. Bonar Law "Conference Memorandum," Bonar Law Papers 39/4/44.
24. Jenkins, *Asquith*, 322.
25. Ibid., 321.
26. NLI MSS 13,174 (3).
27. F. X. Martin, ed., *The Howth Gun-Running* (Dublin: 1964), 68–97.
28. Pearse to Joseph McGarrity (of the Clan na Gael) 12 August 1914: NLI MSS 13,162.
29. Jenkins, *Asquith*, 333.
30. Colonel Moore to Redmond, 31 July 1914: NLI MSS 15,206.
31. Margot Asquith, *Autogiography* (2 vols., London: 1922), II, 163.
32. Percy Illingworth (Liberal Chief Whip) to Redmond, 3 August 1914, in Gwynn, *Redmond*, 353.
33. *Parliamentary Debates*, HC. 5, LXV, 1824.
34. Ibid., 1829.

PART THREE: CHAPTER TEN *(Pages 124–129)*

1. Redmond to Asquith, 4 August 1914: Asquith Papers, 36, fol 62.
2. Carson to Asquith, 4 August 1914: Asquith Papers, 36, fol 64.

3. Redmond to Asquith, 5 August 1914: NLI MSS 15,520.
4. Redmond to Asquith, 6 August 1914: Asquith Papers, 36, fol 70.
5. Dicey to Strachey, October 1913: Strachey Papers, S/5/6/12.
6. Asquith to Redmond, 6 August 1914: NLI MSS 15,520.
7. Redmond to Asquith, 6 August 1914: Asquith Papers, 36, fol 71.
8. Redmond to Asquith, 8 August 1914: Asquith Papers, 36, fol 73.
9. Birrell to Redmond, 14 August 1914: NLI MSS 15,520.
10. F. X. Martin, ed., *The Irish Volunteers*, 146–148.
11. T. P. Gill to W. D'Alton, 6 September 1914: NLI MSS 13,478.
12. Birrell to Redmond, 4 September, 8 September, 13 September 1914: NLI MSS 15,520.
13. *Parliamentary Debates*, HC. 5, LXVI, 893–905.
14. Ibid., 1017–20.

PART THREE: CHAPTER ELEVEN *(Pages 130–147)*

1. A. J. P. Taylor, *English History, 1914–1915* (Oxford: 1965), 33.
2. Kee, *Green Flag*, 524.
3. Mac Giolla Choille, ed., *Intelligence Notes*, 176.
4. Redmond to Asquith, 7 June 1915: Asquith Papers, 36 fol. 89.
5. Healy to Asquith, October 1915: Asquith Papers, 36, fol. 107.
6. Redmond to Asquith, 8 September 1914: Asquith Papers, 36, fol. 77.
7. Gwynn, *Redmond*, 417–18.
8. Pearse to McGarrity, 12 August, 26 September 1914: NLI MS 13, 162.
9. C. Desmond Greaves, *Liam Mellows and the Irish Revolution* (London: 1971), 69.
10. F. X. Martin, ed., *Irish Volunteers*, 169–70.
11. Ó Broin, *Chief Secretary*, 119.
12. A. S. Green to "National Volunteer," October 1914; Redmond to A. S. Green, 23 October 1914: NLI MSS 10,561 (17).
13. Dillon to J. P. O'Donnell, 18 October 1914: NLI MSS 15,458 (5).
14. CO 904.5, 7072/S: October 1914.
15. CO 904.95, 7424/S (November), 7770/S and 7669/S (December) 1914.
16. *Intelligence Notes*, 180.
17. Ibid., 111–12.
18. Moore to Redmond: 6 July 1915: NLI MS 15,206 (7).
19. A. S. Green to Moore, 19 November 1914: NLI MSS 10,561 (17).
20. *Intelligence Notes*, 176.
21. *Intelligence Notes*, 175–76.
22. R. H. West, unpublished dissertation.
23. CO 904.95, 7669/S.
24. M. O'Dubhgaill, *Insurrection Fires At Eastertide* (Cork: 1966), 135.
25. F. X. Martin, ed., *Irish Volunteers*, 194 ff.
26. Maureen Wall, "The Background of the Rising," in Kevin B. Nowlan, ed., *The Making of 1916*, 171.
27. Wall, loc. cit., 177–78.
28. Florence O'Donoghue in F. X. Martin, ed., *Leaders and Men*, 195.
29. Pieras Beaslai, *Irish Independent*, 24 April 1961.
30. David Thornley, "Patrick Pearse" in F. X. Martin, *Leaders and Men*, 152.
31. Pearse, *Political Writings and Speeches* (Dublin: 1966 reprint), 192.
32. Lyons, *Ireland*, 80.
33. Pearse, *Pol. Writings and Speeches*, 24–28.
34. Ibid., 32–34.
35. Ibid., 38–39.
36. J. J. Horgan, *Parnell to Pearse*, 285–86.
37. Pearse, *Pol. Writings and Speeches*, 159 FF.
38. Ibid., 91.
39. Ibid., 63.

40. Martin, ed., *Leaders and Men*, 103, 158.
41. Pearse to McGarrity, 14 August 1914: NLI MSS 13,162.
42. Pearse to McGarrity, 19 October 1914: NLI MSS 13, 162. Italics inserted.
43. Edd Winfield Parks & Aileen Wells Parks, *Thomas McDonagh*, 1.
44. Donagh MacDonagh, "Plunkett and MacDonagh" in Martin, ed., *Leaders and Men*, 171–72.
45. Parks and Parks, *MacDonagh*, 104–106.
46. Padraic Colum, *Poems of the Irish Revolutionary Brotherhood*, xxiii–iv.
47. Parks and Parks, *MacDonagh*, 24.
48. Padraic Colum, xxxviii.
49. MacDonagh to Dominick Hackett, May 1915: NLI MSS 10,843.
50. Michael Hayes in F. X. Martin, ed., *The Easter Rising and U.C.D.*, 40.
51. Earl of Longford and Thomas P. O'Neill, *Eamon De Valera* (Boston: 1971), 24.
52. State Paper Office, CSO RP 1916/491: Report of Superintendent Owen Brien, 17 July 1915.
53. "Casement Vol. 2" (Second volume of Casement's German Diary) NLI MSS 1690, 42–60. The Plunkett Diary has been published in University College, Dublin *Review*, I, No. 11 (December: 1956). The original is in NLI MSS 10,999 (2) with two extra pages, the last apparently stained with blood. The original of the "Declarat" is NLI MSS 10,999 (1).
54. *Irish Independent*, I September 1914.
55. Donal MacCartney in Martin, ed., *Leaders and Men*, 51–54.
56. Lynch, *The IRB and the 1916 Rising*, 27–28.

PART THREE: CHAPTER TWELVE (Pages 148–164)

1. Gollin, *Proconsul in Politics*, 259 ff.
2. Asquith to Redmond, 18 May 1915: NLI MSS 15,165 (5).
3. Redmond to Asquith, 19 May 1915: ibid.
4. Gwynn, *Redmond*, 427.
5. Redmond to Asquith, 7 June 1915: Asquith to Redmond, 9 June 1915: Asquith Papers 36, fol. 89 and 102.
6. Gwynn, *Redmond*, 427.
7. Ó Broin, *Chief Secretary*, 146.
8. Ó Broin, *Dublin Castle*, 16.
9. *Intelligence Notes*, xvii–xxiv.
10. P. S. O'Hegarty, *Sinn Fein: An Illumination* (Dublin: 1919), 50
11. Ó Broin, *Dublin Castle*, 34.
12. Ibid., 33.
13. *Intelligence Notes*, 116, 164.
14. *Workers' Republic*, 25 May, 5 June, 19 June 1915.
15. Kevin B. Nowlan, ed., *The Making of 1916* (Dublin: 1969), 63.
16. *Labour and Easter Week*, 7.
17. Greaves, *Life and Times*, 285.
18. Fox, *Green Banners*, 71.
19. *Labour and Easter Week*, 91.
20. Ibid., 105.
21. O'Dubghaill, *Insurrection Fires*, 109–115.
22. Alan J. Ward, *Ireland and Anglo-American Relations* (London: 1969), 72.
23. Devoy, *Recollections of an Irish Rebel* (Shannon: 1969 reprint), 393.
24. Casement to Moore 30 (?) June 1914: NLI MSS 10,561 (5).
25. Devoy, *Recollections*, 410, 413. Casement "Why I Came to Germany": NLI MSS 13,085 (2), 16 December 1915.
26. Charles Tansill, *America and the Fight for Irish Freedom* (New York, 1967), 177.
27. Devoy, 404.
28. Brian Inglis, *Roger Casement*, 266 Ward, 74–76.
29. Tansill, idem.
30. Alice S. Green to Colonel Moore, 21 October 1914: NLI MSS 10,561 (17).
31. Inglis, 277–78.

32. Giovanni Costigan, "The Treason of Sir Roger Casement," *American Historical Review*, LX (January 1955), 298.
33. Devoy, *Recollections*, 434, gives all ten articles. A rough incomplete draft is Casement's "Formation of an Irish Brigade," undated: NLI MSS 13,085.
34. Devoy, 460.
35. Ibid., 458.
36. *Documents Relative to the Sinn Fein Movement*, 1921 Cmd 1108 xxix, 9–10.
37. Ibid., 11.
38. Devoy, 460.
39. Ward, 106 *n* 15.
40. *Documents*, 11.
41. Idem.
42. Ó Broin, *Dublin Castle*, 28.
43. A. J. P. Taylor, *English History, 1914–1945*, 47.
44. Gollin, *Proconsul*, 393.
45. Gwynn, *Redmond*, 464.
46. CO 904/23.3: G Division DMP for 16 March 1916.
47. *Intelligence Notes*, 207. Greaves, *Liam Mellows*, 80–81.
48. CO 904/23.3: G. Division DMP for 27 March 1916.
49. Idem.
50. CO 904/23.3: G Division DMP for 31 March 1916.

PART THREE: CHAPTER THIRTEEN (*Pages 165–183*)

1. *Documents Relative to the Sinn Fein Movement*, 11.
2. Costigan, loc. cit., 298. Also "Casement 2 vol." (Second volume of his German Diary) NLI MSS 1690, 46.
3. NLI MSS 1690, 52 and 56.
4. Plunkett's Diary had Adler Christiansen — or "Iolar Mac Giolla Chriost" in his private Irish — in Germany as late as 6 June.
5. NLI MSS 1690, p. 60.
6. Casement to Curry, Munich, 26 March 1916. NLI MSS n.d.n.
7. Ward, *Ireland and Anglo-American Relations*, 102.
8. Peter Singleton-Gates and Maurice Girodias, *The Black Diaries and Sir Roger Casement* (New York: 1959), 509.
9. Monteith did his best to dissuade Casement: Martin, ed., *Leaders and Men*, 183.
10. Costigan, loc. cit., 300.
11. *Intelligence Notes*, 228.
12. Devoy, *Recollections*, 461–63.
13. *Documents*, 12.
14. Ward, 108.
15. F. X. Martin, "Eoin MacNeill and the Easter Rising," *Irish Historical Studies*, XIII, No. 47 (March 1961), 230 ff.
16. Martin, loc. cit., 247.
17. Nowlan, ed., *Making of 1916*, 184, 195–96.
18. Hobson, *Ireland Yesterday and Tomorrow*, 74.
19. Martin, loc. cit., 248.
20. Hobson, 75.
21. Martin, 249.
22. Hobson, 76–77.
23. Martin, 249.
24. Martin, 250, 269 *n* 69.
25. Martin, 266 *n* 48, 267 *n* 51.
26. Martin, 267 *n* 69.
27. Martin, 261–63.
28. Dillon to Redmond, 23 April 1916: NLI MSS 15,182 (22).

29. Desmond Fitzgerald, *Memoirs of Desmond Fitzgerald, 1913–1916* (London: 1969), 118ff.
30. *Labour and Easter Week*, 15–16.
31. Ó Broin, *Dublin Castle*.
32. Nathan to Birrell, 20 April 1916: MS/Nathan 466. Italics added.
33. Same to Same, 22 April 1916: ibid.
34. Birrell to Nathan, 23 April 1916: MS/Nathan 449.
35. CO 904/23/3: he also thought of arresting the occupants of a repairing shop in Kimmage and a munition house in Fairview.
36. Dorothy Macardle, *Irish Republic*, 165.
37. Longford & O'Neill, *Eamon de Valera*, 24.
38. Ibid., 52.
39. Ibid., 37.
40. *Labour and Easter Week*, 21.
41. Fitzgerald, *Memoirs*, 137.
42. MS/Nathan 476.32.
43. O'Doubghaill, 221.
44. Fitzgerald, *Memoirs*, 137.
45. Max Caulfield, *The Easter Rebellion* (London: 1964), 69.
46. Pearse, *Political Writings*, 350 ff.
47. Ibid., 338 ff.
48. Greaves, *Life and Times*, 288.
49. *Labour and Easter Week*, 124.
50. Pearse, *Political Writings*, 216.
51. Fitzgerald, *Memoirs*, 142.
52. T. P. Coogan, *Ireland Since The Rising* (New York: 1966), 11.
53. *Workers' Republic*, 5 February 1916.

PART THREE: CHAPTER FOURTEEN *(Pages 186–206)*

1. CSO RP 21285.
2. MS/Nathan 476.16.
3. Ó Broin, *Dublin Castle*, 93.
4. Caulfield, 89.
5. MS/Nathan 476.30, 31, 32.
6. *Rebellion Handbook* (*Irish Times*, 1916), 161.
7. G. A. Hayes-McCoy, "A Military History of the 1916 Rising," in Nowlan, ed., *The Making of 1916*, 274.
8. MS/Nathan 476.118.
9. NLI MSS 15,672.
10. Van Voris, *Markievicz*, 204 *n* 15.
11. Hayes-McCoy, 293.
12. Ibid., 267.
13. *Royal Commission on the Rebellion in Ireland*, 1916 Cd8311 xi, p. 10.
14. Ó Broin, *Dublin Castle*, 97.
15. *Intelligence Notes*, 235–36.
16. Hayes-McCoy, 274.
17. Caulfield, 88; Hayes-McCoy, 178.
18. Longford & O'Neill, *De Valera*, 25–6.
19. Hayes-McCoy, 287.
20. Caulfield, 282.
21. Longford & O'Neill, 43.
22. Ó Broin, *Chief Secretary*, 174.
23. MS/Nathan 476.183.
24. Roger McHugh in Conor Cruise O'Brien, ed., *The Shaping of Modern Ireland*, 125.
25. Ibid., 133.

26. Owen Sheehy-Skeffington, "Francis Sheehy-Skeffington" in O. Dudley Edwards and Fergus Pyle, eds., *The Easter Rising* (London 1968), 142.
27. Idem.
28. Caulfield, 200.
29. Nathan to Birrell, 13 April 1916: MS/Nathan 466.
30. Owen Sheehy-Skeffington, 147.
31. Hayes-McCoy, 284.
32. *Intelligence Notes*, 230.
33. Caulfield, 288–9, 292.
34. *Rebellion Handbook*, 162.
35. Cyril Falls, "Maxwell," in Martin, ed., *Leaders and Men*, 204.
36. Caulfield, 315.
37. Fitzgerald, *Memoirs*, 152.
38. For example CSO RP 916/4446: Deputy Inspector-General, 21 February 1916.
39. W. B. Yeats, *Collected Poems*, 305–06.
40. Fitzgerald, 154.
41. Caulfield, 321.
42. Ibid., 326.
43. Ibid., 328.
44. *Rebellion Handbook*, 210.
45. Roger McHugh, ed., *Dublin 1916*, 207–08.
46. Van Voris, *Markievicz*, 196.
47. Longford & O'Neill, 44–46.
48. *Rebellion Handbook*, 44.
49. CAB 37/156/1: Report of 26 September 1916.
50. Maureen Wall, "The Plans and Countermand: The Country and Dublin," in Nowlan, ed., *The Making of 1916*, 215 and 242 *n* 36.
51. Greaves, *Liam Mellows*, 83.
52. F. X. Martin, *Leaders and Men*, 106.
53. Hobson, *Ireland Yesterday and Tomorrow*, 74; Wall, 210.
54. F. X. Martin, ed., "Extracts from the Papers of the late Dr. Patrick McCartan," *Clogher Record*, 1965, 210.
55. Wall, 206.
56. Wall, 207.
57. Greaves, *Mellows*, 82–83.
58. Ibid., 85–87.
59. O'Dubghaill, *Insurrection Fires*, 205–07.
60. Wall, 208–09.
61. *Rebellion Handbook*, 138.
62. Hayes-McCoy, 301.

PART THREE: CHAPTER FIFTEEN (Pages 207–220)

1. *Intelligence Notes*, 199–200.
2. *Documents Relative to the Sinn Fein Movement*, 14.
3. *S. F. Rebellion Handbook*, 45.
4. Caulfield, *Easter Rebellion*, 357.
5. Ó Broin, *Dublin Castle*, 133.
6. Asquith to George V, 6 May 1916: CAB/37/147/17.
7. Van Voris, *Markievicz*, 210.
8. Longford & O'Neill, *De Valera*, 50.
9. Hobson, *Ireland Yesterday and Tomorrow*, 77.
10. Statement of Major Price, 29 August 1916: NLI MSS 15, 204.
11. SPO CSO RP 21285.
12. Ó Broin, *Dublin Castle*, 162–63.
13. *Rebellion Handbook*, 60.

14. *Parliamentary Debates*, HC., 5 LXXXI 2512.
15. Dillon to Redmond, 30 April; Redmond to Dillon, 1 May 1916: NLI MSS 15,182 (22).
16. Dillon to Redmond, 2 May 1916: ibid.
17. Redmond to Dillon, 4 May 1916: ibid.
18. Dillon to Redmond, 4 May 1916: ibid.
19. Dillon to Redmond, 7 May 1916: ibid.
20. Dillon to Redmond, telegram via Irish Office; Redmond to Dillon, ditto, 7 May 1916: NLI MSS 15,162 (5).
21. Asquith to Redmond, 9 May 1916: NLI MSS 15,165 (2).
22. For General Maxwell's flying columns see *Intelligence Notes*, 240–41, 278 *n* 238.
23. *Parliamentary Debates*, HC. 5 ser. LXXXII, 935–51.
24. CAB 37/150/4: Memorandum of 23 June 1916.
25. CAB 37/148/13: 19 May 1916.
26. CAB 37/148/18: 21 May 1916.
27, Nathan to Asquith, 3 May 1916: Asquith Papers, 36, fol. 149.
28. Birrell to Asquith, 30 April 1916: Asquith Papers 36, fol. 141.
29. Ó Broin, *Chief Secretary*, 176.
30. Ibid., 178–79.
31. Asquith to George V, 6 May 1916: CAB 37/147/17.
32. CAB 37/148/13: 19 May 1916.
33. C. C. O'Brien, "Epilogue: The Embers of Easter, 1916–1966" in Edwards and Pyle, eds., *1916*, 231.
34. Greaves, *Life and Times*, 338 cit. *Voice of Labour*, 10 May 1919.
35. Mansergh, *Irish Question*, 242.
36. Joseph Hone, *W. B. Yeats*, 156, 318.
37. Donald Davie, "The Young Yeats" in Conor Cruise O'Brien, ed., *The Shaping of Modern Ireland*, 143.
38. Yeats, Collected Poems, 177–80.

PART FOUR: CHAPTER SIXTEEN (Pages 223–242)

1. *Intelligence Notes*, 241.
2. Major J. H. Crean to Lord Wimborne, 4 May 1916: SPO CSO RP 7472.
3. Maxwell to Redmond, 15 May, 26 May 1916: NLI MSS 15,206 (1).
4. CAB 37/147/36: Herbert Samuel's Report, 15 May 1916.
5. Macardle, *Irish Republic*, 190. Edwards & Pyle, eds., *1916*, 200.
6. Spring-Rice to Grey, 19 May 1916: CAB 37/148/14.
7. CAB 37/150/11: Lord Lansdowne's Memorandum, 21 June 1916.
8. CAB 37/151/34: "Headings of a Settlement as to the Government of Ireland," 17 July 1916.
9. Asquith to Lloyd George, 22 May; Mrs. Asquith to Lloyd George, 23 May 1916: LGP D/14/1/6 & 7.
10. Jenkins, *Asquith*, 399.
11. Long to Lloyd George, 23 May 1916: LGP D/14/1/9.
12. Midleton to Lloyd George, 26 May 1916: LGP D/14/1/26.
13. O'Brien to Lloyd George, 31 May 1916: LGP D/14/1/44.
14. Long to Lloyd George, 29 May; Stewart to Long (a copy) 31 May 1916: LGP D/14/1/37 & 45.
15. CAB 37/150/11: Lansdowne, "The Proposed Irish Settlement," 21 June 1916.
16. Idem.
17. CAB 37/150/15: Walter Long, "The Irish Difficulty," 23 June 1916.
18. Colvin, *Carson*, III, 166.
19. Ibid., 168–70.
20. Owen to Lloyd George, 14 June 1916: LGP D/14/2/20.
21. Gwynn, *Redmond*, 506.
22. Dillon to Redmond, 5 June 1916: NLI MSS 15,182 (23).

23. T. P. O'Connor to Lloyd George, 9 June encl. Asquith to Lloyd George, 10 June; Lloyd George to Dillon, 9 June 1916: LGP D/14/2/20 & 23.
24. Dillon to Lloyd George, 11 June 1916: LGP D/14/2/25.
25. Lloyd George to Murphy, 8 June 1916: LGP D/14/2/28.
26. Murphy to Lloyd George, 14 June 1916: LGP D/14/2/38.
27. Owen to Lloyd George, 15 June 1916: LGP D/14/2/41.
28. Owen to Lloyd George, 18 June 1916: LGP D/14/3/14.
29. Devlin to O'Connor, 19 June 1916 encl. O'Connor to Lloyd George, 21 June 1916: LGP D/14/3/26.
30. R. Montague Smith of the *Daily Mail* to Lloyd George (a copy), 20 June 1916: Asquith Papers 37, fol., 64.
31. Owen to Lloyd George, 20 June 1916: LGP D/14/3/21.
32. Dillon to Lloyd George, 16 June 1916: LGP D/14/3/2.
33. Owen to Lloyd George, 24 June 1916: LGP D/14/2/38.
34. CAB 37/150/4: 23 June 1916.
35. Lyons, *Dillon*, 388 n1.
36. CAB 37/150/17: "Ulster and the Irish Crisis," 24 June 1916.
37. A. J. P. Taylor, *English History, 1914–1946*, 72.
38. Memorandum n.d.: LGP D/14/2/19. Stewart to Lloyd George, 16 June, 19 June 1916: LGP D/14/3/6 & 16.
39. Memorandum, 31 May 1916: LGP D/14/1/45.
40. Lloyd George to Dillon, 10 June 1916: LGP D/14/2/25.
41. Long to Lloyd George, 11 June 1916: LGP D/14/2/29.
42. Lloyd George to Asquith, 12 June 1916 (a copy): LGP D/14/2/30.
43. Lloyd George to Long, 12 June 1916: LGP D/14/2/31.
44. Long to Lloyd George, 12 June 1916: LGP D/14/2/32.
45. Lloyd George to Asquith, 12 June 1916: LGP D/14/2/33.
46. Lloyd George to Dillon, 12 June 1916: LGP D/14/2/34.
47. Lloyd George to Dillon, 17 June 1916: LGP D/14/3/11.
48. Selborne to Asquith, 16 June 1916, encl. in Asquith to Lloyd George, 17 June 1916: LGP D/14/3/9.
49. Lloyd George to Dillon, 20 June 1916: LGP D/14/3/26.
50. CAB 37/150/11: 21 June 1916.
51. Devlin to Lloyd George, Redmond to Lloyd George, 26 June 1916: LGP D/14/3/39 & 40.
52. Chamberlain to Asquith, Cecil to Asquith, 22 June 1916: Asquith Papers, 36 fol. 58 & 60.
53. CAB 37/150/21: 26 June 1916.
54. Asquith to George V, 27 June 1916: CAB 37/150/23. Italics inserted.
55. T. P. O'Connor to Redmond, 28 June 1916: LGP D/14/3/44.
56. Dillon to Redmond, 29 June, 30 June 1916: NLI MSS 15,182 (3).
57. Lyons, *Dillon*, 400.
58. Blake, *The Unknown Prime Minister*, 287.
59. *Parliamentary Debates*, HL 5 ser. LII, 646.
60. CAB 37/151/38: 18 July 1916. Italics added.
61. Redmond to Asquith and Lloyd George, 18 July 1916: NLI MSS 15,189.
62. Redmond to Asquith, 23 July 1916: Asquith Papers, 37 fol., 107.
63. *Parliamentary Debates*, HC. 5 ser. LXXXIV 1426–34.
64. Asquith to Redmond, 28 July 1916: NLI MSS 15,165 (5).
65. Lloyd George to Lynn, 5 June 1916: LGP D/14/2/13.
66. Blake, *Unknown Prime Minister*, 289. Lord Beaverbrook, *Politicians and the War* (2 vols., London: 1928 and 1932) II, 313.

PART FOUR: CHAPTER SEVENTEEN (Pages 243–263)

1. Brian Inglis, *Roger Casement*, 342.
2. CAB 37/151/35: Memoranda of 15 July (Blackwell) and 17 July (Troup), circulated to Cabinet by the Home Secretary, 18 July 1916.

3. CAB 37/152/8: "American Press Résumé," pp. 3 & 5, 19 July 1916.
4. Tansill, *America and the Fight for Irish Freedom*, 210.
5. CAB 37/153/18: Memorandum of 5 August 1916.
6. A. J. P. Taylor, *English History*, 63.
7. Inglis, 363.
8. Ibid., 366.
9. Eva Gore-Booth to Grey, 17 July 1916: CAB 37/152/4.
10. Rene McColl, *Casement*, 296.
11. Inglis, 370.
12. CAB 37/153/14: 2 August 1916.
13. CAB 37/150/18: Maxwell's report of 24 June 1916.
14. CAB 37/157/15: Maxwell's report of 26 September 1916.
15. Asquith to George V, 19 October 1916: CAB 37/157/38.
16. *Royal Commission on the Rebellion in Ireland*, 1916, Cd. 8311, 26.
17. Robert Kee, *The Green Flag*, 591.
18. Gollin, *Proconsul in Politics*, 380.
19. Cruttwell, *Great War*, 354.
20. Taylor, 75–76.
21. Idem.
22. Idem.
23. Lloyd George, *War Memoirs*, II, 596.
24. Redmond's Memorandum of an interview, 9 December 1916: NLI MSS 15,189.
25. Idem.
26. Cruttwell, *Great War*, 384.
27. CAB 37/157/16 & 33: Memoranda of 9 October and 16 October 1916.
28. CAB 37/159/13: Memorandum of 6 November 1916.
29. Gwynn, *Redmond*, 534.
30. O'Connor to Redmond, "Confidential Memorandum," 22 January 1917: NLI MSS 15,189.
31. CO 904/23/3: 2d part, 1917.
32. *Intelligence Notes*
33. Macardle, *Irish Republic*, 213–14.
34. Kee, *Green Flag*, 599.
35. Lyons, *Dillon*, 599.
36. CO 904/23/3: 2d. part, 1917.
37. CAB 23/2/120: 16 April, 1917.
38. Idem.
39. Gollin, *Proconsul*, Chapter XVI.
40. Cruttwell, *Great War*, 384.
41. Gollin, 422.
42. Crewe to Asquith, 16 May 1917: Asquith Papers, 37, fol. 140.
43. Lloyd George to Redmond, 16 May 1917: CAB 23/2/140, Appendix, G.T.–737.
44. R. B. McDowell, *The Irish Convention, 1917–1918* (London: 1970), 114, 127–28.
45. Redmond to Lloyd George, 13 November; Lloyd George to Redmond, 1917: NLI MSS 15,189.
46. Carson to Lloyd George, 22 January 1918: LGP F/6/3/3.
47. Ian Colvin, *Life of Lord Carson*, III, 327.
48. CAB 23/2/143, 145, 153. G.T.–1027.
49. CAB 23/3/163: 14 June 1917.
50. Macardle, 221.
51. CO 904/23/3, 2d part, East Clare election.
52. Macardle, 229.
53. CAB 23/3/175: 4 July 1917.
54. Roskill, *Hankey*, I, 406–07.
55. CAB 23/2/186: 14 July 1917.
56. Idem.
57. Longford & O'Neill, *De Valera*, 65.

58. CO 904/23/3: Kilkenny election.
59. Macardle, 232.
60. CO 904/23/5: Report of Superintendent Brien, DMP, 14 November 1917.
61. Idem.
62. Idem.
63. Idem.
64. Macardle, 233.
65. Lyons, *Ireland*, 389.
66. *Documents Relative to the Sinn Fein Movement*, 37.

PART FOUR: CHAPTER EIGHTEEN (*Pages 264–304*)

1. John P. Mackintosh, *The British Cabinet*, 372.
2. Cruttwell, *History of the Great War*, 442.
3. CO 904.105: 18085 Secret, 12 February 1918.
4. Idem.
5. Idem.
6. CAB 23/5/345: 13 February 1918.
7. Redmond to Lloyd George, 17 January, 18 January 1918: NLI MSS 15,189.
8. Lloyd George to Plunkett, 21 January 1918: ibid.
9. Carson to Lloyd George, 21 January 1918; Lloyd George to Carson, 21 January 1918: LGP F/6/3/3 & 4. Roskill, *Hankey*, 484.
10. Redmond to Lloyd George, 21 January; Lloyd George to Redmond, 23 January; Redmond to Plunkett, 23 January 1918: NLI MSS 15,189.
11. CAB 24/47/G.T.–4139: 25 February 1918.
12. Idem.
13. CO 904.105: 19001/Secret, 13 April 1918. See also Chief Secretary's Report "Conditions of Ireland," 22 March 1918: CAB 24/46/G.T.–4004.
14. Cruttwell, *Great War*, 501.
15. Roskill, *Hankey*, I, 541.
16. Cruttwell, 506–7.
17. Ibid., 510, *n* 2 & 3.
18. Roskill, *Hankey*, I, 511–12.
19. French to Lloyd George, 5 March 1918: LGP F/48/6/5.
20. NLI MSS 15,190 (3), John Hooper to John Redmond, 17 October 1915. Also H. E. Duke, a year later, in CAB 37/157/33, 16 October 1916.
21. CAB 23/5/372: 25 March 1918.
22. CAB 23/5/373: 26 March 1918.
23. CAB 24/46/G.T.–4049: 27 March 1918.
24. CAB 23/5/374: 27 March 1918. CAB 24/46/G.T.–4052 & 4052 Appendix: Reports of Duke and Byrne.
25. CAB 23/5/376: 28 March 1918.
26. Taylor, *English History, 1914–1946*, 101.
27. CAB 23/5/377: 29 March 1918.
28. Roskill, *Hankey*, 515.
29. CAB 24/46/G.T.–4098: Telegram, Secret, Urgent, Prime Minister to the Dominions, 30 March 1918.
30. Roskill, *Hankey*, I, 521.
31. Lloyd George to Sir Horace Plunkett, 25 February 1918: CAB 24/47/G.T.–4139.
32. CAB 23/6/385: 6 April 1918.
33. Smuts to Lloyd George, 9 May 1918: LGP F/45/9/16.
34. Roskill, *Hankey*, I, 517.
35. *Parliamentary Debates*, HC, 5 ser., CIV, 1337–65.
36. Ibid., CV, 292–305.
37. Cruttwell, *Great War*, 518.
38. Roskill, *Hankey*, I, 521, 538.

39. Longford & O'Neill, *De Valera*, 72; Lyons, *Dillon*, 434.
40. Longford & O'Neill, 73.
41. CAB 24/49/G.T.–4302: Duke's Memorandum of 21 April 1918.
42. CAB 23/6/397: 23 April 1918.
43. Lyons, *Dillon*, 438.
44. CAB 23/6/392: 16 April 1918. Italics inserted.
45. CAB 23/14/381A: 3 April 1918. Italics inserted.
46. CAB 23/6/392: 16 April 1918.
47. Long to Lloyd George, 18 April: LGP F/32/5/34.
48. This was on 3 April — CAB 23/14/481A.
49. CAB 24/49/G.T.–4364: 27 April 1918.
50. CAB 23/14/255A: 23 October 1917.
51. CAB 23/14/379A: 1 April 1918.
52. Ward, *Anglo-American Relations*, 159.
53. W. B. Fowler, *British-American Relations*, 162.
54. Ward, 162.
55. CAB 24/48/G.T.–4128: 13 April 1918.
56. "Secret, Urgent," Memo to War Cabinet, 16 April 1918: LGP F/37/4/51.
57. Wimborne to Lloyd George, 29 March 1918: LGP F/48/1/7.
58. Wimborne to Lloyd George, 28 April; Lloyd George to Wimborne, 6 May; Wimborne to Lloyd George, 9 May 1918: LGP F/48/1/8, 9, 10.
59. French to Lloyd George, 5 May 1918: LGP F/48/6/10.
60. Frederick Guest to Lloyd George, 3 May 1918: LGP F/48/6/10.
61. French to Lloyd George, 18, 19 April: LGP F/48/6/7 & 8.
62. CAB 23/6/391: Report of Sir Eric Geddes, First Lord of the Admiralty, 16 April 1918.
63. Samuels to Lloyd George, 2 May 1918, encl. Major I. H. Price "Short Precis re German help to S.F. rebels. Secret, 2 May 1918": LGP F/42/9/2.
64. CAB 24/51/G.T.–4541: 10 May 1918.
65. CAB 23/14/408A: 10 May 1918.
66. CAB 23/17/X–5: Conversation with Lord Milner and Sir Henry Wilson, 3 May 1918.
67. CAB 23/6/412: 15 May 1918.
68. CAB 23/17/X–2: 16 May 1918.
69. C. C. O'Brien, "The Embers of Easter," in Edwards and Pyle, eds., *1916*, 226–27.
70. Macardle, *Irish Republic*, 254.
71. CAB 23/6/416: 23 May 1918.
72. Ibid., Appendix, G.T.–4621 (revised)
73. Cruttwell, *Great War*, 526.
74. Callwell, *Wilson*, II, 103.
75. CAB 23/6/421: 30 May 1918.
76. CAB 23/6/433, G.T.–4839: 19 June 1918.
77. Jones, *Whitehall Diary*, III, 65.
78. CAB 23/6/392: 16 April 1918.
79. Callwell, *Wilson*, II, 125–26, 130.
80. Ibid., II, 141.
81. CAB 23/13/225A: 23 October 1917, for example, where it was still being said that the Irish problem was "a very small matter."
82. Greaves, *Mellows*, 145.
83. CO 904/106, 21130/Secret: IG for August 1918.
84. CO 904/106, 1997/Secret and 20433/Secret: IG for June and July 1918.
85. CO 904/106: IG for July, Part II, Political.
86. French to Lloyd George, 12 October 1918: LGP F/48/6/20.
87. French to George V, 13 July 1918: LGP F/48/6/17.
88. French to Lloyd George, 7 September 1918: LGP F/48/6/19.
89. Idem.
90. French to Lloyd George, 12 October 1918: LGP F/48/6/20. Also CAB 24/66/G.T.–5919: 8 October 1918.

91. Dillon to T. P. O'Connor, 22 June 1919: Lyons, *Dillon*, 440–41.
92. Dillon to Shane Leslie, 14 June 1918: idem.
93. Hathaway Papers: Report #110, 12 September 1918.
94. Callwell, *Wilson*, II, 137. Wilson put the figures as 9000 "useless men."
95. *Irish Times*, 22 August 1918.
96. CAB 23/17/X–8: 5 June 1918.
97. Ward, *Anglo-American Relations*, 165.
98. Esher to Hankey, 21 August 1918: Roskill, *Hankey*, I 593.
99. CO 904/106: 21130/Secret, Part II, Political, 11 September 1918. Also Hathaway Papers: Report #117, 17 October 1918.
100. Cork *Examiner*, 14 October 1918.
101. The *Times*, 22 November 1918.
102. Macardle, *Irish Republic*, 394.
103. Lyons, *Ireland*, 396.
104. Kee, *Green Flag*, 627.
105. Lyons, *Ireland*, 398.
106. Ibid., 399.
107. Macardle, *Irish Republic*, 926.
108. Ibid., 275–76.

PART FIVE (*Pages 305–350*)

1. Robert Kee, *Green Flag*, 630.
2. CAB 23/9/527: 5 February 1919.
3. CAB 23/9/541: 4 March 1919.
4. Lyons, *Ireland*, 406.
5. CO 904/111: IG for January 1920.
6. Kee, *Green Flag*, 666.
7. CO 904/110: 21796 Secret.
8. Lyons, *Ireland*, cit. *An t-Oglach*, 31 January 1919.
9. CO/904/111. *An t-Oglach*, II, 19 (15 September 1920) 4.
10. CAB 23/18/8 (19): Appendix IV, 1 December 1919.
11. CO 904/23/7: 55/6094.
12. CAB 23/12/628: 7 October 1919.
13. CAB 27/69/C.I. 1: 4 October 1919.
14. CAB 27/69/C.I., 2: 13 October 1919.
15. CAB 23/18/10 (19): 10 December 1919.
16. CO 904/111: IG for July 1920.
17. CAB 23/22/Conclusions of a Conference, 20 September 1920.
18. Thomas Jones, *Whitehall Diary*, III (Ireland, 1918–1925), Keith Middlemas, ed., 14–15.
19. CAB 23/21/23 (20): 30 April 1920.
20. CAB 23/21/29 (20), Appendix II: 19 May 1920.
21. CO 904/111: IG for January 1920.
22. CO 904/112: IG for August 1920.
23. *Whitehall Diary*, III, 28.
24. CAB 23/23/59A: 10 November 1920 — W. O. Memorandum, 3 November 1920.
25. Roskill, *Hankey*, II, 197.
26. CAB 23/23/79A: 29 December 1920.
27. CAB 23/24/7 & 7A: 14 & 15 February 1921.
28. Macready to Under-Secretary Sir John Anderson: CO/904/188/(2).
29. *Whitehall Diary*, III, 39.
30. Marcardle, *Irish Republic*, 380–81.
31. CAB 23/23/53A: 13 October 1920.
32. Roskill, *Hankey*, II, 153, 198.
33. *Whitehall Diary*, III, 31.
34. CAB 23/22/48: 13 August 1920.

35. CO 904/188/1: Anderson to Greenwood, 15 July 1820.
36. *Whitehall Diary*, III, 35.
37. Cabinet Paper 1703, 29 July 1920.
38. Macardle, *Irish Republic*, 412.
39. Cockerill, Memorandum of 29 October 1920: CO 904/188/(1).
40. Kee, *Green Flag*, 693.
41. Anderson to Bonar Law, 2 November & 5 November; Bonar Law to Anderson, 9 November 1920: CO 904/188/(1).
42. CAB 23/23/68: 9 December 1920.
43. Ibid., Appendix III.
44. Healy to Beaverbrook, 23 December 1920: Beaverbrook Papers, Healy Folder 4–8, 4.
45. CAB 23/23/77 and 79A: both 29 December 1920.
46. CO 904/14: IG for January 1921.
47. Lyons, *Ireland*, 415.
48. CAB 23/27/90: 15 December 1921.
49. Macready to Secretary, Army Council, 28 March 1921; CO 904/188/(2).
50. CO 904/110 27196 S: IG for November 1919.
51. Lyons, *Ireland*, 415.
52. *Whitehall Diary*, III, 83: Smuts to Lloyd George, 6 July 1921.
53. CAB 23/24/2: 14 January 1921.
54. Longford & O'Neill, *De Valera*, 116.
55. CO 904/115; IG for May.
56. Macready to Anderson, 25 July 1920: CO 904/188/(1). CO 904/115: IG for April 1921.
57. CO 904/116: IG for June 1921.
58. CO 904/116: IG for May 1921.
59. This correspondence is in CO 904/181/(2), "Miscellaneous."
60. CAB 23/24/12: 8 March 1921. *Whitehall Diary*, III, 54.
61. Longford & O'Neill, *De Valera*, 122.
62. *Whitehall Diary*, III, 76.
63. Ibid., 70.
64. Macardle, *Irish Republic*, 452.
65. E. Clarke, Under-Secretary in Belfast, made this arrangement on 16 April: CO 904/181/(2).
66. R. J. Lawrence, *The Government of Northern Ireland;* (Oxford, 1965) 16.
67. CAB 23/26/47, Cabinet Paper 2925: 2 June 1921.
68. Healy to Lord Beaverbrook, 15 June 1921: Beaverbrook Papers, Healy Folder 4–8, 4.
69. Sir Edward Grigg to Lloyd George, 14 June 1921: E. W. M. Grigg Papers.
70. Greenwood to Lloyd George, 15 June; Grigg to Lloyd George, 16 June 1921: E. W. M. Grigg Papers.
71. A synopsis of these papers, by no means revealing, will be found in CO 904/23/5: 53/6094.
72. Macardle, *Irish Republic*, 471.
73. Maurice Cowling, *The Impact of Labour* (Cambridge: 1971), 120–121. A. J. P. Taylor, *Beaverbrook*, 188–189. Stevenson, *Lloyd George*, 223.
74. Greenwood to Grigg, 29 June 1921: E. W. M. Grigg Papers.
75. Harold Nicolson, *George V*, 356.
76. Macardle, 444.
77. *Whitehall Diary*, III, 89.
78. Longford & O'Neill, *De Valera*, 135.
79. Midleton's Memorandum of 4 July 1921: E. W. M. Grigg Papers.
80. Note dictated 14 July 1921: E. W. M. Grigg Papers.
81. Frank Pakenham (Lord Longford), *Peace by Ordeal* (London: 1935), 84.
82. CAB 23/26/60, C.P. 3149: 20 July 1921.
83. Longford and O'Neill, 137.
84. CAB 23/26/66, C.P. 3214 — De Valera's proposals, 13 August 1921.
85. A. Cope to A. E. Hemming, 7 August 1921: E. W. M. Grigg papers.

86. Lloyd George to Austen Chamberlain, 7 August; Macready to Greenwood, 7 August 1921, E. W. M. Grigg papers.
87. Harold Spender's Memorandum from Dublin, 19 September 1921: E. W. M. Grigg papers.
88. Lloyd George to George V, 18 September 1921: E. W. M. Grigg papers.
89. *Whitehall Diary*, III, 152. John D. Fair, "The Anglo-Irish Treaty of 1921: Unionist Aspects of the Peace," *Journal of British Studies*, XII, (November 1972) 141.
90. *Whitehall Diary*, II, 153–54.
91. Stevenson, *Lloyd George: A Diary*, 234. *Whitehall Diary* III, 160. CAB 23/27/80, 10 November 1921.
92. *Whitehall Diary* III, 160. Stevenson, 236.
93. Blake, *Unknown Prime Minister*, 431, 433.
94. *Whitehall Diary*, III 163.
95. Ibid., 156.
96. Stevenson, 237.
97. CAB 43/4/: 22/N/143, Record of Negotiations, 124–125.
98. Pakenham, *Peace by Ordeal*, 98.
99. CAB 43/4: 22/N/143, S.F.C. 32, 380–81.
100. CAB 43/4: 22/N/143, 115–116. Italics inserted.
101. *Whitehall Diary*, III, 155–56.
102. P. S. O'Hegarty, *History of Ireland Under the Union* (London: 1952), 753.
103. CAB 23/27/89: 5 December 1921.
104. CAB 43/4: 22/N/143, 124–5.
105. CAB 43/4: 22/N/143, 128–29.
106. CAB 43/4: 22/N/143, "Treaty Between Great Britain and Ireland, Articles of Agreement," 402–408.
107. CAB 43/4: 22/N/143, S.F.C. 13, 301–310.
108. CAB 23/27/90: 6 December 1921.
109. Macardle, 596.
110. CAB 43/4: 22/N/143, 7 (1) and (2), 381.
111. Iris Dhail Eireann, *Official Record of the Debate on the Treaty Between Great Britain and Ireland*, especially Collins 30–34, De Valera 24–27, Childers 36–39, Stack 27–28.
112. CAB 23/27/89, Conclusion 1, 5 December 1921.
113. *Whitehall Diary*, III, 83.
114. Macardle, 959.
115. Longford & O'Neill, 180.
116. Macardle, 639n.
117. Riddell, *Intimate Diary of the Peace Conference and After, 1918–1923* (London: 1933), 303; Jones, *Whitehall Diary*, 152, 156; C. P. Scott, *The Political Diaries of C. P. Scott*, Trevor Wilson, ed. (London: 1970), 402–403. Also Stevenson, 234.
118. C. Desmond Greaves, *Liam Mellows*, chapter ten.
119. Pakenham, 270.
120. Coogan, *Ireland Since the Rising*, 256, lists the chief names.
121. *Whitehall Diary*, III, 195.
122. Cowling, *Impact of Labour*, 127.

Bibliography

OFFICIAL DOCUMENTS

A. Public Record Office, London
    1. Cabinet Papers
        (i) CAB 23. This class contains the Cabinet Minutes — the records of the first modern Cabinet (that is to say, a Cabinet equipped with office, secretariat, agenda, files and minutes)

which came into being with David Lloyd George's War Cabinet in December 1916. When the small War Cabinet vanished late in 1919, to be replaced by a regular Cabinet, the Minutes became Conclusions, essentially a verbal change.

(ii) CAB 23/13–17. These volumes within the class 23 contain the secret minutes, running concurrently with the others and distinguished by the letter A. (Thus CAB 23/5/376 refers to a War Cabinet held on 28 March 1918, and CAB 23/14/376A refers to a conference held on the same day but of a more secret nature.) CAB 23/17, however, is designated "CAB 23/17/X-1 Secret" and so on.

(iii) CAB 24. This class contains the G.T. series — the papers and memoranda upon which the Cabinet's discussions were based.

(iv) CAB 27. This class includes the records of the Cabinet's Committees on Ireland.

(v) CAB 37. This class contains some of the memoranda circulated to the Cabinet before the War Cabinet came into being.

(vi) CAB 43/2 contains the documents and CAB 43/4 the record of negotiations leading to the Articles of Agreement of 6 December 1921.

2. Colonial Office Papers

CO 904, or the Dublin Castle Papers: that is to say the documents removed from the Castle archives in 1922. This very important class — necessarily incomplete, since many of the pre-1922 documents and even parts of documents (such as the Connolly 1915–1916 dock strike file) are still with the State Paper Office in Dublin — includes the monthly reports of the Royal Irish Constabulary's County Inspectors and the monthly summaries of the Inspector General or Deputy Inspector General. It also includes many miscellaneous items of great interest.

B. *State Paper Office, Dublin Castle*

Here the researcher is deeply indebted to the Keeper of State Papers, Mr. Breandán Mac Giolle Choilla, M.A., for his "Calendar of Papers Relating to the 1916 Rising," with supporting Documents from the Registered Papers in the Records of the Chief Secretary's Office.

C. *Parliamentary Papers of Special Interest*

Report of the Primrose Committee, 1912–1913 Cd 6153 xxiv 5.

Report of the Departmental Committee on the Housing Conditions of the Working Classes in the City of Dublin, 1914 Cd 7273 xix 61.

Report of the Dublin Disturbances Commission, 1914 Cd 7269 xviii 513.

Royal Commission on the Rebellion in Ireland, 1916 (1) Report: Cd 8279 xi 171 (2) Evidence and Appendix: Cd 8311 xi 137.

Documents Relative to the Sinn Fein Movement, 1921 Cmd 1108 xxix 429.

D. *Dail Eireann*

Official Report: Debate on the Treaty Between Great Britain and Signed in London on 6 December 1921. Dublin, 1922

MANUSCRIPT SOURCES

National Library of Ireland, Dublin
  Redmond Papers
  Maurice Moore Papers
  William O'Brien (Labour) Papers
  Bulmer Hobson Papers
  Alice Stopford Green Papers
  The Joseph Plunkett Diary
  The Roger Casement German Diary, Vol. 2

Beaverbrook Library, London
  Lloyd George Papers
  Bonar Law Papers
  St. Loe Strachey Papers
Bodleian Library, Oxford
  Asquith Papers
  Nathan Papers
With the kind permission of Mr. John Grigg
  Papers of Edward William Macleay Grigg, First Lord Altrincham
University of California, Santa Barbara
  Charles M. Hathaway Papers (American Consul in Cork — Reports to American Ambassador in London.)

BIBLIOGRAPHY

F. X. Martin. "1916: Myth, Fact and Mystery," *Studia Hibernica*, No. 7, 1967 — A fine bibliographical essay on the literature of the Rising.

BOOKS AND PERIODICALS

(A select list, confined to Anglo-Irish problems and their background from 1906 to 1922)

Addison, Christopher *Politics from Within*. 2 vols. London: 1924.

Amery, L. S. *My Political Life*. Vols. 1 & 2, London: 1953.

Asquith, Margot *Autobiography*. 2 vols. London: 1924.

Barry, Tom *Guerilla Days in Ireland*. Cork: 1955.

Beaslai, Pieras *Michael Collins and the Making of a New Ireland*. 2 vols. London: 1926.

Beaverbrook, Lord *The Decline and Fall of Lloyd George*. London: 1963.

Beaverbrook, Lord *Politicians and the War*, 2 vols. London: 1928 and 1932.

Beckett, J. C. *The Making of Modern Ireland*. New York: 1966.

Birrell, Augustine *Things Past Redress*. London: 1937.

Blake, Robert *The Unknown Prime Minister: The Life and Times of Andrew Bonar Law, 1858–1923*. London: 1955.

Bourke, Marcus *John O'Leary: A Study in Irish Separatism*. Tralee: 1967.

Breen, Daniel *My Fight for Irish Freedom*. Dublin: 1926.

Brennan, Robert *Allegiance*. Dublin: 1950.

Byrne, J. J. "AE and Sir Horace Plunkett" in Conor Cruise O'Brien, ed., *The Shaping of Modern Ireland*. London: 1960.

Callwell, Major General Sir C. E. *Field Marshal Sir Henry Wilson, His Life and Diaries*. 2 vols. London: 1927.

Caulfield, Max *The Easter Rebellion*. London: 1964.

Churchill, Randolph *Winston S. Churchill, 1901–1914*. Boston: 1967.

Churchill, Winston S. *The World Crisis, 1911–1918*. 2 vol. ed. London: 1938.

Clarke, Thomas J. *Glimpses of an Irish Felon's Life*, with an Introduction by P. S. O'Hegarty. Dublin: 1922.

Colum, Padraic *Arthur Griffith*. Dublin: 1959.

Colum, Padraic, *Arthur Griffith*. Dublin: 1959.

Colvin, Ian *The Life of Lord Carson*. vols. 2 & 3. London: 1934–36.

Connolly, James *Labour and Easter Week*, Desmond Ryan, ed. With an Introduction by William O'Brien. Dublin: 1949.

Connolly, James *Labour in Ireland: I. Labour in Irish History: II. The Reconquest of Ireland.* Dublin: 1910.

Connolly, James *The Workers' Republic,* Desmond Ryan, ed., with an Introduction by W. McMullen. Dublin: 1951.

Coogan, T. P. *Ireland Since The Rising.* New York: 1966.

Costigan, Giovanni "The Treason of Sir Roger Casement." *American Historical Review,* LX, No. 1. January: 1955.

Cowling, Maurice *The Impact of Labour.* Cambridge: 1971.

Cronin, Sean *Our Own Red Blood.* Dublin: 1966.

Cross, Colin *The Liberals in Power.* London: 1963.

Crozier, Brigadier F. P. *Impressions and Recollections.* London: 1930.

Crozier, Brigadier F. P. *Ireland For Ever.* London: 1932.

Cruttwell, C. R. F. M. *A History of the Great War.* Oxford, 2d ed.: 1936.

Dalton, Charles *With the Dublin Brigade, 1917–1921.* London: 1929.

Daly, Martin (Stephen McKenna) *Memories of the Dead.* Dublin: 1917.

Dangerfield, George *The Strange Death of Liberal England.* New York: 1935.

Devoy, John *Recollections of an Irish Rebel.* Shannon: 1969 reprint.

Dillon, Myles "Douglas Hyde" in O'Brien, ed., *The Shaping of Modern Ireland.* London: 1960.

Douglas, Roy *The History of the Liberal Party, 1895–1970.* London: 1970.

Edwards, Owen Dudley, *Celtic Nationalism.* London: 1968.

Edwards, Owen Dudley, and Pyle, Fergus eds. *1916: The Easter Rising.* London: 1968.

Ensor, R. C. J. *England, 1870–1914.* Oxford: 1936.

Esher, Viscount *Journals and Letters of Reginald Viscount Esher,* Oliver Viscount Esher, ed. 3 vols. London: 1938.

Fair, John D. "The Anglo-Irish Treaty of 1921: Unionist Aspects of the Peace," *Journal of British Studies,* XII (November 1972) 132ff.

Falls, Cyril "Maxwell" in F. X. Martin, ed., *Leaders and Men of the Easter Rising.* Cornell: 1967.

Fergusson, Sir James *The Curragh Incident.* London: 1964.

Fitzgerald, Desmond *Memoirs of Desmond Fitzgerald.* London: 1969.

Forester, Margery *Michael Collins: The Lost Leader.* London: 1971.

Fowler, W. B. *British American Relations: The Role of Sir William Wiseman.* Princeton: 1969.

Fox, R. M. *Green Banners.* London: 1938.

Gilbert, Martin *Winston S. Churchill.* Vol. 3, 1914–1916. London: 1971.

Gollin, A. M. *The Observer and J. L. Garvin: A Study in a Great Editorship.* London: 1960.

Gollin, A. M. *Proconsul in Politics: A Study of Lord Milner in Opposition and in Power.* New York: 1964.

Greaves, C. Desmond *The Life and Times of James Connolly.* London: 1961.

Greaves, C. Desmond *Liam Mellows and the Irish Revolution.* London: 1971.

Greene, David "Michael Cusack and the Rise of the G.A.A." in O'Brien, ed., *The Shaping of Modern Ireland.*

Gregory, Augusta Lady *Lady Gregory's Journals,* Lennox Robinson, ed. New York: 1947.

Grigg, John *The Young Lloyd George.* London: 1973.

Griffith, Arthur *The Resurrection of Hungary,* 3rd edition. Dublin: 1918.

Gwynn, Dennis R. *The Life of John Redmond.* London: 1932.

Gwynn, Stephen *John Redmond's Last Years.* London: 1919.

Hayes, Michael "Thomas MacDonagh and the Rising" in F. X. Martin, ed., *The Easter Rising and University College, Dublin.* Dublin: 1966.

Hayes-McCoy, G. A. "A Military History of the 1916 Rising" in Kevin B. Nowlan, ed., *The Making of 1916: Studies in the History of the Rising.* Dublin: 1969.

Hazelhurst, Cameron *Politicians at War.* London: 1971.

Healy, T. M. *Letters and Leaders of My Day.* 2 vols. London: 1928.

Henry, R. M. *The Evolution of Sinn Fein.* Dublin: 1920.

Heuston, R. F. V. *Lives of the Lord Chancellors, 1885–1940.* London: 1964.

Hobson, Bulmer *Ireland Yesterday and Tomorrow.* Tralee: 1968.

Holt, Edgar *Protest in Arms, 1916–1923* London: 1960.

Hone, Joseph M. *W. B. Yeats.* New York: 1943.

Horgan, J. J. *Parnell to Pearse.* Dublin: 1948.

Hyde, Montgomery *Carson.* London: 1953.

Inglis, Bryan *Roger Casement.* London: 1973.

Irish Times Sinn Fein Handbook, Easter 1916. Dublin: 1917.

Jeffares, Norman and Cross, K. G. W. eds. *In Excited Reverie.* New York: 1965.

Jenkins, Roy *Asquith: Portrait of a Man and an Era.* London: 1964.

Jenkins, Roy *Mr. Balfour's Poodle.* London: 1954.

Jones, Thomas *Lloyd George.* London: 1951.

Jones, Thomas *Whitehall Diary, vol. 3. Ireland,* Keith Middlemas, ed. London: 1971.

Kee, Robert *The Green Flag.* New York: 1972.

Keynes, J. M. *Essays in Biography,* Geoffrey Keynes, ed. London: 1951.

Larkin, Emmet *James Larkin: Irish Labour Leader, 1876–1947.* Cambridge, Mass.: 1965.

Lawrence, R. J. *The Government of Northern Ireland.* London: 1965.

Lloyd George, David *War Memoirs.* 2 vols. London: 1938 ed.

Lloyd George, Frances Countess *The Years That Are Past.* London: 1967.

Longford, the Earl of, and Thomas P. O'Neill *Eamon De Valera.* Boston: 1971.

Lynch, Diarmuid *The I.R.B. and the 1916 Rising,* F. O'Donoghue, ed. Cork: 1957.

Lyons, F. S. L. *Ireland Since the Famine.* London: 1971.

Lyons, F. S. L. *John Dillon: A Biography.* London: 1968.

Macardle, Dorothy *The Irish Republic.* New York: 1965.

MacBride, Mrs. Maud Gonne *A Servant of the Queen.* London: 1938.

McCartney, Donal "The Sinn Fein Movement" in Nowlan, ed., *The Making of 1916.*

McColl, René *Roger Casement.* London: 1956.

McCracken, J. L. *Representative Government in Ireland: A Study of Dail Eireann, 1919–1948.* Oxford: 1958.

MacDonagh, Thomas *The Poetical Works of Thomas MacDonagh.* Dublin: 1916.

MacDonagh, Thomas *Literature in Ireland.* Dublin: 1916.

MacDonagh, Thomas *When the Dawn Is Come: A Tragedy in Three Acts.* Dublin: 1908.

McDowell, R. B. *The Irish Convention, 1917–1918.* London: 1970.

McDowell, R. B. *The Irish Administration, 1801–1914.* London: 1964.

MacEntee, Sean *Episode at Easter.* Dublin: 1966.

Mac Giolla Choille, Breandán *Intelligence Notes, 1913–1916.* Dublin: 1966.

McHugh, Roger ed. *Dublin, 1916.* New York: 1966.

MacInerney, Michael *The Riddle of Erskine Childers.* Dublin: 1971.

Mackintosh, John P. *The British Cabinet.* London: 1968.

MacNeill, R. J. *Ulster's Stand for Union.* London: 1922.

Macready, Sir C. F. Nevil *Annals of an Active Life.* 2 vols. London: 1924.

Mansergh, Nicholas *The Irish Question, 1840–1921.* New and revised ed. Toronto: 1965.

Mansergh, Nicholas "John Redmond" in O'Brien, ed., *The Shaping of Modern Ireland.*

Marjoribanks, Edward *The Life of Lord Carson.* Vol. 1. London: 1932.

Martin, F. X., ed. *The Irish Volunteers, 1913–1915.* Dublin: 1963.

Martin, F. X., ed. *The Howth Gun-Running and the Kilcoole Gun-Running,* with a foreword by Eamon de Valera. Dublin: 1964.

Martin, F. X., ed. *The Easter Rising and University College, Dublin.* Dublin: 1966.

Martin, F. X., ed. *Leaders and Men of the Easter Rising: Dublin.* Ithaca, N.Y.: 1967.

Martin, F. X., "1916: Myth, Fact and Mystery," *Studia Hibernica* No. 7, 1967, 8–126.

Martin, F. X., "The 1916 Rising — A Coup d'Etat or a 'Bloody Protest'?", *Studia Hibernica*, No. 8, 1968, 106–137.

Martin, F. X., "Eoin MacNeill on the 1916 Rising," *Irish Historical Studies*, XII, No. 47 (March, 1961) 226–271.

Martin, F. X., ed. "Extracts from the Papers of the Late Dr. Patrick McCartan," *Clogher Record*, 1965.

Midleton, Earl of *Records and Reactions, 1856–1939*. New York: 1939.

Morgan, Kenneth O. *David Lloyd George: Welsh Radical & World Statesman*. Carditt: 1963.

Morgan, Kenneth O. *The Age of Lloyd George*. London: 1971.

Morris, Lloyd *The Celtic Dawn: A Survey of the Renaissance 1889–1916*. New York: 1917.

Miller, David W. *Church, State and Nation in Ireland, 1898–1921*. Pittsburgh: 1973.

Newton, Lord *Lord Lansdowne, A Biography*. London: 1929.

Nicolson, Harold *George V*. London: 1952.

Norman, Edward *A History of Modern Ireland*. London: 1971.

Nowlan, Kevin B. "Dail Eireann and the Army: Unity and Division, 1916–1922," in T. Desmond Williams, ed., *The Irish Struggle*.

Nowlan, Kevin B. *The Making of 1916*. Dublin: 1969.

O'Brien, Conor Cruise, ed. *The Shaping of Modern Ireland*. London: 1960.

O'Brien, Conor Cruise, *States of Isrland*. New York: 1972.

O'Brien, Conor Cruise, and O'Brien, Maire *The Story of Ireland*. New York: 1972.

O'Brien, Nora Connolly *Portrait of a Rebel Father*. London: 1935.

O'Brien, W., and Ryan D., eds., *Devoy's Post Bag*. 2 vols. Dublin: 1948: 1953.

O'Brien, William *An Olive Branch in Ireland*. London: 1910.

Ó Broin, Leon *Dublin Castle and the 1916 Rising*. Dublin: 1966.

Ó Broin, Leon *The Chief Secretary*. London: 1969.

O'Casey, Sean *The Story of the Irish Citizen Army*. Dublin: 1919.

O'Casey, Sean *Drums Under The Window*. New York: 1947.

O'Connor, Frank *A Short History of Irish Literature*. New York: 1967.

O'Connor, Frank *The Big Fellow*. London: 1937.

O'Dubhgaill, M. *Insurrection Fires at Easter Tide*. Cork: 1966.

O'Faolain, Sean *Constance Marcievicz*. London: 1934.

O'Faolain, Sean *De Valera*. London: 1939.

O'Hegarty, P. S. *Sinn Fein: An Illumination*. Dublin: 1919.

O'Hegarty, P. S. *A History of Ireland Under The Union, 1801–1922*. London: 1952.

O'Kelly, Seamus *The Glorious Seven, 1916–1966*. Dublin: 1966.

O'Malley, Ernie *On Another Man's Wound*. London: 1936.

Owen, Frank *Tempestuous Journey: Lloyd George, His Life and Times*. London: 1954.

Oxford and Asquith, the Earl of *Memories and Reflections, 1852–1927* London: 1928.

Pakenham, Frank (Lord Longford) *Peace by Ordeal*. London: 1935.

Parks, Edd W. and Parks, Aileen W. *Thomas MacDonagh*. Athens, Ga.: 1967.

Paul-Dubois, L. *Contemporary Ireland*, Introduction by T. M. Kettle. London: 1908.

Pearse, Padraic *Political Writings and Speeches*. Dublin: 1966 reprint.

Pearse, Padraic *Plays, Stories, Poems*. Dublin: 1950.

Pearse, Padraic *The Singer and Other Plays*. Dublin: 1960.

Phillips, W. Allison *The Revolution in Ireland*. London: 1923.

Plunkett, Joseph Mary *Poems*, Foreword by Geraldine Plunkett. Dublin: 1916.

Pomfret, C. E. *The Struggle for Land in Ireland*. New York: 1969 ed.

Riddell, Lord *Intimate Diary of the Peace Conference and After, 1918–1923*. London: 1933.

Roskill, Stephen *Hankey: Man of Secrets*. 2 vols. London: 1970, 1972.

Rowland, Peter *The Last Liberal Governments: The Promised Land, 1905–1910*. London: 1968.

Rowland, Peter *The Last Liberal Governments: Unfinished Business, 1911–1914.* London: 1971.

Ryan, A. P. *Mutiny at the Curragh.* London: 1956.

Ryan, Desmond *The Rising: The Complete Story of Easter Week.* Dublin: 1957.

Ryan, Desmond *Remembering Sion.* London: 1934.

Ryan, Desmond *James Connolly.* Dublin: 1924.

Scott, C. P. *Political Diaries,* Trevor Wilson, ed. London: 1970.

Shannon, Martin *Sixteen Roads to Golgotha.* Dublin: 1966.

Singleton-Gates, P., and Girodias, M., eds. *The Black Diaries.* New York: 1959.

Southgate, Donald, ed. *The Conservative Leadership, 1832–1932.* London: 1974.

Spender, J. A. and Asquith, Cyril *The Life of Herbert Henry Asquith, Lord Asquith and Oxford.* 2 vols. London: 1932.

Spindler, K. *The Mystery of the Casement Ship.* Tralee: 1965.

Stansky, Peter, ed. *Churchill: A Profile.* London: 1973.

Stephens, James *Insurrection in Dublin,* Michael Adams, ed. Dublin: 1966.

Stewart, E. *The Ulster Crisis.* London: 1967.

Strauss, E. *Irish Nationalism and British Democracy.* London: 1957.

Tansill, Charles C. *America and the Fight for Irish Freedom, 1866–1922.* New York: 1957.

Taylor, A. J. P. *English History, 1914–1945.* Oxford: 1965.

Taylor, A. J. P. *Beaverbrook.* London: 1972.

Taylor, A. J. P., ed. *Lloyd George, A Diary by Frances Stevenson.* London: 1972.

Taylor, A. J. P., ed. *Lloyd George: Twelve Essays.* London: 1970.

Taylor, Rex *Michael Collins.* London: 1958.

Thompson, William I. *The Imagination of an Insurrection: Dublin, Easter 1916.* New York: 1967.

Torchiana, Donald T. *W. B. Yeats and Georgian Ireland.* Evanston: 1966.

Van Voris, J. *Constance de Markievicz in the Service of Ireland.* Amherst: 1967.

Ward, Alan J. *Ireland and Anglo-American Relations, 1899–1921.* London: 1969.

White, J. R. *Misfit.* London: 1930.

Williams, T. Desmond, ed. *The Irish Struggle, 1916–1926.* London: 1966.

Yeats, W. B. *Essays.* New York: 1924.

Yeats, W. B. *Autobiography.* New York: 1938.

Yeats, W. B. *Collected Poems.* New York: 1951.

Index